二十一世纪普通高等院校实用规划教材·经济管理系列

# 国际贸易实务(英语版)
## (第 2 版)

卢立伟　王　芬　主　编

杨　婷　蔡　静　陈逢丹　副主编

清华大学出版社
北 京

# 内 容 简 介

本书以国际贸易流程为基础框架，介绍了国际贸易术语、商品描述、货物运输、货物运输保险、商品价格、支付工具、支付方式、索赔与不可抗力、谈判与磋商、进出口合同的履行以及国际贸易方式等国际贸易实务中的主要内容，配以相关的案例、流程图、合同条款、法律条文和惯例，结构完整，内容全面，具有较强的实践性和可操作性。

本书既适合高等院校商务英语、国际贸易等涉外专业的本、专科教学，也可供从事外经贸工作的人士及对外贸感兴趣的读者参考学习。

**图书在版编目(CIP)数据**

国际贸易实务(英语版)/卢立伟，王芬主编. —2 版. —北京：清华大学出版社，2018 (2025.1 重印)

(二十一世纪普通高等院校实用规划教材·经济管理系列)

ISBN 978-7-302-50477-1

Ⅰ. ①国… Ⅱ. ①卢… ②王… Ⅲ. ①国际贸易—贸易实务—高等学校—教材—英文 Ⅳ. ①F740.4

中国版本图书馆 CIP 数据核字(2018)第 131683 号

责任编辑：梁媛媛
装帧设计：刘孝琼
责任校对：吴春华
责任印制：杨 艳

出版发行：清华大学出版社
    网  址：https://www.tup.com.cn, https://www.wqxuetang.com
    地  址：北京清华大学学研大厦 A 座    邮  编：100084
    社 总 机：010-83470000    邮  购：010-62786544
    投稿与读者服务：010-62776969, c-service@tup.tsinghua.edu.cn
    质量反馈：010-62772015, zhiliang@tup.tsinghua.edu.cn
    课件下载：https://www.tup.com.cn, 010-62791865

印 装 者：三河市龙大印装有限公司

经  销：全国新华书店

开  本：185mm×230mm  印  张：24.75  字  数：598 千字
版  次：2014 年 3 月第 1 版  2018 年 8 月第 2 版  印  次：2025 年 1 月第 8 次印刷
定  价：59.00 元

产品编号：074544-01

# 再 版 前 言

国际贸易实务是我国普通高等院校涉外经济专业的一门专业基础课程。随着我国经济的快速发展以及全球经济一体化进程的加速,社会亟须兼备专业知识和英语能力的复合型人才。针对这种变化,我国高等院校的教学与时俱进,学科体系、教学措施和教学手段不断完善和创新。2007 年,教育部正式批准成立商务英语专业,用英语教授商务专业课程成为一种必然的趋势。随着改革开放进程的加快,我国对外贸易的限制不断取消,并逐步与国际接轨。由于我国的外贸实务操作有其自身的特色,如一些特定的环节、行业规范和法律法规等,因此,该课程的教学不能完全依赖于外文原版教材,需要编写适合本土教学需要的英文版国际贸易实务教材。本书正是为了适应这一需要而编写的。

本书以国际贸易流程为基础框架,包含绪论、国际贸易术语、商品描述、货物运输、货物运输保险、商品价格、支付工具、支付方式、索赔和不可抗力、谈判与磋商、进出口合同的履行以及国际贸易方式等内容。本书强调学以致用,具有较强的实践性、实用性和可操作性,适合各高校商务英语、国际贸易等涉外专业的本、专科教学以及对外贸感兴趣的读者自学。本书具有如下特点。

(1) 全面性及系统性。本书系统地介绍了进出口贸易的整个流程,结构完整,内容全面,语言浅显易懂。

(2) 新颖性和翔实性。教材融入了国际贸易领域的最新发展与变化,如反映了 *INCOTERMS* 2010 在国际贸易术语解释方面的新内容,以及 2012 年财政部、国家税务总局联合下发通知调整的相关出口退(免)税政策。自 2012 年 8 月 1 日起,取消出口收汇核销单,出口退税由原来的两单两票调整为一单两票,这在第 11 章中也及时加以增补。

(3) 提供开篇案例或新闻导读。教材的每一章都以一个引人入胜的案例或财经新闻开篇,从而提高读者的阅读兴趣,提升学习效果。

(4) 引导对疑难问题的思考。本书将每章的重点、难点、热点问题加以梳理并展开阐述,并配上相应的中文批注,使每章重点突出、内容层次清晰,以提高读者的学习效率,同时解决课时不足或自学困难等问题。

(5) 实践性和可操作性强。本书在各章节适当位置配上相关的案例、流程图、合同条款以及法律条文和惯例,同时,在每章节的末尾配上相应的练习,以增强本书的实践性和可操作性。

随着国际形势的变化,国际贸易的相关内容、惯例以及方式也发生了变化。因此,本书相关章节的内容也作了相应的调整和增补,并出版了第 2 版。相较于 2014 年的第 1 版,第 2 版更新了有关章节的导入案例和课后练习。另外,第 2 章的国际贸易术语作了很大的调整，摒弃了 *INCOTERMS* 2000 通则的相关内容，以 *INCOTERMS* 2010 通则的内容为主；第 4 章的海洋运输突出了集装箱运输以及海运提单的内容，并增补了船东单和货代单的内容；由于近年来进口日趋强劲，所以第 6 章的报价增补了进口报价的内容；第 10 章完善了相关的合同条款的内容；第 11 章增补和完善了相应的单据；近年来跨境电商发展迅猛，所以第 12 章增补了跨境电商的内容。

参加本书编写的有卢立伟(第 1 章、第 7 章、第 8 章、第 9 章)、王芬(第 4 章、第 6 章)、杨婷(第 2 章、第 5 章)、蔡静(第 10 章、第 12 章)、陈逢丹(第 3 章、第 11 章)等。本书由卢立伟和王芬任主编，杨婷、蔡静、陈逢丹任副主编。

在本书编写过程中，编委们参阅了近年来国内外相关学者的研究成果，参考文献仅反映了其中的主要部分，恕不能一一答谢。本书是集体成员努力的成果，受编者学识所限，难免有不足之处，希望广大读者和同行多多批评指正。

编　者

# 目　　录

国际贸易实务(英语版)(第2版)

V

# Chapter 1    General Introduction to International Trade

【Learning Objectives】

By studying this chapter, you should be able to master:

- Definition of international trade
- The importance of international trade
- International trade restrictions
- World Trade Organization (WTO)
- Main procedures of international trade
- Relevant international practice and laws
- Overview of international contract
- Overview of this book

## Lead-in: News Report

### China's Trade Surplus with US Misread

China's large trade surplus is often used by the United States to argue why China should allow its currency to rise. Yet most US officials ignore a very important fact: a majority of China's exports to the US are produced by US-funded companies and huge profits go back into American pockets.

### China's Surplus, Foreign Companies Benefit

Chinese former Premier Wen Jiabao said at Sunday's news conference that half of China's exports came from the processing trade—where imported components were assembled at factories in China and 60 percent were made by foreign-funded companies or joint ventures with foreign partners. "Therefore, to restrict trade with China is tantamount to causing difficulty for the businesses of your own countries," he said.

According to statistics provided by the Ministry of Commerce, 55.9 percent of China's exports were produced by foreign companies last year. The proportions were 83 percent and 75 percent respectively for high-tech products and electronic products. And, over 90 percent of high-tech products exported to the US was made by foreign enterprises.

## Big Surplus, Small Profit

Researchers at the University of California at Irvine conducted a case study of Apple's iPod to examine which countries captured the most economic value from iPod production. The conclusion showed that only four dollars was retained in China, with the bulk going to the designers, retailers and component suppliers.

It seems unfair therefore that the full price of an iPod, roughly $300, instead of four dollars, was counted as part of China's exports to the US.

"China's cheap labor helps foreign companies cut wage costs and increase their profits. Ironically, the rising profits go into foreign bosses' pockets and China is left to take the blame for the trade imbalance," said Tan Yaling, an expert at the China Institute for Financial Derivatives at Peking University.

## Hi-tech Export Controls

Premier Wen said the country's trade imbalance would be much smaller if the US would approve more high-tech exports to China.

The US government unveiled new export control regulations in 2007, which blocked the export of 20 categories of products to China, including airplane engines, lean oil, lasers and avionic devices.

Statistics showed that 18.3 percent of China's high-tech imports came from the US in 2001. The figure dropped to eight percent in 2008, partially reflecting harsh US export controls to China.

"On one hand, the United States asks Beijing to reduce its trade surplus. On the other hand, it refuses to sell high-tech commodities to China. What really does it want?" said Zhang Yansheng, director of the Institute of Foreign Trade of the National Development and Reform Commission.

"I sincerely hope the Europe Union and the United States will recognize China's market economy status and lift restrictions on the exports of high-tech commodities to China because that will help promote trade balance in the world," Wen said Sunday.

*(Source: China Daily, Updated: 2010-03-16 16:26)*

### Class Activities:

1. Why did China's trade surplus shrink in 2010? What were the main reasons?
2. What is the real purpose of the US to control China's exports?

# 1.1 What Is International Trade?

International trade, also known as world trade, foreign trade, overseas trade, etc., is the exchange of goods and services between different countries or regions. Whether a transaction is international trade or not mainly depends on the buyer's and seller's business locations and customs territories.

Depending on what it produces and needs, a country can export and import. Exports refer to that individuals or nations send goods to another country, and imports refer to that individuals or nations bring in goods from another country. Therefore, international trade concerns trade operations of both import and export, and includes the purchase and the sale of both visible and invisible goods, thus international trade can be divided into visible trade, invisible trade and modern barter. The structure of international trade is as shown in Figure 1-1.

国际贸易就是在不同国家或地区之间交换商品和服务。所谓出口商品就是个人或国家卖出商品。而进口商品，则是个人或国家买入商品。判断某笔交易是否属于国际贸易，主要以交易双方营业地和关境为准。

Figure 1-1 The Structure of International Trade

# 1.2 The Importance of International Trade

International trade is not a zero-sum game of winners and losers. It is a game in which everyone wins and, the continued strength of the world economy has been supported by strong growth in international trade. There are the following three main reasons to get into the trade game for every participant:

- Imports can bring profits, while exports can make profits;
- The world is interdependent. People of each nation rely on people of other nations to exchange goods or services;
- International trade can create jobs.

国际贸易并不是一个成功者或失败者的零和游戏，而是一场参与者的共赢盛宴。

Those who are winning the trade game know that, regardless of national deficits or surpluses, the time is right for an import or export business to make profits, thus the whole world welfare will be improved.

## 1.2.1  International Trade Restrictions

It is well known that international trade is very important to the world and national economy. Compared with domestic trade, there are more problems that the imports or exports will have to face in doing international business, including cultural differences, language misunderstandings, trade barriers, etc., which would make international trade more risky.

与国内贸易相比，国际贸易面临文化差异、语言障碍、贸易壁垒等问题。

Governments can control international trade by all means. The most common measures are tariffs (duties) and quotas. A tariff is a tax on imported goods, which is also called tariff barriers, such as specific duties, ad valorem duties and compound duties; a quota is the maximum quantity of a product allowed into a country during a certain period of time, which is a kind of non-tariff barriers to limit the quantity of imports, increase the cost of getting imports into the market, and create uncertainty about the conditions under which imports will be permitted. These measures are protectionist as they raise the price of imported goods to protect domestically produced goods and infant industries.

税收和配额是政府控制国际贸易的常用手段，用于保护国内产品及新生产业。

## 1.2.2  Differences between International Trade and Domestic Trade

The fundamental characteristic that makes international trade different from domestic trade is that international trade involves activities that take place across national borders. Thus when trade is executed beyond national frontiers, it is invariably subject to the political, social, economic and environmental policies of other nations. Such policies have either encouraged or hampered the free flow of merchandise in international trade. Special problems that not normally have been experienced when trading at home may arise in international trade. Below are the major differences between domestic trade and international trade:

与国际贸易相比，国内贸易主要面临生产要素的转移、货物的运输、结算货币、销售市场以及文化差异和语言障碍等问题。

**Mobility in factor of production**

Domestic trade: free to move around factors of production like land, labor, capital and entrepreneurship from one state to another within the same country.

International trade: quite restricted.

**Movement of goods**

Domestic trade: easier to move goods without many restrictions. Maybe need to pay sales tax, etc.

International trade: restricted due to complicated customs procedures and trade barriers like tariffs, quotas or embargo.

**Usage of different currencies**

Domestic trade: same type of currency used.

International trade: different countries use different currencies.

**Broader markets**

Domestic trade: limited market due to limits in population, etc.

International trade: broader markets.

**Language and cultural barriers**

Domestic trade: speak the same language and practice the same culture.

International trade: communication challenges due to language and cultural barriers.

## 1.3　World Trade Organization

In order to reduce trade restrictions between member countries, international organization, like World Trade Organization(WTO), was established to regulate tariffs and deal with the rules of trade between nations.

### 1.3.1　Overview

The World Trade Organization came into force on January 1, 1995. As one of the youngest international organizations, WTO is the successor to the General Agreement on Tariffs and Trade (GATT) established in 1947, and now GATT has become part of it.

WTO is an organization for trade opening and a platform for governments to negotiate trade agreements. It is a place for them to settle trade disputes and operate a system of trade rules. Essentially,

世界贸易组织的目标是帮助商品和服务的生产商和进出口商顺利地开展业务。

WTO is a place where member states try to sort out the trade problems they face with each other.

## 1.3.2　Functions of WTO

The main functions of WTO can be described in very simple terms as follows:

- To oversee implementing and administering WTO agreements;
- To provide a forum for negotiations;
- To provide a dispute settlement mechanism.

The goals behind these functions are set out in the preamble to the Marrakech Agreement, which include:

- Raising standards of living;
- Ensuring full employment;
- Ensuring large and steadily growing real incomes and demands;
- Expanding the production of trade in goods and services.

These objectives are to be achieved while allowing for the optimal use of the world's resources in accordance with the objective of sustainable development, and seeking to protect and preserve the environment. The preamble also specifically mentions the need to assist developing countries, especially the least developed countries, and secure a growing share of international trade.

## 1.3.3　Basic Principles

世界贸易组织的五大原则是非歧视性原则、互惠性原则、约束及承诺机制、透明性原则和安全保护措施。

WTO establishes a framework for trade policies which do not define or specify outcomes, which means, it is concerned with setting the rules of the trade policy game, not with the results of the game.

Five principles are of particular importance in understanding both the pre-1994 GATT and WTO, including nondiscrimination, reciprocity, binding and enforceable commitments, transparency, and safety valves.

## 1.3.4　Missions

WTO's stated goal is to raise people's welfare, reduce poverty, and foster peace and stability among its member states. WTO provides a platform for negotiating agreements aiming at reducing obstacles to international trade and ensuring a level playing field for all, thus contributes to economic growth and development. WTO also provides a legal and institutional framework for the implementation and monitoring of these agreements, as well as for settling disputes arising from their interpretation and application. In a word, its main mission is to help producers of goods and services, exporters and importers, conduct their business and, ensure that flows smoothly, predictably and freely as possible.

## 1.3.5 Formal Structure

All WTO members may participate in all councils, committees, etc., except Appellate Body, Dispute Settlement Panels, and Plurilateral Committees. The formal structure of WTO is illustrated in Figure 1-2.

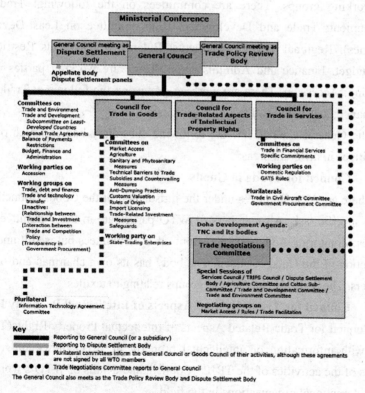

Figure1-2 The Formal Structure of WTO

*Source: www.wto.org*

第一层级：部长级会议

部长级会议是世贸组织的最高权力机构，负责履行世贸组织的职能。休会期间由总理事会代为行使。

第二层级：三种形式的总理事会

在两届部长级会议之间，日常工作由以下三个机构负责处理：总理事会、争端解决机构、贸易政策审议机构。这三个机构实际上是一个，只不过是根据不同的职权范围召开会议而已。总理事会代表部长级会议处理WTO的所有事务。

第三层级：理事会及委员会

另外下设专门委员会、秘书处及总干事。总理事会下设五个专门委员会，负责处理三个理事会的共性事务及其他事务，涉及的议题有：贸易与发展、环境、区域贸易协定以及行政事务。每个较高层次的理事会都有下属机构。货物理事会有11个委员会处理具体议题(如农业、市场准入、补贴、反倾销措施等)。纺织品监督机构也向货物理事会报告。

## First level: Ministerial Conference

The topmost level is ministerial conference which has to meet at least once every two years. The Ministerial Conference can make decisions on all matters under any of the multilateral trade agreement.

## Second level: General Council in three guises

Day-to-day work in the ministerial conferences is handled by three bodies. They are **the General Council, the Dispute Settlement Body and the Trade Policy Review Body.** All three are in fact the same. The Agreement Establishing WTO states they are all the General Council, although they meet under different terms of reference. Again, all three consist of all WTO members. They report to the Ministerial Conference.

## Third level: councils for each broad area of trade

The General Council has several different committees, working parties, and working groups. There are committees on the following: Trade and Environment; Trade and Development (Subcommittee on Least-Developed Countries); Regional Trade Agreements; Balance of Payments Restrictions; and Budget, Finance and Administration. There are working parties on the following: Accession. There are working groups on the following: Trade, debt and finance; and Trade and technology transfer.

The General Council has the following subsidiary bodies which oversee committees in different areas:

- **Council for Trade in Goods**

There are 11 committees under the jurisdiction of the Goods Council, each with a specific task. All members of WTO participate in the committees. The Textiles Monitoring Body separates from other committees but is still under the jurisdiction of the Goods Council. The body has its own chairman and only 10 members. The body also has several groups relating to textiles.

- **Council for Trade-Related Aspects of Intellectual Property Rights**

Council for Trade-Related Aspects of Intellectual Property Rights(TRIPS) deals with information on intellectual property in WTO, news and official records of the activities of the TRIPS Council, and details of WTO's work with other international organizations in the field.

- **Council for Trade in Services**

The Council for Trade in Services operates under the guidance of the General Council and is responsible for overseeing the functioning of the General Agreement on Trade in Services (GATS). It is open to all WTO members, and can create subsidiary bodies as required.

The Service Council has three subsidiary bodies: financial services, domestic regulations, GATS rules and specific commitments.

- **Trade Negotiations Committee**

The Trade Negotiations Committee (TNC) is the committee that deals with the current trade talks round. The chair is WTO's director-general. As June of 2012, the committee was tasked with the Doha Development Round.

# 1.4  Main Procedures of International Trade

International trade practice, which we can understand as international trade transaction, complies with two parts: export transaction and import transaction.

## 1.4.1  Basic Procedures of Export

The basic procedures of export include preparing for export, business negotiation and the performance of export contract. The main flow chart of export procedures is as shown in Figure 1-3.

### 1. Preparation for Export

Before exporting, the exporter needs to make careful preparations for the negotiation. At first, the exporter needs to do some market research to select the target market and decide the methods of export. When selecting the target market, the exporter needs to do a lot of market research, which is a process of conducting research into a specific market for a particular product. Market research is necessary, especially for companies entering into international business for the first time. Through market research, the exporter can learn the needs of the market and the methods by which the products can be supplied. At the same time, by doing the market research, the exporter may find some potential buyers for their products.

秘书处由总干事负责。部长级会议任命总干事并明确规定其权力、职责、服务条件及任期，总干事任命副总干事和秘书处工作人员，并按部长级会议通过的规则确定他们的职责。

在总理事会一级，争端解决机构还有两个下属机构，即对争端进行裁决的争端解决专家组及处理上诉的上诉机构。

出口流程主要包括出口贸易前的准备、出口贸易磋商和出口合同的履行。

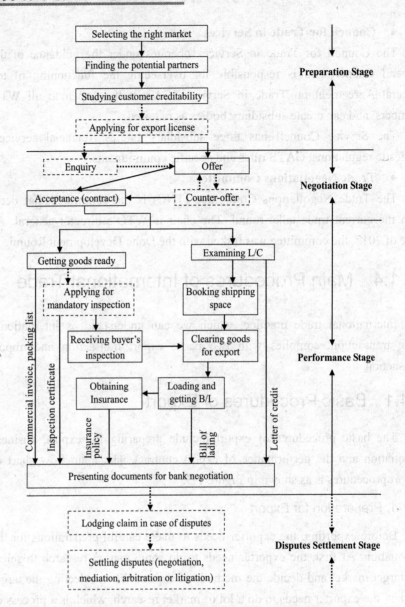

Figure 1-3   The Flow Chart of Export Procedure

When selecting the target market, several aspects must be taken into consideration:

- The economic and political environment of the foreign market. One must consider whether the country or district which the market is in has a stable political situation and whether it has a friendly foreign policy with one's own country. At the same time, one will have to know what the country's economic situations is. Find out whether that country is undergoing growing economy and what the people's purchasing powers are, etc.;

● The demand of the product in the local market;

● The rivals or competitors exist in this market. One has to know the size of market, and whether there is still market share left for him/her to enter the market.

## 2. Business Negotiation

After the exporter has selected the target market, the potential buyers, and has prepared sufficiently for the negotiation, the next step would be the negotiation. In international trade, business negotiations are quite important and unavoidable. During the negotiation, the relevant parties will negotiate matters pertaining to the major terms and conditions of the contract, such as quality, quantity, packing, price, transport, insurance, payment or even some clauses involving inspection, claim, force majeure and arbitration, etc. Through these negotiations, the exporters and importers can bridge their differences and reach a fair and mutually satisfactory deal.

Usually, business negotiation consists of four stages: inquiry, offer, counter-offer and acceptance. Among them, offer and acceptance are the two indispensable stages, which are required for reaching an agreement and concluding a sales contract.

商务谈判主要包括询盘、发盘、还盘和接受四个环节。其中发盘和接受两个环节不可缺少。

## 3. The Performance of Export Contract

The export performance process will differ a little in different transactions, especially the transactions under different trade terms. Normally, we reach the export deal under trade terms CIF(Cost, Insurance and Freight). And the process of the export contract performance would involve the following: getting the goods ready; examining the L/C(Letter of Credit); amending the L/C; shipping; customs clearance; arranging the insurance; preparing the required documents and getting paid; claims (if any) .

## 4. Disputes settlement of Export

Disputes between the buyers and the sellers occur frequently in international trade. Usually a claim will be made by the injured party after the disputes. Sometimes the transaction parties often resolve the disputes through amicable negotiations to maintain the goodwill and friendly business relations. But in case no settlement can be reached by negotiation, the relevant two parties can resort to mediation, arbitration or even litigation.

## 1.4.2　Basic Procedures of Import

进口贸易的基本业务程序主要包括进口贸易前的准备、进口贸易的磋商和进口合同履行。

The basic procedures of import are similar to those of export, which involve preparation before import, negotiation and the performance of the sales contract. Because the preparation and negotiation are so similar to those of export, we will mainly focus on the performance of the contract here.

Normally, the procedures for the importer to perform the contract will involve the following steps:

### 1. Applying for Import License

进口合同的履行主要包括进口许可证的申请、信用证的开立、海洋运输的准备、保险和结算的安排与进口检验及海关清关等手续。

Generally, an import company needs to apply for the import license from the authority after the contract is signed. He will submit the license application letter to the import office of the local government to get the license. If the authority signs the import license after having checked the application form, the importer can start to send his order, make payment and submit application for customs clearance based on the import license.

### 2. Opening L/C

The importer should open the letter of credit(L/C) within the set period of time stipulated in the contract and make appropriate amendment if it is needed.

The importer should follow the time of opening L/C which stipulated in the contract. No earlier or later than that. If earlier, the importer will increase his expense. While later, it will cause his failure in contract obligation and may delay the exporter's shipping operation.

### 3. Preparing for Shipment

Under FOB(free on board), it is the importer's obligation to book the shipping space and accept goods at the stipulated place. The procedure is similar to the procedure operated by exporter under CIF terms. After booking shipping space, the importer should advise the exporter within 45 days to deliver and load the goods in time.

### 4. Arranging Insurance and Payment

Under FOB terms, the importer should arrange the marine insurance for the goods on board on receipt of the shipping advice from the exporter.

When the bank receives the relevant documents required by the L/C from the seller, it will make the payment if these documents are in exact conformity with the L/C.

### 5. Import Inspection and Customs Clearance

If necessary, the importer or his agency would apply for the inspection for the import goods. He will submit the import contract, invoice, packing list, B/L(Bill of Lading), quality certificate, usage illustration, relevant standards, technical data and weight list after completion of the application forms. The inspection institution would carry out the inspection at the stipulated place according to the contracts and relevant laws. If the goods are qualified, the institution will issue the inspection qualification certificate and sign it.

After the inspection, the importer can apply for customs clearance and pay for import duties according to the customs requirement.

## 1.5　Relevant International Practices and Laws

In international trade transaction, to ensure the fulfillment of the contract and to protect the respective rights and obligations of both parties, the regulation of the business by laws or international trade conventions applicable are absolutely necessary. The laws applicable in international trade transaction are of the following three kinds:

国际贸易买卖合同中使用的法律主要有国内法、国际贸易惯例和国际条约。

### 1. Domestic Laws

Domestic laws are laws made by the legislative body of a country and are effective within that country only. In international trade transaction, to reach the contract, the relevant parties will have to obey the domestic laws in their own countries first. The *Contract Law of China*, which was adopted at the second session of the ninth National People's Congress on March 15, 1999, specifies in the Article 126 that "The parties to a contract involving foreign interests may choose the law applicable to the settlement of their contract disputes, except as otherwise stipulated by law. If the parties to a contract involving foreign interests have not made a choice, the law of the country to

国内法是指由国家制定或认可并在本国主权管辖范围内生效的法律。国际货物买卖合同必须符合国内法，即符合某个国家制定或认可的法律。在中国主要是指1999年颁布的《中华人民共和国合同法》。

which the contract is most closely connected shall be applied." Therefore, usually both parties to a contract may choose either the law of the exporting country or the importing country, or that of a third country. If both parties to a contract agree to choose to be governed by the law of a certain country, then the contract should stipulate it clearly. If the contract does not make it clear as to which law is applicable in case of contract dispute, then according to the *Contract Law of China*, "the law of country to which the contract is most closely connected shall be applied".

### 2. International Trade Practice

International trade practice is among the most important legal rule that applies to the international trade of goods. It is composed of general provisions, norms and rules prescribed by some international organizations and commercial groups. It is accepted and used extensively in the world and can be treated as trade custom. The international trade custom is not a law. It does not have coercive power. However, if the relevant parties agree to obey the relevant custom, their actions will be bound to it.

在实践中被广泛使用的国际贸易惯例有《国际贸易术语解释通则》、《跟单信用证统一惯例》和《托收统一规则》等。

The most famous international organization in international trade is the International Chamber of Commerce (ICC). It is an international organization that works to promote and support global trade and globalization. It serves as an advocate of world business in the global economy, in the interests of economic growth, job creation and prosperity. As a global business organization, made up of member states, it helps the development of global outlooks on business matters. ICC has direct access to national governments worldwide through its national committees. ICC contributes large efforts to promoting the international trade, and the conventions published by it are widely used today. Among them, the widely used ones are *INCOTERMS, Uniform Custom and Practice for Documentary Credit (UCP)* and *Uniform Rules for Collection (URC)*. The ICC has developed and molded the *UCP* by regular revisions. The current version called *UCP 600* was formally commenced on 1 July 2007. The result is the most successful international attempt at unifying rules ever, as the *UCP* has substantially universal effect.

These trade practices have a set of rules, which do not apply obligatorily as laws. However, when the text of the credit expressly indicates that it is subject to these rules, they are binding on all parties to the credit or the contract unless expressly modified or excluded by the credit or the contract.

### 3. International Trade Laws

*The United Nations Convention on Contracts for the International Sale of Goods (CISG)* has been recognized as the most successful attempt to unify a broad area of commercial law at the international level. The self-executing treaty aims to reduce obstacles to international trade, particularly those associated with choice of law issues, by creating even-handed and modern substantive rules governing the rights and obligations of parties to international sales contracts. At the time this was written (February 2009), the *CISG* has attracted more than 70 contracting states that account for well over two thirds of international trade in goods, and that represent extraordinary economic, geographic and cultural diversity.

《联合国国际货物销售合同公约》被认为是目前全世界最重要的一项国际条约。

## 1.6　Overview of Contract

A contract is an agreement that creates an obligation, which is a binding, legally enforceable agreement between two or more competent parties.

## 1.6.1　The Functions of a Written Contract

A written contract is normally preferred in international transaction, because it has the following functions:

### 1. The Evidence of a Contract

A written contract endorsed by both parties of the transaction serves as legally effective evidence of a contract. The contract needs to be evidenced in case there is any dispute about it or whenever arbitration or litigation occurs. And written evidence will make it easy to present the evidence, especially when the business has been done by verbal means. It will be necessary for the parties to sign a written contract.

### 2. The Condition of Effectiveness

A written contract sometimes is the necessary condition of effectiveness of a contract. Although Article 23 of CISG stipulated "a contract is concluded at the moment when an acceptance of an offer becomes effective in accordance with the provisions of this Convention", the contract usually takes effect only when it is signed by both parties.

### 3. The Guidance of Performance

As the performance of contract should be in strict conformity with the conditions stipulated in the contract, without a written contract, a verbal offer is almost impossible to be executed. Therefore, it will be necessary to stipulate all the terms of a deal in a written contract to guide the performance of the contract.

## 1.6.2 The Essential Features of a Legally Binding Contract

We've talked about how a contract is concluded at the moment when an acceptance of the offer becomes effective. Please be noted that it doesn't mean the contract is effective upon its conclusion. There are prerequisites for the effectiveness of a legal contract.

### 1. Legal Capacity to Contract of the Parties

The parties to a contract must have the legal capacity and competency to contract. Minors, namely persons under the legal age of 18 years old, have limited capacity to contract. At the same time, contracts with persons under guardianship or who lack sufficient mental capacity to contract are voidable. We say that these contracts are voidable, not void, which means that the contract may be disaffirmed by the person who lacks capacity (or his guardian).

### 2. Consideration

Consideration, in legal terminology, is what one party to a contract will get from the other party in return for performing contract obligations. Particularly, in international trade transaction, the seller provides the commodity and the buyer makes the payment for what he purchases in return. A contract with no consideration is void.

## 1.6.3 The General Contents of a Sales Contract

合同的内容主要包括约首、本文和约尾。

In an ordinary contract, to ensure both parties' fulfillment of contractual obligations, a sales contract for international commodities usually covers the following contents:

- Title.
- Preamble—contract date, number, place, parties concerned.
- Name of commodity.
- Quality clauses—the method and standard by which to determine the quality, the time and the place to determine the quality, and tolerance clause, etc.
- Quantity clauses—the unit of measurement, the place and time to deliver the agreed quantity, calculation of weight, and more or less clause, etc.
- Price clauses—the terms of price, the currency used, commission and discount, etc.
- Packing clauses—inner packing, outer packing, lining material, packing measurement, weight and marking, etc.
- Insurance clauses—insurant, conditions, the insured amount and place for claim.
- Shipment and delivery—place, time, mode of shipment and delivery, shipping advice, etc.
- Payment clauses—time, terms, currency for payment, stipulation for deferment and dishonor, etc.
- Inspection clauses—place of inspection, standard, the authorized inspection institution, etc.
- Claim clauses—validity of claim, claim certificate, etc.
- Arbitration clauses—location of arbitration, applicable arbitral rules of procedure, arbitration organization, etc.
- Force majeure clauses—scope of force majeure accidents, time and means of notification, certified statement, reports and documents, the escape clause, etc.
- Breach and cancellation of contract clauses—settlement of breach, compensation amount, etc.
- Applicable laws.
- Miscellaneous clauses.
- Language Versions of contract and legal force.

合同约首包括合同名称、合同编号、合同签订日期、订约地点、订约双方名称和地址、序言等。

合同本文包括品质条款、数量条款、价格条款、包装条款、保险条款、交货条款、支付条款、商检、索赔、仲裁条款、不可抗力、违约和废弃条款、法律适用条款等。

合同约尾包括合同文字及其效力、合同附件及其效力，订约双方签字等。

- Appendix and legal force.
- Witness clauses—signature of the parties concerned, etc.

## 1.7 Overview of This Book

This book is intended to enable readers to understand and have a clear knowledge of international trade practices. It is written for those who want to attain more information about what is going on in international transactions.

In total, there are 12 chapters in this book. Chapter 1 is about a general idea of international trade and what it is about. Chapter 2 is about international trade terms, including the introduction of trade terms, international trade usage concerning trade terms, the introduction to *Incoterms 2010* and brief introduction to *Incoterms 2000*. Chapter 3 is about terms of commodity. The main contents are about name of commodity, quality of commodity, quantity of commodity and package of commodity. Chapter 4 is about international cargo transport. The main contents are modes of transport, shipping documents, the clause of shipment and international cargo agent. Chapter 5 is about international cargo transport insurance including the definition of insurance, parties to the insurance, marine insurance, the scope of insurance coverage, coverage of marine cargo insurance of *CIC* and *ICC*, the procedures of marine insurance and insurance clauses in contract. Chapter 6 is about price of goods including price elements, conversion of major trade terms, export and import cost accounting, commission and discount, avoidance of foreign exchange risk, and clause of price. Chapter 7 is about credit instruments, mainly including bill of exchange, promissory note and check. Chapter 8 is about international payment and settlement, including remittance, acceptance, the Letter of Credit, banker's Letter of Guarantee and standby Letter of Credit, and factoring and export credit insurance. Chapter 9 is about inspection, claim, force majeure and arbitration. Chapter 10 is about business negotiation and establishment of contract including enquiry, offer, counter-offer, acceptance and conclusion of contract. Chapter 11 is about exporting and importing procedures. Chapter 12 is about modes of international trade, and the main contents are agency and distribution, tenders, bids and auction, improvement trade, future trading and cross-border e-commerce.

International trade practice is a very practical subject. This book doesn't just describe international trade theories. In addition to explanatory cases throughout the chapters and a great deal of explanations in Chinese, by cooperating with companies, and absorbing and drawing on the experiences of businessmen, we provide the readers with blended international trade theories together with practical trade experiences.

Specimen 1-1 is the Sample of Sales Confirmation.

Specimen 1-1　The Sample of Sales Confirmation

# SALES CONFIRMATION

S/C No.: KX-MIGSC11

Date:

The Seller: TRIUMPH IMP. & EXP. CO., LTD.
Address: 2103  INT'L TRADE CENTER
2200 YAN-AN ROAD (W)
SHANGHAI, 200335, CHINA
E-Mail: BOX11@SIFT.SIFT.EDU

The Buyer: MIGUEL ANGEL ORFEI
Address: 20 DE SETIEMBRE 1758
7600 MAR DEL PLATA
BUENOS AIRES, ARGENTINA
E-Mail: MIGUEL@SIFT.SIFT.EDU

| Item No. | Commodity | Unit | Quantity | Unit Price (US$) | Amount (US$) |
|---|---|---|---|---|---|
| | FOREVER BRAND FOOTBALL | | | | |
| 1 | SWB32S | PIECE | 2400 | 20.90 | 50160.00 |
| 2 | KS32S | PIECE | 3600 | 11.20 | 40320.00 |
| 3 | KOWB532 | PIECE | 2700 | 6.40 | 17280.00 |
| 4 | KWB32 | PIECE | 2700 | 8.20 | 22140.00 |
| | | | | | 129900.00 |

| TOTAL CONTRACT VALUE: | SAY US DOLLARS ONE HUNDRED AND TWENTY |
|---|---|
| CIFC5% BUENOS AIRES | NINE THOUSAND AND NINE HUNDRED ONLY |

PACKING:　　　　　SWB32S AND KS32S ARE PACKED IN CTNS OF 24 PCS EACH;
　　　　　　　　　　KOWB532 AND KWB32 ARE PACKED IN CTNS OF 50 PCS EACH;
　　　　　　　　　　TOTAL 358 CTNS.

PORT OF LOADING &
DESTINATION:　　　FROM SHANGHAI CHINA  TO BUENOS AIRES ARGENTINA

TIME OF SHIPMENT:　TO BE EFFECTED BEFORE THE END OF
　　　　　　　　　　PARTIAL SHIPMENT NOT ALLOWED;July,2013.
　　　　　　　　　　TRANSHIPMENT ALLOWED

TERMS OF PAYMENT:　THE BUYER SHALL OPEN THOUGH A BANK ACCEPTABLE
　　　　　　　　　　TO THE SELLER AN IRREVOCABLE L/C AT  SIGHT TO REACH
　　　　　　　　　　THE SELLER 30 DAYS BEFORE THE DATE OF SHIPMENT, VALID
　　　　　　　　　　FOR NEGOTIATION IN CHINA 15 DAYS AFTER THE DATE OF
　　　　　　　　　　SHIPMENT.

Confirmed by:

| THE SELLER | THE BUYER |
|---|---|
| TRIUMPH IMP. & EXP. CO., LTD. | MIGUEL ANGEL ORFEI |
| MANAGER | |
| ( signature) | ( signature) |

# 【Key Terms and Words】

acceptance 接受

Enquiry 询盘

Offer 发盘

Tariff 关税

Quota 配额

*INCOTERMS*《国际贸易术语解释通则》

ICC 国际商会

*UCP*《跟单信用证统一惯例》

*CISG*《联合国国际货物销售合同公约》

NTB 非关税贸易壁垒

International trade 国际贸易

Visible trade/merchandise trade 有形贸易

Invisible trade/service trade 无形贸易

International trade dependency ratio 国际贸易依存度

Comparative advantage 比较优势

International trade practice 国际贸易实务

Trade barrier 贸易壁垒

Specific duty 从量税

Ad valorem duty 从价税

Compound duty 复合税

Counter-offer 还盘

# 【Exercises】

## I. Answer the following questions.

1. What is international trade?

2. What are the differences between international trade and domestic trade?

3. What are the risks in international trade?

4. What are the barriers to international trade?

5. What are the real functions of tariffs?

6. What are the functions of WTO?

7. What are the main relative international practice and laws?

8. What are the main functions and essential features of a written contract?

## II. Case study.

Suppose that an America-based multinational company set up two subsidiaries in China. The parent company signed a sales contract between the subsidiaries, which stipulated that the parent company would make the delivery to one of the subsidiaries in Shanghai, which should forward some of the goods to another subsidiary at Chengdu.

**Questions:**

1. Is the transaction between the parent company and the two subsidiaries international trade? Why?

2. Is the transaction between the two subsidiaries international trade? Why?

# Chapter 2　International Trade Terms

【Learning Objectives】

By studying this chapter, you should be able to master:

● The role of trade terms in International trade

● The *Incoterms 2010*

● The differences between *Incoterms 2010* and *Incoterms 2000*

● The relations between Incoterms and sales contract

● How to choose trade terms

## Lead-in: News Report

### Freight Charges are the Focus for Steelmakers

BEIJING — The focus of iron ore negotiations between Chinese steelmakers and global iron ore producers this year will shift to freight price stabilization, to keep steelmakers' costs low, the Economic Observer Newspaper reported.

China's steel mills and its steel lobby body, the China Iron and Steel Association (CISA), have accepted the mechanism of quarterly iron ore pricing, the report said. In January, the Australian miner BHP Billiton Ltd. moved to a monthly set-pricing system after three mining companies abandoned a 40-year tradition of annual iron ore negotiations in March 2010 and turned to a quarterly pricing mechanism linked to iron ore indexes.

The CISA has previously insisted that Chinese steel mills should have long-term iron ore prices, which could stabilize their raw material costs.

The report said this year's negotiations are no longer about whether to accept quarterly pricing, but have shifted to freight costs. Shipping costs from Australia to China can vary widely, from $6 to $50 per ton.

The big three miners, BHP, Vale SA, and Rio Tinto Group currently offer FOB (free on board)

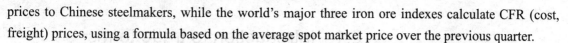

prices to Chinese steelmakers, while the world's major three iron ore indexes calculate CFR (cost, freight) prices, using a formula based on the average spot market price over the previous quarter.

According to historical records, ocean freight costs will fall before the annual negotiations, but once they are completed, the price is likely to rise dramatically.

The recent rally in spot iron ore prices is likely to push up second-quarter contract rates to a record $165 a ton for ore FOB from Australian mines with an iron content of 62 percent, a Reuters poll reported.

Platts'62 percent iron ore remains at $187.3 a ton, including freight, delivered to China, a record reached last week.

The Steel Index (TSI) 62 percent iron ore benchmark was also steady at $185.6 and Metal Bulletin's 62 percent ore was unchanged at $183.4.

The CISA is in discussion with Australian miners about the stabilization of freight charges to reduce volatility and keep costs stable, said an executive with a State-owned steelmaker, who declined to be named as the issue is sensitive.

The Brazilian company, Vale, in 2009 signed independent ore contracts with Chinese steel mills for fixed freight charges to further expand its presence in the country.

Some Chinese steelmakers have signed pricing contracts valid for three to four years with Vale for fixed freight, according to earlier reports.

Unlike BHP and Rio, which ship ore from Australia, Vale needs to transport iron ore from Brazil to China, resulting in much higher freight costs.

Vale is building 16 large ore carriers to reduce transportation costs between China and Brazil.

Freight costs from Brazil to China can vary from $10 to $110 per ton, based on historical records.

*(Source: http://europe.chinadaily.com.cn/business/2011-02/10/content_11976995.htm)*

### Class activities:

1. Why do steelmakers put much focus on freight charges?
2. If the freight charges are fixed, which trade term will the steelmakers choose?

国际贸易实务(英语版)(第2版)

# 2.1 Introduction to trade terms

For hundreds of years, businessmen have learned the business from practice and began to form the base of international sales contracts. The forms of contract have been developed to the standards and always contain a code of certain conditions of what is known today as trade terms. Trade terms are combinations of letters or words, specifying the responsibilities and obligations of a seller and a buyer under international trade agreements.

Firstly, trade terms define the place of risk transfer, that is to say, the seller or the buyer has to bear the damage in case of bad performance of the carriage; secondly, they distribute between the seller and the buyer the logistic and administrative expenses at the various stage of the process; finally, they specify where and how the seller must make the goods available to the buyer and how the buyer must take delivery of the goods.

All above mentioned mean that the buyers know exactly at what time and in which place, they should bear the risks of losing goods during the delivery; the sellers know exactly when and where they should bear the costs and expenses of delivery; and the sellers know where they must deposit the merchandise.

The trade terms make international trade easier and help traders in different countries to understand one another so as to avoid or reduce conflicts between the relevant parties. When a sales contract names the price of the goods followed by an Incoterm code and a name of the place, the line of liability becomes very clear. For example, a buyer has ordered 1,000 bicycles from a manufactory in China for US$20,000 FOB Port of Shanghai. This price and Incoterm plus the name of the place have outlined the liability of the seller and the buyer.

The top three influential international trade rules are *Warsaw-Oxford Rules 1932, Revised American Foreign Trade Definitions 1941* and *International Commercial Terms*.

## 2.1.1 *Warsaw-Oxford Rules 1932*

In 1928, The International Law Association held a meeting in Warsaw, the

贸易术语又称贸易条件、价格术语，用来说明价格的构成及买卖双方有关费用、风险和责任的划分，以确定买卖双方在交货和接货过程中各自应尽的义务。

24

capital of Poland and worked out *Warsaw Rules 1928,* with a total of 22 provisions. The Rules were revised into 21 provisions, after New York meeting in 1930, Paris meeting in 1931 and Oxford meeting in 1932, and was renamed as *Warsaw-Oxford Rules 1932.* The Rules govern the rights and obligations of the parties to the sales of goods on CIF (Cost, Insurance and Freight) terms.

The seller's obligations stipulated in *Warsaw-Oxford Rules 1932* are as follows:

- The seller must provide the goods of the contractual description, and have them loaded on board the vessel at the port of shipment in the manner of customary at the port. The risk shall be transferred to the buyer from the moment the goods are loaded on board the vessel.

- It shall be the duty of the seller to procure, at his own cost, a contract of carriage that is reasonable having regard to the nature of the goods and the terms current on contemplated route or in a particular trade. Moreover, the contract of carriage must be evidenced by a "shipped" bill of lading issued by the ship owner or his official agent.

- It shall be the duty of the seller to procure at his own cost from an underwriter or insurance company of good repute a policy of marine, evidence a valid and subsisting contract which shall be available for the benefit of the buyer, covering the goods during the whole of the course of transit contemplated in the contract of sale, including customary transshipment. The seller shall not be bound to procure a policy covering War Risk unless special provision to this effect shall have been made in the contract of sale. The value of the goods for insurance, shall be fixed in accordance with the usage of the particular trade, but in the absence of any such usage it shall be the invoice CIF value, of the goods to the buyer, less freight payable if any, on arrival and plus a marginal profit of 10 percent of the said invoice CIF value, after deduction of the amount of freight, if any payable on arrival.

- The seller shall give notice to the buyer that the goods have been shipped, or delivered into the custody of the carrier, as the case may be, stating the name of the vessel, if possible, the marks and full particulars. The cost of giving such notice shall be borne by the buyer. The non-receipt of such notice by, or the accidental omission

本协议以英国的贸易惯例和案例为基础，对 CIF 买卖合同的性质、买卖双方承担的费用、责任、风险作了说明。

to give any such notice to, the buyer shall not entitle the buyer to reject the documents tendered by the seller.

- The seller must exercise all the due diligence and send forward the documents. By the term "documents", it means the bill of lading, invoice, and policy of insurance, or other documents validly tendered in lieu thereof in accordance with the provisions of these Rules.

Besides, the buyer's obligations stipulated in *Warsaw-Oxford Rules 1932* are as follows:

- Should any import license be required by the country of destination for goods of the contractual description, it shall be the duty of the buyer to procure the same at his own expense and to notify the seller that such license has been obtained prior to the time for shipment of the goods.

- When the proper documents are tendered, it shall be the duty of the buyer to accept such documents and to pay the price in accordance with the terms of the contract of sale. The buyer shall be entitled to a reasonable opportunity of examining the documents and to a reasonable time in which to make such examination. The buyer, however, shall not be entitled when the proper documents are tendered to refuse to accept such documents or to refuse to pay the price in accordance with the terms of the contract of sale.

### 2.1.2 *Revised American Foreign Trade Definitions 1941*

In 1919, nine business communities in America made *The U.S. Export Quotations and Abbreviations*. As time went by, many changes in practice had occurred, which contributed to the further revision at the 27th National Foreign Trade Convention in 1940. The new edition was adopted by a joint committee representing the Chamber of Commerce of the United States of America, National Council of American Importers Inc. and National Foreign Trade Council, Inc. in the following year, known as *Revised American Foreign Trade Definitions 1941*. The Definitions defines six terms: Ex Point of Origin, FOB, FAS, C&F, CIF, Ex Dock.

《1941 年美国对外贸易定义修正本》是 1919 年在美国举行泛美贸易会议时所制定的出口报价定义，原名为《美国出口报价及其缩写》。

1941 年经美国商会、全国对外贸易委员会等三个民间团体所组成的联合委员会修订并改名。

本规则主要在北美大陆使用。因其 FOB 的定义与 INCOTERMS 不同，所以在与该区域客户贸易时应注意 FOB 术语的定义。

A. Ex (Point of Origin)

Under this term, the price quoted applies only at the point of origin, and the seller agrees to place the goods at the disposal of the buyer at the agreed place on the date or within the period fixed. The origin of the goods shall be indicated, i.e. Ex Factory, Ex Mill, Ex Mine, Ex Plantation, Ex Warehouse, etc.

Under this quotation, the seller must bear all costs and risks of the goods until such time as the buyer is obliged to take delivery thereof. The buyer must take delivery of the goods as soon as they have been placed at the agreed place on the date or within the period fixed and bear all costs and risks of the goods from the time when he is obliged to take delivery thereof.

B. FOB (Free on Board) (named inland carrier at named inland point of departure)

Under this term, the price quoted applies only at inland shipping point, and the seller arranges for loading the goods on, or in, railway cars, trucks, lighters, barges, aircraft, or other conveyance furnished for transportation.

本术语指在指定国起运地点的指定国内运输工具上交货。

- FOB (named inland carrier at named inland point of departure) freight prepaid to (named point of exportation)

Under this term, the seller quotes a price including transportation charges to the named point of exportation and prepays freight to named point of exportation, without assuming responsibility for the goods after obtaining clean bill of lading or other transportation receipts at named inland point of departure.

本术语是指在指定出口地点的指定运输工具上交货，运费预付至指定出口地点。

- FOB (named inland carrier at named inland point of departure)

Under this term, the seller quotes a price including the transportation charges to the named point, shipping freight collect and deducting the cost of transportation, without assuming responsibility for the goods after obtaining a clean bill of lading or other transportation receipts at named inland point of departure.

本术语是指在指定国内起运地点的指定运输工具上交货，扣除至指定地点运费。

- FOB (named inland carrier at named point of exportation)

Under this term, the seller quotes a price including the costs of transportation of the goods to named point of exportation, bearing any loss or damage, or both, incurred up to that point.

本术语指在指定出口地点的指定国内运输工具上交货。

- FOB Vessel (named point of shipment)

Under this term, the seller quotes a price covering all expense up to, and including delivery of the goods upon the overseas vessel provided by, or for,

本术语指在指定装货港船上交货，在使用 FOB Vessel 术语时，卖方无须负责取得出口许可证，无须负担出口捐税及费用，除非买方提出请求并负担费用和税捐的情况下，卖方才有义务协助买方取得各种出口证件。

本术语是指在进口国指定国内地点运输工具上交货。

the buyer at the named port of shipment.

Under this quotation, the seller must pay all charges incurred in placing goods on board the vessel designated and provided by, or for, the buyer on the date or within the period; provide clean ship's receipt or on-board bill of lading. The buyer must give seller adequate notice of name, sailing date, loading berth of, and delivery time to, the vessel; provide and pay for insurance, ocean and other transportation.

- FOB (named inland point in country of importation)

Under this term, the seller quotes a price including the cost of the merchandise and all costs of transportation to the named inland point in the country of importation.

Under this quotation, the seller must provide and pay for marine insurance; provide and pay for war risk insurance, unless otherwise agreed between the seller and buyer; be responsible for any loss or damage, or both, until arrival of goods on conveyance at the named inland point in the country of importation; pay the costs of certificates of origin, consular invoice, or any other documents issued in the country of origin, or shipment, or of both; pay all costs of landing, including wharfage, landing charge, and taxes, if any; pay all costs of customs entry in the country of importation.

The buyer must take prompt delivery of goods from conveyance upon arrival at destination; bear any cost and be responsible for all loss or damage, or both, after arrival at destination.

C. FAS (Free Along Side)

Under FAS Vessel (named port of shipment), the seller quotes a price including delivery of the goods alongside overseas vessel and within reach of its loading tackle.

《1941年美国对外贸易定义修订本》的 FAS 是 Free alongside，适用于各种运输工具，其 FAS Vessel 和 INCOTERMS 的 FAS 基本相同。

D. C&F (Cost and Freight) (named point of destination)

Under this term, the seller quotes a price including the cost of transportation to the named point of destination.

E. CIF (Cost, Insurance, and Freight) (named point of destination)

Under this term, the seller quotes a price including the cost of the goods, the marine insurance, and all transportation charges to the named point of destination.

F. Ex Dock (named port of importation)

Under this term, the seller quotes a price including the cost of the goods and all additional costs necessary to place the goods on the dock at the named port of importation, duty paid, if any.

### 2.1.3  *International Commercial Terms*

The most internationally accepted trade terms are *International Commercial Terms* or called *INCOTERMS*, developed by the International Chamber of Commerce (ICC) in Paris, defining the costs, risks, and obligations of buyers and sellers regarding the delivery of goods in international transactions.

The first set of Incoterms was published in 1936 and has been periodically updated for 7 times to adapt to temporary commercial practice. The first version remained in use for nearly 20 years before the second one was published in 1953. Amendments followed in 1967, 1976, 1980, 1990 and 2000. The latest version referred to as *INCOTERMS 2010* was published on January 1, 2011.

Incoterms benefit seller and buyer because they avoid misunderstandings about who should do what, as below:

- Who should clear the job for export or import;
- Who should pay the costs of loading, transporting and discharging the goods;
- Who should bear risk of loss or damage to the goods in transit;
- Who should take out insurance as a protection against these risks?

Responsibilities are simply and clearly defined by referring to one of the ICC Incoterms. And these terms are accepted by governments, legal authorities and businesses worldwide. Therefore, the risk of misunderstanding and subsequent disputes is eliminated.

## 2.2  Introduction to *INCOTERMS 2010*

The ICC's *INCOTERMS 2010*, the eighth revision of the Incoterms Rules, came into force on January 1, 2011. The new Rules have been revised to take into account developments in international trade over the last decade as both the volume and complexity of global sales have increased greatly. *INCOTERMS 2010* also aims to address security issues arising in recent years

ICC 于 1936 年首次公布通则后，分别在 1953 年、1967 年、1976 年、1980 年、1990 年、2000 年不同版本中作了 6 次修订和补充。

2007 年，ICC 组织 7 人小组，开始启动新的修订工作和新版规则定名为 *INCOTERMS 2010* 的起草，2011 年正式推出并使用。

国际贸易术语有利于买卖双方洽商交易和订立合同、有利于双方核算价格和成本、有利于解决履行过程中的争议。

and provides for ongoing changes in electronic communications. Finally, the new Rules recognize the growth of customs-free areas.

*INCOTERMS 2010* are categorized into two groups based on method of delivery:

a. Rules in relation to any mode or modes of transport.

b. Rules for sea and inland waterway transport.

Table 2-1 shows Categories of *INCOTERMS 2010*.

*INCOTERMS 2010* 对于 11 种术语按照适用的运输方式分为两大类：①适用于任何或多种运输方式的术语；②适用于海运和内陆水路运输方式的术语。

Table 2-1　Categories of *INCOTERMS 2010*

| Deliveries by any mode of transport (sea, road, air, rail) | Deliveries by sea and inland water transport |
|---|---|
| EXW (Ex Works) | FAS (Free Alongside Ship) |
| FCA (Free Carrier) | FOB (Free on Board) |
| CPT (Carriage Paid To) | CFR (Cost and Freight) |
| CIP (Carriage and Insurance Paid To) | CIF (Cost, Insurance and Freight) |
| DAT (Delivered at Terminal) | |
| DAP (Delivered at Place) | |
| DDP (Delivered Duty Paid) | |

## 2.2.1　Mode of transport

Not all Incoterms are appropriate for all modes of transport. Some terms were designed with waterborne transport, such as sea, ocean, and inland waterway while others were designed to be applicable to all modes. The use of trade terms in connection with different modes of transport in the export and import of goods is described in Table 2-2.

Table 2-2　The mode of transport of Incoterms 2010

●= Yes

○= No

| Incoterms | Mode of Transport | | | | | |
|---|---|---|---|---|---|---|
| | Sea | Road | Rail | Air | Inland waterway | Multimodal |
| EXW | ● | ● | ● | ● | ● | ● |
| FCA | ● | ● | ● | ● | ● | ● |

continued

| Incoterms | Mode of Transport | | | | | |
|---|---|---|---|---|---|---|
| | Sea | Road | Rail | Air | Inland waterway | Multimodal |
| FAS | ● | ○ | ○ | ○ | ● | ○ |
| FOB | ● | ○ | ○ | ○ | ● | ○ |
| CFR | ● | ○ | ○ | ○ | ● | ○ |
| CIF | ● | ○ | ○ | ○ | ● | ○ |
| CPT | ● | ● | ● | ● | ● | ● |
| CIP | ● | ● | ● | ● | ● | ● |
| DAT | ● | ● | ● | ● | ● | ● |
| DAP | ● | ● | ● | ● | ● | ● |
| DDP | ● | ● | ● | ● | ● | ● |

## 2.2.2   The six most popular trade terms

In international transactions, FOB, CFR, CIF, FCA, CPT and CIP are the most frequently used trade terms. Their definitions, expenses distribution between the seller and buyer, and responsibilities of the seller and buyer will be illustrated in this part.

### 1. FOB (Free on Board…named port of shipment)

Figure 2-1 shows the responsibilities of the seller and the buyer under FOB.

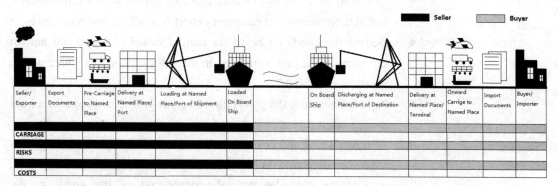

Figure 2-1   Responsibilities of the seller and buyers under FOB

FOB 术语下卖方在指定装运港将货物交到买方指定的船上，或取得已如此交付的货物，卖方完成交货义务。

Under FOB term, the seller fulfills his obligation when the goods are delivered on board the vessel at the port of shipment named in the sales contract. The risk of loss or damage to the goods is transferred from the seller to the buyer when the goods are placed on board the vessel. The buyer bears all costs from that point forward, including freight, insurance, unloading and the transportation from the arrival port to the final destination. This term requires the seller to clear the goods for export. The key document involved in FOB transaction is the On Board Bill of Lading.

修订后的 *INCOTERMS 2010* 取消了以往"船舷"的概念：规定卖方承担货物装上船为止的一切风险，买方承担货物自装运港装上船后的一切风险。

With FOB, the seller has the option to deliver the goods on board the vessel, or to "procure goods already so delivered." This is a reference to so-called "string sales," where a single shipment might be resold multiple times during transport, as is common in the commodity trade.

If the shipment is containerized or to be containerized, common practice is to deliver the shipment to the carrier at a terminal and not on board a ship. In such situations, the FCA term is recommended.

FOB 术语的风险转移点和费用划分点都在装运港指定船只上，两者是重合的。

Sellers and buyers often misuse the FOB term. FOB does not mean loading goods onto a truck or train at the seller's place of business. FOB is used only in reference to delivering the goods on board a ship in ocean or inland waterway transport. The FCA term, on the other hand, is applicable to all modes of transport.

**The seller's obligations:**

- Provide the goods, commercial invoice, and other documentation as required by the sales contract.
- Obtain at own risk and cost all required export licenses, documents, and authorizations and carry out export formalities and procedures.
- Deliver the goods on board the named vessel at the named port of shipment at the time stipulated in the sales contract, or "procure the goods so delivered."
- Pay all costs until the goods have been delivered on board the vessel at the named port of shipment.
- At buyer's risk and cost, provide notice to the buyer that the goods have been delivered on board the ship at the named port of shipment, or that the ship did not take possession of the goods at the agreed-upon time.
- Provide the buyer with a proof of delivery that the goods have been

delivered on board the ship at the named port of shipment.

**The buyer's obligations:**

- Pay for the goods as provided in the sales contract.
- Obtain any import licenses or authorizations and handle all import customs formalities.
- Contract at own expense for the carriage of the goods from the named port of shipment.
- Pay all costs for carriage and insurance from the time the goods have been delivered on board the ship at the named port of shipment.
- If the buyer nominates the ship, give sufficient notice to the seller of the name of the vessel, the loading point, and the time or period for delivery.

**Attentions:**

**(1) The transfer of risks in advance.** Normally, when the goods are delivered on board the vessel at the named port of shipment, the risk of loss of or damage to the goods is transferred from the seller to the buyer.

If the buyer fails to notify the seller of the name of the vessel, and the port of shipment within the prescribed period, the buyer would bear all the consequential costs and risks from the expiry date of the notification period.

买方应负责租船订舱并将船期、船名及时通知对方，而卖方负责在规定期限内将货物装上买方指定的船上，否则到期后买方要承担相应的风险和费用。

*Case study*

*On FOB term basis, Seller A prepared the goods at the stipulated time, meanwhile, Buyer B informed A of the name of vessel and the date of shipment. When the goods are lifted to the ship, they fell down on deck. Now who shall take the responsibility?*

**(2) The problems of the loading of goods.** To avoid any dispute of loading expenses, the derived form of FOB occurs. In order to indicate who shall bear the loading charges, the most used variations of FOB are as follows:

a. FOB liner terms

b. FOB under tackle

c. FOB stowed

d. FOB trimmed

e. FOB stowed & trimmed

Table 2-3 shows five derived forms of FOB.

由于装船费用的负担问题，2010 通则的 FOB 术语变形为 5 种。

Table 2-3    Variations of FOB.

| Derived Form | Seller | Buyer | Remarks |
|---|---|---|---|
| FOB Liner Terms (FOB ) | | √ | The shipping company is responsible for loading, so the buyer pays loading expenses. |
| FOB Under Tackle (FOB) | | √ | The seller only needs to send and place the goods on wharf within the reach of the ship's tackle. Loading expense incurred thereafter will be borne by the buyer. |
| FOB Stowed (FOBS) | √ | | The seller loads the goods into the ship's hold and pays loading expenses including stowing expenses. |
| FOB Trimmed (FOBT) | √ | | The seller pays all loading expenses including trimming expenses. |
| FOB Stowed & Trimmed(FOBST) | √ | | The seller pays all loading expenses including stowing and trimming expenses. |

买方有时指定卖方为租船订舱的代理，但即使这样，风险和费用仍由买方承担。

**(3) Contract of carriage.** The seller has no obligation to the buyer to make a contract of carriage. However, if requested by the buyer or if it is commercial practice and the buyer does not give an instruction to the contrary in due time, the seller may contract for carriage on usual terms at the buyer's risk and expense. In either case, the seller may decline to make the contract of carriage and, if it does, shall promptly notify the buyer.

## 2. CIF (Cost, Insurance and Freight…named port of destination)

Figure 2-2 illustrates the responsibilities of the seller and buyer under CIF.

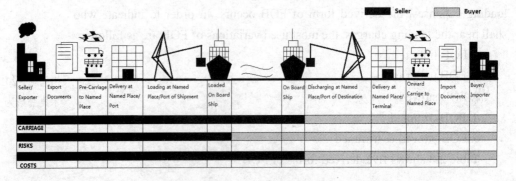

Figure 2-2    Responsibilities of the seller and buyer under CIF.

Under CIF term, the seller is responsible for delivering the goods on board the ship at the port of shipment (not destination). This is where risk passes from seller to buyer. The seller pays the costs and freight of the goods to the named port of destination. This is where costs transfer from seller to buyer. It is important to note that the transfer of risk from seller to buyer occurs at a different point from the transfer of costs. The seller also has to procure and pay for minimum cover marine insurance on behalf of the buyer against the buyer's risk of loss or damage to the goods during the carriage. The CIF term requires the seller to clear the goods for export.

The buyer should note that under the CIF term, the seller is required to obtain insurance only on minimum cover. Should the buyer wish to have the protection of greater cover, he would either need to agree as such expressly with the seller or to make his own extra insurance agreement.

When using the CIF term, it is advisable to clearly specify in the contract of sale and contracts of carriage, not only the named port of destination, but also the precise point at or within the named port of destination.

With CIF, the seller has the option to deliver the goods on board the vessel, or to "procure goods already so delivered." This is a reference to so-called "string sales" where a single shipment might be resold multiple times during transport, as is common in the commodity trade.

If the shipment is containerized or to be containerized, common practice is to deliver the shipment to the carrier at a terminal and not on board a ship. In such situations, the CIP term is recommended.

**The seller's obligations:**

- Provide the goods, commercial invoice, and other documentation as required by the sales contract.
- Obtain at own risk and cost all export licenses, documents, and authorizations and carry out export formalities and procedures.
- Contract or procure a contract for the carriage of the goods from the point of delivery to the named port of destination.
- Obtain and pay for minimum cover cargo insurance as agreed in the contract.
- Deliver the goods on board the ship at the port of shipment or "procure goods already so delivered."
- Pay all costs until the goods have been delivered on board the ship at

CIF 术语下卖方必须在合同规定的装运期内在装运港将货物交至运往指定目的港的船上，负担货物装上船为止的一切费用和货物灭失或损坏的风险，并负责办理货运保险，支付保险费，以及负责租船或订舱，支付从装运港到目的港的运费。

国际贸易实务(英语版)(第2版)

the port of shipment.

- Provide notice that enables the buyer to take timely possession of the goods at the named port of destination.
- Provide the buyer with a transport document, dated within the period agreed, that allows the buyer to claim the goods at the named port of destination.

**The buyer's obligations:**

- Pay for the goods as per sales contract.
- Obtain any import licenses or authorizations and handle all import customs formalities.
- Pay any additional costs for the goods, other than main carriage, once they have been delivered on board the ship at the port of shipment.
- If, according to the sales contract, the buyer is entitled to specify a time for shipping or the point of receiving the shipment at the named port of destination, give seller sufficient notice.

**Attentions:**

**(1) About Insurance.** The seller must obtain at his own expense cargo insurance as agreed in the contract. If not, the seller is required to obtain insurance only on minimum cover.

**(2) Symbolic Delivery.** Symbolic delivery means that the seller fulfills his obligation when he delivers the goods on board the vessel at the port of shipment within the agreed period and provides the buyer with shipping documents in conformity with the contract of sale.

**(3) Notice to the seller.** The seller must give the buyer sufficient notice that the goods have been delivered as well as any other notice required in order to allow the buyer to take measures which are normally necessary to enable him to take the goods.

**(4) About the landing fee.** As the unloading of goods is a continuous process, it is hard to divide the responsibilities and costs. To avoid any dispute of unloading expenses, the derived form of CFR and CIF occurs. In order to indicate who shall bear the unloading charges, the most used variations of CFR and CIF are as shown in Table 2-4:

卖方应被要求按照合同规定及时投保，否则卖方只按最低责任投保。

36

Table 2-4 Variations of CFR and CIF

| Derived Form | Seller | Buyer | Remarks |
|---|---|---|---|
| CFR/CIF Liner Terms | √ | | The shipping company is responsible for unloading, so the seller pays unloading expenses. |
| CFR/CIF Ex Tackle | √ | | The seller loads the goods into the ship's hold and pays loading expenses including stowing expenses. |
| CFR/CIF Landed | | √ | The seller needs to send and place the goods on wharf within the reach of the ship's tackle. Unloading expense incurred will be borne by the buyer. |
| CFR/CIF Ex-ship's Hold | | √ | The buyer pays the cost for discharging the goods from the ship's hold. |

*Case study*

A Chinese import and export company concluded a Sale Contract with a Holland firm on August 5, 2017, selling a batch of certain commodities. The contract was based on CIF Rotterdam at USD 2,500 per metric ton. The Chinese company delivered the goods in compliance with the contract and obtained a clean on board Bill of Lading. During transportation, however, 100 metric tons of goods got lost because of rough sea. Upon arrival in Rotterdam, the price of the contracted goods went down quickly. The buyer refused to take delivery of the goods and effect payment and claimed damages from the seller.

How would you deal with the case?

## 3. CFR (Cost and Freight…named port of destination)

Figure 2-3 shows the responsibilities of the seller and buyer under CFR.

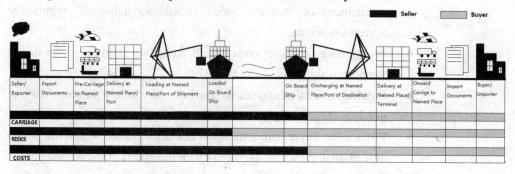

Figure 2-3 Responsibilities of the seller and buyer under CFR

CFR 术语下卖方必须在合同规定的装运期内,在装运港将货物交至运往指定目的港的船上,负担货物装上船为止的一切费用和货物灭失或损坏的风险,并负责租船或订舱,支付抵达目的港的正常运费。

Under CFR term, the seller delivers when the goods are delivered on board the vessel at the port of shipment (not destination). This is where risk passes from seller to buyer. The seller is responsible for contracting and paying for the cost and freight necessary to bring the goods to the named destination. This is where costs transfer from seller to buyer. It is important to note that the transfer of risk from seller to buyer occurs at a different point than the transfer of costs. The CFR term requires the seller to clear the goods for export.

When using CFR term, it is advisable to clearly specify in the contract of sale, and contracts of carriage, not only the named port of destination, but also the precise point at or within the named port of destination.

With CFR, the seller has the option to deliver the goods on board the vessel, or to "procure goods already so delivered." This is a reference to so-called "string sales" where a single shipment might be resold multiple times during transport, as is common in the commodity trade.

If the shipment is containerized or to be containerized, common practice is to deliver the shipment to the carrier at a terminal and not on board a ship. In such situations, the CPT term is recommended.

**The seller's obligations:**

- Provide the goods, commercial invoice, and other documentation as required by the sales contract.
- Obtain at own risk and cost all required export licenses, documents, and authorizations and carry out export formalities and procedures.
- Contract or procure a contract for the carriage of the goods from the point of delivery to the named port of destination.
- Deliver the goods on board the ship at the port of shipment (not destination) or "procure goods already so delivered" within the agreed-upon time.
- Pay all costs until the goods have been delivered on board the ship at the port of shipment.
- Provide notice that enables the buyer to take timely possession of the goods at the named port of destination.
- Provide the buyer with a transport document, dated within the period agreed, that allows the buyer to claim the goods at the named port of destination.

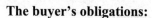
**The buyer's obligations:**

- Pay for the goods as provided in the sales contract.
- Obtain any import licenses or authorizations and handle all import customs formalities.
- Pay any additional costs for the goods, other than main carriage, once they have been delivered on board the ship at the port of shipment.
- If, according to the sales contract, the buyer is entitled to specify a time for shipping or the point of receiving the shipment at the named port of destination, to give seller sufficient notice.

**Attentions:**

**(1) Notice to the seller.** The seller must give the buyer sufficient notice that the goods have been delivered as well as shipping advice and any other notice required in order to allow the buyer to insure the goods.

卖方装船后要及时给买方发装运通知书,便于买方及时投保。

**(2) Who pays landing fee.** To avoid any dispute of landing fee, the derived form of CFR occurs. In order to indicate who shall bear the landing fee, the most used variations of CFR are as follows:

a. CFR Liner Terms

b. CFR Landed

c. CFR Ex Tackle

d. CFR Ex Ship's Hold

由于卸货费用的负担问题,2010 通则的 CFR 术语变形为 4 种。

***Case study***

*A merchant in South America placed an order with a Chinese export company for a certain commodity on CFR Asuncion (亚松森) terms. With a view to develop new markets, the export company immediately made an offer abroad on the basis of CFR Asuncion, and the transaction was soon concluded. When shipping the goods, however, this company came to realize that Asuncion is an inland city. As was the case, if the company had the goods transported to Asuncion, it had to, first of all, have the goods transported by sea to a seaport in Argentina or some other South American neighboring countries. After that, the goods might be transported to Asuncion through river transportation or inland transportation. As a result, this company had to pay a considerable sum of freight charges.*

*What can we learn from this case?*

### 4. FCA (Free Carrier…named place of delivery)

Figure 2-4 illustrates the responsibilities of the seller and buyer under FCA.

FCA 术语是指卖方在其所在处所或另一指定地，将货物交给由买方指定的承运人或另一人，即完成交货。如买方不通知在指定地内的特定交货地点，卖方可选择在指定地内他认为最合适的地点交货。

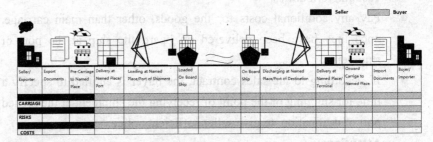

Figure 2-4　Responsibilities of the seller and buyer under FCA

Under FCA term, the seller clears the goods for export and delivers them to the carrier nominated by the buyer at the named place of delivery. The risk of loss or damage to the goods is transferred from seller to buyer at that time.

In this term, the chosen place of delivery has an impact on the obligation of loading and unloading the goods at that place. If delivery occurs at the seller's place of business, the seller is responsible for loading the goods onto the transport vehicle. If delivery occurs at any other place, such as the loading dock of the carrier, the seller is not responsible for unloading. When using the FCA term, it is advisable to clearly specify in the contract of sale and contracts of carriage the precise point of delivery. If no precise point is indicated at the time of the contract of sale, the seller may choose within the place or range where the carrier should take the goods into his charge.

**The seller's obligations:**

● Provide the goods, commercial invoice, and other documentation as required by the sales contract.

● Obtain at own risk and cost all required export licenses, documents, and authorizations and carry out export formalities and procedures.

● Deliver the goods to the carrier at the named place of delivery at the time stipulated in the sales contract.

● Pay all costs until the goods have been delivered to the carrier at the named place of delivery.

● At buyer's risk and cost, provide notice to the buyer that the goods have been delivered to the carrier, or that the carrier did not take possession of the goods at the agreed-upon time.

- Provide the buyer with a proof of delivery.

**The buyer's obligations:**

- Pay for the goods as provided in the sales contract.
- Obtain any import licenses or authorizations and handle all import customs formalities.
- Provide for carriage of the goods from the named place of delivery.
- Pay all costs for carriage and insurance from the time the goods have been delivered to the carrier at the named place of delivery.
- Give sufficient notice to the seller of the name of the carrier, the delivery point, the time or period for delivery, and the mode of transport.

**Attentions:**

**(1) About carrier.** "Carrier" means any person who, in a contract of carriage, undertakes to perform or to procure the performance of transport by rail, road, air, sea, inland waterway or by a combination of such modes. If the buyer nominates a person other than a carrier to receive the goods, the seller is deemed to have fulfilled his obligation to deliver the goods when they are delivered to that person. The risk of loss of or damage to the goods is transferred from the seller to the buyer at the time the nominated carrier accepts the goods at the prescribed place.

**(2) About delivery.** The seller must deliver the goods to the carrier or another person nominated by the buyer at the agreed point, if any at the named place on the agreed date or within the agreed period.

Delivery is completed:

a) If the named place is the seller's premise, when the goods have been loaded on the means of transport provided by the buyer.

b) In any other case, when the goods are placed at the disposal of the carrier or another person nominated by the buyer on the seller's means of transport ready for unloading.

c) The seller must deliver the goods by placing them at the disposal of the buyer at the agreed point, if any, at the named place of delivery, not loaded on any collecting vehicle.

To be concluded, according to *INCOTERMS 2010*, if delivery occurs at the seller's premises, the seller is responsible for loading. If delivery occurs at

如果指定地点是在卖方所在地，则卖方必须将货物装上买方指定的承运人或其代理人提供的运输工具上，这时装货义务及有关费用由卖方承担。

如果指定地点是在其他任何地点，则当货物在卖方的运输工具上，尚未卸货而交给买方指定的承运人或其代理人处置时，卸货义务及有关费用由买方承担。

any other place, the seller is not responsible for unloading.

### 5. CPT (Carriage Paid To...named place of destination)

Figure 2-5 shows the responsibilities of the seller and buyer under CPT.

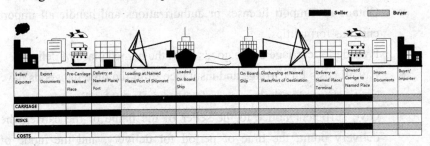

Figure 2-5   Responsibilities of the seller and buyer under CPT

CPT 术语下卖方支付货物运至指定目的地的运费。在货物被交由(第一)承运人保管时,货物灭失或损坏的风险,即从卖方转移至买方,买方负责由于货物交给承运人后发生的事件引起的额外费用;卖方负责办理出口清关手续,并支付有关费用和税捐。

注意:

(1) 明确装运期、装运地点和目的地。

(2) 当由买方确定交货时间时,买方要及时通知卖方。

(3) 当具体交货地点未确定时,卖方可在最适合要求的地点交货。

(4) 一般情况下,装货费由卖方承担,卸货费由买方承担。

(5) 卖方需特别注意的是装运通知问题。(与 CFR 相同,运输与保险分离。)

Under CPT term, the seller clears the goods for export and is responsible for delivering the goods to the carrier at an agreed-upon place of shipment (not the destination). This is where risk passes from seller to buyer. Like CFR, the buyer bears all risks and any other additional costs once the seller delivers the goods to the first carrier (if subsequent carriers are used for the carriage to the agreed destination, the risk passes when the goods have been delivered to the first carrier). The seller, however, is responsible for contracting for and paying the costs associated with transport of the goods to the named place of destination. This is where costs transfer from seller to buyer. It is important to note that the transfer of risk from seller to buyer occurs at a different point from the transfer of costs.

As mentioned previously, "Carrier" is defined as any person who, in a contract of carriage, undertakes to perform or to procure the performance of transport by rail, road, sea, inland waterway or by a combination of methods.

The seller is also responsible for the costs of unloading, customs clearance, duties, and other costs if such costs are included in the cost of carriage. But the seller is not responsible for procuring and paying for insurance cover.

It is noted that the CPT term requires the seller to clear the goods for export. CPT is almost the same as CFR except that CFR is only applied to sea and inland waterway transportation while CPT may be used irrespective of the mode of transport including multi-modal transport.

**The seller's obligations:**

- Provide the goods, commercial invoice, and other documentation as required by the sales contract.

- Obtain at own risk and cost all required export licenses, documents, and authorizations and carry out export formalities and procedures as well as those required for transshipment through any country prior to delivery.

- Contract or procure a contract for the carriage of the goods from the point of delivery to the named place of destination. No obligation to provide insurance.

- Deliver the goods to the (first) carrier at the named place of shipment (not place of destination).

- Pay all costs until the goods have been delivered to the (first) carrier at the named place of shipment. Pay all costs of loading and carriage to the named place of destination.

- Give the buyer sufficient notice that the goods have been delivered to the agreed point at the named place of destination.

- Provide timely notice that the goods have been delivered to the (first) carrier and notice that enables the buyer to take timely possession of the goods at the named place of destination.

- Provide the buyer with a transport document, dated within the period agreed, that allows the buyer to claim the goods at the named place of destination.

**The buyer's obligations:**

- Pay for the goods as provided in the sales contract.

- Obtain any import licenses or authorizations and handle all import formalities.

- Pay costs other than main carriage after the goods have been delivered to the (first) carrier at the place of shipment.

- If, according to the sales contract, the buyer is entitled to specify a time or point of taking delivery at the named place of destination, to give seller sufficient notice.

## 6. CIP(Carriage and Insurance Paid to…named place of destination)

Figure 2-6 shows the responsibilities of the seller and buyer under CIP.

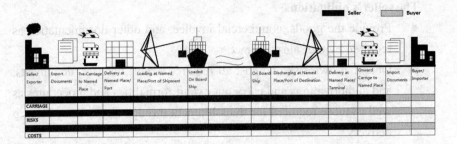

Figure 2-6  Responsibilities of the seller and buyer under CIP

CIP 术语下卖方除了须承担在 CPT 术语下同样的义务外，还须对货物在运输途中灭失或损坏的买方风险取得货物保险，订立保险合同，并支付保险费。

Under CIP term, the seller clears the goods for export and is responsible for delivering the goods to the carrier at an agreed-upon place of shipment (not the destination). This is where risk passes from seller to buyer. The seller, however, is responsible for contracting for and paying the costs associated with transport of the goods and minimum cover insurance to the "named place of destination." This is where costs transfer from seller to buyer. It is important to note that the transfer of risk from seller to buyer occurs at a different point than the transfer of costs.

When using the CIP term, it is advisable to clearly specify in the contract of sale and in contracts of carriage, not only the named place of destination, but also the precise point at or within the named place of destination.

Should the buyer wish to have the protection of greater cover, he would either need to agree as such expressly with the seller or to make his own extra insurance arrangements.

The CIP term requires the seller to clear the goods for export. Its only difference from CIF is that CIP may be used irrespective of the mode of transport including multi-modal transport.

注意：
货物运输途中的风险属于买方，但保险责任由卖方承担。卖方应按双方约定的险别、保险额投保；若无约定，卖方按最低责任险投保，最低保险金额为合同价款加成 10%，并以合同货币投保。

**The seller's obligations:**

- Provide the goods, commercial invoice, and other documentation as required by the sales contract.
- Obtain at own risk and cost all required export licenses, documents, and authorizations and carry out export formalities and procedures as well as those required for transshipment through any country prior to delivery.
- Contract or procure a contract for the carriage of the goods from the point of delivery to the named place of destination.
- Obtain and pay for minimum cover cargo insurance as agreed in the

contract.

- Deliver the goods to the (first) carrier at the named place of shipment (not place of destination).
- Pay all costs until the goods have been delivered to the (first) carrier at the named place of shipment.
- Provide timely notice that the goods have been delivered to the (first) carrier and notice that enables the buyer to take timely possession of the goods at the named place of destination.
- Provide the buyer with a transport document, dated within the period agreed, that allows the buyer to claim the goods at the named place of destination.

**The buyer's obligations:**

- Pay for the goods as provided in the sales contract.
- Obtain any import licenses or authorizations and handle all import formalities.
- Pay any additional costs for the goods, other than main carriage, once they have been delivered to the (first) carrier at the place of shipment.
- If, according to the sales contract, the buyer is entitled to specify a time or point of taking delivery at the named place of destination, to give seller sufficient notice.

## 2.2.3  The other five trade terms

Compared with the six trade terms mentioned above, EXW, FAS, DAT, DAP and DDP are less frequently used trade terms in international transactions.

### 1. EXW (Ex Works…named place of delivery)

Figure 2-7 illustrates the responsibilities of the seller and buyer and EXW.

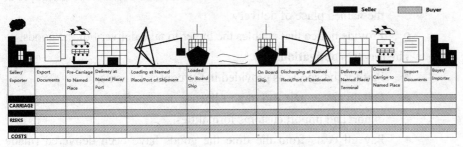

Figure 2-7   Responsibilities of the seller and buyer under EXW

EXW 术语下卖方在其所在处所(工厂、工场、仓库等)将货物提供给买方时，即履行了交货义务，除非另有约定。卖方不负责将货物装上买方备妥的车辆，也不负责出口清关，买方要负担自卖方所在处所提取货物后至目的地的一切费用和风险，这是卖方责任最小的一种术语。

Under EXW term, the seller fulfills his obligation to deliver when he has made the goods available at "named place of delivery", which is commonly, but not necessarily, the seller's place of business (i.e. works, factory, warehouse, etc.). This term represents the minimum obligation for the seller that he is not responsible for clearing the goods for the export and loading the goods onto a truck or other transport vehicle at the named place of departure. Responsibility for the seller is to put the goods in a good package which is adaptable and disposable by the transport.

The buyer arranges insurance for damage transit goods and the buyer has to bear all costs and risks involved in taking the goods from the seller's premises.

However, if the parties wish the seller to be responsible for the loading of the goods on departure and bear the risk and all the costs of such loading, this should be made clear by adding explicit wording to this effect in the contract of sale. This EXW term should not be used when the buyer cannot handle the export formalities directly or indirectly. Under such circumstances, a better solution is to use the FCA (Free Carrier) term, provided that the seller agrees that he will load at his cost and risk.

**The seller's obligations:**

- Provide the goods, commercial invoice, and other documentations as required by the sales contract.
- Provide the buyer, at the buyer's request, risk and expense, assistance in securing any license, documents, authorizations, and security clearance required for the export of the goods.
- Make the goods available to the buyer at the named place and point of delivery at the time stipulated in the sales contract.
- Pay all costs until the goods have been made available to the buyer at the named place of delivery.
- Provide notice that enables the buyer to take delivery of the goods.

**The buyer's obligations:**

- Pay for the goods as provided in the contract of sale.
- Obtain any export and import license or authorizations and handle all export and import customs formalities.
- Pay all costs from the time the goods have been delivered (made available) at the named place of delivery.

- If, according to the sales contract, the buyer is entitled to specify a time for taking delivery or the point of taking delivery at the named place of delivery, give seller sufficient notice.

### 2. FAS (Free alongside Ship…named port of shipment)

Figure 2-8 shows the responsibilities of the seller and buyer under FAS.

| | | | | | Seller | | Buyer | | | | | |
|---|---|---|---|---|---|---|---|---|---|---|---|---|
| Seller/Exporter | Export Documents | Pre-Carriage to Named Place | Delivery at Named Place/Port | Loading at Named Place/Port of Shipment | Loaded On Board Ship | | On Board Ship | Discharging at Named Place/Port of Destination | Delivery at Named Place/Terminal | Onward Carriage to Named Place | Import Documents | Buyer/Importer |
| CARRIAGE | | | | | | | | | | | | |
| RISKS | | | | | | | | | | | | |
| COSTS | | | | | | | | | | | | |

Figure 2-8　Responsibilities of the seller and buyer under FAS

Under FAS term, the seller fulfills his obligation to deliver when the goods have been placed alongside the vessel (on a dock or barge) at the named port of the shipment. The buyer has to bear all costs and risks of loss or damage to the goods from that moment. The FAS term requires the seller to clear the goods for export. This term is typically used for heavy-lift or bulk cargo.

When using the FAS term, it is advisable to clearly specify in the contract of sale and contracts of carriage, not only the named port of shipment, but also the precise loading point at or within the named port of shipment, particularly when the named port of shipment is large and options abound for delivery points.

With FAS, the seller has the option to deliver the goods alongside the ship, or to "procure goods already so delivered." This is a reference to so-called "string sales" where a single shipment might be resold multiple times during transport, as is common in the commodity trade.

If the shipment is containerized or to be containerized, the common practice is to deliver the shipment to the carrier at a terminal, and not alongside a ship. In such situations, the FCA term is recommended.

**The seller's obligations:**

- Provide the goods, commercial invoice, and other documentation as required by the sales contract.
- Obtain at own risk and cost all required export licenses, documents,

FAS 术语下卖方在装运港将货物放置在码头或驳船上(a quay or a barge)靠船边,或为配合大宗货物在运送途中的转售,取得已按上述交付方式的货物,即履行交货义务。买方必须自该时刻起,负担一切费用和风险。

and authorizations and carry out export formalities and procedures.

- Deliver the goods alongside the ship at the named port of shipment, or "procure the goods so delivered," within the agreed-upon time stipulated in the sales contract.
- Pay all costs until the goods have been delivered alongside the ship at the named port of shipment.
- At buyer's risk and cost, provide notice to the buyer that the goods have been delivered alongside the ship at the named port of shipment, or that the ship did not take possession of the goods at the agreed-upon time.
- Provide the buyer with a proof of delivery that the goods have been delivered alongside the ship at the named port of shipment.

**The buyer's obligations:**

- Pay for the goods as provided in the sales contract.
- Obtain any import licenses or authorizations and handle all import customs formalities.
- Contract at own expense for the carriage of the goods from the named port of shipment.
- Pay all costs for carriage and insurance from the time the goods have been delivered alongside the ship at the named port of shipment.
- If the buyer nominates the ship, give sufficient notice to the seller of the name of the ship, the loading point, and the time or period for delivery.

**Attentions:**

(1) According to *INCOTERMS*, FAS is Free alongside ship (named port of shipment), this term can be used only for sea or inland waterway transport.

According to *Revised American Foreign Trade Definitions, 1941*，FAS is Free Along Side, and this term can be used for any transport.

There are differences in the rights and the obligations of the parties concerned and the transfer of risks between them. Therefore, when we trade with the US, Canada, or other American countries, we should pay more attention to these differences.

(2) The transfer of risks in advance. Normally, when the goods are placed alongside the vessel at the named port of shipment, the risk of loss of or damage to the goods is transferred from the seller to the buyer.

与《1941 美国对外贸易定义修订本》的不同：后者规定的 FAS 是 Free Along Side，适用于各种运输工具，其 FAS vessel 和 INCOTERMS 的 FAS 基本相同。

If the buyer fails to notify the seller of the name of the vessel, and the port of shipment within the prescribed period, the buyer would bear all the consequential cost and risk from the expiry date of the notification period.

### 3. DAT (Delivered at Terminal...named terminal at port or place of destination)

Figure 2-9 shows the responsibilities of the seller and buyer under DAT.

| | | | | | | | | | | | |
|---|---|---|---|---|---|---|---|---|---|---|---|
| Seller/ Exporter | Export Documents | Pre-Carriage to Named Place | Delivery at Named Place/ Port | Loading at Named Place/Port of Shipment | Loaded On Board Ship | | On Board Ship | Discharging at Named Place/Port of Destination | Delivery at Named Place/ Terminal | Onward Carriage to Named Place | Import Documents | Buyer/ Importer |
| **CARRIAGE** | | | | | | | | | | | |
| **RISKS** | | | | | | | | | | | |
| **COSTS** | | | | | | | | | | | |

Figure 2-9   Responsibilities of the seller and buyer under DAT

DAT (Delivered at Terminal) replaces DEQ (Delivered ex Quay) in *INCOTERMS 2000*. DAT may be used irrespective of the mode of transport selected and may also be used where more than one mode of transport is involved.

Under DAT term, the seller delivers when the goods, having been unloaded from the arriving means of transport, are placed at the buyer's disposal at a named terminal at the named port or place of destination. The seller pays for the carriage to the terminal, except for costs related to import clearance, and assumes all risks prior to the point that the goods are unloaded at the terminal. It is considered that DAT would prove more useful than DEQ in the case of containers that might be unloaded and then loaded into a container stack at the terminal, awaiting shipment. There is previously no term clearly dealing with containers that are not at the buyer's premise.

**The seller's obligations:**

- Provide the goods, commercial invoice, and other documentation as required by the sales contract.
- Obtain at own risk and cost all required export licenses, documents, and authorizations and carry out export formalities and procedures as well as those required for transshipment through any country prior to delivery.

买方必须把船名、交货地点、时间及时通知卖方。卖方货抵船边后,应通知买方。否则自负相关风险。

FAS 下卖方不负责装船费。

DAT 术语为 *INCOTERMS 2010* 的新增术语,可适用于任何运送方式,包含运送全程适用一种以上的运输方式。

卖方交货:卖方须在合同议定日期或期间交货,在(进口地)目的港或目的地的指定终站将已运送抵达指定地点并已从承运的运输工具上完成卸载(once unload)但尚未办妥进口通关的货物,交付买方处置。

- Contract and pay for the carriage of the goods to the named terminal at port or place of destination.
- Make the goods available to the buyer, unloaded from the arriving means of transport, at the named terminal at port or place of destination, within the agreed-upon time.
- Pay all costs until the goods have been made available to the buyer, unloaded from the arriving means of transport, at the named terminal at port or place of destination.
- Provide timely notice that enables the buyer to take possession of the goods at the named terminal at port or place of destination, within the agreed-upon time.
- Provide the buyer with a document that will allow the buyer to claim the goods at the named terminal.

**The buyer's obligations:**

- Pay for the goods as provided in the sales contract.
- Obtain any import licenses or authorizations and handle all import formalities.
- Pay any additional costs after the goods have been made available at the named terminal at port or place of destination, within the agreed-upon time.
- If, according to the sales contract, the buyer is entitled to specify a time or point of taking delivery at the named place of destination, to give seller sufficient notice.

## 4. DAP (Delivered at Place…named place of destination)

Figure 2-10 illustrates the responsibilities of the seller and buyer under DAP.

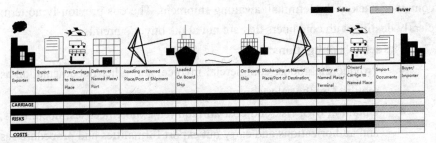

Figure 2-10    Responsibilities of the seller and buyer under DAP

DAP (Delivered at Place) replaces DAF, DES and DDU in *INCOTERMS 2000*. Under Delivered at Place, the seller clears the goods for export and is responsible for their delivery to the named place of destination. The seller makes the goods available to the buyer on the arriving means of transport at the named place of destination, not unloaded. The arriving vehicle under DAP could be a ship and the named place of destination could be a port.

When using the DAP term, it is advisable to clearly specify in the contract of sale and contracts of carriage, not only the named place of destination, but also the precise point at or within the named place of destination.

**The seller's obligations:**

- Provide the goods, commercial invoice, and other documentation as required by the sales contract.
- Obtain at own risk and cost all required export licenses, documents, and authorizations and carry out export formalities and procedures as well as those required for transshipment through any country prior to delivery.
- Contract and pay for the carriage of the goods to the named place of destination.
- Make the goods available to the buyer, not unloaded, from the arriving means of transport, at the named place of destination, within the agreed-upon time.
- Pay all costs until the goods have been made available to the buyer, not unloaded from the arriving means of transport, at the named place of destination.
- Provide timely notice that enables the buyer to take possession of the goods at the named place of destination, within the agreed-upon time.
- Provide the buyer with a document that will allow the buyer to claim the goods at the named place of destination.

**The buyer's obligations:**

- Pay for the goods as provided in the sales contract.
- Obtain any import licenses or authorizations and handle all import formalities.
- Pay any additional costs after the goods have been made available at the named place of destination within the agreed-upon time.

DAP 术语为 *INCOTERMS 2010* 通则的新增术语，与 *INCOTERMS 2000* 的 DDU 相当，可适用于任何运送方式，包含运输全程适用一种以上的运输方式。

卖方交货：卖方须在合同议定日期或期间交货，在（进口地）指定目的地将已运送抵达指定地点，但未从承运人的运输工具上卸载但准备卸载且未办妥进口通关的货物，交于买方处置。风险和费用也在此划分。

- If, according to the sales contract, the buyer is entitled to specify a time or point of taking delivery at the named place of destination, to give seller sufficient notice.

## 5. DDP (Delivered Duty Paid...named place of destination)

Figure 2-11 shows the responsibilities of the seller and buyer under DDP.

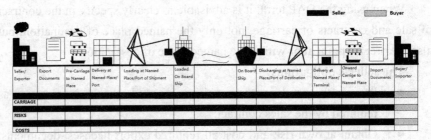

Figure 2-11   Responsibilities of the seller and buyer under DDP

DDP 术语下卖方将货物运至进口国指定地点，可供买方收取时即履行交货义务。卖方负担货物交至该处的一切风险和费用(包括关税、税捐和其他费用，并办理货物进口清关手续)。

卖方承担在指定目的地约定地点将尚未卸下的货物交给买方控制之前的一切费用和风险。卖方自负费用和风险，取得出口和进口许可证及其他官方文件，并办理货物出口和进口的一切海关手续，承担相关费用。DDP 是 11 个贸易术语中唯一需要卖方办理进口通关手续的；如果卖方无能力在进口地办理通关手续，不宜采用 DDP。

In Delivered Duty Paid, the seller clears the goods for export and is responsible for making them available to the buyer at the named place of destination, cleared for import, but not unloaded from the transport vehicle. Therefore, the seller bears all responsibilities for delivering the goods to the named place of destination, including clearing the goods for import and paying for duties, and other costs payable upon import.

The buyer's role is to accept the goods at the named place of destination and he is responsible for all the subsequent costs of the goods including the handling. The buyer has the minimum obligation under this term. This term should not be used if the seller is unable directly or indirectly to obtain the import license.

If the parties desire that the seller not be obliged to pay for VAT (Value-added Tax), explicit wording to that effect should be added to the contract of sale.

While the EXW term represents the minimum obligation for the seller, DDP represents the maximum obligation.

DDP term is typically used when the named place of destination is the buyer's place of business, or the place of business of the buyer's client.

**The seller's obligations:**

- Provide the goods, commercial invoice, and other documentation as required by the sales contract.

- Obtain at own risk and cost all required export and import licenses, documents, and authorizations and carry out export and import formalities and procedures as well as those required for transshipment through any country prior to delivery.
- Contract and pay for the carriage of the goods to the named place of destination.
- Make the goods available to the buyer, not unloaded, from the arriving means of transport, at the named place of destination, within the agreed-upon time.
- Pay all costs until the goods have been made available to the buyer, not unloaded from the arriving means of transport, at the named place of destination.
- Provide timely notice that enables the buyer to take possession of the goods at the named place of destination, within the agreed-upon time.
- Provide the buyer with a document that will allow the buyer to claim the goods at the named place of destination.

**The buyer's obligations:**
- Pay for the goods as provided in the sales contract.
- Provide the seller, at the seller's request and cost, assistance in securing licenses, documentation, and authorizations required to import the goods.
- Pay any additional costs after the goods have been made available at the named place of destination within the agreed-upon time.
- If, according to the sales contract, the buyer is entitled to specify a time or point of taking delivery at the named place of destination, to give seller sufficient notice.

## 2.3　*INCOTERMS 2010* vs. *INCOTERMS 2000*

*INCOTERMS 2000* are categorized into 4 groups, 13 terms in total, ranging from the minimum obligation for the seller (Ex-Works) to the maximum obligation of Delivered terms.

- The "E" term (EXW)—The only term where the seller makes the goods available at his or her own premises to the buyer.
- The "F" terms (FCA, FAS and FOB)—Terms where the seller is responsible to deliver the goods to a carrier named by the buyer.
- The "C" terms (CFR, CIF, CPT and CIP)—Terms where the seller is responsible for contracting and paying for carriage of the goods, but not responsible for additional costs or risk of loss or damage to the goods once they have been delivered to the carrier. The "C" terms evidence "shipment" (as opposed to "arrival") contracts.
- The "D" terms (DAF, DES, DEQ, DDU and DDP)—Terms where the seller is responsible for all costs and risks associated with bringing the goods to the named place (usually of destination).

♦ **The revised categories**

*INCOTERMS 2000* contain 13 rules, which have been reduced to 11 ones in *INCOTERMS 2000*. Two new rules replace four current terms. The "D" terms in *INCOTERMS 2000* have been consolidated to reduce the number of terms that were considered to have little real difference between them.

The replaced terms of *INCOTERMS 2000* are as shown in Table 2-5.

Table 2-5　The replaced terms of *INCOTERMS 2000*

| Replaced Incoterms | New Incoterms |
| --- | --- |
| DAF (Delivered at Frontier) | DAP (Delivered at Place) |
| DES (Delivered Ex Ship) | |
| DDU (Duty Unpaid) | |
| DEQ (Delivered Ex Quay) | DAT (Delivered at Terminal) |

*INCOTERMS 2010* 对涉及运输和保险合同的A3/A4款中有关保险的内容作了修改，这在 CIF 和 CIP 术语中均有体现。

♦ **Institute cargo clause updated and insurance obligations clarified**

In 2009, insurance markets adopted the revised *Institute Cargo Clauses (LMA/IUA) (2009)*. Incoterms Cost Insurance and Freight (CIF) and Carriage and Insurance Paid (CIP) have been amended to reflect this. The amendments also clarify information obligations regarding insurance.

♦ **New security obligations**

The seller and the buyer will be compelled to co-operate as they have not done previously. This is because *INCOTERMS 2010* will allocate the obligations to supply the necessary information in order to obtain export and import clearance (e.g., chain of custody information).

♦ **Using Incoterms for domestic sale of goods contract**

*INCOTERMS 2010* have been adopted for use in domestic contracts and reference is made in a number of the Rules that export and import formalities will only need to be complied with where applicable. This will make it easier to incorporate Incoterms in contracts relating to the movement of goods domestically — for example, within a trading bloc such as the EU where the export and import formalities have largely disappeared, and in the US where there has been an increasing preference to use Incoterms rather than the *Uniform Commercial Code* in domestic sales.

♦ **Electronic Communication**

The *INCOTERMS 2000* provided for the use of EDI(Electronic Data Interchange) messages, where the parties had agreed to use them. A new sentence in article A1 of each Incoterm of *INCOTERMS 2010* accepts the functional equivalence of paper and electronic documents. This does not mean, of course, that electronic bills of lading are now automatically provided for where the sale contract is governed by English law: regulations under the *Carriage of Goods by Sea Act 1992* are still awaited to bring about that all-embracing result. It does mean, however, that where *INCOTERMS 2010* are incorporated, the parties will be precluded from objecting as against each other that a document has been tendered in electronic rather than paper form. This was intended to be the case under *INCOTERMS 2000*. The drafting technique there was, however, quite different: references to various types of electronic documents were strewn across *INCOTERMS 2000*; the method adopted in *INCOTERMS 2010* was to state the principle of functional equivalence boldly at the start of each rule.

♦ **On Board**

The *INCOTERMS 2010* also eliminate the concept of delivery "over the ship's rail" or "pass the ship's rail" for the FOB, CFR and CIF terms. The concept of goods being loaded over the ship's rail dates back to a time when most cargoes were loaded in break bulk fashion and actually hoisted by cranes over the ship's rail. Previous versions of the *INCOTERMS* have specified that

如今对货物在转移过程中的安全关注度很高，因而要求检定货物不会因除其自身属性外的原因而造成对生命财产的威胁。因此，*INCOTERMS 2010* 在各种术语的 A2/B2 和 A10/B10 条款内容中包含了取得或提供帮助取得安全核准的义务。

*INCOTERMS 2010* 赋予电子通信方式和纸质通信方式相同的效力，更适合当今国际贸易的新变化及新特点。

补充说明：在 *INCOTERMS 2010* 中，国际商会正式认可所有的贸易规则既可适用于国际贸易也可适用于国内贸易。

the seller's risk of loss, for example, passed to the buyer at the specific point when the goods passed over the ship's rail on their way to being loaded. Today, most cargo is loaded in containers and, although those containers are also loaded over the ship's rail, the International Chamber of Commerce has decided to employ the term "On Board" for *INCOTERMS 2010*, and presumably into the future, because this is a concept that is more familiar to parties dealing with modern transportation and bill of lading terminology. It is hoped that this change, which attracted little attention in the consultation process leading to the revision of the rules, will cause little difficulty in practice.

♦ **Requirements and obligations associated with string sales recognized**

*INCOTERMS 2010* now make it clear that the rules can be adopted where a sale contract forms part of a string. It is well-known that the main trade associations operating in the dry commodities markets exclude Incoterms from their standard forms. It is equally true that commodities traders have over the past few years, regardless of such standard exclusions, expressly incorporated Incoterms into their contracts. Such incorporation did, however, cause a problem: a CIF seller in the middle of a string could not meaningfully be said to be under a duty to ship goods already shipped by another seller upstream or to make a contract of carriage already concluded by another seller upstream. *INCOTERMS 2010* now cater for these possibilities: rather than ship goods and make a contract of carriage, a seller in string can procure goods shipped and procure a contract of carriage in performance of his duties towards his buyer downstream. It is hoped that a possible obstruction to the incorporation of Incoterms in commodities sales has thus been removed.

♦ **Obligations around terminal handling charges clarified**

Under certain *INCOTERMS 2000* Rules (e.g. CIF, CFR), the buyer potentially faced paying for the same service twice. The seller was including freight costs as part of the sale price, yet the buyer was sometimes expected by the carrier or terminal operator to pay the costs of handing and moving the goods within the port or container terminal facilities. *INCOTERMS 2010* seek

---

*INCOTERMS 2010*把原来的风险转移点由越过船舷为界改成装运港船上,此改变更准确地反映了现代商业现实,避免了以往风险围绕船舷这条虚拟垂线来回摇摆而发生货物的损失或纠纷。

连串销售的中间销售商对其买方应承担的义务不是将货物装船,而是"设法获取"已装船货物。着眼于贸易术语在这种销售中的应用,*INCOTERMS 2010*的相关术语中同时规定了"设法获取已装船货物"和"将货物装船"的义务。

*INCOTERMS 2010*加入终端处理费用的归属,以保证不出现真空;在相关术语的 A6/B6 条款中对这种费用的分配做出了详细规定,旨在避免上述情况的发生。

to reduce the potential for buyers to be charged twice for terminal handling charges. Pass through of the cost of carriage of goods to an agreed destination, which often resulted in buyers being charged twice, should disappear as a result of amendments to CIP, CPT, CFR, CIF, DAT, DAP and CCP Incoterms.

# 2.4　Incoterms and Contract

Incoterms are shorthand in international sales contracts, namely risk of loss and responsibility for delivery. If the merchandise is lost at sea, for example, who bears the loss? Where are you supposed to deliver the merchandise to? Who is handling export and customs clearance, and things like that? These issues are important, but Incoterms do not:

- Determine ownership or transfer title to the goods, nor evoke payment terms.

- Apply to service contract, nor define contractual rights or obligations (except for delivery) or breach of contract remedies.

- Protect parties from their own risk or loss, nor cover the goods before or after delivery.

- Specify details of the transfer, transport, and delivery of the goods. Container loading is not considered packaging, and must be addressed in the sales contract.

Incoterms are not law. These issues are dealt with by the sales contract. Different countries have different business cultures and languages. It's a good idea to make sure a clear written contract is made to minimize the risk of misunderstandings.

The contract should set out where the goods are being delivered. It should cover who is responsible for every stage of the journey, including customs clearance, and what insurance is required. It should also clarify who pays for each different cost.

To avoid confusion, internationally agreed Incoterms should be used to spell out exactly what delivery terms are being agreed, such as:

虽然贸易术语能够说明买卖双方费用、风险和责任的划分，但在贸易实务中，贸易术语不等同于法律，贸易双方还需签订合同来保护自己的利益。

- Where the goods will be delivered;
- Who arranges transport;
- Who is responsible for insuring the goods, and who pays for insurance;
- Who handles customs procedures, and who pays any duties and taxes.

For example, an exporter might agree to deliver goods, at the exporter's expense, to a port in the customer's country. The customer might then take over responsibility, arrange and pay for customs clearance and make delivery to their premises. The exporter might also be responsible for arranging insurance for the goods until they reach the port, but pass this cost on to the customer.

As well as including delivery details, the contract should cover payment. This should include what currency payment will be made in, how much will be paid, when payment is due and what payment method will be used.

# 2.5   Choice of Trade Terms

FOB, CFR and CIF are the most popular price terms of Incoterms used in international transactions. They are the first three terms adopted and defined by the trade organization and have been used worldwide. Furthermore, the seller and the buyer involved in international transaction would like to have the risks covered in his or her own country, and these three terms happen to have the risks transferred from the seller to buyer when the goods are placed on board the ship at the port of shipment.

In international trade practice, the selection of the trade terms is determined by the particular circumstance that the seller and buyer are under. It is of great importance for the parties to take all the aspects into consideration when choosing the trade terms. Neither party should take the trade term which actually requires performances beyond his abilities.

选用贸易术语主要考虑以下几个因素：运输条件、货源情况、运费因素、运输过程中的风险、关税制度、市场优势以及办理进出口手续有无困难等情况。

Some suggestions are proposed for different scenario in the following part:

- Exporters are advised to choose CIF or CFR over FOB to make more foreign exchange, but importers shall choose FOB over CIF or CFR to save foreign exchange on freight.

- If one of the parties wishes to have the goods delivered by air, railway or road, he is advised to choose FCA, CPT or CIP, as they are used irrespective of mode of transport including multi-modal transport.

- For inland export companies, they are advised to choose CIP instead of CIF. By doing so, they could lower the risks and save much freight. Moreover, inland export companies are suggested to choose FCA over FOB.

- If the exporter has the last word in the transaction, he may choose trade terms like EXW, FAS or FOB which are to his advantages.

- If the government at the import's end exempts tariff on imported goods, the transactions is advised to be concluded on DDU basis. If the importer happens to be in the bonded area, then DDU should be used.

- If the transaction is concluded on the FOB contract, the exporter will have to make sure if the importer might have the slightest possibility to take delivery of the goods without bill of lading.

- If the transaction is concluded on CFR contract, the importer must examine the bill of lading provided by the exporter carefully to see if it is a forged one.

There might be chances that one of the parties has to make some concessions on the selection of trade terms for some financial causes or certain government regulations.

# 【Key Terms and Words】

Trade Terms  贸易术语

Price Terms  价格术语

Delivery Terms  交货术语

Warsaw-Oxford Rules 1932  1932 年华沙–牛津规则

International Law Association  国际法律协会

*Revised American Foreign Trade Definitions 1941*  《1941 年美国对外贸易定义修正本》

*INCOTERMS 2000*  2000 年国际贸易术语解释通则

International Chamber of Commerce (ICC)  国际商会

United Nations Commission on International Trade Law (UNCITRAL)  联合国国际贸易法律委员会

Carrier  承运人

Frontier  边境

Clear  清关

Quay  码头

EXW  工厂交货

FCA  货交承运人

FOB  装运港船上交货

FAS  货交船边

CFR  成本加运费

CIF  成本加保险费加运费

CPT  运费付至

CIP  运费、保险费付至

DAF  边境交货

DES  目的港船上交货

DEQ  目的港码头交货

DDU  未完税交货

DDP  完税后交货

DAP  目的地交货

DAT  终点站交货

Value added tax(VAT)  增值税

Ship's Rail  船舷

Multi-modal Transport  多式联运

# 【Exercises】

## I. Answer the following questions.

1. What are trade terms?

2. What are Incoterms?

3. What are the differences between *INCOTERMS 2010* and *INCOTERMS 2000*?

4. How to choose trade terms in international transactions?

5. What is the relation between Incoterms and contract?

## II. Short answers.

1. Who pays for loading for shipment under FOB?

2. Who pays for unloading under CIF?

3. Please compare and contrast FOB, CFR and CIF.

4. What are the two types of trade terms concerning the transfer of risks?

5. What are the differences and similarities between CPT and CFR?

6. What are the differences and similarities between CIP and CIF?

7. If you trade with an American, is the sales contract subject to Incoterms without any doubt? And what should you do?

8. What are the most commonly used trade terms?

9. Who is responsible for carrying out customs formalities for exports under an FOB contract?

10. If a Chinese trader signs a FOB Hamburg contract, is he exporting or importing?

## III. Please explain the following trade terms.

1. EXW

2. FCA

3. DAT

4. DAP

5. DDP

IV. Please complete the following diagram.

### The mode of transport of *INCOTERMS 2010*

| Deliveries by any mode of transport (sea, road, air, rail) | Deliveries by sea and inland wcaterway transport |
|---|---|
| EXW — (　　) | FAS — (　　　) |
| FAC — (　　) | FOB — (　　) |
| CPT — (　　) | CFR — (　　) |
| CIP — (　　) | CIF — (　　) |
| DAT — (　　) |  |
| DAP — (　　) |  |
| DDP — (　　) |  |

V. Case study.

1. In 2002, a Chinese exporter exported 500M/T walnut to a Canadian importer on the basis of US$ 4,800 per M/T CIF Quebec. As it was a seasonal commodity, the importer required and both parties agreed to stipulate the following in the contract:

a) L/C Issuing Date: to be issued by the end of September.

b) Shipment: Not later than October 31, partial shipment and transshipment prohibited.

c) Arrival Date: Not later than November 30. Otherwise, the buyer is entitled to refuse the goods.

d) Terms of Payment: Draft at 90 days under L/C.

Due to the bad weather, the liner arrived at Quebec on December 5. Consequently, the importer refused to take the delivery of the cargo unless 20% discount of the total value of the goods was made for the loss incurred to the importer. After painful negotiations, the transaction came to an end with the exporter's loss of US$ 360,000 by the discount of 15% of the total value of the goods.

**Question:**

What is the crux of this case?

2. A Chinese import and export company concluded a Sale Contract with a German firm on October 5,2006, selling a batch of certain commodity. The contract was based on CIF Hamburg at USD 2,500 per metric ton; The Chinese company delivered the goods in compliance with the contract and obtained a clean on board B/L. During transportation, however, 100 metric tons of the goods got lost because of rough sea. Upon arrival of the goods, the price of the contracted goods

went down quickly. The buyer refused to take delivery of the goods and effect payment and claimed damages from the seller.

**Questions:**

(1) Is the buyer's refusal reasonable? Why?

(2) How should the buyer deal with the loss?

3. One import and export company exported his goods under the CIF term. The seller delivered the goods on board the vessel on time and prepared all necessary documents. But the vessel stranded and sank in a few hours after departure. The next day, when the seller asked for payment with full set of documents in conformity with the contract, the buyer refused to accept the documents and rejected payment because his goods have been lost.

**Question:**

Is it reasonable for the buyer to do so? Why?

4. A Shanghai company signed a CIF contract to sell Christmas goods to a British company. The $1,000,000 contract stipulated, "The seller guarantees that the goods arrive at the port of destination by December 1, 2008. If the carriage is late, the buyer can cancel the purchase, and get the refund for the payment." So the shipment was made. Unfortunately, due to mechanical problems, the vessel arrived at the destination a few hours late. The buyer refused to accept the goods. As a result, the goods had to be sold on the spot, and the seller lost $700,000.

**Questions:**

(1) Was the "arrival date" clause consistent with the CIF term under *INCOTERMS 2010*?

(2) What trade term is proper for the obligation concerning arrival time?

5. An FOB contract stipulated, "The shipment will be effected in March 2008. If the vessel fails to arrive at the port of shipment on time, the seller agrees to set aside the goods for additional 27 days, and the buyer will bear all costs of delay." It turned out that under the seller's repeated requests, the vessel named by the buyer finally arrived at the port of shipment on May 1. As a result, the seller refused to make the shipment.

**Questions:**

(1) Was the seller entitled to compensation for the warehouse rent, insurance and interest due to the delay?

(2) If the seller had sold the goods to a third party on April 25, should the buyer pay for the delay?

(3) If the seller had sold the goods to a third party on May 1 with a better price, was he entitled to any compensation?

6. Chinese company finalized a transaction with a German company under CIF price and L/C payment. Both sales contract and L/C received stipulated that transshipment was not allowed. The

Chinese company made the shipment on a direct vessel within the validity period of the L/C and negotiated the payment with a direct Bill of Lading successfully. After departing from the Chinese port, in order to take another shipment, the shipping company unloaded the goods from the original vessel and reloaded them onto another one. Due to the delay and the poor condition of the second vessel, the goods arrived two months later than the expected time. The German company suffered and claimed compensation from the Chinese company with the reason that the Chinese side cheated them with a direct B/L. The Chinese company believed that since they signed the contract under a "到岸价格" and they booked the shipping company, they would be responsible for what happened. As a result the Chinese side compensated.

**Question:**

Please comment on this case.

# Chapter 3   Terms of Commodity

【Learning Objectives】

By studying this chapter, you should be able to master:

- The importance of name, quality, quantity and packing of commodity in the contract
- Different ways of naming the commodities
- Different ways of stipulating quality of the commodities
- The importance of quality latitude and quality tolerance clauses in the contract
- Different ways of calculating weight of the commodities
- More or less clause
- Marks of transport packing
- How to make and recognize shipping marks
- How to stipulate name, quality, quantity and packing terms in the contract

## Lead-in: Case Study

Just as Brazil's mysterious, acai berries once were to Western health fanatics, so are jujubes to China. Known as red date or hongzao in Chinese, jujube has long been regarded as a superfood or "the king of nuts". There is an old Chinese saying, "three red dates a day keeps you young for ever." In China, red dates are accustomed to make regular appearance on traditional Chinese medicine prescription pads. Also, they are used in kitchen to decorate buns, porridge, soup or desert for its rich nutritional value. Since red dates have enjoyed such a high reputation in China, they are now exported to other countries in Southeast Asia including Japan, Korea, Thailand and Singapore, as well as some American countries.

### A Case of Xinjiang Red Dates Export

Xinjiang province, due to its unique geographical environment and climate, is destined to output abundant of fruits, and red date is one of them. Because of sufficient sunshine (at least 8 hours daily) and the large temperature gap between day and night (about 30℃ even more), Xinjiang red dates are famous all over the world.

There is a Xinjiang exporter who had entered an agreement with a Singapore company to sell two metric tons of red dates. Both the L/C and sales contract specified that "the red dates should be grade 3". Usually the Xinjiang seller has a supply ability of 5 metric tons per month. However, when preparing goods for shipment, the seller found that red dates of grade 3 were out of stock. In order to make timely delivery, he delivered grade 2 red dates instead of grade 3 red dates without the approval of the buyer, and later wrote in the commercial invoice that "Grade 2 red dates, price is the same." Unfortunately, when receiving the goods, the Singapore buyer refused to pay.

*Class Activities:*

1. Do you think it is legal and reasonable for the Singapore buyer to refuse to pay for the red dates?

2. As far as the exporter's interest is concerned, what lesson should be taken?

# 3.1  Name of Commodity

Name of commodity is a concept that can distinguish one goods from others. To some degree, it can reflect natural attributes or performance characteristics of a product. That is to say, products with low processing level usually reflect more natural attributes, while products with high processing level more performance characteristics.

商品的名称，又称商品的品名，它是某种商品区别于其他商品的一种称呼或概念。商品的名称在一定程度上体现了商品的自然属性及主要性能特征。

Name of commodity clause is one of the main terms of the contract, relatively simple but important. It is a fundamental base of business negotiation. If the goods delivered by the seller do not conform to the agreed name of commodity in the contract, the buyer will be entitled to lodge a claim, reject the goods or even terminate the contract.

## 3.1.1  Commodity Naming Methods

In international trade, different commodities show different characteristics. Accordingly, commodity names differ greatly from each other. Table 3-1 presents the most frequently used ways of naming the commodities.

Table 3-1  Commodity Naming Methods

| Commodity naming methods | Examples |
| --- | --- |
| 1. Naming the commodity by use | Sewing Machine, Fax Machine, Travel Bag |
| 2. Naming the commodity by raw materials of ingredients | Chiffon Dress, Cashmere Sweater, Silk Pajamas, Ginseng Pearl Cream, Cog Liver Oil |
| 3. Naming the commodity by appearance or shape | Green Tea, White Sugar, Cocktail Dress |
| 4. Naming the commodity by personal and place names | Confucius Family Liquor, Scotch Whisky, Xinjiang Dried Golder Raisin |
| 5. Naming the commodity by the manufacturing process | Handmade Writing Paper, Refined Oil, Fermented Soy Sauce |

同样的商品采用不同的品名和 HS 编码，征收的关税也会不同。

Every product exported or imported from a country is given a HS code. When naming the commodity, both parties should take reference from the HS, which might help to make trade and customs clearance easier. For the same commodity, the trader may apply different names with different HS codes, which probably results in different customs taxes or tax refund rates. For instance, tax rate for furniture is 15%, while tax rate for furniture K.D. (Knock Down) is only 8%. For barber's chair exported to Africa, it would be taxed with the name of "barber's chair", and free of tax with the name of "hospital chair".

## 3.1.2　HS Code

各国海关、商品出入境管理机构确认商品类别、进行商品分类管理、审核关税标准和检验商品品质指标的基本要素就是进出口商品通用的身份证明，即 HS 编码。

The "HS Code" or simply "HS", short for the "Harmonized Commodity Description and Coding System", is an internationally standardized system of names and numbers for classifying traded products developed and maintained by the World Customs Organization (WCO). HS codes are essentially the language of international trade. They are the numerical codes that describe "what" is being shipped to and from countries worldwide, and they form the basis upon which all modern customs management systems operate. The first 6 digits of the HS are used universally. Each country may then add to the original 6 to suit its own tariff and statistical needs, creating 8, 10, and sometimes 12 digit national codes.

The harmonized system is based on a fundamental principle that goods are classified by what they are, not according to their stage of fabrication, use, status, or any other criteria. It has been used by more than 200 countries and economies as a basis for customs tariffs and the collection of international trade statistics. China began to adopt HS in 1992.

## 3.1.3　Name Clauses in the Contract

As a main component of the description of goods, name of commodity is usually stated out at the beginning of the contract. Usually, it is specified in the contract under the subject "*name of commodity*", or listed under the subject "*description of commodity*" together with the quality clause. Sometimes it is just described in the beginning of the contract, such as "*The seller agrees to*

*sell and the buyer agrees to buy...on the terms and conditions stated below."*

> **Example**
> Name of Commodity: Floor Lamp
> Description of Commodity: Floor Lamp, E14, 25W Max, IP20
> The seller agrees to sell and the buyer agrees to buy floor lamp on the terms and conditions stated below.

To avoid possible conflicts, the name of commodity clause should be clearly stipulated. The following points are to be noted in naming the commodities.

(1) The name of commodity must be clear and specific, not too vague or general in stipulation. For instance, *"Chinese Tea"* is too general for the buyer and the seller to reach an agreement on name. In contrast, *"West Lake Longjing Tea"* by adding its type and place of origin, is a more concrete name for two parties to clearly understand each other.

(2) The name of commodity must be practical, not too belittled or exaggerated in expression. It should express real condition of the goods. For example, "defectless" in *"Defectless Cotton Fabric"* is an unnecessary modifier, because it is extremely difficult for the seller to fulfill the obligation of producing completely flawless cotton fabric.

(3) The name of commodity should be internationally standardized. A product may have different names in different countries and regions. Take *"pineapple"* as an example. It is known as *"nanas"* in Malaysia, *"abacaxi"* in Brazil and *"nanasi"* in East Africa. Both parties should choose one of them as the name of commodity, possibly *"pineapple"* for it is internationally accepted.

(4) The name of commodity should be properly chosen, if more than one is available. Both parties should select the name by taking reference from the HS, so as to reduce customs tariff and freight of the same product.

同样的商品不同的品名能以不同的 HS 编码报关，以达到合理避税。

## 3.2   Quality of Commodity

Quality of commodity refers to the totality of internal properties and external appearance of a product. The former includes shape, structure, flavor, color and luster of the goods, while the latter includes chemical composition, physical and mechanical properties, and biological features of the goods.

Quality is a matter of capital importance in international trade. The quality

商品的质量是商品的内在质量和外观形态的综合。内在质量包括商品的化学成分、物理和机械性能、生物特性等。外观形态包括商品的外形、结构、味觉、色泽等。

of a certain product determines to a great degree its market and price. Hence winning the market with high quality becomes an effective way for the seller to raise the competitiveness of products. According to Article 35(1) & (2) in *United Nations Convention on Contracts for the International Sale of Goods* (CISG), the seller must deliver the goods which are of the quality required by the contract. If the goods received by the buyer are not in accordance with the quality stipulated in the contract, the buyer reserves the right to claim damage or even declare the contract null and void. Thus, great efforts need to be made on specifying quality clause in the contract so as to avoid unnecessary disputes in practice.

## 3.2.1 Quality Stipulation Methods

商品质量规定方法主要分为两大类：①商品质量用实物样品表示，②商品质量用文字说明表示。

Different commodities have different qualities, and even the same commodity may have various qualities in the market due to different raw materials, technologies and market conditions. In general, ways of stipulating quality of commodity fall into two categories: sale by actual goods and sale by description (see Figure 3-1).

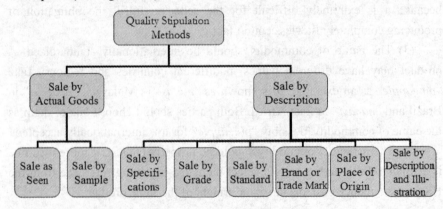

Figure 3-1　Quality Stipulation Methods

### 1. Sale by Actual Goods

看货买卖，是指买卖双方根据成交商品的实际品质进行交易，一般适用于珠宝、字画、特定工艺品等。

1) Sale as Seen

"Sale as seen" is a sale made on the basis of the actual quality of the goods that already exists at the time of contracting. The buyer or his agent normally examines the quality of the goods at the seller's place. He will then buy the goods under the condition of this inspection without any guarantee of quality from the seller. And the seller does not promise that the goods he is selling are in good condition or are right for a particular purpose. This method is often used in consignment, auction and exhibition, which applies to items such as jewelry, paintings, arts and crafts and most products in stock.

2) Sale by Sample

Sample is the article drawn from a whole lot, shown as evidence of the quality of the whole, or the article specially designed and processed to encourage prospective transactions. "Sale by sample" refers to the transaction concluded on the basis of the sample representing the quality of the whole lot. Samples are either provided by the seller or the buyer. Sale by sample can be further divided into three kinds, i.e., sale by seller's sample, sale by buyer's sample and sale by counter sample.

(1) Sale by Seller's Sample

"Sale by seller's sample" is the sale made based on the sample provided by the seller. The seller usually supplies an original sample (or representative sample, or type sample) to the buyer, and the buyer makes the selection. Meanwhile, the seller keeps a duplicate sample (or keep sample) for the convenience of verification if any quality dispute happens or for future transaction needs. When the sample is accepted by the buyer in quality, the seller is obliged to deliver the goods of the same quality as shown in the original sample.

It is important to stipulate in the contract *"quality as per seller's sample"* or *"quality to be strictly as per sample submitted by the seller on July 1, 2012"*. If the quality of mass products fails to conform to that of the sample, the buyer is entitled to claim compensation for losses or decline the goods.

(2) Sale by Buyer's Sample

When buyer's sample serves as the quality standard for the goods to be produced and delivered by the seller, we call it "sale by buyer's sample". Under such condition, *"quality as per buyer's sample"* is to be clearly stated in the contract.

When confirming buyer's sample, the seller should take into full consideration the feasibility of raw material supply, equipments, processing technology, and delivering the goods on time. Also, he should be aware

样品无论是由卖方提供，还是由买方提供，一经双方凭以成交便成为履行合同时的交接货物的质量依据。卖方须承担交付的货物质量与样品完全一致的责任，否则买方有权提出索赔甚至拒收货物。

whether the buyer's sample involves any infringement of industrial property rights of a third party, such as trademark right, patent right. If so, the seller is not encouraged to accept this method of quality stipulation.

(3) Sale by Counter Sample

Sometimes the buyer may send a sample to the seller, who is asked to supply the goods in accordance with it. When possible, the seller will do accordingly. If impossible, the seller may send the buyer a sample of goods in similar quality, called **counter sample** or **return sample**, as a proposal for the buyer's consideration. Under such circumstance, even the buyer later finds the counter sample does not match with the original, the seller will not hold any responsibility as the counter sample has been confirmed by the seller.

In international trade practice, when a sale is made by sample, the following should be noted.

i. If it is hard to keep the goods in strict accordance with the sample, the seller might add some flexible terms in the quality clause such as "*Quality to be about equal to the sample.*", "*Quality to be nearly the same as the sample.*" and "*Quality to be similar to the sample.*"

ii. If necessary, sealed samples can be adopted serving as the proof of quality when quality disputes arise. **Sealed samples** are several samples of the same quality drawn from the whole lot by a third party or a notary party. Each sample is sealed and identified. Among these samples, one is reserved by a third party or a notary bureau; others are at the user's disposal.

iii. Normally samples are used to represent the overall quality of a product. But in international transactions, there are some samples just reflecting a certain part or some parts of the quality of the goods, such as color sample, pattern sample.

### 2. Sale by Description

#### 1) Sale by Specifications

Specification of goods refers to a detailed and exact description of the quality of goods such as composition, content, purity, volume and dimensions. It is simple and accurate in quality stipulation, and thus becomes the most frequently used method in international trade.

凭样品成交:

i.如对货样难以做到严格一致的商品, 应在合同中订明, "品质与样品大致相同"。

ii.为避免买卖双方在履约过程中产生质量争议, 必要时可使用"封样"。

iii.以样品作为规定商品某项或几项质量指标的依据, 如色样、款式样等。

[Example 1]

Real Leather Oak Framed Dinning Chair

Width: 46 cm

Height: 87 cm (Seat Height 51 cm)

Depth: 60 cm

Material: Solid wood, leather

2) Sale by Grade

Grade of goods refers to the classifications of the commodity which is indicated by words, numbers or symbols. The classifications are usually decided by different qualities, weights, compositions, appearances, properties, etc. When sale by grade is adopted, you just simply state the grade of the goods, and don't bother to mention its specification.

[Example 2]

**Yellow Corn, U.S. Grade 2**

Official U.S. Standards for Grain

| U.S. Grade | Test Weight Per Bushel (Min.) | Moisture (Max.) | Broken Corn and Foreign Material (Max.) | Total Damaged Kernels (Max.) | Heat Damaged Kernels (Max.) |
|---|---|---|---|---|---|
| 1 | 56 pounds | 14% | 2% | 3% | 0.1% |
| 2 | 54 pounds | 15.5% | 3% | 5% | 0.2% |
| 3 | 52 pounds | 17.5% | 4% | 7% | 0.5% |

[Example 3]

Fresh Hen Eggs, shell light brown and clean, even in size

Grade AA: 60-65 gm per egg

Grade A: 55-60 gm per egg

Grade B: 50-55 gm per egg

Grade C: 45-50 gm per egg

Grade D: 40-45 gm per egg

Grade E: 35-40 gm per egg

3) Sale by Standard

Standard refers to specifications or grades, which are stipulated and announced in a unified way by government departments or commercial organizations of a country. There are international standards such as ISO (International Standards Organizations) and IEC (International Electrotechnical

国际贸易中，标准可分为国际标准、国家标准、行业标准和企业标准。

Commission). And countries have their own standards, like BS in Britain, ANSI in the U.S.A., DIN in Germany, JIS and JAS in Japan. In China, there are national standards, professional standards, provincial standards and company standards.

It is worthy to note that standards of commodities are subject to change and amendment and a new standard often takes place of the old one. Thus it is important to mark the year or name of edition, when certain standard is applied.

**[Example 4]**

Monosodium Dihydrogen Citrate, BP 93, USP 32.

In Example 4, "BP 93" stands for the 1993 edition of British Pharmacopoeia, while "USP 32" is short for the 32th edition of the United States Pharmacopoeia published in 2009.

**[Example 5]**

China Northeast Soybean, 1995 New Crop, F.A.Q.:

| | |
|---|---|
| Moisture | (Max.)15% |
| Admixture | (Max.)1% |
| Imperfect granules | (Max.)7% |
| Oil Content | (Min.)17% |

In international trade, terms like F.A.Q. and G.M.Q. are often employed to indicate the quality of goods. F.A.Q., short for "Fair Average Quality", refers to the average quality level of agricultural products within a certain period of time. This kind of standard is quite ambiguous and does not represent any fixed, accurate specification. G.M.Q., short for "Good Merchantable Quality", means the goods sold are free from defects and good enough for use or consumption. It is employed to indicate the quality in trading of wood or aquatic products.

4) Sale by Brand or Trade Mark

Brand is a name, term, design, symbol or any other feature that identifies one product or service as distinct from others. Trade mark is a  legal term. It is a distinctive symbol that identifies particular products of a trader to the general public. Goods with stable quality and sound reputation

大路货(F.A.Q.),一般指农副产品每个生产年度或季度的中等货。合同中除表明"F.A.Q."外,最好再订有具体规格。上等可销品质(G.M.Q.),一般指卖方所交货物为"品质尚好,合乎商销"。

may sell well by brand or trade mark. The Coca-Cola logo is an example of a widely-recognized trademark and the name "Coca-Cola" is a global brand.

**[Example 6]**

White Rabbit Brand Creamy Candy

Butterfly Brand Sewing Machine

Nordic Natural Baby's DHA

5) Sale by Place of Origin

As to some agriculture products and by-products, origins may well indicate their qualities. They enjoy a high reputation, such as France perfume, German beer and China plum wine. These products with unique processing technologies can be sold by place of origin.

**[Example 7]**

Yongquan Tangerine

Jinhua Ham

Dezhou Braised Chicken

6) Sale by Description and Illustration

In the sales of machines, appliances, instruments, complete sets of equipments and the like, technical manuals, booklets of directions, drawings or illustrations are quite necessary for the seller to indicate qualities of the goods. It is because they are complicated in structure, performance, installation and maintenance. Expressions are to be stipulated in the contract, i.e., "*Quality and technical data as per seller's catalogue.*" or "*Quality as per technical feature indicated in illustrations by the seller.*"

To sum up, when the transaction is made by description, several methods can be adopted simultaneously, so as to make a complete and specific quality stipulation. Yet, it is not recommended to apply sale by actual goods and sale by description simultaneously in the transaction. As CISG Article 35 states, if a transaction is made both by description and by sample, the seller must deliver the goods not only conforming to quality description required by the contract, but also possessing the same quality of the sample. In other words, the more criteria the seller sets, the more difficulties he will meet when fulfilling his obligation.

在销售某一商品时，原则上，可用文字说明表示质量的，就不再同时用样品表示，反之亦然。

Moreover, in the case of sale by description, the seller is usually required to send samples for the buyer's reference. Such samples are known as **reference samples**, which are for sales promotion only and not binding upon

如样品仅供参考，应订明"参考样品"(reference sample)或"样品仅供参考"(only for reference)。

the seller. It should be noted that standard sample is very different from reference sample. Standard sample is the basis of delivery of the goods, while the reference sample is "for reference only".

## 3.2.2  Quality Latitude and Quality Tolerance

Due to natural, technical and productive reasons, quality deviations of some kinds of goods are unavoidable. Such goods include agricultural products, industrial raw materials and some light industrial products. When trading those kinds of products, both parties can adopt quality latitude or quality tolerance in the contract.

**Quality latitude** means that both parties agree that the quality of the goods delivered can vary within an agreed range. The following three ways are commonly used to express quality latitude.

i. A given range. Certain quality index can change within a given range.

**[Example 8]**

Yarn-dyed Gingham: Width 42/43

ii. Maximum or minimum. It is to stipulate the maximum and minimum of the specifications.

**[Example 9]**

Chinese groundnut 1997 new crop, F.A.Q.:

| | |
|---|---|
| Moisture | (max.) 13% |
| Admixture | (max.) 5% |
| Oil content | (min.) 44% |

iii. An allowed deviations. It is to stipulate a more or less allowance for a certain quality index.

**[Example 10]**

South China grey duck down with 19% down content, allowing 1% more or less

**Quality tolerance** is the quality deviation internationally recognized. Tolerance is the allowed deviation from a given standard of size, content, performance, purity, or some other measurable characteristics in the specifications of a product. As long as the quality of the product is still within the range of the tolerance, the seller is deemed to have fulfilled his obligation. Sometimes, price adjustment is needed if the tolerance goes beyond a certain limit.

品质机动幅度是指特定质量指标可以机动的幅度。

品质公差是指国际上公认的产品品质的误差标准。

**[Example 11]**

Specifications of Chinese sesame 1995 crop:

| | | |
|---|---|---|
| Moisture | 8%–1% | price +5% |
| Oil content | 20%+1% | price +5% |
| Admixture | 2%+1% | price–5% |

## 3.2.3  Quality Clauses in the Contract

As an essential term of a sales contract, the quality description is normally written under *"quality of commodity"* or *"description of goods"*. In quality clause, name, specification, grade, standard or brand name etc. should be clearly stated. In the case of sale by sample, the serial number and sending date of the sample are to be carefully marked.

Examples of quality clauses in the contract are to be shown as follows:

a. Quality of commodity: Wilson brand football, article number WS18, size 5, genuine leather, hand sewn, FIFA approved.

b. Description of goods: Art. No. S312 16cm Christmas bear with cap and scarf, details as per the sample dispatched by the seller on August 8,2012.

Thus the traders need to be aware of the following points in stipulating quality clause.

1. Quality of commodity should be clear and specific in the contract. When it is sold by standard, the year and name of edition should be noted. And when it is sold by description and illustration, technical manuals, booklets or illustration should be clearly described and easy to understand.

2. Quality stipulation should be practical and flexible in the contract. If necessary, the parties can make a tolerance clause to stipulate the allowed deviations from the standard. Such deviations are usually unavoidable and commonly accepted as the usage of the same special trade.

3. Proper quality stipulation methods can be chosen based on different characteristics of the goods. For instance, teas are usually sold by sample, by place of origin or by grade, while computers are often sold by brand and trademark or by description and illustration.

## 3.3  Quantity of Commodity

As one of the major indispensable terms of the contract, quantity of commodity lays the foundation for both parties to conclude a valid contract. It is the seller's obligation to deliver the quantity of goods required in the contract. According to CISG Article 35(1), "the quantity of the goods delivered should be identical to that called for in the contract". Article 52(2) of CISG further explained that "If the seller delivers a quantity of goods greater than that provided for in the contract, the buyer may take delivery or refuse to take delivery of the excess quantity. If the buyer takes delivery of all or part of the excess quantity, he must pay for it at the contract rate."

### 3.3.1　Unit of Measurement

国际上常用的度量衡制度有：公制、英制、美制和国际单位制。

In the business world, different countries adopt different **Systems of Weights and Measures**. The commonly used systems are the Metric System, the British System, the American System and the International System of Units (S.I.). Some units in different systems may carry the same name, but they involve different quantities. For instance, 1 British long ton = 1016 kilograms; 1 American short ton = 907 kilograms; 1 metric ton = 1000 kilograms. Thus foreign traders should have a good knowledge of the units of measurement in different systems and the way how they are converted into another.

Units of measurement usually applied are listed as follows.

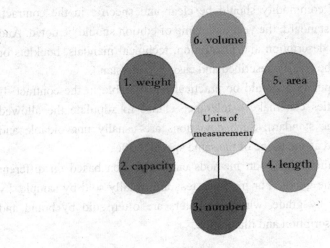

**(1) Unit of weight**: gram (g.), kilogram (kg.), ounce (oz.), pound (lb.), metric ton (m/t), long ton (l/t), short ton(s/t), quintal (q.), etc. They are usually used for mineral products, agricultural and by-products such as wool, cotton, grain, minerals, oil and medicine.

1 pound = 0.4536 kilogram

1 pound = 16 avoirdupois ounces / 12 troy ounces

1 avoirdupois ounce = 28.35 grams

1 troy ounce = 31.106 grams

**(2) Unit of capacity**: liter (l.), gallon (gal.), pint (pt.), bushel (bu.), etc. They are often used for cereals, fluid products and gas products, such as wheat, corn, gas, gasoline and beer.

1 bushel = 8 gallons

1 gallon = 4.545 liters (British System)

1 gallon = 3.785 liters (American System)

1 bushel = 36.368 liters (British System)

1 bushel = 35.238 liters (American System)

bushel(蒲式耳)，是英美国家用来计量谷物、蔬菜、水果的容量单位，和我国旧时的斗类似。

**(3) Unit of number**: piece (pc.), package (pkg.), pair, set, dozen (doz.), gross (gr.), ream (rm.), roll, case, bale, barrel, bag, etc. They are constantly used for daily industrial products and general products such as stationery, paper, toys, ready-made clothes, vehicles and live animals.

1 gross = 12 dozen

1 great gross = 12 grosses = 144 dozen

1 ream = 480 sheets (British System)

1 ream = 500 sheets (American System)

**(4) Unit of length**: meter (m.), centimeter (cm.), yard (yd.), foot (ft.), inch (in.), mile, etc. They are mostly used for textiles, electric wires, metal cords and ropes.

1 mile = 1760 yards

1 yard = 3 feet = 0.9144 meter

1 foot = 12 inches

1 inch = 2.54 centimeters

**(5) Unit of area**: square meter ($m^2$), square foot ($ft^2$), square yard ($yd^2$), square inch, etc. They are often used for glass, textile products such as carpets.

1 square yard = 0.8361 square meters

1 square inch = 6.452 square centimeters

**(6) Unit of volume**: cubic meter ($m^3$), cubic foot ($ft^3$), cubic yard ($yd^3$), cubic inch, etc. They are mostly used for chemical gas and wood.

1 cubic meter = 1.308 cubic yards = 35.315 cubic feet

### 3.3.2　Calculation of Weight

In international trade, many commodities are measured by weight. The methods to calculate the weight of commodity are stated as follows.

#### 1. Gross Weight

以毛作净，即把货物的毛重当作净重来计算价格。在国际贸易中，有些价值较低的农产品可用"以毛作净"来计重。

Gross weight is the sum of total weight of the commodity itself and the tare (the package weight). That is to say, it refers to the net weight plus the tare of the goods.

$$Gross\ Weight = Net\ Weight + Tare$$

Sometimes, "gross for net" is used for weight calculation. For some low commodities, we may price them by gross weight instead of net weight. For instance, Chinese rice, 1,000 metric ton, sack, gross for net.

#### 2. Net Weight

Net weight is the actual weight of the commodity without the addition of the tare. CISG Article 56 stipulates that "if the price is fixed according to the weight of the goods, in case of doubt it is to be determined by the net weight" So if the contract does not stipulate definitely by gross weight or by net weight, it is customary to calculate the weight by net weight.

$$Net\ Weight = Gross\ Weight - Tare$$

Tare is the weight of the package, and it can be calculated in the following ways.

**(1) By actual tare.** It is the actual weight of the packages of the whole commodities.

**(2) By average tare.** In this way, the weight of packages is calculated based on the average tare of a part of the packages.

**(3) By customary tare.** The weight of standardized package has a generally recognized weight, which can be used to represent the weight of such packages.

**(4) By computed tare.** The weight of package is calculated according to the tare previously agreed upon by the seller and the buyer instead of actual weight.

#### 3. Conditioned Weight

Conditioned weight equals to dry weight of a commodity plus the standard moisture content. It is the weight obtained by first deducting the actual moisture content from the actual weight of the commodity and then adding the standard moisture content both by scientific methods. Conditioned weight is often applicable to commodities as raw silk, wool and cotton, which are of high economic value and with unsteady moisture content. The weight of these commodities is likely to be unstable and varies greatly from time to time and from place to place.

公量是用科学的方法抽出商品中所含水分，然后加上标准水分，所求得的重量。

The formula of calculating conditioned weight is as follows:

> Conditioned Weight = Dry Weight + Standard Moisture Content
>
> Conditioned Weight = $\dfrac{\text{Actual Weight} \times (1 + \text{Standard Moisture Regain Rate})}{1 + \text{Actual Moisture Regain Rate}}$

公量=干量+标准含水量

公量=$\dfrac{\text{实际重量}(1+\text{标准回潮率})}{(1+\text{实际回潮率})}$

（注：回潮率是水分与干量之比。）

An exporter has signed a contract to export a consignment of raw silk. The net weight of one pack of raw silk is 58 kg. When shipment is made, the actual moisture regain rate obtained by the scientific method is 12.24%, and the agreed standard moisture regain rate is 11%. So what is the conditioned weight of that pack of raw silk?

**[Calculation]**

$$\text{Conditioned Weight} = \frac{\text{Actual Weight} \times (1 + \text{Standard Moisture Regain Rate})}{1 + \text{Actual Moisture Regain Rate}}$$

$$= \frac{58\,\text{kg} \times (1 + 0.11)}{1 + 0.1224} = 57.36\,(\text{kg})$$

## 4. Theoretical Weight

Theoretical weight is obtained by multiplying the unit weight with the total quantity of the commodities. It is applicable to commodities with regular specifications and regular sizes, such as galvanized iron and steel plate. These commodities are of identical or standardized sizes and specifications, and the weight of each unit is almost the same, thus the total can be obtained by means of theoretical calculation.

纯商品的重量加上直接接触商品的包装材料,如内包装的重量,即为法定重量。而扣除这部分内包装的重量及其他包含杂物的重量即为净净重。

### 5. Legal Weight

Legal weight is the weight of the goods and the immediate package of the goods. Goods packed by cans, small paper boxes, small bottles, etc., might be counted by legal weight. Net net weight is the weight of the commodity by deducting the weight of the immediate packages from the legal weight.

## 3.3.3　Quantity Allowance Clauses

In International business some products such as gold and silver, medicine, raw silk etc., can be precisely weighed. Yet it is difficult to measure accurately those bulk goods of agricultural and mineral products, like corn, soybean, wheat, coal etc. Influenced by natural conditions, packing patterns, loading and unloading methods, the quantity of such goods delivered by the seller may not be in accordance with the quantity definitely stipulated in the contract. To facilitate the implementation of the contract, the seller and the buyer generally agree to use quantity allowance clauses in the contract.

Quantity allowance is the allowed deviation in quantity on delivery from that stipulated in the contract. It can be stipulated in two ways: more or less clause and approximate clause.

### 1. More or Less Clause

溢短装条款,就是在规定具体数量的同时,再在合同中规定允许多装或少装的百分比。

The most commonly used way to stipulate quantity allowance is **more or less clause (or plus or minus clause).** It means that over-load and under-load are permitted but should not surpass a certain percentage of the stipulated quantity. In other words, both parties agree to allow certain percentage more or less of the goods delivered, which does not exceed the fixed quantity agreed upon.

If the clause writes:"Chinese long-shaped rice, 100,000 m/t, 10% more or less at seller's option." It means that the quantity delivered can range from 90,000 m/t (=100,000 m/t ×(1−10%)) to 110,000 m/t (=100,000 m/t ×(1+10%)) in accordance with the seller's requirement.

溢短装条款一般包括机动幅度、机动幅度的选择权及溢短装部分的计价方法。

Usually, the more or less clause includes the following: the allowance percentage of the goods, which party determines the quantity allowance and the price of the over-load or under-load quantity.

The quantity allowance is mostly determined at seller's option, and sometimes at buyer's option or at carrier's option. And under more or less clause, the payment for the over-load and under-load is usually made according to the contract price or at the market price at the time of shipment.

> ***Example***
> - 800 metric tons, 5% more or less at seller's option.
> - 20,000 metric tons, the carrier is allowed to load 5% more or less; the price shall be calculated according to the unit price in the contract.
> - 1,000 metric tons, 5% more or less, at buyer's option with more or less portion priced at the market price at the time of shipment.

### 2. Approximate Clause

Sometimes we can put words such as "about", "approximately" or "circa" in front of the quantity in the contract to indicate the quantity allowance, i.e., **approximate clause**.

由于"约"数在国际贸易中有不同的解释，合同中的数量条款尽量避免使用该词。

Article 30 of UCP600 stipulates that the words "about", "approximately" used in connection with the amount of the credit or the quantity or the unit price stated in the credit are to be interpreted as allowing a tolerance not to exceed 10% more or 10% less than the amount, the quantity or the unit price to which they refer.

However, up to now there is no uniform interpretation of the "about" or "approximately" in international trade practice. These words may have several different interpretations in different nations: some refer to 2.5% more or less, some 5%, and some 10%. Thus it is not advisable to employ this method in international trade practice.

## 3.3.4   Quantity Clauses in the Contract

The quantity clause in a contract includes specific quantity, unit of measurement and method of measurement, if necessary. Mutual understanding of the quantity, unit of measurement and method of measurement is of key importance to both parties.

Examples of quantity clauses in the contract are to be shown as follows.

(1) 3000 cartons, 6000 dozens, 20 doz/ctn.

(2) 800 metric tons, 5% more or less at seller's option.

(3) 1000 m/t with 3% more or less at seller's option. Such excess or deficiency to be at the contracted price.

When stipulating the quantity clause, both parties should bear in the mind the following points.

First, quantity terms may be ambiguous, so careful definition in the contract is very important. For instance, an avoirdupois ounce is different from a troy ounce. Similarly, a ton has a different actual weight depending on whether it is a short ton, a long ton or a metric ton.

Then when it is difficult to stipulate definitely the quantity in the contract, more or less clause can be adopted. In doing so, the seller can fulfill the contract more smoothly. However, it is not advisable to apply approximate clause in the contract in international trade practice. It is because words like "about" or "approximate" have ambiguous interpretations, which might result in future quantity disputes.

# 3.4   Packing of Commodity

进出口货物根据是否加以包装可以分为三大类：裸装货、散装货和包装货。

In the international trade, while cargoes are transported, they fall into three groups based on whether they need packing or not: nude cargo, bulk cargo and packed cargo.

**Nude cargoes** refer to cargoes with stable qualities, either being difficult to be packed or need no packing, such as timber, steel plates, lead ingots, cars, livestock etc. **Bulk cargoes** are shipped without packages on the conveyance in bulk, such as mineral ore, grain, coal, etc. **Packed cargoes** are commodities which need packing in the process of handling, transport and storage. In international trade practice, most of commodities belong to packed cargoes, so the packing of packed cargoes will be the focus of this part.

Proper packing is of great importance and necessity in business practice. It is one of the most important problems which merchants may confront with. And packing has several functions as follows.

i. Physical protection. Packing protects the products from various hazards during handling, storing and transportation from the factory to the consumer. Such hazards can be natural calamity or fortuitous accidents, e.g., tsunami, earthquake, flood, ship collision, ship stranding, ship sinking, fir, explosion, etc.

ii. Convenience. Packing is an art of protecting products in distribution, handling, storage, sale and use. It not only reduces the security risks of shipment, but also facilitates the loading and unloading, transport and storage process.

iii. Marketing. Packing can make the products look appealing and encourage potential buyers to make the purchase. By adding value to products, packing also plays a positive impact upon the buyers' purchasing decision.

iv. Information transmission. The information printed on packing provides consumers with details about the contents, use, transport and recycle of a particular product.

# 3.4.1  Transport Packing

According to its function in the commodity circulation, packing can be classified into two types: **transport packing** and **sales packing**.

**Transport packing**, also called outer packing or big packing, is mainly adapted to protect the goods from being damaged or stolen in the handling, transport and storage process. To stand ocean transportation and rough handling, the outer packing should be solid and durable, easy to store and ship, convenient to load and unload.

根据在商品流通过程中所起的不同作用, 包装可分为销售包装和运输包装。

## 1. Types of Transport Packing

Based on the method of packing, transport packing falls into two kinds: unit transport packing and collective transport packing.

1) Unit Transport Packing

Unit transport packing means that the cargoes are packed as a single unit, i.e., a measuring unit, in the transportation process. Containers for unit transport packing can be sub-divided into the following types.

(1) Case: wooden in structure and various in size and capacity. It usually provides strong protection for cargoes as equipment and car accessories. Cases include wooden case, crate, carton, corrugated carton, skeleton case. The carton is widely used in export packing because it is light, resilient, cheap and most suitable when carried within a metal container.

(2) Drum, cask: made of wood, plastic or metal, and used for carrying liquids, powder or granular cargoes. Drums or casks include wooden drum,

根据包装方式不同, 单件运输包装主要可区分为: 箱(case)、桶(drum, cask)、袋(bag)和包(bundle, bale)。

iron drum, plastic case, barrel, hogshead, etc.

(3) Bag: made of cotton, plastic, paper or jute, and ideal for cement, fertilizer, flour, chemicals, etc. Bags include gunny bag, cloth bag, paper bag, plastic bag, etc.

(4) Bundle, bale: a package of soft goods (e.g., wool, cotton, carpets and raw silk) tightly pressed together, wrapped in a protective material (e.g., linen) and usually strengthened by metal bands or plastic strips.

2) Collective Transport Packing

Collective transport packing means a certain number of single pieces are grouped together to form a big packing or are packed in a big container. It is designed to optimize the carriage of goods by one or more modes of transportation without intermediate handling of the contents. Containers for collective transport packing usually include pallet, flexible container and container.

集合运输包装，主要指托盘(pallet)、集装袋(flexible container)和集装箱(container)。

(1) Pallet. It is used to hold a number of packages or pieces. A pallet is a flat transport structure that supports goods in a stable fashion while being lifted by a forklift or pallet jack. It is the structural foundation of a unit load which allows handling and storage

efficiencies. Goods are often placed on a pallet secured with strapping and shipped. Most pallets are made of wood, and some others are plastic or metal.

(2) Flexible container. Flexible containers are bags in large dimensions for storing and transporting dry, flowable products, for example, sand, fertilizers, and granules of plastics. Flexible Intermediate Bulk Containers (FIBCs), most often made of synthetic fibers or compound materials, normally measure around 110 cm in diameter and vary in height from 100 cm up to 200 cm. Its capacity is normally around 1-4 m/t, but the

larger units can store even more. The maximum capacity can reach about 13 m/t.

(3) Container. It is used to transport goods by road, rail, sea or air. A container is a large reusable receptacle that can accommodate smaller cartons or cases in a single shipment, designed for efficient handling and shipping of

cargoes. Containers are built to standardized dimensions, and can be loaded and unloaded, stacked, transported efficiently over long distances, and transferred from one mode of transport to another without being opened.

At present, the universally used ISO standard containers in the international trade are 20ft container ($20' \times 8' \times 8'6''$), 40ft container ($40' \times 8' \times 8'6''$) and 40ft high-cube container ($40' \times 8' \times 9'6''$). The 20ft container is often taken as a measuring unit, i.e., *twenty-foot equivalent units* (TEU). In

practice, it has a maximum weight of 17,500 kg and a capacity of 25 cubic meters. Similarly, the 40 ft container is commonly designated as two TEU.

As to a container, there are "Full Container Load" (FCL) and "Less Than Container Load" (LCL). A **full container load** (FCL) is an ISO standard container that is loaded and unloaded under the risk and account of one shipper and only one consignee. A **less than container load** (LCL) is a shipment that is not large enough to fill a standard cargo container. It is grouped with other consignments for the same destination in a container at a container freight station.

根据托运货物是否装满一个集装箱,可分为整箱货(FCL)与拼箱货(LCL)。

Besides, there are different types of containers satisfying different needs: dry cargo container, refrigerated container, open top container, tank container, flat rack container, livestock container, etc.

## 2. Marks of Transport Packing

Marking means to have some designs, letters, words or figures stenciled on the transportation packing of cargoes. The purpose of marks on transport packing is to identify goods, to understand the place of origin, to simplify the examination of documents, to keep the secret of business, and to protect the cargoes. According to its function, marks can be classified into the following types: shipping marks, indicative marks, warning marks, weight and volume marks and marks of origin.

包装标志可分为运输标志、指示性标志、警告性标志、重量体积标志和产地标志。

### 1) Shipping Marks

Shipping marks of goods are analogous to identification cards of people. They are also the essential means of identifying cargoes and documents, and linking them together, so as to assure efficient and correct handling during transport and upon arrival at destination. As one of the most important elements agreed on by both parties concerned, shipping marks are stenciled not only on the transport packing of cargoes, but also on the invoices, bills of lading, packing lists and some other documents.

**Shipping marks** usually consist of a simple geometric figure, some letters, numbers and simple words. To promote the application of electronic data interchange, International Standards Organization and some major trading nations have developed new standard shipping marks, which have been adopted in China. International standard shipping marks are made up of the following four parts.

(1) Abbreviations of consignee or buyer

There are usually the initials or abbreviations of a consignee. No full name is to be used here. But in railway or highway transportation, full names are required.

(2) Reference No.

It is one of the numbers of the shipping documents and should not be too long. For example, reference No. can be order No., invoice No., S/C No. or L/C No., etc.

(3) The name of the unloading port

It is used to show the port of destination, and must be clear and complete. In case the name refers to more than one place, it should be followed by the name of its country, so as to avoid wrong delivery. For example, there are 8 different ports sharing the same name "*Victoria*" in different countries, i.e., in Brazil, Canada, Guinea, Cameroon, Australia, Seychelles, Malaysia and Grenada. If transshipment is needed, the port of the transshipment should be indicated, e.g., "*In transit Hong Kong*" or "*London via Hong Kong*".

(4) Package No.

Exporters should list in the shipping mark the total number of the whole lot of cargoes and number the individual packages consecutively so as to facilitate the verification of each individual consignment of the whole patch.

运输标志的主要内容如下：

(1) 收货人或买方的名称首字母或简称，有时加简单的几何图形；

(2) 参考号码；

(3) 目的港或目的地名称；

(4) 件数号码。

An example of shipping marks is illustrated as follows. 标准唛头的式样：

| SMCO | ...... Abbreviation of consignee | ·····收货人代号 |
| 2002/C NO.245789 | ...... Reference No. | ······参考号 |
| NEW YORK | ......The name of the unloading port | ·····目的地 |
| NO.1—20 | ...... Package No. | ·····件数代号 |

Generally, shipping marks are made by sellers. The parties need not discuss this during the negotiation. However, the shipping mark must appear in shipping documents. Should the shipping mark be made by the importer, the seller should get it before the shipping documents are made, and also the marks must be identical with that designated by the buyer, especially under the payment of L/C.

2) Indicative Marks

Indicative marks are eye-catching figures and concise instructions concerning manner of proper handling, storing, loading and unloading. They are used to remind the porters and the container-openers that improper handling might cause damage to the goods. Some commonly used pictorial marking for handling of goods are to be shown in Figure 3-2.

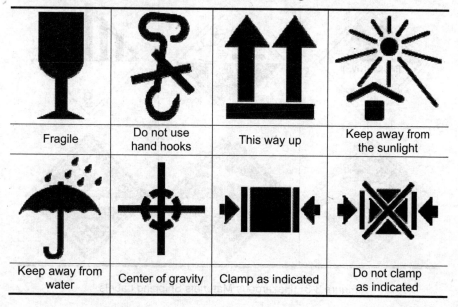

Figure 3-2　Some Pictorial Marking for Handling of Goods

警告性标志，是指在装有爆炸品、易燃物品、腐蚀物品、氧化剂和放射性物质的运输包装上用图形或文字表示各种危险品的标志。

3) Warning Marks

Warning marks are obvious symbols or words to warn people against the hidden danger of hazardous materials or dangerous goods, such as explosives, inflammables, corrosives, oxidizers and radioactives. Shipments of hazardous materials or dangerous goods have special information and symbols as required by UN, country, and specific carrier requirements. Such symbols are printed on the shipping packages of hazardous materials to give warnings for the handling, shipping and storing personnel to take protective measures according to the characters of commodities. Shipping labels for hazardous materials are listed in Figure 3-3.

Figure 3-3   Hazardous Materials Shipping Labels

重量体积标志的用途是方便储运过程中安排装卸作业和仓位。

4) Weight and Volume Marks

Upon the request of the importers, it is the practice of the sellers to supply some supplementary marks, such as marks of weight and volume. Weight and volume marks indicate the volume or gross/net weight of the package to facilitate loading and unloading, or booking shipping space.

**For example:**

Gross weight: 60 kg

Net weight: 56 kg

Measurement: 50 cm×32 cm×40 cm

5) Marks of Origin

In accordance with the rules and regulations laid down by the importing or exporting countries, marks of origin are required by many countries for customs statistics and taxation. Some countries view marks of origin as an indispensable part of goods description, and require the name of origin to be marked on both transport packing and inner packing. For instance, Chinese export commodities are always printed with "Made in China".

## 3.4.2  Sales Packing

**Sales packing**, also called inner packing or small packing, is designed to provide protection for commodities against damage and pilferage, but primarily used to aid marketing. Increasingly fierce market competitiveness and gradually diversified customers' demands bring great challenges to the traders. Good sales packing helps make the goods visible and distinctive, and thus enables potential buyers to identify, to select, to carry and to buy the goods. In this way, sales packing becomes an important factor directly affecting the sales volume and the price.

### 1. Types of Sales Packing

In practice, sales packing can be realized in various forms and with different materials, as long as it is portable, beautiful and helpful to promote sales. Based on different characteristics of the commodities, various types of sales packing have been developed so as to meet the demands of consumers and compete with marketing competitions.

(1) Hanging packing: Packing can be hung on the store shelves for display, with hooks, suspenders, hitches, and string bags, etc.

(2) Stacking packing: Packing can be stacked or piled up so as to save space, such as cans and bottles.

(3) Portable packing: Packing easy for consumers to carry, e.g. paper and plastic bags with handles.

商品产地是海关统计和征税的重要依据，由产地证说明。

常见销售包装有挂式包装、堆叠式包装、便携式包装、一次用量包装、易开包装、喷雾包装、配套包装和礼品包装。

(4) One-off packing: Packing designed to be consumed once such as one-off medicine, one-off drinks and one-off dressing.

(5) Zip-top/Ring-pull packing: Packing with tight-sealed tops that can be opened without the help of tools, such as zip-top cans, bottles and boxes.

(6) Spraying packing: Packing suitable for goods such as perfume and cleanser.

(7) Set packing: Packing with auxiliary items packed in, for example, boxes for complete sets of china.

(8) Gift packing type: Packing especially designed for gifts, which shall create impressions of richness, luxury, and exclusiveness.

### 2. Bar Code for Commodities

条码是商品能够流通于国际市场的一种统一代码和通用的"国际语言",是商品进入超市和大型商场的通行证。

Bar code was first put forward by American N.T. Woodland in 1949. In recent years, the application of the bar code gets very big development with the increasing popularity use of computer. In the international market, each product is assigned a unique numeric code and printed as a bar code on its packing. Only with bar codes, commodities can be sold in the supermarkets.

条码一般由反射率相差较大的黑条(条)和白条(空)组成。商品条码是一种代码,由一组规则排列的条、空及对应代码组成,表示商品特定信息的标识。

Basically, bar code is composed by the reflective black bar (hereinafter referred to as bar) and the white bar (hereinafter referred to as space). Bar code for commodities consists of a group of printed and variously patterned bars and spaces and sometimes numerals which contains information about the commodity it labels.

There are many types of bar codes, and the two commonly adopted universal product codes are Universal Product Code (UPC) and European Article Number (EAN).

UPC 条码,由美国统一代码委员会编制。

UPC, compiled by Universal Code Council (UCC), is mainly used in the United States and Canada. There are five versions of UPC (version A, B, C, D and E), while UPC-A is the basic version and UPC-E is the most common version.

EAN or the International Article Numbering System (EAN International system), compiled by European Article Number Association which is later called International Article Number Association (IANA), is widely used around the world. In November 2002, UCC officially joined EAN International. Then in 2004, EAN international system was renamed GS1 (Global Standard No.1) system, and became an internationally accepted method of identifying products.

There are two versions of EAN, i.e., EAN-13 and EAN-8, and EAN-13 is the standard international commodity bar code. EAN-13 has 13 digits, which falls into two halves — the former containing 7 digits and the latter 6 digits. The first 3 digits designate the country of the EAN International organization. The next 4 digits relate to the manufacturer's code. Similarly, the first 5 digits of the right half are the product code and the final digit is the check digit.

EAN 条码，由国际物品编码协会(前身：欧洲物品编码协会)编制，是当今使用最广泛的条形码。2002 年，UCC 加入 EAN International，共同组成了 EAN·UPC 全球统一标识系统。

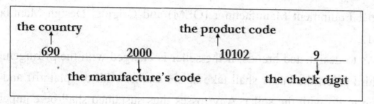

In order to meet the rapid development of economic and technological exchange between China and other countries and regions, China set up Article Numbering Center of China (ANCC) in 1988. In April 1991, China joined IANA and has taken responsibility for promoting application of the code technology and unifying code management. Up to now, GS1 has allocated numbers 690, 691, 692, 693, 694 and 695 to China, while 978 for books, and 977 for magazines.

国际物品编码协会规定我国出口商品的编码为 690 系列。我国的书籍代码为 "978"，杂志代码为 "977"。

### 3.4.3 Neutral Packing and Designated Brand

**Neutral packing** is a special type of packing, which makes no mention of the country of origin, the name and address of the manufacturer, the trade mark and the brand on the inner and outer packing.

Neutral packing can be divided into **neutral packing with designated brand** and **neutral packing without designated brand**. The former means the brand and trade mark designed by the buyer are marked out on the product and package, but with no indication of the country of origin. The latter means neither brand and trade mark nor the country of origin are marked out on the product or package.

The purpose of using neutral packing by the exporters is to break down

中性包装，指既不标明生产国别、地名和厂商名称，也不标明商标或品牌的包装。

the high tariff duties or to avoid problems caused by the import quota imposed by the importing countries on their exports, or for other marketing reasons. It may also help the manufacturer in exporting countries to increase the competitiveness of their products, expand the exports and market profitably in the importing countries. Thus neutral packing becomes a usual practice in international trade, but in recent years it has been restricted by some countries.

**Designated brands** or **brands designated by the buyer,** means that the seller marks trade marks or brands on the package of the commodity or the commodity itself at the buyer's request. It mainly consists of two types: Original Equipment Manufacturer (OEM) and Original Design Manufacturer (ODM).

As to designated brands, if the seller is charged with the infringement by any third party, the buyer shall take up the matter with the plaintiff and it has nothing to do with the seller. Any losses thus sustained shall be compensated by the buyer.

### 3.4.4　Packing Clauses in the Contract

Packing, as one of the major terms of the contract, is the essential content of business in negotiation. According to CISG Article 35(1), the seller must deliver the goods which are contained or packaged in the manner required by the contract. Otherwise, even if the goods are in conformity with the quality, the buyer still has the right to reject the goods and lodge a claim.

The packing clause should be carefully stipulated in the contract. It usually includes packing material, packing method and quantity of the goods. Examples are to be shown as follows.

(1) In cloth bales each containing 20 pcs of 42 yds.

(2) 20 pcs to a box, 10 boxes to one carton. Total 500 cartons only.

(3) In packets of 5 pieces each, 20 packets to a carton, 144 cartons to a 40′ container.

(4) Each set packed in one export carton, each 810 cartons transported in one 40′ container.

(5) Packed in wooden cases, each containing 12 five-pound tins, net

定牌生产，指卖方按买方要求在其出售的商品或包装上表明指定的商标或牌号。

包装条款通常包括包装材料、包装方式和每件包装的商品数量等。

weight 60 pounds, gross weight 90 pounds.

(6) Each piece to be wrapped with paper and to a plastic bag, each dozen then to a new strong wooden case brushed with the marks specified in the relevant L/C. Total 400 cases only.

When specifying the packing clause, both parties should pay attention to the following aspects.

(1) Stipulation in the packing clause should be concrete and not too vague. For instance, ambiguous terms such as "seaworthy packing", "customary packing" or "seller's usual packing" should be avoided, because such terms have no uniform interpretations and disputes may arise.

(2) Appropriate packing should be chosen according to the nature of the commodity and transportation modes. For example, packing for ocean transportation should be seaworthy and protective against squeezing and bumping, while packing for air transportation should be light and compact.

(3) Packing forms to be adopted should be clearly stated in the contract. Detailed requirements for packing materials and techniques should be specified in the contract, depending on characteristics of the goods, modes of transportation and the climate in the course of transportation and so on.

(4) Which party provides shipping mark should be stated out. According to international practice, shipping mark is always given by the seller. If the buyer has any requirements on shipping marks, that should be stipulated in sales contract.

(5) Packing expenses are usually included in the price, and shall be borne by the seller. If the buyer has special requirements for the packing, which is beyond the seller's ability, the buyer himself should undertake the expenses.

# 【Key Terms and Words】

Bushel (bu.)　蒲式耳

Ream (rm.)　令

Corrosive　腐蚀物品

Radioactive　放射性物质

Oxidizer　氧化剂

Name of commodity　商品名称，品名

Description of goods　商品描述

World Customs Organization (WCO)　世界海关组织

HS code　海关编码，"商品名称及编码协调制度"简称

Original sample/representative sample　原样/代表样品

Duplicate/ keep sample　留样

Sale by sample　凭样品买卖

Sale by seller's/buyer's sample　凭卖方/买方样品买卖

Counter sample　对等样品

Sealed sample　封样

Reference sample　参考样品

Sale as seen　看货买卖

Sale by specification　凭规格买卖

Sale by brand or trade mark　凭牌名或商标买卖

Sale by place of origin　凭产地名称买卖

Sale by description and illustration　凭说明书或图样买卖

Fair average quality (F.A.Q.)　良好平均品质

Good merchantable quality (G.M.Q.)　上等可销品质

Quality latitude　品质机动幅度

Quality tolerance　质量公差

Systems of Weights and Measures　度量衡制度

The Metric System　公制

The International System of Units (S.I.)　国际单位制

Avoirdupois ounce　常衡盎司

Troy ounce　金衡盎司

Average tare　平均皮重

Customary tare 习惯皮重

Computed tare 约定皮重

Conditioned weight 公量

Moisture regain rate 回潮率

Dry weight 干量

Theoretical weight 理论重量

Net net weight 净净重

Quantity allowance 数量机动幅度

More or less clause 溢短装条款

Approximate clause "约"数条款

Nude cargo 裸装货

Bulk cargo 散装货

Unit transport packing 单件运输包装

Collective transport packing 集合运输包装

Corrugated carton 瓦楞纸箱

Skeleton case 漏孔箱

Gunny bag 麻袋

Full container load (FCL) 整箱货

Less than container load (LCL) 拼箱货

Shipping mark 运输标志，唛头

Indicative mark 指示性标志

Warning mark 警告性标志

Stacking packing 堆叠式包装

Zip-top packing 易开包装

Spraying packing 喷雾包装

Neutral packing with designated brand 定牌中性包装

Neutral packing without designated brand 无牌中性包装

# 【Exercises】

I. Please briefly explain the meaning of the following terms.

1. Gross for net

2. More or less clause

3. G.M.Q.

4. Shipping marks

5. Neutral packing

II. Please translate the following terms into Chinese.

1. Packed cargo ＿＿＿＿＿＿＿＿＿＿＿　　2. Bulk cargo ＿＿＿＿＿＿＿＿＿＿＿

3. Outer packing ＿＿＿＿＿＿＿＿＿＿＿　　4. Inner packing ＿＿＿＿＿＿＿＿＿＿＿

5. Neutral packing ＿＿＿＿＿＿＿＿＿＿＿　6. Full container load ＿＿＿＿＿＿＿＿＿＿

7. Corrosive ＿＿＿＿＿＿＿＿＿＿＿　　　8. Radioactive ＿＿＿＿＿＿＿＿＿＿＿

9. Shipping mark ＿＿＿＿＿＿＿＿＿＿＿　　10. Indicative marks ＿＿＿＿＿＿＿＿＿＿

III. Commodities are given in the left column and quality stipulation methods in the right column. Please match each commodity with the most suitable method.

| 1. Grade A fresh hen eggs | A. Sale by standard |
|---|---|
| 2. Calligraphic works | B. Sale by place of origin |
| 3. Fish | C. F.A.Q. |
| 4. Gree Air-co | D. G.M.Q. |
| 5. Robot lawn mover | E. Sale by brand or trademark |
| 6. Rice | F. Sale by grade |
| 7. Jingdezhen Porcelain | G. Sale as seen |
| 8. Rifampicin B.P. 1993 | H. Sale by description and illustration |

IV. Please translate the following sentences into English.

1. 每20件装一盒子，10盒子装一纸箱，共500纸箱。

2. 每24套装一纸箱，共676纸箱，装入一个20尺小柜。

3. 800公吨，卖方可溢装或短装3%。溢短装部分价格按合同价核算。

4. 每只包纸，并套塑料袋，每一打装一坚固新木箱，并刷信用证规定的唛头。共计400箱。

V. Shipping Marks

Shanghai Light Industrial IMP & EXP Corp. enters into an agreement with an American importer ABC Co. for selling cloth doll. Description of commodity: "Cloth Doll, Art. No. 612, 10 dozens to one carton. Total 70 cartons only." S/C No.: SHLI950310, L/C No.: 95LCA0220, and port of destination: New York.

Please make a shipping mark according to the above information.

VI. Calculation

1. The specification of steel plate A is 1m×1m×1mm, and its theoretical weight is 7.85 kg. And

steel plate B's specification is 2m×1m×1mm. Then what is the theoretical weight of 400 sheets of steel plate B?

2. An exporter has signed a contract to export 10 metric tons of raw silk to Spain. It is stipulated in the contract that conditioned weight is used and the standard moisture regain rate is 10%. If the actual moisture regain rate is 21% when shipment is made, how many metric tons of raw silk should the exporter deliver in order to fulfill the contract?

## VII. Case Study

1. A Shanghai exporter signed a sales contract with a British company for selling paper. The quality clause in the contract stipulated: "Handmade Writing Paper". The exporter had sent its sample to the importer for confirmation before production. However, upon receipt of the goods, the British importer lodged a claim against the exporter on the ground that: the inspection certificate shows that the paper was partly made by machine; in the legal sense, it constitutes "over-publicity" according to British Law; the importer suffered a great loss.

The exporter argues: the buyer accepted the sample sent by the seller; the deal should be deemed as "sales by sample", and the quality of the goods was fully in line with the sample; the seller bore no responsibility for the loss.

**Questions:**

(1) What is the focus of the dispute?

(2) Who is responsible for the loss? Give reasons to support your argument.

2. One company in Beijing planned to export frozen Beijing duck to Iraq. The clause in the contract was "all ducks should be killed in Muslim way". But, in fact, the company hadn't exactly nown the Muslim way, and in the processing, they used another way by killing the ducks through the mouth and cleaned the inner parts of the duck. Then they froze the ducks to keep a good shape. After that, the company got a certificate from an association concerned to certify that they killed the ducks according to the Muslim way without the actual inspection of that association. When the goods reached the buyer, they found that the ducks were not killed in the agreed way and refused to accept the consignment. They broke the contract. The seller should either destroy all the goods or ship them back.

**Questions:**

(1) What is the cause of the seller's loss?

(2) What should they do about this?

3. The quantity clause in the contract stipulates "10,000 M/T, 5% more or less at seller's option". Assume that the international market price is rising sharply when the seller is about to deliver the goods.

**Questions:**

(1) If you were the seller, how many goods do you think you would deliver? Why?

(2) If you were the buyer, what should you pay attention to when negotiating the more or less clause in the contract?

4. A bicycle manufacturer based in Shanghai signed a contract with a Hong Kong merchant, selling 1,000 bicycles. When the countersigned copy returned, the exporter noticed the merchant had added "C.K.D." to packing requirement "packed in wooden case".

**Questions:**

(1) What does C.K.D. mean?

(2) What would you recommend the exporter to do?

5. A Chinese company concluded a sales contract with a Singapore buyer. The packing clause stated "packed in plywood box, net weight 10 kg, and two boxes in a bale, covered with jute bag". When the L/C arrived, the packing requirement said "packed in plywood box, net weight 10 kg, and two boxes in a bale", without the phrase "covered with jute bag". The exporter packed the goods as the L/C requested and shipped them. When they arrived, the buyer refused to accept them.

**Questions:**

(1) What are the problems in this deal?

(2) What will you suggest to the exporter?

# Chapter 4  International Cargo Transport

【Learning Objectives】

By studying this chapter, you should be able to master:

- Containerization
- Freight of Container Transportation
- Marine Transport
- Liners Transportation
- Freight of Liners
- Bill of Lading
- Shipment Clause

## Lead-in: News Report

### Sub-anchor: Eurasian Land Bridge

The new Eurasian land bridge, also called the Second Eurasian land bridge, is a new rail line running through China and Europe. It starts in the coastal city of Lianyungang in China's eastern Jiangsu province, crosses almost 12 thousand kilometers through Kazakhstan and Russia, and ends in Rotterdam in The Netherlands. The old land bridge, which is almost a hundred years old now, starts at the Russian coast in Vladivostok and ends in Rotterdam after crossing Siberia, so the new route covers different ground, including China and Kazakhstan.

Kazakhstan is the largest inland country in the world. As Chinese rails and highways have expanded west, trade between Kazakhstan and China has been booming. From January to October this year, goods passing through the Khorgas port between the two nations reached 880,000 tons—that's over 250% growth compared with the same period last year. And trade between China and Kazakhstan is expected to grow 3 to 5 fold over the next 4 years. As of November 2007, however, only about 1% of the goods shipped from Asia to Europe were delivered by overland routes. So there is a lot of potential in the new link.

Transportation is one of important steps in international trade. Without transportation, goods sold by the seller are not able to be delivered to the buyer aboard. An increase in trade increases the transport of the goods. Meanwhile, with the development of modern technology in transportation, speed and capacity for shipment has been largely improved and modes of transportation have been greatly varied. Obviously, all these contribute a lot to the expansion of international trade. There are several ways to carry the goods to their destination, including marine transport, land transport, air transport and multi-modal transport. It is stressed that containers as special equipment are widely used in different modes of transportation because they offer higher efficiency in loading and unloading and enable quick transit and better quality. Thus goods usually arrive in better condition.

*(Source: China 24 from CCTV.com, Updated: 2011-12-03 09:37)*

**Class Activities:**

1. Tell more background information on the so-called new Eurasian land bridge?

2. The new Eurasian land bridge connects Europe and China through Kazakhstan. Tell more about these two neighboring economies.

# 4.1　Containerization

Containerization is considered as the key innovation in the field of logistics in the twentieth century. Today, nearly 90% of non-bulk cargo is handled by containers. And one fourth of world's total containers start from China. Containerization is a system of inter-modal freight transport using standard ISO (International Standards Organization) containers that can be loaded and sealed intact onto container ships, railroad cars, planes, and trucks.

集装箱化是使用标准集装箱进行货物运输的多式联运系统，使其能适用于船舶、铁路、公路等多种运输方式。

ISO Technical Committee defines the Container as "Article of transport equipment which is

(1) of a permanent character and accordingly strong enough to be suitable for repeated use;

(2) specially designed to facilitate the carriage of goods, by one or more modes of transport, without intermediate reloading;

(3) fitted with devices permitting its ready handling, particularly its transfer from one mode of transport to another;

(4) so designed as to be easy to fill and empty;

(5) stackable;

(6) having an internal volume of 1 cubic meter or more . "

Exporters and importers can decide which methods will be the best for the goods to be transported according to the commodity features, transport cost, speed and so on.

按国际标准化组织的规定，集装箱应具备下列条件：

(1) 能长期反复使用，具有足够的强度。

(2) 途中转运不用移动箱内货物，就可以直接换装。

(3) 可以进行快速装卸，并可从一种运输工具直接方便地换装到另一种运输工具。

(4) 便于货物的装满和卸空。

(5) 可堆叠。

(6) 具有 1 立方米(即 35.32 立方英尺)或以上的容积。

## 4.1.1　Features of Container Transportation

Container transportation is highly efficient in terms of reliability, cost, quality of service and advanced technology. Features of container transportation are as follows.

- It offers a door to door service under FCL/FCL (Full Container Load/Full Container Load), door to container freight station (CFS) service under FCL/LCL (Full Container Load/Less than Container Load), CFS/CFS service under LCL/LCL, or CFS to door service under LCL/FCL conditions.

- It can be handled quickly by standardized equipment and can thus save labors and loading and unloading charges.
- The low risk of cargo damage and pilferage enables more favorable cargo premiums to be obtained, compared with break-bulk cargo shipments.
- Less packing is required for containerized consignment. In some cases, particularly with specialized ISO containers such as refrigerated ones or tanks, no packing is required. This produces substantial cost savings in the international transit and raises service quality.
- Faster transits, coupled with more reliable maritime schedules, and ultimately increased service frequency, produce savings in warehouse accommodation needs, lessen risks of obsolescent stock and speed up capital turnover.

## 4.1.2  Types of Container

There are many kinds of container such as dry cargo container, bulk container, reefer container, open top container, flat rack container, tank container and so on. They are used to serve the different needs for cargo transportation.

Container transport falls into two kinds: full container loads (FCL) and less than container loads (LCL). A full container load is an ISO standard container that is loaded and unloaded under the risk and account of one shipper and only one consignee. In practice, it means that the whole container is intended for one consignee. FCL consignments are usually packed into the container by the consignor himself at the production site or the warehouse, and then sent to the container yard (CY) ready for shipment by the carrier. After arrival at the place or port of destination, the consignee can directly accept the goods at the container yard of destination. Less than container load is a shipment that is not large enough to fill a standard cargo container. LCL

整箱货(FCL)是指由货方在工厂或仓库进行装箱，然后直接交集装箱堆场等待装运，货到目的地(港)后，收货人可直接从目的地集装箱堆场提走。适用的交货方式通常为集装箱堆场到集装箱堆场(CY to CY)。

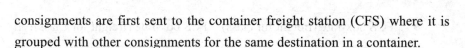

consignments are first sent to the container freight station (CFS) where it is grouped with other consignments for the same destination in a container.

The main sizes of containers are as follows:

- 1A: 40′ GP (40 feet general purpose, 8′×8′×40′), it can hold the goods of about 24.5 M/T or 55M³;
- 1AA: 40′ HQ (40 feet high cube container, 8.6′×8′×40′), it can hold the goods of about 24.5 M/T or 68M³;
- 1C: 20′ GP (20 feet general purpose, 8′×8′×20′), it can hold the goods of about 17.5 M/T or 25 M³.

## 4.1.3   Freight of Container Transportation

There are two major freight rates used for calculation of container transportation freight. One is similar to those of general cargo, that is to say, measurements are made in freight ton. The other is box-rate. Its freight rate is determined largely by the capacity of the container and the destination of the consignment, irrespective of the quantity of commodity carried. The box-rate will gradually replace the former and become the mainstream.

There are three kinds of box-rate:

- FAK box-rate (freight for all kinds)   FAK box-rate (freight for all kinds): It is a term for a carrier's tariff classification for various kinds of goods that are pooled and shipped together at one freight rate. Consolidated shipments are generally classified as FAK. Table 4-1 shows the FAK box-rate of China-Singapore lines.

Table 4-1   China–Singapore Lines Box-rate          (in US $)

| Shipment Port | Type of Cargo | CFS/CFS | CY/CY | |
| --- | --- | --- | --- | --- |
| | | Per F/T | 20′ FCL | 40′ FCL |
| Dalian | General Cargo | 78.50 | 1250.00 | 2310.00 |
| Xingang | General Cargo | 70.00 | 1150.00 | 2035.00 |
| Shanghai | General Cargo | 70.00 | 1150.00 | 2035.00 |
| Huangpu | General Cargo | 63.00 | 950.00 | 1750.00 |
| … | … | … | … | … |

拼箱货(LCL)是指货量不足一整箱，须由承运人在集装箱货运站负责将不同发货人的少量货物拼装在一个集装箱内，货到目的地(港)后，由承运人拆箱后分拨给各收货人。适用的交货方式通常为集装箱货运站到集装箱货运站(CFS to CFS)。

● FCS box-rate (freight for class)  FCS box-rate (freight for Class)：It is a term for a carrier's tariff classification for different classes of goods at different freight rate. Table 4-2 shows the FCS box-rate of China-Australia lines.

Table 4-2  China–Australia Lines Box-rate          (in US $)

| Base Port: Brisbane, Melbourne, Sydney, Fremantle | | | | |
|---|---|---|---|---|
| Class | Basis | 20′(CY/CY) | 40′(CY/CY) | LCL(per F/T) |
| 1-7 | W/M | 1700 | 3230 | 95 |
| 8-13 | W/M | 1800 | 3420 | 100 |
| 14-20 | W/M | 1900 | 3510 | 105 |

● FCB box-rate (freight for class & basis)  FCB box-rate (freight for Class & basis)：It is a term for a carrier's tariff classification for different classes of goods and different basis for freight calculation at different rate. Table 4-3 shows the FCB box-rate of China-Mediterranean lines.

Table 4-3  China–Mediterranean Sea Lines Box-rate        (in US $)

| Base Port: Algiers, Genoa, Marseilles-FOS | | | | |
|---|---|---|---|---|
| Class | LCL Per W | LCL Per M | FCL 20′(CY/CY) | FCL 40′(CY/CY) |
| 1-7 | 131.00 | 100.00 | 2250.00 | 4200.00 |
| 8-13 | 133.00 | 102.00 | 2330.00 | 4412.00 |
| 14-20 | 136.00 | 110.00 | 2450.00 | 4640.00 |

In addition to the basic freight, various additional surcharges can be charged as well. They are composed of:

● Inland transport charges;

● LCL services charge;

● Terminal handling charge;

● Fee for using container and other equipments.

*Example 1*

Suppose: The goods are packed in cartons, which dimensions are 50cm×40cm×30cm. The gross weight is 52Kg/CTN. Please calculate the number of packages separately according to payload capacity of 20′GP and 40′GP.

*Calculation:*

Weight:

The maximum packages of 20′GP=17.5/0.052=336.538/CTNS, The rounded number is 336.

The maximum packages of 40′GP=24.5/0.052=471.154/CTNS, The rounded number is 471.

Measurement:

The maximum packages of 20′GP=25/(0.5×0.4×0.3)=416.667/CTNS, The rounded number is 416.

The maximum packages of 40′GP=55/(0.5×0.4×0.3)=916.667/CTNS, The rounded number is 916.

*Example 2*

Company A exports 600 PCS of Wrench to Kobe, Japan. The total gross weight is 16.2 M/T, and the measurement is 23.316 M³. The goods is packed into a container of 20′ GP. For Wrench, the freight rate is W/M, and the Freight Tariff (Shanghai—Kobe) for 20′ GP is USD 870/M or USD 850/W, the packing charge is USD 120/20′ GP. How much is the total freight?

*Calculation*

Measurement > Weight, "M" is the freight calculation basis, that is USD 870/M per 20′ GP

Total freight = Basic freight+ surcharge

Total freight = USD 870+USD 120 = USD 990

# 4.2 Modes of Transportation

At present, the commonly used modes of transportation are marine transportation, rail transportation, road transportation, air transportation and international multimodal transportation. When more than one mode is available, careful consideration should be made to decide the right method of transportation. You will have to consider the time needed for the transport, the quantity of the goods, the safety of the goods, the availability of the transport vehicles and so on.

## 4.2.1 Marine Transport

Marine transportation, also called ocean transportation, is the most widely used mode of transportation in international trade. It is cheap for delivering large quantities of goods over long distances. About 2/3 of the world trade volume and 90% of China's trade volume now are transported by sea.

It has the following advantages:

(1) The easy passage since about 70% of the earth is covered by water.

(2) It has a large capacity.

(3) It is a relatively low-cost way to transport goods.

However, compared with road or air transportation, marine transportation is slow, vulnerable to bad weather and less punctual.

### 1. Types of Cargo Vessels

Different types of cargo vessels are used to suit the needs of shipping different cargoes. In general, marine transport can fall into two groups: liners and tramps.

1) Liners

班轮运输是指在一定航线上，在一定停靠港口，定期开航的船舶运输。"四固定"和"一负责"是其基本特点。

*Liners* operate over regular route according to an advertised time-table. It has the following characteristics: fixed schedule, route, ports and relatively fixed freight, loading and unloading charges (included in freight). Shipment made on liners is relatively small but frequent. Meanwhile the scheduled services enable shipping, industrial and marketing operations to be planned well in advance.

## 2) Tramps

A *tramp* is a freight carrier that doesn't sail on firm schedule and regular routes, but goes all over the world in search of cargoes, primarily bulk shipments, like grain, timber, steel, coal, ores, fertilizers, etc., which are carried in complete shiploads. Tramp vessels are engaged under chartering on a time and voyage basis, and occasionally are chartered to supplement existing liner services to meet peak cargo shipment demands. Generally, there are three kinds of chartering as follows: voyage charter, time charter and demise charter.

A *voyage charter* is the hire of a ship for a particular trip, which might be for one single or consecutive single voyage or for one return or consecutive return voyages. The charterer should pay the freight for his shipment of cargoes on an agreed rate. Should he fail to provide sufficient cargo to fill the ship, he is liable for what is termed dead freight, a prorate payment for the space not used. The ship owner should provide a ship that is seaworthy and avoid unjustifiable deviation en route.

A *time charter* is the hire of a ship for a specified period of time, from a few months up to many years. During the time of chartering, the business of the ship is under the management of the charterer.

*Demise charter* is also called bare boat charter. Under demise charter, the ship owner only rents the charterer the boat, while the charterer is responsible for crewing, provisioning and fuelling, and the boat is under complete control of the charterer. To some extent, it is a form of time charter.

## 2. Freight Rates

### 1) Freight of Liners

The freight of liners varies with bulk cargo transport or container service. The freight of bulk cargo transportation comprises basic charges and additional charges. The following rules are concluded in relation to the calculation of basic charges.

- *W*　For items marked with "W", it is called weight ton. The freight is to be calculated per metric ton or long ton which is decided by liner companies.
- *M*　For items marked with "M", it is called measurement ton. The freight is to be calculated per cubic meter or 40 cubic feet.

租船运输指租船人向船东租赁船舶用于货物运输的业务。租船方式主要有定程租船、定期租船和光船租船。

在实际业务中，基本运费的计算标准以按货物的毛重（"W"）或按货物的体积（"M"）或按重量、体积从高选择（"W/M"）三种方式居多。贵重物品较多是按货物的价格，即按 FOB 总值（"A.V."）计收。

- *A.V.*   For items marked with "A.V. " or "Ad Val.", the freight is to be calculated on the basis of the price or value of the cargo concerned.

- *W/M*   For items marked with "W/M", the freight is to be calculated on the basis of either weight ton or measurement ton, subject to the higher rate.

- *W/M or A. V.*   For items marked with "W/M or A.V.", the highest rate is applicable.

- *Unit*   For items marked "Unit", the freight is to be calculated according to the number of the cargo carried.

- *Minimum Rate*   For carriage of cargo in extremely small quantities, a minimum freight is adopted for the obtainment of freight.

- *Open Rate*   For items marked "Open", the freight is to be calculated according to the temporary or special agreement entered into between the carrier and the consignor. Usually, shipment of cargo in extremely large quantity such as grains, ores, and coal is subject to open rate.

---

***Examples***

<u>Typical Rate Basis</u>

| | |
|---|---|
| * W: Weight Ton | USD100 Per M/T |
| * M: Measurement Ton | USD100 Per M$^3$ |
| * A.V. | 1% of FOB Value |
| * W/M | USD100 Per F/T |
| * Unit | USD100 Per Unit |
| * Minimum rate | USD150 Per B/L |
| * Open rate | To be negotiated |

---

In practice, the shipping company often calculate the basic charges by weight ton ("W"), measurement ton ("M") or freight ton ("W/M"). Meanwhile we should not overlook the additional charges in the quotation of the goods. A few of them are listed here:

---

**Surcharges**

* BAF: Bunker Adjustment Factor

* CAF: Currency Adjustment Factor

---

* Port Congestion Surcharge

* Transshipment Surcharge

* Deviation Surcharge

* Port Surcharge

**Additionals**

* Heavy Lift Additional

* Lengthy Cargo Additional

* Bulky Cargo Additional

* Additional on Direct

* Additional on Optional Discharging Port

* Additional for Alternation of Destination

To get the freight of cargoes, we need to

●　Know the grade of the goods and the basis of freight calculation by looking up the goods in the freight tariff;

●　Get the basic freight rates of the goods, which is given in number of US $ for each unit of the goods;

●　Get additional charges of the route and the ports that will be called upon, which is given in percentage of the basic freight rates;

●　Get the total freight by adding the additional charges to the basic freight charges.

*Example*

Company A exports 15 cartons of Diesel Engine to Hong Kong. The total gross weight is 5.65 M/T, and the volume is 10.676 M³. For Diesel Engine, the freight rate is W/M, and the Freight Tariff (Qing Dao—Hong Kong) is USD 22 per F/T, with a 10% port surcharges. How much is the total freight?

*Calculation:*

Measurement＞Weight, "M" is the freight calculation basis

Total freight = Basic freight rate　(1+ surcharge) × Total Measurement

Total freight = 22 × (1+10%) × 10.676 = USD 258.3592

2) Freight of Charter

The freight of charter is usually stipulated according to the tonnage of the ship and the freight rate on the current chartering market.

There are three methods of stipulating the freight:

- Tonnage of the goods loaded;
- Tonnage of the goods unloaded;
- On all-round contract basis.

The freight may be stipulated in the charter party as follows:

- Freight can be paid in advance;
- Freight can be paid after the goods have arrived at the port of destination;
- Part of freight is paid in advance, the rest of which is paid after the goods have arrived at the port of destination.

Before the charterer pays off freight and other charges, the ship owner is entitled to refuse to deliver the goods. This kind of right is called lien.

There are four methods to be used to stipulate the expenses of loading and unloading:

- The ship owner bears gross terms;
- The ship owner is free in (F.I.);
- The ship owner is free out (F.O.);
- The ship owner is free in and out (F.I.O.).

When adopting this method, the interested parties should indicate who will bear the expenses of stowing and trimming. If they agree the charterer shall be responsible for them, the interested parties shall stipulate "ship owner is free in and out, stowed, trimmed (F.I.O.S.T.)."

**Demurrage and Dispatch Money**

The time of loading and unloading will affect the turnover rate of the ship, and this, will affect the interest of the ship owner. Therefore it is the main clause specified in the charter party. The time limit of loading and unloading may be indicated by

- days or running or consecutive days/hours;
- working days;
- weather working days;
- weather working days of consecutive 24 hours.

在规定的装卸期限内，如果租船人未能完成装卸作业，为了弥补船方的损失，超过时间的租船人应向船方支付一定的罚款，这种罚款称为"滞期费"。

During the time limit of loading and unloading, in case the charter does not finish the work of loading and unloading, in order to compensate the ship owner for his losses, the charter should pay a certain amount of fine for the exceeding time. This is the *demurrage*.

During the time limit of loading and unloading, in case the charter finish the work of loading and unloading ahead of schedule, then the ship owner shall pay certain amount of bonus to the charter. This is called the *dispatch money*.

反之，如果租船人在规定的期限内，提前完成装卸作业，则船方要向租船人支付一定的奖金，这种奖金称为"速遣费"。

---

**Example**

Suppose: We import the goods of 10000 M/T based on FOB. The contract stipulates the goods of 500 M/T loading on board every day. For each day the demurrage is RMB600 and the dispatch money is RMB300. Finally, all the goods are shipped on board for 22 days and 6 hours. Who is going to be charged? How much to charge for it?

Calculation:

$600×(22.25-20)=$ RMB1350

So we should pay the ship RMB1350 as the demurrage.

---

### 3. Bill of Lading

Bill of Lading, shortened as B/L, is a document issued by a carrier which details a shipment of merchandise and gives title of that shipment to a specified party. Bills of lading are one of three important documents used in international trade to help guarantee that exporters receive payment and importers receive merchandise.

1) Functions of Bill of Lading

A bill of lading is issued by the captain or the shipping companies to testify that the goods have been received or shipped on board for delivery to a certain port of destination. It has three major functions as follows:

- A Receipt of Cargo

A bill of lading is a cargo receipt. It is a receipt issued by a carrier evidencing that a consignment of goods has been received at his disposal for shipment, or actually loaded on board the ship. Thus a bill of lading will show the quantity and apparent condition of the cargo loaded.

In international trade practice, the information about goods is normally

海运提单的性质：
一是货物收据，二是运输合同的证明，三是货物所有权的凭证。

provided by the shipper and confirmed by the carrier as the goods are transferred to him or loaded aboard the ship. However, the carrier is responsible only for the apparent compliance rather than the contents packed inside, that is, a carrier simply makes sure that the labels comply with the goods listed and that the packages are in good condition.

- An Evidence of the Contract of Carriage

A bill of lading is the evidence of the contract of carriage between the consignor and the carrier. Listed on the B/L are the rights and liabilities of the carrier and the consignor, though under a charter party, the rights and liabilities are to be decided by the charter party.

- A Document of Title to the Goods

A bill of lading is a document of title to the goods, that is, the legal owner of a bill of lading holds legal possession of the goods described in it. The legal holder of the bill of lading is given the right to take delivery of the goods at the port of destination. For this function, the goods still in transit can be transferred from one owner to another by means of selling and buying of a bill of lading.

2) Content of Bill of Lading

The basic terms are usually shown on the face of the bill while some general terms and conditions are printed on the back. The items on the face of a bill of lading are usually the information concerning the contracted parties, full particulars of the cargo and terms of carriage contract. The general terms and conditions of the contract of carriage are printed on the back of the bill of lading. They are the basis for the rights and obligations of all the parties concerned.

Different shipping companies have different forms of B/L, but any B/L contains the following information:

- Carrier. Not only the captain of the ship should be presented, but also the shipping companies should be given.
- Shipper, or consignor, generally the exporter.
- Consignee. This column should be filled in with great care and in accordance with the instructions of L/C.
- Notify party, generally the consignee. This is the party to be notified by the ship upon the arrival at the port of destination. If so required by the L/C, the complete address of the consignee should be filled here; if not required, the full address of the consignee should be

given here in duplicate. If "only" is required by the L/C following the name of consignee, there should be "only" there. If two or more than two names and addresses are required here by L/C, there should not be only one here.

- Number of B/L.
- The name of the carrying vessel and voyage number.
- The date when the goods were received for the shipment and/or loaded on the vessel.
- Port of discharge. If the B/L has another column "final destination" or "port of delivery" as in a combined transport bill of lading, the port of discharge should be the transshipment port. If not, this is the port of destination.
- Port of delivery. This is the port of final destination. If there will be transshipment, there should be a remark here "with transshipment at …".
- Shipping marks.
- Description of the goods.
- Gross weight.
- Measurement.
- Numbers and kinds of packages.
- Freight, whether it is prepaid as under CIF and CFR or to collect as under FOB.
- Number of B/L signed on behalf of the Master or his agent. Generally there should be two or three originals with many copies. One of the copies will be retained by the carrier and the originals are kept by the shipper after they are duly signed by the Master or his agent for negotiation. With one of the originals used for taking delivery of the goods at the port or place of destination, the other originals will stand void.
- The signature of the Master or his agent and the date.

3) Types of Bill of Lading

Bill of lading can be classified into various forms according to different standards.

(1) On Board B/L and Received for Shipment B/L

According to whether the goods have been loaded on board the carrying

已装船提单是指承运人在货物已经装上指定船舶后所签发的提单。已装船提单必须以文字表明货物已装上或已装运于某具名船只,提单签发日期即为装船日期。

vessel, bill of lading can be classified into on board (or shipped) B/L and received for shipment B/L.

*On board B/L* refers to the one that shall be issued after the cargo has been actually shipped on board vessel. It is issued by the shipping company, on which both the loading date and the name of the vessel shall be indicated in detail. Since shipped bills of lading provide better guarantee for the arrival of the goods at the destination, they are usually preferred by the importer.

*Received for shipment B/L* is the one that acknowledges that goods have been received for shipment but not been loaded on board the carrying vessel yet. It is issued when the goods have been placed in the custody of the carrier awaiting shipment. Such a bill does not show the name of the carrying vessel and the date of shipment. The absence of date of shipment makes it difficult to anticipate the date of the goods, therefore it is generally not favored by the buyer, and usually the L/C will require the seller to present on board B/L for negotiation at the bank. But it can become a shipped on board B/L by adding an on board notation, and signed by the carrier or agent on the received B/L.

(2) Clean B/L and Unclean B/L

According to the apparent condition of the received cargo, bill of lading can be classified into clean B/L and unclean B/L.

清洁提单是指货物在装船时表面状况良好,承运人在提单上不带有明确宣称货物受损及/或包装有缺陷状况的不良批注的提单。

A *clean B/L* refers to the one that does not contain any notation declaring a defective condition of the exterior packing of goods. It is a proof that the goods have been "shipped in apparent good order and condition" or "clean on board" or the like.

A clean B/L is usually issued to the shipper when goods do not show any defects on their exteriors at the time of loading. By issuing a clean bill of lading, the carrier undertakes full liability for the goods in transit. A clean B/L is favored by buyers and banks for settlement, and therefore it is usually stipulated in the sales contract that the seller should obtain a clean bill of lading for presentation.

An *unclean B/L*, also named a dirty B/L, is the one that contains unfavorable notation about the apparent condition of the cargo. An unclean B/L is usually issued by the carrier when the goods received for shipment are found in a damaged condition. It is generally marked "carton old and stained", "two cases missing and one case broken" and so on. By issuing an unclean B/L, carrier's liability can be reduced if damage to the goods is due to these deficiencies. An unclean B/L is usually not acceptable to the buyer and banks

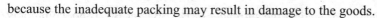
because the inadequate packing may result in damage to the goods.

(3) Straight B/L, Order B/L and Bearer B/L

According to whether the B/L is transferable, it is divided into three kinds: straight B/L, order B/L and bearer B/L (blank B/L).

A *straight B/L* is made out so that only the named consignee at the destination is entitled to take delivery of the goods under the bill. The consignee is designated by the shipper. The carrier has to hand over the cargo to the named consignee, not to any third party in possession of the bill. This kind of B/L is not transferable. The shipper cannot pass the bill to a third party by endorsement. So the bill is of very restricted application. When the goods are shipped on a non-commercial basis, such as samples or exhibits, or when the goods are extremely valuable, a straight bill of lading is generally issued.

> **NOTE: Endorsement**
>
> *There are two types of endorsement: special endorsement and blank endorsement. In the case of special endorsement, an order B/L must be signed by the shipper (endorser or transferor) showing both the names of the endorser and the endorsee. While in the case of a blank endorsement, only the signature of the shipper (endorser or transferor) is required (without indicating the endorsee of transferee). An order B/L with blank endorsement serves the purpose of the further transfer of the B/L from one to another.*

An *order B/L* refers to the one that is made out in such a way that the goods are consigned or destined to the order of a named person instead of a definite consignee. Order bills are usually issued by carriers to the shipper/consignor by making "To order", "To order of the shipper", or "To order of the consignor" in the box of consignee. This means that the carrier will deliver the goods to any consignee designated by the shipper/consignor at the port of destination. An order B/L is a negotiable and transferable document, but to transfer the title to the goods, the transferor, being the shipper in the case of "To order" or "To order of the shipper", should endorse the bill at the back of the B/L. If he does not endorse the bill, he then reserves the right to put the goods at the disposal of himself.

指示提单是指提单上的收货人栏内填写"凭指示"或"凭某人指示"字样的提单。注意,"凭指示"和"凭托运人指示"的含义相同,在托运人背书转让前,物权仍归托运人。这种提单经过背书后可以转让,故其在国际贸易中使用最广。

A *bearer B/L* (Blank B/L or Open B/L) refers to the bill in which the name of a definite consignee is not mentioned. There usually appears in the box of consignee words like "to bearer" and the holder of the B/L can take delivery of the goods against the surrender of B/L. Bearer B/L is not commonly used in international trade due to the high risk involved.

(4) Master B/L and House B/L

According to the issuer of B/L, it can be divided into master B/L and house B/L. The issuer of master B/L is the shipping company or the actual carrier. And the latter is issued by the forwarder.

The differences between master B/L and house B/L are as follows:

a. The issuer of master B/L is the shipping company. And the house B/L is issued by the forwarder based on master B/L. The issuer should have its agent on port of destination.

b. The title of master B/L is the shipping company. But the title of house B/L is the forwarder.

c. The consignee can directly take the delivery of the goods by master B/L. If it is the house B/L, the consignee should use his house B/L in exchange for the master B/L from the agent on port of destination at first. Then he can take the delivery of the goods by master B/L.

(5) Direct B/L, Transshipment B/L and Through B/L

According to the modes of transport, the B/L can be divided into direct B/L, transshipment B/L and through B/L.

A *direct B/L* is the evidence that the goods are shipped and carried by the steamer and transported from the port of loading directly to the port of destination without transshipment during the voyage. The buyer usually prefers such a B/L, because the possible cargo damages or losses are usually caused by transshipment.

A *transshipment B/L* is a document showing that when there is no direct service between two ports, the goods are transited by another steamer during the voyage, generally at the port of transshipment mentioned in the B/L, to the port of destination.

A *through B/L* is issued when the entire voyage involves more than one carrier. The first carrier issues the bill and collects the freight for the entire voyage, and arranges transshipment and forwarding of the goods at the international port. The shipper prefers this kind of B/L because the trouble has been saved to deal with other carriers by himself.

(6) Long Form B/L and Short Form B/L

According to the contents of the B/L, it can be divided into long form B/L and short form B/L.

A *long form B/L* refers to the bill of lading on the back of which all the detail terms and conditions about the rights and obligations of the carrier and the consignor are listed as an integral part of the bill.

A *short form B/L* is a document which omits the items and conditions on the back of the B/L.

(7) Original B/L and Copy B/L

According to the validity, bills of lading are divided into original B/L and copy B/L.

An *original B/L* refers to one that is signed and dated by either the shipping company or by a duly authorized agent. The bill of lading must show how many signed originals were issued. The originals are marked "Original" on their face and they become valid only after being signed by the carrier. The original B/L is a piece of evidence showing the ownership of goods, one of which must be presented to the carrier at the destination in exchange for the goods.

In some cases, a "full set" of rather than just one original bill of lading is required to be presented. In practice, bill of lading is normally made out in a set of three originals and if a full set is required, all three originals are to be delivered to the buyer or the consignee. When one of the originals is used, the others automatically become null and void.

A *copy B/L* is marked "Copy", "Duplicate" or "Non-negotiable" instead of "Original". For easy distinction, copy and original B/L are usually designed and printed in two different colors. Copy bills of lading are mainly used for reference or for records.

(8) Freight Prepaid B/L and Freight to be Collected B/L

According to the time for payment of freight, it can be divided into freight prepaid B/L and freight to be collected B/L.

A *freight prepaid B/L* indicates that the freight has been paid by the consignor. This type of B/L is usually issued only after the freight has been paid.

A *freight to be collected B/L* refers to the B/L on which "freight payable at destination" or "freight to be collected at destination" is indicated.

(9) Other Types of B/L

Other forms of bill of lading also exist according to different circumstances. They are stale B/L, ante-date B/L, advanced B/L and on-deck B/L.

A *stale B/L* is a B/L presented to the consignee or the bank later than the latest presentation date specified in the L/C or later than the goods' arrival at the destination. Sometimes, especially in the case of short voyages, it is a

过期提单是指提单签发后超过信用证规定期限才交到银行的提单或者晚于货物到达目的港的提单。

common occurrence that a bill of lading arrives late and in this case, it is necessary to add a clause that a "Stale B/L is acceptable" in the contract.

Without the bill of lading, the cargo normally cannot be released. Thus in order to facilitate the smooth claim of the goods, a bill of lading is usually required to be presented to the consignee or their bank within a specified time (i.e., presentation period). The late arrival of this important document may lead to additional costs, such as warehousing expenses and sometimes even loss or damage. Therefore, the buyer and the bank usually refuse to accept a stale B/L. According to UCP600, the B/L shall be presented within 21 days after issuance, unless otherwise stipulated in the credit.

A B/L is antedated when the shipment date shown on the bill is earlier than the actual one. An *ante-dated B/L* is issued at the request of the shipper when the actual shipment date is later than that stipulated in the credit.

When the actual loading date is later than the date of shipment stipulated in the L/C, the bank would decline the bill because the bill fails to meet the L/C stipulation. Therefore, in order to negotiate payment, the seller sometimes may ask the carrier to issue an ante-dated B/L where the loading date is in line with the L/C stipulation.

An *advanced B/L* is the one that is issued before actual loading of the goods is completed or even before the commencement of the actual loading operation. An advanced B/L is usually issued when the time of shipment stipulated in the L/C is almost due but the actual loading of the goods is not yet completed or the goods are not ready for shipment. An advanced B/L is similar to an ante-dated B/L in that both of them are issued at the request of the seller, both carry false information as to the actual date of loading and finally both are for the avoidance of a non-acceptance for negotiation of payment at the bank. The difference between them is that an advanced B/L is issued before actual loading is finished while an ante-dated B/L is issued after it.

In both cases, the carrier is liable for all risks arising from the issuance of such bills of lading because the buyer will find out the actual loading date in the sails log. Therefore, carrier normally will avoid these practices.

In practice, when the carrier agrees to issue an advanced B/L or ante-dated B/L, the shipper should first submit to the carrier a letter of indemnity thereby undertaking all responsibilities for risks that may derive from the issuance of such a bill. However, since the letter is not considered to be a lawful document, the carrier usually finds it difficult to avoid liability for issuance of either an

倒签提单是指承运人应托运人的要求在货物装船后，提单签发的日期早于实际装船完毕日期的提单。

advanced B/L or ante-dated B/L when disputes arise or when the consignee brings an arbitration or even a lawsuit against him for conducting a fraud.

An *on-deck B/L* is issued when the goods are stowed on deck. Some cargoes, such as inflammable goods, explosive goods and poisonous goods, cargoes in large volume or of backward sizes, live cattle, plants, etc., must be loaded on to the deck. Some world-famous shipping companies are as figure 4-1.

| MAERSK<br>Maersk Line | m sc<br>Mediterranean Shipping Company |
|---|---|
| EVERGREEN<br>Evergreen Marine Corp. | CHINA OCEAN SHIPPING GROUP<br>China Ocean Shipping Company |
| OOCL<br>*We take it personally*<br>Orient Overseas Container Line | APL<br>American President Lines |

Figure 4-1  World-famous Shipping Companies

It must be noted that the above-mentioned types of bill of lading are not independent of each other. One bill may, at the same time, be in more than one form. For example, a shipped B/L can be a clean order bill as well. In trade practice, the most common bill of lading is a clean, shipped direct bill of lading made out to order with a blank endorsement.

## 4.2.2  Air Transportation

Air transportation offers quick transit of the goods with low risk of damage and pilferage, and very competitive insurance rates. It can also save packing cost and reduce amount of capital tied up in transit. But it has limited capacity of overall dimensions together with weight restrictions. It is the best choice for the carriage of goods with high value and limited dimensions.

The airway bill is the document testifying that the goods have been sent by air. With this the seller can settle the payment at the bank. Upon arrival of the destination, the carrier will send the buyer an arrival notice with which the buyer is supposed to get the goods at the airport. The airway bill has the following features:

- It is a transport contract signed between the consignor/shipper and the carrier/airline;
- It is a receipt from the airline acknowledging the receipt of the consignment from the shipper.

## 4.2.3  Railway Transportation

Railway transportation of China now comprises three parts: domestic railway transport, railway transport to Hong Kong and Macao, and international combined railway transport. Though train charges are needed to effect the arrival of the goods, the consignor needs only to get the cargo receipt to settle payment at the bank.

The goods belonging to the export country shall be transported to the place of destination with a railway bill of lading issued at the place of dispatch. During the delivery, the railway department is responsible for transportation and the consignor and consignee do not have to care for it.

The main transport documents are the *railway bill* and its duplicate. The railway bill is the transportation contract and binding upon the consignee, the consignor and the railway department. The railway bill together with the goods is transported from the place of dispatch to the place of destination and then is delivered to the consignee after he has paid off the freight and other charges. The consignor may make exchange settlement with the bank against the duplicate of the railway bill.

## 4.2.4  International Multi-modal Transport

International combined transport means the conveyance of cargo includes at least two modes of transport by which the goods are carried from the place of dispatch to that of destination on the basis of combined transport or a multimodal transport contract. Under this method, the container is used as an inter-medium and makes up of an international multimodal and joint transport mode by sea, air and land.

The basic conditions of international multi-modal transport are as follows:

- Transport documents, i.e., combined transport documents shall cover the whole journey;
- It includes two or more different modes of successive transportation;
- It shall be international transportation;
- The multi-modal transport operate (MTO) shall be responsible for the whole journey;
- The whole journey shall use a single factor rate.

## 4.2.5　Land Bridge Transport

Land bridge transport is a mode of transport that connects the ocean transport on the two sides of the land by the railway and land which runs across the continent, i.e., ship-train-ship. Land bridge transport uses the container as a medium, so it has all advantages of container transport.

There are three main land bridges in the world: American land bridge; Siberian land bridge and the New European-Asia land bridge.

## 4.2.6　Postal Transport

According to international trade practice, the seller fulfils the duty of delivery only if he delivers the parcel to the post office, pays off the postage, and gets the receipt. The post office is responsible for the delivery of the goods to the destination, and the consignee goes to the post office for picking up his goods. Postal transport falls into two kinds: regular mail and air mail.

## 4.2.7　Pipelines Transport

Pipelines are used for transporting commodities, such as crude oil and gases etc., long distances over land and under the sea. Rising fuel costs make pipelines an attractive economic alternative to other forms of transport in certain circumstances. Safety in transferring flammable commodities is another important consideration.

# 4.3　Shipment Clauses in Sales Contract

When negotiating a transaction, the buyer and the seller should reach an agreement on time of shipment, port of shipment and port of destination, shipping advice, partial shipment and transshipment, dispatch and demurrage, etc., and specify them in contract of sale. Clear stipulation of shipment clause is an important condition for the smooth execution of the contract. The following is an example of shipment clause in sales contract.

> **Example**
>
> Shipment: To be shipped on or before Sept. 31, 2012 subject to acceptable L/C reaching the seller by the end of Sept. 15, 2012, and partial shipments prohibited, transshipment allowed.
>
> Port of shipment: Shanghai, China
>
> Port of destination: London optional Liverpool, U.K.

## 4.3.1　Time of Shipment and Time of Delivery

在国际贸易中，存在着"装运时间"和"交货时间"两种不同的提法。值得注意的是，在装运合同项下，"装运时间"等同于"交货时间"。而在到达合同项下，"装运时间"和"交货时间"则完全是两个不同的概念。

*Time of shipment* is the deadline by which the seller makes shipment of the contracted goods. *Time of delivery* is the deadline during which the seller shall deliver the goods to the buyer at agreed place.

For all shipment contracts, time of shipment is equal to time of delivery and they can be used interchangeably in the contract. According to Incoterms 2010, contracts concluded on the basis of such terms as FOB, CFR, CIF, FCA, CPT, CIP are shipment contracts. Under shipment contracts, the seller fulfills his obligation of delivery when the goods are shipped on board the vessel or delivered to the carrier and the seller only bears all risk prior to shipment. The delivery goods under a shipment contract imply a symbolic delivery. Delivery is a symbolic one when the delivery of goods is symbolically made by means of the transfer of documents instead of the actual transfer of goods.

For all arrival contracts, time of shipment and time of delivery are two completely different concepts and time of delivery should be stipulated in contract. According to Incoterms 2010, contracts concluded on the basis of terms such as DAT, DAP and DDP are arrival contracts. Arrival contracts differ from shipment contract in that seller should be responsible for all risks of bringing the goods to the named destination. Arrival contracts usually suggest actual delivery. Actual delivery is made when the goods are actually delivered from the seller to the buyer.

Time of shipment is a very important clause in a contract as any delay or advance of delivery constitutes a violation of contract. There are basically two ways of stipulating time of shipment in contract: one is clearly specifying a period of time or a deadline, and the other is setting a time period between the shipment and the deadline by which the relevant L/C must reach the seller.

- Specifying a fixed period of time or deadline

**Examples:**

Shipment is to be made during January/February/March 2017.

Shipment not later than July 31, 2017.

- Setting a time period upon receipt of payment

**Examples:**

Shipment is to be made within 30 days after receipt of the L/C. The relevant L/C must reach the seller not later than June 30, 2017.

In case of payment by L/C, the seller should stipulate the time of delivery based on the time of receipt of L/C. By so doing, the seller is able to reduce his risks of losses resulted from the buyer's failure in opening the L/C required.

## 4.3.2　Port of Shipment and Port of Destination

Port of shipment is the port where goods are shipped and depart, while port of destination is the port at which goods are ultimately discharged. Both of them should be specified in the contract. Normally, one specific port of shipment and one specific port of destination are stipulated, but sometimes two or more of each are stated to meet special requirements. In case a decision cannot be made, several alternatives should be listed, such as "One port out of London/Hamburger/Rotterdam as the port of destination at the buyer's location" or perhaps a general scope is stated such as "EMP (European Main Port)", "China Port". As "EMP" or "China Port" is too vague, we had better try to avoid using them. In choosing port of shipment and port of destination, try to make them as clear as possible; provide some flexibility by allowing optional ports especially when it is hard to make a final decision; take into account port regulation, facilities, charges and possible sanctions; and be alert to the possibility of different ports having the same time.

### 4.3.3　Shipping Advice

When the goods are shipped on board the vessel, the seller needs to give the buyer prompt notice of the port of shipment, the date of sailing, the name of the carrying vessel, the estimated time of arrival of the vessel and send the buyer the copies of the necessary documents to enable the buyer to get ready to take delivery of the goods. In the event of the seller failing to send shipping advice to the buyer within the prescribed time period, the seller would bear the consequential cost incurred. Under FOB terms, the seller should also send notification of cargo readiness to the buyer 30 days or 45 days before the time of shipment so that the buyer can charter ships and send them to the shipment port to take cargoes in time. On the other hand, after receipt of the notification of cargo readiness from the seller, the buyer should inform the seller within the agreed time the name of the nominated vessel and the date of the vessel taking cargoes so as to enable the seller to arrange shipment.

### 4.3.4　Partial Shipment and Transshipment

根据国际商会《跟单信用证统一惯例》的规定，除非信用证另有规定，否则准许分批装运。

*Partial shipment* means shipping the commodity under one contract in more than one lot. It should be defined in the clause of shipment whether "Partial shipment is (or is not) allowed". Meanwhile, the time and quantity of each shipment should be specified, such as "shipment during March to June in four equal monthly lots". The seller should strictly follow the regulations. Otherwise, the buyer has the right to reject goods.

《跟单信用证统一惯例》中的禁止转运，实际上仅是禁止海运港至港除集装箱以外的货物运输的转运。

*Transshipment* means when there is no direct ship between the port of shipment and the port of destination, or no suitable ships available at that particular period, the goods have to be transferred from one ship to another at an intermediate port. The clause must also specify whether "Transshipment is (or is not) allowed". In addition, it should also be indicated that who pays the cost of transshipment.

## 4.3.5   Lay Time, Demurrage and Dispatch

*Lay time* is the time allowed for the completion of loading and unloading, and it is usually expressed by days or hours. There are several ways of stipulating lay time:

- Days or Running Days: including bad weather days, Sundays or any other holidays, unfavorable to the shipper.
- Weather Working Days of 24 Hours: excluding Sunday, holidays and rainy days, favorable for shipper but unfavorable for ship owner.
- Weather Working Days of 24 Consecutive Hours: excluding the bad weather time period, suitable for ports that operate day and night.

As lay time concerns the interests of ship owner, consignor or consignee, it is important to make it clear in the contract. Vague phrase as "to load/discharge in customary quick dispatch" should be avoided. If loading and unloading are not completed within the agreed lay time, demurrage should be paid at an agreed rate by the party that charters ships to the ship owner to compensate for the cost sustained. *Demurrage* is an extra charge a shipper pays for detaining a freight car or ship beyond time permitted for loading or unloading. On the other hand, if loading and unloading are completed in advance, the ship owner will pay dispatch money as a reward to the party who charters ships. *Dispatch* is an amount paid by a vessel's operator to a charter if loading or unloading is competed in less time than stipulated in the charter agreement. Demurrage and dispatch are considered as a way of encouraging timely shipment, and are sometimes specified in the shipment clause.

## Specimen 4-1 The Sample of Bill of Lading

| Shipper | | B/L No. |
|---|---|---|
| NINGBO HUANCHI IMP. & EXP. CO. LTD<br>HENGHE INDUSTRY ZONE, CIXI CITY, NINGBO, CHINA | | RGL29180113 |

**CRGL Freight System**

**Consignee (Complete name and address)**

A.G INDIA RETAIL PVT LTD
H-3/113-114 VARDMAN PLAZA
NETAJI SUBASH PLACE PITAMPURA
NEW DELHI-110034 INDIA
IEC NO:0512065586
GST NO: 07AAACM0611Q1ZU

**COMBINED TRANSPORT**
**BILL OF LADING**

**Notify Party (Complete name and address)**

SAME AS CONSIGNEE

SHIPPED on board in apparent good order and condition (unless otherwise indicated) the goods or packages specified herein and to be discharged at the mentioned port of discharge or as near thereto as the vessel may safely get and be always afloat.

The weight, measure, marks and numbers, quality, contents, and value, being particularly furnished by the Shipper, are not checked by the Carrier on loading.

The Shipper, Consignee and the Holder of this Bill of Lading hereby expressly accept and agree to all printed, written or stamped provisions, exceptions and conditions of this Bill of Lading, including those on the back hereof.

IN WITNESS whereof the number of original Bills of Lading stated below have been signed, one of which being accomplished, the other(s) to be void.

| Pre-carriage by | Place of receipt | | |
|---|---|---|---|
| **Ocean vessel**<br>MAERSK TAURUS 1802 | **Port of loading**<br>NINGBO, CHINA | | |
| **Port of discharge**<br>NHAVA SHEVA, INDIA | **Place of delivery**<br>NHAVA SHEVA, INDIA | **Freight payable at** | **Number of original B/L**<br>THREE(3) |

| Marks and Nos. | Number and kind of packages | Description of goods | Gross weight (kgs.) | Measurement (M³) |
|---|---|---|---|---|
| KF201117/15118<br>NO. 1-UP | 30PALLETS | BEARINGS | 21,414.520KGS | 21.322CBM |

*ORIGINAL*

FREIGHT PREPAID
SHIP ON BOARD DATE
20. Jan. 2018

MSKU0952236/CN9240903/20GP/30PALLETS/21414.52KGS/21.322CBM

TOTAL: ONE (1×20GP) CONTAINER(S) ONLY

ABOVE PARTICULARS FURNISHED BY SHIPPER

| For delivery of goods please apply to: | IN WITNESS whereof the number of original Bills of Lading stated above have been signed, one of which being accomplished, the other(s) to be void. |
|---|---|
| RAJ GLOBAL LOGISTICS<br>OFFICE NO. 613, 7TH FLOOR, CENTRAL FACILITY BUILDING,<br>A.P.M.C<br>FRUIT MARKET, SECTOR - 19, VASHI TURBHE, NAVI MUMBAI -<br>400705<br>TEL: (022) 41238064<br>EMAIL ID : CSM.MNRAJLOGISTICS.IN<br>KIND ATTN : MR.GAURAV BHARADWAJ | **Place and date of issue**<br>SHENZHEN 2018/01/20 |
| | For and on behalf of the Carrier SYSTEM<br>深圳市盒贸通国际物流有限公司<br>*Signed for or on behalf of the Carrier*<br>Authorized Signature as Agent |

TERMS AND CONDITIONS AS PER ORIGINAL BILL OF LADING    No.

# 【Key Terms and Words】

Transshipment　转运

Demurrage　滞期费

Dispatch　速遣费

Containerization　集装箱化

Full container load (FCL)　整箱货

Less than container load (LCL)　拼箱货

Container yard (CY)　集装箱堆场

Container freight station (CFS)　集装箱货运站

Marine transportation　海洋运输

Liner terms　班轮条件

Charter transportation　租船运输

Clean B/L　清洁提单

Order B/L　指示提单

Stale B/L　过期提单

Master B/L　船东单

House B/L　货代单

Freight ton (F/T)　运费吨

Time of shipment　装运期

Time of delivery　交货期

Optional port　选择港

Partial shipment　分批装运

Lay time　装卸时间

# 【Exercises】

I. Review and discuss the following questions.

1. What are the major types of transportation in international cargo transport?

2. What are the characteristics of liner transport?

3. What are the differences between voyage charter and time charter?

4. What are the main functions of B/L?

5. What should be considered when choosing port of shipment and port of destination?

6. Why can the advice of shipment coordinate the responsibilities of the exporter and the importer?

国际贸易实务(英语版)(第2版)

7. What are the main responsibilities of multi-modal transport operator?

8. What main points are included in the clause of shipment?

II. Choose the right answer from each of the following.

1. _____ can be freely bought and sold just like commodities.
   A. Railway bill　　B. Airway bill　　C. Shipping advice　　D. Ocean bill of lading

2. Freight under liner transportation _____.
   A. needs to stipulate demurrage and dispatch money between the shipper and the carrier
   B. does not include loading and unloading cost
   C. consists of basic charges and additional charges
   D. is collected based on gross weight of the goods

3. Airway bill is NOT _____.
   A. a transport contract between the consignor and the carrier
   B. a document for customs clearance
   C. a document for bank negotiation
   D. a document of title

4. _____ is the most commonly used transportation mode, which occupies 2/3 of international transportation.
   A. Railway transportation　　　　B. Maritime transportation
   C. Air transportation　　　　　　D. Parcel transportation

5. In international trade, the importer often does not require _____.
   A. shipped B/L　　B. clean B/L　　C. blank B/L　　D. order B/L

6. _____ can be transferred after endorsement.
   A. Straight B/L　　B. Blank B/L　　C. Order B/L　　D. Through B/L

7. Multi-modal transport operator is responsible for _____.
   A. the first voyage　　　　B. the whole voyage
   C. the ocean transport　　D. the last voyage

8. Under _____ charter, the ship owner only rents the charterer the boat.
   A. demise　　B. time　　C. voyage　　D. booking

9. _____ is suitable for conveying fresh, emergent and seasonal goods.
   A. Scheduled airlines　　　　B. Chartered carriers
   C. Consolidated consignment　　D. Liners

10. If items marked with "AD Val.", the freight is to be calculated on the basis _____ of the cargo concerned.
    A. weight　　B. price or value　　C. measurement　　D. volume

130

III.  Judge whether the following statements are true or false.

1. The loading and unloading charges are included in the freight of the liners.                    (    )

2. Demurrage is the extra charge a shipper pays to detain a freight ship beyond time permitted for loading or unloading.                    (    )

3. Dispatch money is a fine imposed on the charterer for the delay in the loading and unloading of the goods.                    (    )

4. A straight B/L can be transferred through endorsement.                    (    )

5. A bill of lading is both a receipt for merchandise and an evidence of contract to deliver it as freight.                    (    )

6. Advantages of containerization include less handling of cargo, more protection against pilferage, less exposure to the elements, and reduced time of shipping.                    (    )

7. An order B/L can be transferred with or without endorsement.                    (    )

8. In international multi-modal transportation, a multi-modal transport operator will issue a combined transport document and be responsible for the safe carriage of the whole voyage.    (    )

9. In order to clarify who will bear the loading and unloading charges in voyage charter transportation, the clause "Free in and out" is set forth in the Voyage Charter Party. This means the charterer shall be responsible for both loading and unloading charges.                    (    )

10. Free in and free out means that the ship owner is responsible for both loading and unloading charges.                    (    )

## IV. Calculation

1. There is one consignment of 10 cartons of leather shoes. Measurement of each carton is 50×50×50 cm, and gross weight of each is 15 kg. Freight basis is W/M and the quotation is USD100 per F/T. How much is the total freight?

2. Company A is to export their goods by three 20′ FCL containers from Shanghai, China to Felixstowe, UK. The quotation is as follows:

O/F rate: USD 750.00/20′

BAF: USD 500.00/20′

CAF: 12% on the freight rate

ISPS (International ship and port facility security): USD 10.00/20′

How much is the total freight?

## V. Case Study

Company A in the mainland of China reached an FOB contract with Company B in Hong Kong, exporting steel sheets. To resell the goods, Company B signed another CFR contract with Company C in South Korea. Later, Company A received the relevant L/C from Company B for the transaction. The price showed in the L/C was FOB as contracted. The L/C also stipulated that Busan (in South Korea) should be the port of destination. What's more, the L/C stipulated that the B/L should be marked with "Freight Prepaid".

**Questions:**

(1) Why did Company B have such requests?

(2) Should Company A accept these clauses?

# Chapter 5　International Cargo Transport Insurance

【Learning Objectives】

By studying this chapter, you should be able to master:

- The principles of cargo insurance
- The losses, risks and expenses covered by Marine insurance
- The scope of the Ocean Marine Cargo Clauses of CIC
- The procedure of Marine insurance
- The insurance clauses in sales contract

## Lead-in: Case Study

### Hurricane Sandy-Struck Businesses Sue Insurance Brokers over Uncovered Losses

A pair of Hurricane Sandy-struck businesses have sued their insurance brokers after the immense losses they suffered from the Oct. 29 super storm went largely uncovered.

One business, which runs an Ethan Allen furniture store in River Edge, said it lost $1.5 million worth of inventory after flood waters deluged its warehouse in Carlstadt. The other, the Raritan Yacht Club in Perth Amboy, was a scene of devastation after Sandy, which left bay-level buildings on the marina smashed.

At the heart of both complaints — filed a day apart in separate counties late last month — is essentially the same argument: the businesses say they relied upon their brokers' expertise to buy the right level of coverage based on the risks they faced. But in both cases, the suits allege, the brokers failed to procure for them the flood insurance they needed.

The cases highlight some of the legal pressures facing insurance brokers after the storm. Attorneys for policyholders have said that New Jersey courts have found brokers to have a heightened duty to their clients, particularly if they have presented themselves as risk-management experts. Brokers are independent insurance agents who are licensed by the state to sell and advise on insurance.

The complaint involving the Ethan Allen store was filed May 22 in Superior Court of Bergen County. It pitted the store's operator, Landau Holding, against its insurance broker, Richard Kohlhausen, and his company, Capitol Risk Management Services of Nanuet, N.Y.

The Raritan Yacht Club suit was filed a day later in Superior Court of Middlesex County. In it, the club claimed its broker, Randolph Winston, and his company, Exemplar International, failed to procure for its flood insurance even though the club, as its name implies, is located on the water. The club's board of governors was named a co-defendant. On the basis it failed its "basic responsibility" to obtain the correct insurance coverage for the club.

In the matter of Landau Holding, which also runs an Ethan Allen-branded store in New York State, the company said Capital Risk was familiar with Landau's insurance program after it was hired in 2011. Among other things, Capital Risk knew Landau wanted protection against floods and other risks.

But when Landau relocated its warehouse operation to Carlstadt, Capital Risk never told the company of the need for, or even absence of, flood insurance for the inventory it would keep there. Instead, it gave Landau assurances that the necessary coverage was in place. That turned out to not be the case after Sandy passed.

Kohlhausen did not return a call seeking comment. Landau also sued Aspen American Insurance Co., claiming a breach of contract. A spokesman for the insurer declined to comment. Landau's attorney, Alexander Anglim, also declined to comment.

The Raritan Yacht Club did not quantify in its lawsuit the "significant" damages it suffered during Hurricane Sandy. But it alleged its broker, Exemplar, failed to even suggest that the club needed flood insurance, according to the suit filed by its attorney Eugene Killian.

Also named a co-defendant was the yacht club's insurer, Federal Insurance Co., a unit of Chubb Corp. The club claims the policy sold to it was deemed the "'Cadillac' of insurance policies for yacht clubs." That led club officials to believe the policy covered all risks typically encountered by yacht clubs. Yet Federal Insurance ended up denying much of the club's claims because of a clause in the policy that said coverage was not granted for damage from "waves, tidal water or tidal waves."

Warren Bigos, a commodore of the yacht club and a member of its governing board, declined to comment. A Chubb spokesman also declined to comment. Winston, the insurance broker, could not be reached through a Fort Lee phone number listed for him. According to state records, his insurance license is no longer active, which could mean he failed to renew it or voluntarily gave it up.

*(Source: http://www.nj.com/business/index.ssf/2013/06/sandy-struck_businesses_sue_in.html)*

**Class Activities:**

1. Why did the businesses fail to procure the flood insurance?
2. What role does a broker play in insurance?

# 5.1　Principles of Cargo Insurance

As stipulated in Insurance Law of The People's Republic of China issued in 1995, there are mainly four types of principles related to marine insurance: the Insurable Interest Principle, the Utmost Good Faith Principle, the Indemnity Principle and the Proximate Cause Principle.

## 5.1.1　Principle of Insurable Interest

保险利益又称可保权益，是指投保人对保险标的具有的法律上承认的利益。

Insurable interest means that the insured should have interests in the subject when it is to be insured. He should be benefited by the safe arrival of commodities and he should be prejudiced by loss or damage of goods. The insured may not have an insurable interest at the time of acquiring a marine insurance policy, but he should have a reasonable expectation of acquiring such interest.

When the goods are lost or damaged and the owner of the goods (i.e., the title holder in the goods) suffers a loss, fails to realize an expected profit, or incurs liability from the loss or damage, the owner (the title holder) is deemed to have an insurable interest in the goods.

When the exporter delivers the goods, the insurable interest in such goods transfers at the point and time where the risk shifts from the exporter to the importer, as determined by the international commercial terms used. For example, under CIF (Cost, Insurance and Freight to the named port of destination) contract, the point the risk shifts is on board the ship at the named port of loading, as such the insurable interest transfers from the exporter to the importer at the time the goods pass over the ship's rail.

## 5.1.2　Principle of Utmost Good Faith

最大诚信原则是指投保人和保险人在签订保险合同以及在合同有效期内，必须保持最大限度的诚意，双方都应恪守信用，互不欺骗隐瞒。

The principle of utmost good faith is indispensable in any insurance contract. Under the open policy the insurer usually knows only of the shipments made by the exporter after the receipt of the insurance declaration form and/or the copy of the insurance certificates. Under such circumstances, a consignment may have reached the importer without sustaining any loss or damage, before the insurer knows of such consignment. If the exporter knows that the consignment has safely reached the importer and deliberately does not declare such consignment in the insurance declaration form in order to avoid paying the insurance premium, such action is a breach of good faith. Consequently, the insurer may cancel the insurance policy issued to the exporter when the exporter's bad faith is known. On the contrary, a consignment reaches the importer in bad condition, that is, sustaining loss or damage, before the insurer knows of such consignment. Whether or not the exporter knows that the consignment has not safely reached the importer and fails to declare such consignment in the insurance declaration form, the insurer is liable to pay for the loss or damage out of good faith.

## 5.1.3   Principle of Indemnity

This principle means that the insured will be compensated only to the extent of loss suffered. Under no circumstances is an insured allowed to make a profit out of a claim. The underwriter provides to compensate the insured in cash and not to replace the cargo or the ship. In the absence of the principle of indemnity it was possible to make a profit.

This value may be either the insured or insurable value. If the value of the subject matter is determined at the time of taking the policy, it is called "Insured Value". When loss arises, the indemnity will be measured in the proportion that the assured sum bears to the insured value.

In fixing the insured value, the cost of transportation and anticipated profits are added to original value so that in case of loss the insured can recover not only the cost of goods or properties but also a certain percentage of profit.

The insured value is called agreed value because it has been agreed between the insurer and the insured at the time of contract and is regarded as sacrosanct and binding on both parties to the contract. In marine insurance, it has been customary for the insurer and the assured to agree on the value of the insured subject matter at the time of proposal.

Having, agreed of the value or basis of valuation, neither party to the contract can raise objection after loss on the ground that the value is too high or too low unless it appears that a fraudulent evaluation has been imposed on either party.

Technically speaking, the doctrine of indemnity applies where the value of

补偿原则又称损害赔偿原则，是指当保险标的遭受保险责任范围内的损失时，保险人应当依照保险合同的约定履行赔偿义务。

subject-matter is determined at the time of loss. In other words, where the market price of the loss is paid, this doctrine has been precisely applied.

Where the value for the goods has not been fixed in the beginning but is left to be determined by the time of loss, the measurement is based on the insurable value of the goods. However, in marine insurance the insurable value is not common because no profit is allowed in estimating the insurable value.

Again, if the insurable value happens to be more than the assured sum, the assured would be proportionately uninsured. On the other hand, if it is lower than the assured sum, the underwriter would be liable for a return of premium of the difference.

### 5.1.4　Principle of Proximate Cause

近因原则是指保险人只对承包风险与保险标的损失之间有直接因果关系的损失负赔偿责任，而对保险责任范围外的风险造成的保险标的的损失，不承担赔偿责任。

This is a Latin word which means the nearest or proximate cause. It helps to decide the actual cause of loss when a number of causes have contributed to the loss. The immediate cause of loss should be determined to fix the responsibility of the insurer. The remote cause for a loss is not important in determining the liability. If the proximate cause is insured against, the insurer will indemnify the loss.

Unfortunately, when a loss occurs there will be a series of events leading up to the incident and so it is sometimes difficult to determine the nearest of proximate cause. There is a general rule that applies to the burden of proof. The policyholder must demonstrate that an insured peril has caused the loss or damage and, having done so, it is then for the insurer to demonstrate the operation of any exclusion.

## 5.2　The Definition of Insurance

保险是指投保人根据合同规定，向保险人支付保险费，保险人对于合同约定的可能发生的事故因其发生所造成的财产损失承担赔偿保险金责任的商业保险行为。

Insurance is a form of risk management primarily used to hedge against the risk of a contingent, uncertain loss. Insurance is defined as the equitable transfer of the risk of a loss, from one entity to another, in exchange for payment.

In international trade, during cargo transportation from the port of shipment to port of destination, there are a lot of risks, which, if they occur, will involve traders in financial losses. The goods can be damaged even if they are well packed and wrapped, and they can disappear during handling, fall overboard in bad weather, be destroyed by fire and in addition be considerably delayed. And the forwarding agents' legal responsibility for action is limited and varies depending upon the type of transport being used. Although these risks cannot be avoided, they can be transferred to insurance company by covering the goods for various basic risks or insurance clauses with the insurer.

Cargo insurance, also known as marine cargo insurance, is a type of insurance against physical damage or loss of goods during transportation. Cargo insurance is effective in all the three cases whether the goods have been transported via sea, land or air.

Cargo insurance is an insurance for export, import and domestic transports:

- The insurance provides coverage for all goods and all forms of transport.
- Insurance of goods is an object insurance which is released in the event of a claim regardless of who has caused the damage.
- The insurance, if nothing else has been agreed upon, normally provides coverage for the value of the goods, plus freight, plus 10% imaginary profit and covers the ordinary chain of transport.
- The agreed trade terms stipulates if the buyer or the seller are to effect an insurance.

The purpose of cargo insurance is to cover goods in transit—during land transport as well as transport by sea or air. It is essential for cargo insurance that a loss is recoverable only by an insured who at the time of loss has an insurable interest in the goods.

# 5.3　Parties to the Insurance

There are usually two parties involved in insurance—insurer and insured, but sometimes a third party is involved, the broker.

## 5.3.1　Insurer

The Insurer is the party who assumes or accepts the risk of loss and undertakes for a consideration to indemnify the insured or to pay him a certain sum on the happening of a specified contingency or event. The business of insurance may be carried on by individuals just as much as by corporations and associations. The state itself may go into insurance business.

### 5.3.2 Insured

The insured, or the second party to the contract, is the person in whose favor, the contract is operative and who is indemnified against, or is to receive a certain sum upon the happening of a specified contingency or event. He is the person whose loss is the occasion for the payment of the insurance proceeds by the insurer.

### 5.3.3 Brokers

保险经纪人是基于投保人的利益，为投保人与保险人订立保险合同提供中介服务，并依法收取佣金的保险公司从业人员。

Brokers play an important role in marine insurance. The broker will meet with the assured to determine its insurance requirements. The broker will then canvass the market to find insurers willing to insure the assured and will negotiate terms with those underwriters. The broker may also become involved in the event of a loss by presenting the loss to insurers and negotiating on behalf of the insured.

## 5.4 Marine Insurance

国际货物运输保险主要包括国际海上货物运输保险、国际铁路货物运输保险、国际公路货物运输保险、国际航空货物运输保险和邮包运输保险等。其中，历史最悠久、业务量最大、法律规定最全的是海上货物运输保险。

Of all the international cargo transportation insurances, ocean marine cargo insurance is of the longest history and of the greatest significance. Ocean marine insurance is insurance used to protect cargo, vessels and other items while they are being transported across the ocean. Marine insurance covers the loss or damage of ships, cargo, terminals, and any transport or cargo by which property is transferred, acquired, or held between the points of origin and final destination. Both the vessel owner and the owner of the cargo are able to benefit from this type of insurance. Ocean marine insurance is not limited to ships, but can also cover items traveling by air and land as well. Since the cargo is being moved through international territories, this insurance is not regulated by any particular countries.

In practice, China Insurance Clauses (C.I.C.) of the People's Insurance Company, and Institute Cargo Clauses (I.C.C.) of Lloyd are most applied in marine cargo insurances.

The insurance company covers risks, losses and expenses and compensates for the losses according to different risks.

## 5.4.1　Risks

There are many hidden risks when it comes to trading internationally. Marine insurance generally deals with two categories of risks: perils of the sea and extraneous risks.

The categories of marine risks can be divided into perils of the sea and extraneous risks. The perils of the sea include natural calamities and fortuitous accidents, while extraneous risks include general extraneous risks and special extraneous risks as well.

### 1. Perils of the Sea

Perils of the sea refer to natural calamities and fortuitous accidents of the sea. A peril of the sea must be both fortuitous and of the sea. Fortuitous means that the cause of the loss is not intentional or inevitable.

- **Natural calamities** refer to earthquakes, volcanic eruptions, tsunami, floods and heavy weather, etc.
- **Fortuitous accidents** include fire, explosion, vessel being stranded, grounded, sinking, or colliding with icebergs, etc.

A sinking resulting from the ingress of sea water due to a fortuitous act is an accident of the sea. But ordinary wear and tear is excluded from the definition of fortuitous.

### 2. Extraneous Risks

Extraneous risks are categorized into general extraneous risks and special extraneous risks.

- **General extraneous risks** include theft or pilferage, shortage, rain, leakage, breakage, contamination, taint of odor, rusting, hook damage, heating, non-delivery and short-delivery.
- **Special extraneous risks** include war risks, strikes, failure to deliver due to certain regulations.

## 5.4.2　Losses

Marine losses can be divided into two broad types, including Total Loss

需要指出的是，按照国际保险市场的一般解释，海上风险并非局限于海上发生的灾害和事故，还包括那些与海上航行有关的，发生在路上或海路、海河或与驳船相连接之处的灾害和事故。

按各国保险业习惯，海上损失和费用也包括与海运相连接的陆上或内河运输中所发生的损失和费用。

and Partial Loss.

### 1. Total Loss

Total loss can be subdivided into two categories: actual total loss and constructive total loss.

- **Actual Total Loss**

实际全损是指该批被保险货物在运输途中完全灭失，或者受到严重损坏完全失去原有的形体、效用，或者不能再归被保险人所用。

The actual total loss takes place when the cargo or ship insured against the perils of sea is totally destroyed. An actual total loss also occurs when the insured losses the possession of his property. The amount of total will be paid by the underwriter on all policies issued on that ship.

When a ship is sunk or is completely destroyed by fire, it will be a case of actual total loss. There may be a case when the goods are badly damaged. For example, if crockery is broken into pieces, it is a case of actual total loss. In another case, if the ship is missing and there is no trace of it, it is also a case of actual total loss. In case of actual total loss, the insured is entitled to recover full amount of the loss. When the insured has been compensated the title of goods and passes it on to the insurer, if some amount is received from the sale of damaged goods, the amount will go to the insurer and not to the insured.

- **Constructive Total Loss**

推定全损是指被保险货物在运输途中受损后，实际全损已经不可避免，或者为避免发生实际全损所需支付的费用与继续将货物运抵目的地的费用之和超过保险价值。

This occurs when the ship is abandoned for certain reasons. It is not commercially viable to retrieve the ship or cargo. The ship or the cargo is not wholly destroyed but it is not practicable to get it repaired and restore to its original position. When a ship is badly damaged, and the cost of repairs is expected to be more than the value of ship, it will be advisable to abandon the ship. In the same way, if the cargo is safe in the abandoned ship but the cost of bringing the cargo to the coast is more than the cost of cargo, then it will be proper to leave the cargo.

In the case of constructive total loss, the insured gives a notice of abandonment and surrenders its interest in the subject-matter to the insurer. The insured can claim damage for total loss.

### 2. Partial Loss

When the subject-matter is partially damaged, it will be a case of partial loss. It is of two types: general average loss and particular average loss.

● **General Average Loss**

A ship sailing in the open water faces some perils. Ship masters have to incur several expenses in order to carry ship cargoes safely to their destination. A general average loss is caused voluntarily to avoid an impending danger. A general average loss is one that is caused by an extra-ordinary sacrifice or expenditure voluntarily and reasonably made or incurred under fortuitous circumstances, for the sole purpose of preserving the common interest from an impending peril.

共同海损是指在同一海上航程中，船舶、货物和其他财产遭遇共同危险，为了共同安全，有意地、合理地采取措施所直接造成的特殊牺牲、支付的特殊费用。

If a ship is sinking because of overload, some of the cargo may be thrown out of the ship with a purpose to save the ship and the crew. It will be a case of general average loss.

Some conditions are to be satisfied before deciding about a general average loss:
- There must be an extra-ordinary situation.
- The peril must be real and not imaginary.
- The loss must be voluntary and deliberate.
- The sacrifice must be made prudently.
- The purpose should be to save the whole adventure.
- The act should be successful at least partially.

● **Particular Average Loss**

A particular average loss has been defined as, a partial loss of subject-matter insured, caused by a peril insured against, and which is not general average loss. A particular average loss is not caused voluntarily. The insured subject-matter should be damaged and this damage should be caused by marine peril which is insured. For example, if some bales of cotton are damaged by fire, it is a particular average loss.

单独海损是指除共同海损以外的部分损失，即被保险货物遭遇海上风险受损后，其损失未达到全损程度，而且该损失应由受损方单独承担。

## 5.4.3  Expenses

Marine cargo insurance covers the expenses incurred for the rescue of the insured cargo. There are mainly two types, one is salvage charge, and the other is sue and labor expenses.

### 1. Salvage Charges

Subject to any express provision in the policy, salvage charges incurred in preventing a loss by perils insured against may be recovered as a loss by those perils.

"Salvage charges" means the charges recoverable under maritime law by a salvor independently of contract. They do not include the expenses of services in the nature of salvage rendered by the assured or his agents, or any person employed for hire by them, for the purpose of averting a peril insured against. Such expenses, where properly incurred, may be recovered as particular charges or as a general average loss, according to the circumstances under which they were incurred.

### 2. Sue and Labor Expenses

Sue and labor expenses are extraordinary costs and expenses reasonably incurred after any casualty for the purpose of avoiding or minimizing any liabilities, costs or expenses.

The assured has a duty, under the insurance contract, to take all reasonable steps to avert or minimize any loss for which a claim would be payable under the policies.

Sue and labor expenses are to be distinguished from general average expense. The former are incurred to avert or minimize the loss to a single interest (e.g., ship) rather than for the common safety of more than one interests (e.g., ship, cargo and freight).

## 5.5  Coverage of Marine Cargo Insurance of *CIC*

*China Insurance Clauses (CIC)* are insurance clauses of the People's Insurance Company of China (PICC). Established in 1949, PICC is a state-owned insurance company in China. It underwrites almost all kinds of insurance and has agents in almost main ports and regions in the world.

In accordance with the Ocean Marine Cargo Clauses of the People's Insurance Company of China dated on January 1st, 1981, there are mainly two types of insurance coverage: basic coverage and additional risks. Basic coverage consists of F.P.A., W.A. and All Risks, and Additional Risks include General Additional Risks and Special Additional Risks.

救助费用是指保险标的在遭遇保险责任范围内的灾害事故时，由保险人和被保险人以外的第三者采取了救助措施并获得成功而向其支付的报酬。

施救费用是指保险标的在遭遇保险责任范围内的灾害事故时，被保险人或其代理人、雇用人员和保险单受让人对保险标的所采取的各种抢救、防止或减少货损的措施而支出的合理费用。

## 5.5.1　Basic Coverage

### 1. Free from Particular Average (F.P.A)

In insurance parlance, the phrase "free from" means the insurer (the insurance company) is not liable for whatever follows it. When being used for insurance, the word of average means loss, so "particular average" means partial loss. As such, "free from particular average" means excluding partial loss. F.P.A. is the lowest coverage level of marine cargo insurance. It is the narrowest form of cover as the insurance company does not cover the partial loss or damage to the cargo. The insured is only covered if the entire consignment is lost or damaged. For example, when a ship sinks, or is burned down by fire, the insured will be covered. F.P.A. cover is usually purchased to cover used goods, such as scrap metal.

To be specific, F.P.A. covers:

- Actual total loss or constructive total loss of the whole consignment insured caused in the course of transit by natural calamities: heavy weather, lightning, tsunami, earthquake and flood. Constructive Total Loss refers to the loss where an actual total loss appears to be unavoidable or the cost to be incurred in recovering or reconditioning the goods together with the forwarding cost to the destination named in the policy would exceed their value on arrival.

- Total or partial loss caused by accidents: carrying conveyance being grounded, stranded, sunk or in collision with floating ice or other objects as fire or explosion.

- Partial loss of the insured goods attributable to heavy weather, lightning and/or tsunami, where the conveyance has been grounded, stranded, sunk or burnt, irrespective of whether the event or events took place or after such accidents.

- Partial or total loss consequent on falling of entire package or packages into the sea during loading, transshipment or discharge.

- Reasonable cost incurred by the insured on salvaging the goods or averting or minimizing a loss recoverable under the policy, provided that such cost shall not exceed the value of consignment being salvaged.

被保险货物用驳船运往或运离海轮时，每一驳船所装的货物可视作一个整批。

- Losses attributable to discharge of the insured goods at a port of distress following a sea peril as well as special charges arising from loading, warehousing and forwarding of the goods at an intermediate port of call or refuge.
- Sacrifice in and contribution to General Average and Salvage Charges.
- Such proportion of losses sustained by the ship owners as is to be reimbursed by the cargo owner under the Contract of Affreightment "Both to Blame Collision" clause.

### 2. With Average (W.A.)

**With average (W.A.)** is sometimes called the With Particular Average. In insurance, the words "with average" and "with particular average" mean including partial loss. W.A. is similar to the All Risks coverage except that it is not normally written on a warehouse-to-warehouse basis. W.A. covers against total loss and partial loss caused by the perils of the sea, jettison of cargo, barratry, and other like perils.

### 3. All Risks (A.R.)

**All risks (A.R.)** is the most comprehensive cargo insurance, providing protection against loss or damage from external causes. The term "all risks", is misleading, as it does not cover loss or damage arising from delay, inherent vice (deterioration or damage without outside help, e.g., milk souring), or the nature of the goods insured. Losses as a result of inadequate packaging, weight loss from drying out, or market changes are also not covered. Risks from war, strikes, riots and civil unrest are also not covered, but can be covered at extra cost.

*Case study:*

*A candy exporter signed a CIF contract with a Canadian company. The goods were insured against "All Risks". But in the course of the long voyage, candies absorbed sweating in the ship's hold and degraded. Was the insurance liable for the loss? Why or why not?*

## 5.5.2 Additional Risks

Additional risks include general additional risks and special additional

与国际保险市场的习惯做法一样，我国的海洋运输货物保险条款规定的保险责任起讫期限，也是采用"仓至仓"条款。

risks.

### 1. General Additional Risks

According to Ocean Marine Cargo Clauses of the People's Insurance Company of China, there are eleven general additional risks. All these eleven risks are included in All Risks. Therefore, if the goods have been insured against All risks, the insured need not effect the general additional risks. Furthermore, these risks cannot be covered alone. They must be insured together with W.A. or F.P.A.

- Theft, Pilferage and Non-delivery (T.P.N.D.)

When the insured cargo is stolen or pilfered in the valid period of insurance or when the whole cargo fails to be delivered after the arrival in destination, the insurance company will pay the compensation. Theft is usually referred to the situation that the whole cargo is stolen. Pilferage refers to that a part of cargo is pilfered. Non-delivery is referred to the situation that the whole cargo is not delivered to the consignee.

- Fresh Water Rain Damage (F.W.R.D.)

The insurance company will compensate for the damage and loss caused by fresh water, rain and snow thaw. The fresh water includes the fresh water in cabin on vessel, the leaked water in pipes, and sweat on vessel, etc.

- Risk of Shortage

This risk is to cover the shortage of goods occurring during the transport due to the breakage in the outer package. For break bulk cargo, the shortage can be counted according to the difference in weight between loaded cargo and unloaded cargo. However, it is exclusive of normal shortage of weight during the transport.

- Risk of Intermixture and Contamination

This risk is to cover the damage and loss caused by the intermixture of impurities in the transportation of insured cargo. Additionally it is for the contamination caused by the exposure of insured cargo to other substances, such as piece goods, paper sheets, food, costumes, etc. Furthermore, it is also for the financial loss caused by the pollution of oil and colored substances, etc.

- Risk of Leakage

This risk is to cover the damage and loss of leakage from wet and oil goods in fluidities and semi-fluid caused by the breaking of container in transportation. It is also for the damage and loss of substances stored in liquid,

当投保险别为平安险或水渍险时，可加保11种一般附加险中一种或数种险别。但是，如果已经投保了一切险，就不需要再加保一般附加险，因为保险公司对于承保一般附加险的责任已包含在一切险的责任范围内。

such as pickled vegetables.

- Risk of Clash & Breakage

This risk is to cover the clash and breakage occurring during the transport caused by shock, collision or press of the insured goods.

- Risk of Odor

The insurance company will compensate for the loss of odor mixture due to the influence of other cargo odor on the insured cargo. For example, tea, flavor, medical materials are damaged on quality due to the adverse influence of odor mixture from piles of pelts and camphor in transit. However, the loss of odor mixture is mainly caused by the wrong loading, so the carrier should be responsible for the consequence and be claimed for compensation.

- Risk of Sweating & Heating Damage

This risk is to cover the loss caused by damp and heat on the insured cargo. For example, the loss of cargo is caused by steam condensation, damp, heating in cabins due to the sudden change in temperature or malfunction in equipments in vessels in transit.

- Risk of Hook Damage

This risk is to cover the loss caused by hand hooks and other hooks in loading and unloading the insured cargo.

- Risk of Packing Breakage

This risk is to cover the loss and damage of the shortage and stain caused by the breaking of packing. Furthermore, it is also for the extra cost incurred by repairing and exchanging packing for the sake of safety in any further transportation.

- Risk of Rust

This risk is to cover the risk of rusting on the insured cargo in transportation. This kind of loss is not referred to the one which occurred before loading, but happened in the validity of insurance. It should be pointed out that this insurance is not for the metal plate, block, bar or pipe without packing, because it is evitable for these cargo to incur rust.

## 2. Special Additional Risks

**Special additional risks** cover the loss or damage caused by special extraneous reasons, such as politics, regulation or war, which differs from general additional risks that are not in the coverage of all risks. Moreover, special additional risks cannot be insured alone. They can be insured only after the insured has covered W.A. or F.P.A. Special additional risks include:

- Risk of Failure to Deliver

The insurance company will compensate for all the damage and loss, if the insured cargo fails to be delivered to the destination within 6 months as from the loading date, no matter what reason it is. Such situation is usually not caused by the problems in transportation, but by some political factors.

- Risk of Import Duties

It is responsible for the loss caused by the Customs import duties imposed according to the original value, regardless of how much damage the cargo suffers.

- Deck Risk

The cargo transported by sea is usually loaded inside the cabin, irrespective of whether the vessel is for dry cargo or break bulk cargo. However, there are some products with large measurement or poisons or pollution, which have to be loaded on deck according to the convention of shipping. In that case, this risk will be responsible for the loss and damage of the cargo due to wind and wave.

- Rejection Risk

It is responsible for the loss caused by confiscation of the authorities in destinations who refuse to import cargo for any certain reasons when the cargo arrives.

- Aflatoxin Risk

Aflatoxin is the poisonous bacterium substance in peanuts. If its proportion exceeds the standard of limitation in destination countries, it will be inevitable to be rejected or to be confiscated, or to be forced to change its usage. Aflatoxin risk is responsible for the loss caused by the above consequences.

- Fire Risk Extension Clause for Storage of Cargo at destination Hong Kong, including Kowloon, or Macao

For the cargo from mainland to Hong Kong and Macao, if they are unloaded into the warehouse designated by the bank of ownership transfer directly shown on the insurance policies, this clause should be added and stamped to extend the Fire Risk during storage. The insurance term is from the time that the cargo enters into the warehouse designated by the banks of ownership transfer, until 30 days the banks' unclaiming the ownership of cargo or the termination of transportation responsibility. This kind of risk is to protect the interests of the banks of ownership transfer.

- Strikes Risk

The Strikes Risk is responsible for the loss of cargo caused by the actions of strikers, workers, the people participating in the strike movement, the insurrection and mob battle.

- War Risk in Shipping

It refers to all kinds of War Risk covering sea, inland, air, post transportation. This risk is responsible for the direct loss and damage caused by war.

## 5.6　Coverage of Marine Cargo Insurance of ICC

与 CIC 条款不同的是，ICC 条款中除了恶意损害险以外，其余条款均可以单独投保。ICC 一切险不等于 ICCA 险。

Chinese companies usually follow CIC in business practice, but CIC is not the only option for companies worldwide. Companies in other countries have their own clauses as the guidance of insurance practice, and the most influential one is London Institute Cargo Clauses (ICC).

ICC was first published in 1912 and has been revised for many times in order to adapt to modern commercial practice. The latest revision was put into effect on January 1st, 1982, which includes 6 clauses:

- Institute Cargo Clause A
- Institute Cargo Clause B
- Institute Cargo Clause C
- Institute War Clause—Cargo
- Institute Strike Clause—Cargo
- Malicious Damage Clause

### 5.6.1　Institute Cargo Clauses A

(A)险条款对承保风险的规定采用 "一切风险减除外责任" 的方式，即除了在除外责任项下所列风险所致损失不予负责任外，其他风险所致损失均予负责。

- Insured Clause: The insurance covers all risks of loss of or damage to the subject-matter insured except those excluded.
- General Average Clause: This insurance covers general average and salvage charges incurred to avoid loss from any cause except those excluded.
- "Both to Blame Collision" Clause: This insurance is extended to indemnify the Insured against such proportion of liability under the contract of affreightment "Both to Blame Collision" Clause as in respect of a loss recoverable hereunder.

## 5.6.2　Institute Cargo Clauses B

- The insurance covers, except those excluded,
  - ◆ loss of or damage to the subject-matter insured reasonably attributable to
  —fire or explosive
  —vessel or craft being stranded, grounded, sunk or capsized
  —overturning or derailment of land conveyance
  —collision or contact of vessel, craft or conveyance with any external object other than water
  —discharge of cargo at a port of distress
  —earthquake, volcanic eruption or lightning
  - ◆ loss of or damage to the subject matter insured caused by
  —general average sacrifice
  —jettison or washing overboard
  —entry of sea, lake or river water into vessel, craft, hold, conveyance, container, lift-van or place of storage
- Total loss of any package lost overboard or dropped whilst loading on to, or unloading from, vessel or craft.
- General Average Clause: This insurance covers general average and salvage charges incurred to avoid loss from any cause except those excluded.
- "Both to Blame Collision" Clause: This insurance is extended to indemnify the Insured against such proportion of liability under the contract of affreightment "Both to Blame Collision" Clause as in respect of a loss recoverable hereunder.

（B)险条款对承包风险的规定是采用"列明风险"的方式，即把所承保的风险一一列举，凡属承保责任范围内的损失，无论是全部损失还是部分损失，保险人按损失程度均负责赔偿。

## 5.6.3　Institute Cargo Clauses C

- The insurance covers, except those excluded,
  - ◆ loss of or damage to the subject matter insured reasonably attributable to
  —fire or explosive
  —vessel or craft being stranded, grounded, sunk or capsized
  —overturning or derailment of land conveyance
  —collision or contact of vessel, craft or conveyance with any

（C)险条款的风险责任规定也和(B)险条款一样，采用"列明风险"的方式，只是仅对"重大意外事故"所致损失负责，对非重大意外事故和自然灾害所致损失均不负责。

external object other than water

—discharge of cargo at a port of distress

◆ loss of or damage to the subject matter insured caused by

—general average sacrifice

—jettison

● General Average Clause: This insurance covers general average and salvage charges incurred to avoid loss from any cause except those excluded.

● "Both to Blame Collision" Clause: This insurance is extended to indemnify the insured against such proportion of liability under the contract of affreightment "Both to Blame Collision" Clause as in respect of a loss recoverable hereunder. Summary of Institute Cargo Classes Coverage is shown in Table 5-1.

Table 5-1    Summary of Institute Cargo Clauses Coverage

●= included

○= excluded

| Loss or Damage Caused by | Clause A | Clause B | Clause C |
|---|---|---|---|
| General Average | ● | ● | ● |
| Both to Blame Collision | ● | ● | ● |
| Fire or explosion | ● | ● | ● |
| Vessel or craft being stranded | ● | ● | ● |
| Overturning or derailment of land conveyance | ● | ● | ● |
| Collision or contact of vessel, craft or conveyance with any external object other than water | ● | ● | ● |
| Discharge of cargo at a port of distress | ● | ● | ● |
| General average sacrifice | ● | ● | ● |
| Jettison | ● | ● | ● |
| Earthquake, volcanic eruption or lightning | ● | ● | ○ |
| Washing overboard | ● | ● | ○ |
| Entry of sea, lake or river water into vessel, craft, hold, conveyance, container, lift-van or place of storage | ● | ● | ○ |
| Total Loss of any package lost overboard or dropped whilst loading on to, or unloading from, vessel of craft | ● | ● | ○ |
| Theft or Pilferage | ● | ○ | ○ |
| Contamination (own damage) | ● | ○ | ○ |
| Rain &/or fresh water damage | ● | ○ | ○ |

### 5.6.4　Major Exclusion

The Company will not indemnify the insured in respect of loss, damage or expense:

- Attributable to willful misconduct of the insured;
- Of ordinary leakage, ordinary loss in weight or volume or ordinary wear and tear of the subject matter insured;
- Caused by insufficiency or unsuitability of packing or preparation of the subject-matter insured;
- Arising from unseaworthiness of vessel or craft;
- Caused by war, civil war, revolution, rebellion, insurrection, or civil strife arising therefrom, or any hostile act by or against a belligerent power;
- Resulting from strikes, lock-outs, labor disturbances, riots or civil commotions;
- Caused by any terrorist or any person acting from a political motive.

## 5.7　Procedures of Marine Insurance

In international trades, the one who will cover the insurance is based on which trade term is adopted. For example, if the business is concluded on the basis of CIF or CIP terms, the seller will effect the insurance. But under FOB or CFR term, the buyer will arrange the insurance.

How to insure the cargo and how much to insure are discussed in the next few paragraphs.

### 5.7.1　Gather Information

The potential insured should first gather all the information needed for an insurance quote, because the potential insurer will need to know what item the insured is shipping, how much it is valued at, how it will be packed for shipment, where it is being shipped from and where it will be sent to.

It is a common practice to insure for 10% above the CIF value of the goods, in order to allow for problems involved in replacing the goods, waiting for the money, etc. The goods may be insured for even higher amounts — for example, to cover loss of import duty paid on products

为简化计算程序，我国保险公司制定了保险费率常用表，将 CFR 或 CPT 价格直接乘以表内所列常数，便可算出 CIF 或 CIP 价格。

which have subsequently disappeared. The formula for the calculation of insurance amount is:

> *Insurance amount = CIF (CIP) × (1 + markup rate)*

### 5.7.2  Choose the Insurance Coverage

The potential insurer determines the insurance coverage based on the information gathered about the goods, such as the nature of the goods, how the goods are packed, shipping route, where they are being sent, etc. These factors are closely related to what insurance coverage will be chosen.

### 5.7.3  Get Quotes

Cargo insurance is available from freight and shipping companies, brokers and insurance agents. The potential insured can call these places directly for a quote or check online. Many sites have Web-based systems for quotes.

### 5.7.4  Pay the Insurance Premium

目前，我国的出口货物保险费率按照不同商品、不同目的地、不同运输工具和不同险别，分别有"一般货物费率"和"指明货物加费费率"。

When applying for marine cargo insurance, the applicant has to pay the premium to the insurer. Insurance premium refers to the fees charged to the insured by the insurer for the indemnity liability undertaken. The insurance premium is determined by the insurance amount and the insurance rate. The formula is shown as follows:

> *Insurance Premium = insurance amount × premium rate*
> *= CIF (CIP) × (1 + markup rate) × premium rate*

> **Example:**
> Suppose the value of CIF invoice is USD10,000 and goods are covered against All Risks and War Risks with premium rate to be 0.5% and 0.05%, respectively. If the markup rate is 10%, the insurance premium would be:
> Insurance Premium $= 10,000 × (1+10\%) × (0.5\% + 0.05\%)$
> $= 11,000 × 0.0055$
> $= USD60.5$

## 5.7.5   Purchase the Insurance Policy

Often, this can be done right from the insurer or shipping company's web site and certainly by phone.

Since insurance documents are the evidence of insurance contract between the insurer and the insured, they are mainly classified as the following four types: Insurance Policy, Insurance Provision, Insurance Certificate and Open Policy.

Insurance policy is a written legal contract between the insurer and the insured containing all terms and conditions of the agreement. It shows full details of the risks covered, and is also called formal insurance documents.

### 1. Insurance Policy (See Specimen I)

Key elements of insurance policy are illustrated as follows:

- Name of the insurer with a signature identified as that of insurance company, or underwriter, or insurance agent.
- Name of the insured, both the seller and the buyer might be the insured if they have insured interest and with good faith.
- The insured goods which include description of subject matter.
- Type of risks covered which should be one of the three basic risks, i.e., F.P.A., W.P.A. and All Risks.

保险单俗称大保单，是使用最广的一种保险单据。它具有法律上的效力，对双方当事人均有约束力。

### 2. Insurance Certificate

An insurance certificate is a document issued to the insured certifying that the insurance has been effected. It contains the same details as an insurance policy except that version of provisions is abbreviated. If a documentary credit requires an insurance policy, issuing bank will refuse an insurance certificate for payment.

保险凭证俗称小保单，是一种简化的保险单。保险凭证和保险单据有同等法律效力。

### 3. Open Policy

This is a pre-contract concluded between the insurer and the insured by which the insurer offers insurance to the insured for the consignments he

预约保单又称预约保险合同，它是被保险人和保险人之间订立的合同。

dispatches within a certain period of time.

Open policy is only applicable to the imported goods from foreign countries to China. As soon as the carriage for the consignment under the open policy is made, it is under the insurance cover of the open policy in accordance with the terms listed on the open policy.

### 4. Insurance Endorsement

保险批单是保险公司在保险单出立后，根据投保人的需求，对保险内容进行补充或变更，而出具的一种凭证。它是保险单的组成部分。实务操作中，保险批单应粘贴在保险单上，并加盖骑缝章，其效力优先于保险单。

An insurance endorsement is an added provision to a policy that changes the policy's terms or conditions. Common types of endorsements add coverage for special events, name additional parties to the policy or restrict coverage based on specific criteria. Endorsements are a legally binding change to a policy and should be kept with the original policy documents.

## 5.7.6  Lodge an Insurance Claim

In the event something happens to the cargo, there are a few procedures the insured will need to follow and some principles to observe to make a claim at the insurance company.

对易碎和易短量货物的索赔，应了解是否有免赔的规定，即所谓不论损失程度均予赔偿，或规定免赔率。

- As soon as the cargo is lost, damaged or missing, the insured should make a written claim to the carriers, or other responsible persons immediately. Under no circumstances should he lose any receipts or paperwork handed to him.

- Do not sign any receipt documents and receipt before inspecting the cargo to ensure that it is in order. Be sure to check serial numbers and other identifying numbers that distinguish different cargos. It is not uncommon for people to mix up numbers and receive cargo not intended for them.

- Examine the cargo for damages or losses within three days on receiving the shipment. Make sure that the goods are in good condition and not tampered with.

- Check the container seals to see whether they are broken, missing or tampered with in any way. If the seals are in any way tampered with, broken or missing, or in any way not in the condition that was stated in the shipping documents, it is the responsibility of the claimant or agent to apply for a joint survey with the port authorities or carriers before the cargo or container is taken out of the port.

- It is advisable that clean receipts are not given when the goods are delivered in doubtful conditions.

- The cargo should not be unpacked until they are fully inspected by the surveyors. If they have already been unpacked, the original packing materials should not be discarded.

- Supply full documentations of the claim promptly to enable the insurance company to deal with the matter fast enough. The required documents may include: Certificate of Insurance; packing lists and commercial invoices; original Bills of Lading; copies of delivery receipts; correspondence with the carriers and third parties holding them responsible for the losses or damages; claim statement with details of effected goods; and any other relevant correspondence in respect to the cargo in question.

## 5.8　Insurance Clauses in Sales Contract

The main risks that arise in international trade are loss, damage and delay. How these risks are shared between buyers and sellers should be covered in the contract of sale. The terms of sale agreed in a commercial transaction outline who is responsible for the cost of goods being transported. The most commonly used terms for delivery in an international sales contract are those found in Incoterms. It should be stressed that the standard set of trading terms are limited to matters relating to the contract of sale and do not apply to contracts of carriage. When signing the sales contract, both the seller and the buyer should clearly stipulate the relative insurance clauses.

应注意避免使用"通常险"(usual risks)、"惯常险"(customary risks)或"海运保险"(marine clause)等笼统的规定方法。

If the business is concluded on the basis of the FOB, CFR, FCA or CPT term, it is the buyer to purchase transport insurance to cover the risk of loss or damage. The insurance clause in the contract may be stipulated as **"Insurance: to be effected by the buyer."** Sometimes, the buyer may request the seller to insure the goods at the seller's end. For example, the seller makes it clear in the letter that **"We shall be pleased if you will arrange to insure the goods on our behalf against All Risks for invoice value plus 10%"**, and the insurance clause in the contract is stipulated as **"Insurance: to be effected by the seller on behalf of the buyer for 110% of the invoice value against All Risks as per Ocean Marine Cargo Clauses of People's Insurance Company of China dated Jan. 1, 1981"**.

The insurance should be effected by the buyer if the contract is concluded on FOB or CFR basis. However, the seller should, immediately after the goods are completely loaded at port of shipment, notify the buyer of the consignee of the contract number, name of the commodity, quantity, gross weight, measurement, invoice value and number of B/L, name of the vessel, the date of shipment, etc. In case the goods are not insured in time, owing to the seller's failure to give shipping advice timely, any and all consequent losses should be borne by the seller.

If the business is concluded on the basis of CIF or CIP terms, the sales contract shall indicate the specific insurance amount and the risks covered. For example, **"Insurance: to be effected by the seller for the amount of seller's CIF invoice value plus 10% against All Risks as per Ocean Marine Cargo Clauses of the People's Insurance Company of China dated Jan. 1, 1981"**. Any additional insurance required by the buyer shall be at his own expense. The seller may insure against War Risk at the buyer's request and at his expense. In case the rate of relevant insurable premium shall be raised between the time of concluding contract and that of shipment, this excess premium shall be on the buyer's account.

# 【Key Terms and Words】

Broker   保险经纪人

Perils of the sea   海上风险

Extraneous risks   外来风险

Natural calamities   自然灾害

Fortuitous accidents   意外事故

General extraneous risks   一般外来风险

Special extraneous risks   特殊外来风险

Total loss   全部损失

Actual total loss   实际全损

Constructive total loss   推定全损

Partial loss   部分损失

General average loss   共同海损

Particular average loss   单独海损

Salvage charges   救助费用

Sue and labor expenses   施救费用

Free of particular average   平安险

With average   水渍险

All risks   一切险

Additional risks   附加险

General additional risks   一般附加险

Theft, pilferage and non-delivery   偷窃、提货不着险

Fresh water rain damage   淡水雨淋险

Risk of shortage   短量险

Risk of intermixture and contamination   混杂、沾污险

Risk of leakage   渗漏险

Risk of clash & breakage   破损、破碎险

Risk of odor   串味险

Risk of sweating & heating damage   受潮受损险

Risk of hook damage   钩损险

Risk of packing breakage   包装破裂险

Risk of rusk   锈损险

Special additional risks   特殊附加险

Risk of failure to deliver   交货不到险

Risk of import duties   进口关税险

Deck risk　舱面险

Rejection risk　拒收险

Aflatoxin risk　黄曲霉素险

Fire risk extension clause — for storage of cargo at destination Hong Kong, including Kowloon, or Macao　货物出口到香港(包括九龙)或澳门存仓火险责任扩展条款

Strikes risk　罢工险

War risk　战争险

Insurance policy　保险单

Insurance certificate　保险凭证

Open policy　预约保单

Insurance endorsement　保险批单

# 【Exercises】

## I. Answer the following questions.

1. What is insurance?

2. What parties are involved in insurance?

3. What risks are covered by marine insurance?

4. How is insurance claim lodged?

5. What documents are needed in filing a claim?

## II. Give the definition to the following terms.

1. Free from particular average

2. With average

3. All risks

4. Theft pilferage and non-delivery

5. Partial loss

6. General average

7. Salvage charge

8. Sue and labor expenses

## III. Judge whether the following statements are true or false.

1. If the insured has insured the goods against F.P.A., it means that the insurance company would cover the partial loss or damage to the cargo.　　　　　　(　　)

2. If the insured has insured the goods against All Risks, the insurance company would cover the loss of the goods caused by war.　　　　　　(　　)

3. According to China Insurance Clause, the general additional risks have to be insured together with W.P.A. or W.A.                                                                                    (   )

4. In the international practice, the insurance policy and the insurance certificate have the same legal effect.                                                                                                              (   )

5. General extraneous risks include war risks, strikes, failure to deliver due to certain regulations.                                                                                                                     (   )

6. Sue and labor expenses are extraordinary costs and expenses reasonably incurred after any casualty for the purpose of avoiding or minimizing any liabilities, costs or expenses.        (   )

7. Generally speaking, the insured will cover the goods for 100% of the invoice value against certain risk.                                                                                                          (   )

8. The With average is written on a warehouse-to-warehouse basis.                                         (   )

9. The actual total loss takes place when the cargo or ship insured against the perils of sea is totally destroyed.                                                                                                      (   )

10. Fortuitous accidents refer to earthquakes, volcanic eruptions, tsunami, floods and heavy weather, etc.                                                                                                              (   )

## IV. Case Study.

1. A Chinese exporter signed an FOB contract with an American company and a CIF contract with a Korean company. All the cargoes were covered for marine cargo insurance. Unfortunately, the goods were damaged in the transit from the factory to the port of departure.

**Question:**

Under this circumstance, which party should obtain insurance and which party should bear the loss?

2. A ship started on its voyage after loading, but in the course of the journey a fire broke out during transit in Hold A, which had been loaded with stationary and tea. The caption ordered his crew to pour water on the fire. It was found out, after the fire was extinguished, that part of the stationery had been burned, the remainder and all the tea had been soaked through.

**Questions:**

(1) What were the natures of the respective losses?

(2) What risks would you have covered if you had wanted to be compensated for the losses?

3. A Chinese company exported 600 cases of tableware on CIF basis. The export company covered the insurance on the goods against FPA for 110% of the CIF value. Before the goods were loaded on the ship, 20 cases were off the hook and fell into the sea.

**Questions:**

(1) Do you think the insurance company should undertake to compensate for the loss?

(2) If this transaction was concluded on FOB or CFR basis, should the insurance company compensate for the loss? Why or why not?

# 国际贸易实务(英语版)(第2版)

## Specimen 5-1  The Insurance Policy

# Chapter 6   Price of Goods

【Learning Objectives】

By studying this chapter, you should be able to master:

- Pricing principles
- Pricing consideration
- Pricing methods
- Pricing composition
- Currency option
- Calculation of price
- Export cost accounting
- Price including commission
- Price with discount

## Lead-in: News Report

### Vietnam Won't Reduce Rice Export Price

The Vietnam Food Association (VFA) collects the winter-spring crop rice at VND4,500 per kilo only, which is VND700 per kilo lower than in 2011.

The association said its member export companies have to pay low for rice materials because Vietnam's export prices have decreased sharply.

Experts have affirmed that Vietnam's rice is the most competitive in the world. Thai rice is at least $170 per ton more expensive than Vietnam's. India's exports remain moderate. The country with high population and high demand for food is believed to be not be capable enough to compete with Vietnam in the long term.

Meanwhile, Myanmar's rice, though being cheap, has lower quality than Vietnam's. Meanwhile, it can export no more than 900,000 tons a year. Professor Vo Tong Xuan, a well-known Vietnamese rice expert, affirmed that Myanmar's rice with low quality and low output cannot be comparable to Vietnam's.

However, despite the great advantages, Vietnam's rice prices have been falling down dramatically in the world market. In the first quarter of 2013, Vietnam exported 1.45 million tons of rice, up by 350,000 tons over the first quarter of 2012, but the export turnover was 6 percent lower.

VFA, which says Vietnam now has to compete fiercely with Thailand, Myanmar and India, has been attempting to ease the rice export prices.

The information has made relevant parties in the rice production and distribution chain, especially farmers, worried stiff.

Experts have affirmed that there is no reason for Vietnam to ease the export prices any more. Thailand, which exports 10 million tons of rice every year, has been determined to keep the 5 percent broken rice price at approximately $600 per ton in order to protect farmers' benefits.

Meanwhile, India only exports many-year inventories when it is sure that it can ensure the domestic food security. Therefore, Indian rice's quality is certainly lower than Vietnam's.

In such conditions, experts say, Vietnam should follow Thailand when defining the rice export policy to protect Vietnamese farmers' benefits, instead of following India, which exports rice at low prices.

They also said that Vietnam and Thailand control 50 percent of the world market with 18 million tons of rice provided every year.

Rice import countries, which cannot let their people stay hungry with the empty rice storehouses, would have to buy Vietnamese rice, which is cheaper than Thai rice (at $550 per ton), because they fear the rice price may go up further.

It would be good if India also raises its export price like Vietnam. But it would not matter, if it does not. When India sells out its cheap rice, it would be the time for Vietnam's rice.

In fact, the experts said, importers just try to force the prices down by threatening Vietnamese exporters. If Vietnam eases the export prices now, the prices would go down further and further.

Vietnamese farmers have suffered heavily from the rice price decreases. Rice exporters have been selling rice at surprisingly low prices after VFA removed the floor prices for 5 percent broken rice products. At present, the floor price is still applied to 35 percent broken rice, but this kind of product must not be the reference for defining the export price.

*(Source: http://english.vietnamnet.vn/, Updated: 2013-05-15 15:00)*

***Class Activities:***

1. What happens to the effect of price fluctuation on commodity export of the country?
2. Why won't Vietnam reduce rice export price in this case?

The price of the goods is certainly among the chief terms discussed in business negotiation. The price clause is an important part of a contract, where the buyer and seller argue most because it is directly related to the interests of both parties involved. Therefore, having a full knowledge of the composition of the price and the methods of pricing to make proper decision of pricing is important in international transaction.

商品的价格是国际货物买卖的主要交易条件；价格条款是买卖合同中必不可缺的合同条款。

# 6.1   Price Elements

Pricing means a series of techniques relating to a single product or a group of products. Price is the amount of money that is needed to acquire some combination of a product and its accessorial services. Price is also a critical ingredient in consumer evaluation of the product. In this section, we will explore price both as an ingredient of the value package and as a strategic marketing tool.

## 6.1.1   Pricing Principles

It is very complicated to make a good price for a product in the import and export business. In order to do it well, you should carry out correctly your pricing principles and be sure to master the changing trend of the international market. All the factors that may influence pricing should be taken into account. The calculation of cost, profit and loss must be reinforced.

In order to pricing properly, the following three principles should be adhered to:

● To price according to the international market

The international market price is made on the basis of international merits and formed in the international market competition, which can be accepted both by the buyer and the seller.

● To price based on the situations of different policies of various countries and regions

In order to let the foreign trade work in accordance with the diplomatic policies, you should consider the policies of different countries and regions in the reference with the international market.

● To price based on purpose of purchasing

The price of goods to be imported and exported can be made according to the international market, and be made based on the purpose of purchasing. That's to say, the price can be a little higher and lower than the international market.

The international market price is subject to the supply and demand, so it is not so stable. Therefore, in order to make the price of the goods, we should pay a great attention to the ups and downs of the international market and make good prediction so as to avoid blindness of the making correct use of pricing.

## 6.1.2 Pricing Consideration

There are many factors to affect the fluctuation of price. And even for the same goods, its price varies from different factors in different situation. To set the proper price of goods, we should take into account the following factors:

● The quality and grade of commodities

In general, the price of goods depends on the quality in international market. There are many factors to affect the price of goods such as quality, grade, design, packing, brand and so on.

● The transport distance

The goods can be conveyed from one place to another only by sea or other modes of transport in international trade. The transport distance will affect the freight and premium and then influence the price of goods. So we should figure up the costs of transportation when setting the price of goods.

● The place of delivery and the conditions of delivery

In international trade, the responsibilities, expenses and risks of the seller and buyer vary from different places and terms of delivery. So we should take into account these factors when setting the price of goods.

● Seasonal changes in demand

In international markets, some seasonal goods can sell for a high price if reaching the named destination before the holidays. If not, the goods can just sell at a low price even less than cost. Therefore, we should take advantage of seasonal changes in demand to set the proper price of seasonal goods.

● The trading volume

The trading volume will affect the price of goods according to the international practice. If the order is big enough, the seller can sell at a

国际市场上，某些节令性商品如果赶在节令前到货，抢先应市，就能卖出好价钱。一旦过了节令，则售价往往很低。

favorable price or give a discount. On the contrary, if the order is small even below the minimum quantity, the seller can fairly raise the price.

- The payment terms and the risks of exchange rate

The Payment terms and risks of exchange rate will also affect the price of goods. For example, the price of same commodities will be different under the different terms of payment. The price will be higher on credit, while the price will be reduced under the payment by L/C. Moreover, we should try to reach a deal by a currency of advantage to us. Otherwise, we must take into account the risks of foreign exchange when setting the price of goods.

## 6.1.3　Pricing Methods

The pricing methods of goods in international trade are very varied. And the commonly used ways are as follows:

- Fixed price

It is the most popular method in international trade. The seller delivers and the buyer accepts the goods at a fixed price agreed by both parties. Neither party shall have the right to change the agreed price after conclusion of the contract. The standard format of a price in international trade has four components including the type of currency, the unit of price, the unit of measurement and the trade term. An example is shown as follows.

国际贸易中的报价，通常由计量单位、单位价格金额、计价货币和贸易术语四部分组成。买卖合同中的价格，如无特殊约定，应理解为固定价格。

---

**Example**

| USD | 15.00 | PER YARD | CIF NEW YORK |
|-----|-------|----------|--------------|
| Type of currency | Unit of price | Unit of measurement | The trade term |
| | | | (每码15美元CIF 纽约) |

---

Payment currency in international trade should be a freely convertible currency. What is a freely convertible currency? It is defined that a country shall impose no restriction on its currency being converted into another currency in any international transaction. According to Article VIII of agreement of the international monetary fund, a freely convertible currency should meet the following requirements:

(1) No member shall, without the approval of the fund, impose restrictions on the making of payments and transfers for current international transactions;

根据《国际货币基金协定》的规定，可自由兑换货币，必须具备以下三个条件。

(1) 对国际上经常往来的付款和资金转移不得施加限制。

(2) 不施行歧视性货币措施或复汇率。

(3) 在另一成员国要求下，随时有义务换回对方在经常往来中所结存的本国货币。

(2) No member shall engage in any discriminatory currency arrangements or multiple currency practices;

(3) Each member shall buy balances of its currency held by another member if the latter, in requesting the purchase.

Figure 6-1 shows common currency in foreign trade.

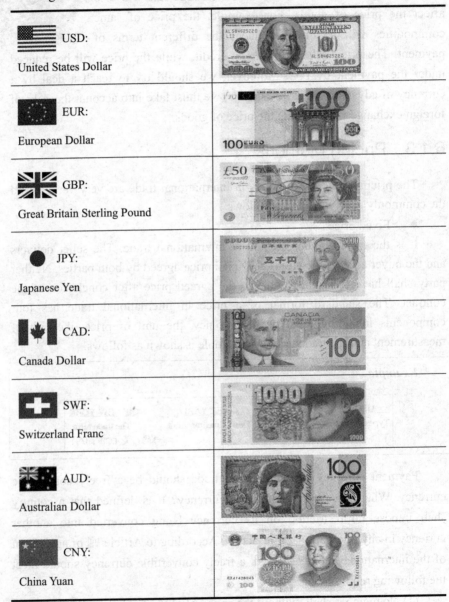

| | |
|---|---|
| USD:<br>United States Dollar | |
| EUR:<br>European Dollar | |
| GBP:<br>Great Britain Sterling Pound | |
| JPY:<br>Japanese Yen | |
| CAD:<br>Canada Dollar | |
| SWF:<br>Switzerland Franc | |
| AUD:<br>Australian Dollar | |
| CNY:<br>China Yuan | |

Figure 6-1    Common Currency in Foreign Trade

CNY, also known as RMB, is accepted as a payment currency in foreign trade even though it is not a completely free convertible currency. In April 2009, Chinese government put forward the policy of Cross-border RMB Trade Settlement to encourage enterprises to adopt RMB as the settlement currency in foreign trade.

- Flexible price

The pricing time and the pricing method are specified in the price terms, but no exact amount of price is shown on the contract.

> **Note:**
> *The price will be negotiated and decided by both parties within 60 days before the shipment according to the international price level.*

- Partial fixed price and partial unfixed price

The parties concerned only fix the price for the commodities to be delivered recently, and leave the price of goods to be delivered in the long term open.

- Floating price

The pricing method is especially for resource-intensive commodity transactions, and project-oriented transactions which may take over six months or more time to complete. When the macro economic environment is highly volatile, the market price of resource type of goods like oil, steel and rubber may experience dramatic upward and downward movements. In order to protect the interest of both sellers and buyers and promote fairness, a contract can leave the prices unfixed and subject to adjustment according to the market prices of certain variables. At the time of pricing, the price adjustment is also stipulated.

滑动价格是指先在合同中规定一个基础价格，交货时或交货前一定时间，按工资、原材料价格变动的指数作相应调整，以确定最后价格。

> **Note:**
> *The above basic price will be adjusted according to the following formula based on the wage and price indexes published by National Bureau of Statistics of China as of March 2013.*
>
> Adjustment Formula:
>
> $P=P_0(A+B\times M/M_0+C\times W/W_0)$
>
> *P: Final price after adjustment*
>
> $P_0$: *Basic price at the time of conclusion of contract*
>
> *A: Administration overheads, the fixed portion of basic price*

> *B: Materials cost, the changeable portion of basic price*
>
> *C: Labor cost, the changeable portion of basic price*
>
> *M: Materials wholesale price indexes at the time of delivery three months later*
>
> *$M_0$: Materials wholesale price indexes at the time of conclusion of contract*
>
> *W: Wage index at the time of delivery three months later*
>
> *$W_0$: Wage index at the time of conclusion of contract*

## 6.1.4  Pricing Composition

When deciding the price of goods, an export price list will be necessary to avoid the catastrophe of getting a heavy loss because of failing to take many additional factors into consideration. In many cases, the following costs should be added to each item in the product line.

> ★ **Price list**
> ***Item:***
> * Production costs
> * Profit
> * Selling and delivery costs
> * Export credit insurance and marine insurance
> * Customs duties
> * Financial charges
> * Other charges

● **Production costs**

Production costs embrace all those elements in the product manufacture, including labor, raw materials, component parts, heating, lighting, general maintenance of the factory building and plant and any other ancillary cost which could be directly allocated to the product. This could include warehousing, distribution involving inter-factory transfer handling and assembly costs.

● **Profit**

Normally, profit will have already been included in the domestic price. However, if it is insufficient for the risk involved in selling abroad, an extra allowance for profit can now be added.

● **Selling and delivery costs**

Selling and delivery costs can be divided into both fixed costs like salesmen's salaries, and variable costs like packaging cost, agent's commission abroad, labeling cost, marking cost, strapping cost, cost of taking goods to the seaport, loading and unloading cost, terminal cost, cost of documents, ocean freight, freight forwarder's fee and so on. All these contribute to the total costs of the products contracted.

- Export credit insurance and marine insurance

The exporter may decide to take out insurance on its credit sales abroad. Exporter credit is always given by the exporter's bank.

The exporter must choose the coverage most suitable for the shipment as stipulated in the contract while they are being shipped abroad. Usually ocean shipments are insured for 110% of their total costs. If he/she wishes, the exporter may include the insurance premium in the amount on which insurance is taken on certain for basis.

- Customs duties

Customs duties are the other cost factors that should be taken into account by the exporter when he/she prices his/her products.

- Financial charges

Until he/she receives payment, the exporter will have part of his/her working capital tied up in the export merchandise. Even if no credit is given, he/she will give credit to the foreign customer, and he/she may have to wait for several months for payment. Consequently, the export price should include an amount to cover the cost of this working capital as well as the interest.

- Other charges

Here, space is left for the inclusion of unexpected additional expense such as the cost of overseas telegrams or phone calls, fax charges, extra storage charges.

The above costs are now available for consolidation into a properly printed price list. These are the ones being used by most of the Chinese trading companies. To guard against complications, it is advisable to print the words on all price lists: " All prices are subject to change without notice. " In the case of certain countries, there are special charges which have to be paid for the legalization and certification of export document or for having B/L visited and for certificates of origin. It is good to make the situation quite clear by having the following words printed on the list "Free for certification and legalization of documents are not included in the above prices." The export price is a multi-dimensional variable. Whether or not you can export your merchandise with price calculated from the above costing sheet, the foreign consumer is always the final controller of your price. Accurate calculation does not imply right exporting. That is dependent upon your pricing strategies and policies.

## 6.1.5　Currency Option

计价货币是指买卖双方在合同中规定用来计算和清偿彼此债权债务的货币，一般与结算货币相同，如果双方在合同中只规定了计价货币，没有规定结算货币，则计价货币就是结算货币。

There are two kinds of currency adopted in international trade. One is quote currency which is used for price calculation; the other is settlement currency which is used for settlement. Normally, quote currency is settlement currency if no otherwise is stipulated in the contract. In international trade, the price of goods may be quoted in the buyer's currency, the seller's currency or in a third currency agreed by both parties.

汇率是一国货币兑换另一国货币的比率，是以一种货币表示另一种货币的价格。汇率的标价一般分为直接标价法和间接标价法。前者是以外币为基准，折算成若干单位的本币；后者则是以本币为基准，折算成若干单位的外币。

Moreover, the exchange rate is one of the most important factors in international trade. It is defined as the price of one currency in terms of another. There are generally two methods of exchange rate quotation, one is *direct quotation*, which means one unit of a foreign currency is worth a given number of currency of the home country, and the other is *indirect quotation*, which means one unit of a home currency is equal to a given number of foreign currency. The former (direct quotation) is now used by most countries in the world including China. And the latter (indirect quotation) is adopted by a very few but important countries such as America and Britain.

| Direct Quotation | Indirect Quotation |
| --- | --- |
| CAD1=RMB5.9701 | USD1=CAD1.0327 |

汇率有买入价和卖出价之分。买入价是指银行买入外汇的价格，卖出价则是指银行卖出外汇的价格。

In addition, there are differences between buying exchange rate and selling exchange rate. The *buying rate*, also called bid rate, is the price used by a bank to purchase the foreign exchange needed from its customers or cooperative banks. While the *selling rate*, also called offer rate, is the price used by a bank to sell the foreign exchange. In practice, we should use the selling rate to convert home currency into foreign currency when making a quotation to our foreign business partners.

Table 6-1 shows buying rate and selling rate.

Table 6-1   Buying Rate and Selling Rate

Unit:100

| Currency Name | Buying Rate | Selling Rate | Pub Time |
|---|---|---|---|
| USD | 680.56 | 683.29 | 2017-05-31 |
| EUR | 763.79 | 769.15 | 2017-05-31 |
| GBP | 877.09 | 883.25 | 2017-05-31 |
| JPY | 6.1390 | 6.1821 | 2017-05-31 |
| CAD | 503.55 | 507.08 | 2017-05-31 |
| HKD | 87.30 | 87.64 | 2017-05-31 |

(Source: *http://www.boc.cn/sourcedb/whpj/*)

Since the exchange fluctuation of the selected currency may directly affect their financial interests, the parties concerned should choose the currency favorable to them during pricing. In general, hard currency as settlement currency is more favorable to the exporter, while the importer prefers to pay in weak currency. In practice, the selection of currency shall depend on the business practices and intentions of both parties. If the unfavorable currency has to be adopted for the conclusion of a deal, the following two remedies may be taken: to make corresponding adjustment to the quotation according to the possible trend of the currency in the future, and to get the price protected against the currency risks.

出口商要尽可能地采用"硬币"作为计价和结算货币，而进口商则要尽可能地采用"软币"。

## 6.2   Calculation of Price

Generally speaking, an export price shall cover costs and contribute a certain portion of profit. Otherwise, it is meaningless to export. In addition, the price components of the same commodity are different when adopting different trade terms. The calculation of price requires one to analyze in detail costs involved. Using a worksheet can make the process easier and clear to stand. Table 6-2 provides a sample calculating chart for different terms if marine transport is employed. Here only three terms (FOB, CFR and CIF) are listed because they are most commonly adopted in practice. The actual application of such a worksheet may be subject to specific cost variations among different transaction.

Table 6-2　Pricing Worksheet

| Item | Amount | Total |
|---|---|---|
| Production cost | | |
| +Anticipated profit | | |
| +Local transport costs from works to port of shipment | | |
| +Local transport insurance if applicable | | |
| +Storage costs, THC, loading costs | | |
| +Costs for export clearance | | |
| =Sale price under FOB | | |
| +Main ocean freight to port of destination | | |
| =Sale price under CFR | | |
| +Marine cargo insurance premium | | |
| =Sale price under CIF | | |

As shown in Table 6-2, the relationship of these three terms is as follows:

CFR=FOB+F

CIF=CFR+I=FOB+F+I

*F*: *Main ocean freight from port of shipment to destination*

*I*: *Marine cargo insurance premium from port of shipment to destination*

---

***Example***

You are an export agent for children shoes. Suppose you have got the following information from different parties.

***Factory***:

Product sale price: RMB23.00/Dozen

Standard packing details:

20 Dozen/Carton, 45×30×50cm/Carton

Quantity: 7000 Dozens

***Shipping company***:

Freight charge for FCL 1×20′: USD1050.00

Freight charge for LCL:USD50/CBM

***Insurance company***:

All risks, premium rate as 0.5%

*Your company pricing policy:*

Required profit margin as 10%

---

**Bank**:

Exchange rate on the day of quotation: USD1.00=RMB6.20

**Questions**:

What is the FOB price for 1×20′container of goods?

What about CIF price for 1×20′container?

What about CFR price for quantity less than 1×20′container?

**Answer**:

1. FOB= (Product sale price + Profit)/ Exchange rate

   =(23.00+23.00×10%)/6.20

   =USD4.08/Dozen

2. CIF=FOB+F+I

I=CIF×110%×0.5%

Hence:

CIF=FOB+F+( CIF×110%×0.5%)

   =(FOB+F)/(1 − 110%×0.5%)

Since:

FOB= USD4.08/Dozen

F=USD1050.00/7000=USD0.15/ Dozen

So:

CIF=(4.08+0.15)/( 1 − 110%×0.5%)

   =USD4.25/Dozen

3. Measurement of the goods:

   45×30×50cm/Carton=0.0675 CBM/Carton

   The number of Carton: 7000/20=350 Cartons

   The total Measurements:350×0.0675=23.625 CBM

Hence:

F=(50×23.625)/7000=USD1181.25/7000=USD0.17/Dozen

So:

CFR=FOB+F=USD(4.08+0.17)=USD4.25/Dozen

# 6.3　Export Cost Accounting

In general, our exporters should account costs of goods before trading. They hope to make sure whether the company is profitable. In addition to the profit and loss rate of well-known, the foreign exchange cost of export products is an important measurable indicator. If the foreign exchange cost of export products is more than the buying rate of foreign exchange, it means that the deal has made a loss.

**Formulas:**

- The Foreign Exchange Cost of Export Products

= Total costs of export products (RMB) / Net FOB incomes of export exchange (USD)

- The Profit and Loss Rate of Export Products

= (Net RMB incoming of export distribution — Total costs of export products)/Total costs of export products ×100%

在我国，出口换汇成本是指商品出口后净收入每 1 美元所耗费的人民币成本。出口盈利越大，则换汇成本越低；反之，亏损越大，则换汇成本越高。

---

*Example*

Goods: Baby Stroller

Quantity: 598 sets

Income and Cost: USD42988.80 CIF Hamburg, Freight USD2400, Insurance premium USD308, Total Purchase price (including VAT 17%) RMB275880, Rate of expense standard 5%, Rate of Export Tax Rebate 14%.

Rate of foreign exchange: USD1.00=RMB6.50

*Question*:

What is the foreign exchange cost of export products?

*Answer*:

Total costs of export products (RMB)

=275880+(275880×5%)−[275880÷(1+17%)×14%]

=RMB256662.72

Net FOB incomes of export exchange (USD)

=42988.80−2400−308=USD40280.80

The foreign exchange cost of export products

= RMB256662.72/USD40280.80

=RMB6.372 < 6.50

So this deal is profitable.

---

## 6.4   Commission and Discount

A price shown in the contract directly comes from the calculation of basic costs and profit, which is called a "net price". But occasionally traders have to make some adjustments to the net prices to achieve the goal of promoting sales. These adjustments include commission and discount.

## 6.4.1   Price Including Commission

Commission is an incentive payment made to the middlepersons or brokers for their intermediary service. Modern international trade has been getting more and more specialized. Therefore any party who might be involved in facilitating the transaction can be a commission receiver. A price which contains a proportion as commission payment is called a "price including commission". It is normally expressed by mentioning a percentage as the commission rate at the end of the price with commission.

佣金是卖方或买方付给中间商为其对货物的销售或购买提供中介服务的酬金。

**For example:**

*USD335 per M/T CIF New York including 2% commission*

It is called as "*USD335 per M/T CIFC2% New York*" for short.

The calculation of commission is comparatively easy. The formula is as following:

$$\text{Commission} = \text{Contract value} \times \text{Commission Rate}$$

A note to remember is that the contract value of above formula refers to price including commission instead of net price. And the relationship between "net price" and "price including commission" is as follows:

$$\text{Net price} = \text{Price including commission} - \text{Commission}$$

$$\text{Price including commission} = \text{Net price} / (1 - \text{Commission Rate})$$

---

*Example*

If the net price is USD100 per piece, the commission rate is 5%, what is the price including commission?

*Answer*:

*Price including commission = USD100/ (1−5%)*

*= USD105.26*

---

### 6.4.2 Price with Discount

折扣是卖方按照原价给予买方的一定的价格减让。

Similar to commission in the sense that it is also used to promote the transaction, the discount, however, has a different nature. It is a deduction from the net price rather than a mark-up. The reasons for providing discount can de multifold. The most common one is to increase the competitiveness of the product in the market. Providing a price with discount can be considered as lowering a product price, which is a frequently used approach to increasing sales. Importers may use discount as a motivator to introduce products into new markets. In some cases, discount is useful for enterprises to get rid of their stocked goods and speed up cash flow. More often than not, discount is used as compensation for settling previous disputes between traders.

If discount is applied, it should be clearly expressed in the contract as a percentage of the total value or a fixed amount. For example:

USD200 per M/T FOB Ningbo less 2% discount

The calculation of discount is simple, which is:

Discount = contract price × discount rate

Then the actual price of the product will be:

Actual price = contract price − discount

= contract price × (1 − discount rate)

It is normally deducted before the buyer pays.

## 6.5 Import Cost Accounting

The costs of imported goods refer to the full costs on imported goods, including the contract price, the total domestic expenses, as shown in the following formula:

The cost of imported goods = Import contract price + Total domestic expenses of importing country + import taxes

进口货物成本=进口合同价+进口国内总费用+进口税费

## 6.5.1  Import contract price

The import contract price is an estimation of the price before the import contract is established. It is the contract price that the buyer and seller can obtain agreement through negotiation. Sometimes it is the price that the importer strives to trade with the exporter. After the contract has been established, it is the commodity price stated in the contract.

在合同成立后，进口合同价格一般就是合同写明的商品价格。

## 6.5.2  Total Domestic Expenses of Importing Countries

The domestic expenses of importing country include:

1. Fees for unloading, barge, dock construction and wharf warehouse

2. Inspection fees and other notary fees for imported goods

3. Bank charge such as issue charge and other service charges

4. Customs brokerage charges

5. Domestic freight and warehouse rental fee

6. Interest payments incurred during the period from issuance of L/C to receipt of payment

7. Other costs

The accounting of domestic expenses of importing countries is the same as the domestic cost of exporting countries. It is worth noting that the transportation and insurance are handled by the importer under FOB terms. So the total domestic costs should include freight and insurance premium. And the calculation method is the same as that of the freight and insurance premium when exporting. In the same way, the insurance premium should be covered when calculating the total domestic under CFR terms.

值得注意的是，FOB术语下运输和保险事宜是由进口方负责办理的，故国内总费用中还应加上运费和保险费，其计算方法与出口中运费和保险费的核算方法相同。同理，如果是 CFR 术语，则应在核算国内总费用时加上保险费。

## 6.5.3  Calculation of Imported Goods Tariff

The Customs shall not only determine the applicable tax rate at which the goods are to be taxed after classifying the import and export goods, but also examine the tax rate charged for the duty in order to achieve the rate of account. The tax price is the customs duty-paid price, which is the basis for Customs to levy tariffs.

计税价格即海关完税价格，是海关计征关税的依据。

### 1. Customs dutiable price of imported goods

It is determined by the customs on the basis of the transaction price of imported goods, including the price of goods, the freight and insurance premium of the goods before discharging at the Customs of the importing country. Usually it is based on CIF price. It should be deducted from the transaction price if the seller pays at a normal discount during the course of transaction.

The imported goods are traded under CFR terms. And the premium shall be added to the dutiable price. The formula is:

Dutiable price = CFR ÷ (1 − insurance rate)

The imported goods are traded on FOB terms. So the premium and freight shall be added to the dutiable price. The formula is:

Dutiable price = (FOB + freight) ÷ (1 − insurance rate)

### 2. Tariff calculation of import goods

After the duty-paid price has been determined, the applicable tax rate can be obtained accordingly. The formula is:

Tariff amount = taxable import goods quantity × dutiable price × applicable tariff rate

## 6.5.4 Calculation of Value-added Tax and Consumption Tax

The Customs shall impose Value-added tax (VAT) on imported goods. Value-added tax is carried out by way of tax excluded in price. The formula is:

VAT = Composite assessable price × Tax rate

Composite assessable price = Customs dutiable value + Customs Duty + Consumption Tax

The Customs shall impose consumption tax on consumer goods from abroad. If the goods are not taxable consumer goods, the consumption tax is not levied. Consumption tax is carried out by way of tax within price. Its amount may be calculated ad valorem, at a flat rate or by a combination of the two.

进口货物完税价格由海关以进口货物的成交价格为基础审核确定。一般包括货价、货物运抵进口国境内指定地点起卸前的运费和保费。通常以CIF价为基础。

应纳关税额=应纳税进口货物数量 × 完税价格 × 适用关税税率

增值税属于价外税。计算公式为：
应纳增值税额=组成计税价格 × 适用税率

我国消费税采用价内税，即计税价格组成中包括消费税税额。

### 6.5.5 Total Import Cost

Total import cost = FOB + freight + insurance + total domestic expenses + tariff + consumption tax + VAT

= CFR + insurance + total domestic expenses + tariff + consumption tax

+ VAT

= CIF + total domestic expenses + tariff + consumption tax + VAT

## 6.6 Price Clause in Sales Contract

As previously mentioned，the price of commodity is composed of four parts: currency unit, unit price figure, measurement unit and trade term. The common way of price stipulation is to define a fixed price mutually agreed. Besides, commission or discount used in the price should also be clearly stipulated in the contract.

> **Examples**
> GBP500 per M/T CIF London
> USD100 per M/T FOB Shanghai gross for net
> USD300 Per set CIF New York including commission 5%
> HKD50 per dozen CFR Hong Kong less 1% discount

# 【Key Terms and Words】

Commission　佣金

Discount　折扣

Fixed price　固定价格

Flexible price　可变价格

Floating price　滑动价格

Price adjustment　价格调整

Quote currency　计价货币

Settlement currency　结算货币

THC (Terminal Handling Charge)　集装箱码头装卸作业费

Cost accounting　成本核算

Foreign exchange cost of export products　出口换汇成本

Value-added tax (VAT)　增值税

Export rebate rate　出口退税率

Net price　净价

Price including commission　含佣价

# 【Exercises】

## I. Please answer the following questions.

1. While making pricing decision, what major factors should be considered?

2. What are the differences and similarities between commission and discount?

3. Do you know how to convert the price under different trade terms?

4. What does the price clause include in the contract?

5. Do you know how to stipulate the price in the contract?

## II. Choose the right answer from each of the following.

1. If the CIF price of a product is USD100 per set, freight charge USD10 per set, insurance premium USD10 per set, the FOB price should be (　　).

　　A. USD110/set　　　　　　　　　　B. USD90/set

　　C. USD80/set　　　　　　　　　　　D. USD120/set

2. If the CIF price of a product is USD100 per set, commission rate 2%, the commission payment based on CIF price should be (　　).

A. USD1.60/set        B. USD1.63/set        C. USD2.00/set        D. USD2.04/set

3. Which one of the following prices is correctly expressed? (      )

A. CNY3.50 CIF Hong Kong

B. USD3.50 per piece CIF

C. RMB3.50 per piece CIFC London

D. USD3.50 per piece CIFC2 London

4. The standard form of a price consists of the following items EXCEPT (        ).

A. currency                    B. port or place of destination

C. unit                        D. amount

5. If we import commodities from Germany, what kind of currency we'd better choose to make the payment? (        )

A. Hard currency, which exchange rate is stable and would increase continuously.

B. Weak currency, which exchange rate is unstable and would decrease continuously.

C. A third country's currency that the two parties didn't agree to use.

D. Currency that can't convert freely.

## III. Judge whether the following price terms are correct or not. If not, why?

1. GBP 500 per carton CFR England

2. USD1000 per M/T FOB London

3. Yuan3.50 per yard CIFC Hong Kong

4. EUR100 per dozen FOB less than 1% discount

5. JPY2000 CIF Shanghai including 2% commission

## IV. Calculations

1. A company exports commodity X to Canada. The total amount is USD38500 CIF Vancouver, including USD1700 of freight and USD217 of insurance premium. If the total purchase price (including VAT 17%) is RMB245700, the rate of expense standard is 5% and the rate of export tax rebate is 14%, what is the foreign exchange cost of export products? (Rate of foreign exchange: USD1.00=RMB6.50)

2. The price quoted by a Shanghai exporter was "USD1200 per M/T CFR Liverpool". The buyer requested a revised FOB price including 2% commission. The freight for Shanghai to Liverpool was USD200 per M/T. To keep the export revenue constant, what would be FOB 2% price?

3. A company offered to sell goods at "USD2000 per M/T CIF Toronto with all risks for 110% of the value". The importer requested a revised quota for FOB Ningbo. The freight for Ningbo to Toronto was USD50 per M/T, and the premium rate was 1%. To get the same export revenue, what FOB price should be the exporter offer?

# Chapter 7　Credit Instruments

【Learning Objectives】

By studying this chapter, you should be able to master:

- Essential features of negotiable instruments
- Functions of negotiable instruments
- The legal System of Instruments
- Bill of Exchange
- Promissory note
- Check

## Lead-in：Case Study

### What Is a Credit Instrument?

A credit instrument is a term used in the banking and finance world to describe any item agreed upon that can be used as currency. Banks issue credit instruments in the form of credit cards. Customers, in turn, use these credit instruments to make purchases "on credit" and pay the amount "borrowed" back to the bank either at the end of the month, quarter, or whatever term has been agreed upon.

Any item can serve as a credit instrument, so long as both parties (the borrower and the lender) have agreed on the use of that instrument. The instrument is basically a promise by the debtor that he/she will pay back the debtor.

A simpler example of a credit instrument is the cheque. When one person gives you a cheque, he/she is basically saying that this piece of paper proves he/she owes you a certain amount of cash. And if you take it to the bank, the bank will gladly pay you on his/her behalf. Even simpler than the cheque is the promissory note, which is also very similar in nature.

Credit instruments are ever popular due to their convenience by not having you carry around piles of cash everywhere you go.

## What Are the Classifications of Credit Instruments?

The basic purpose of Credit instruments is their use in place of currency.

**Forms of Credit Instruments:**

Check is one of the earliest credit instruments and is used by people as a way of paying for products and services from the funds placed in your bank account.

The second one is Credit Card in which the basic idea is creating a contract between the buyer and the seller, and the seller extends credit and expects the card issuer to cover it. In return, the card holder has to pay back the debt to the card issuer along with the applied interest and other charges.

The third form of a credit instrument is the promissory note in which the lenders give funds to debtors with the expectation that the amount would be paid in full in the future. These are called notes and they sometimes have date on which the payment has to be done.

*(Source: http://www.blurtit.com/q830752.html)*

***Class Activities:***

1. What is a credit instrument?

2. What are the two parties involved in a credit instrument?

3. What are the main different forms of credit instruments?

# 7.1　Summary of Instruments

Due to the long distance between the parties concerned and the long time needed to handle the transaction, international payment heavily relies on the use of documents. There is a special category of financial documents which are called credit instruments.

## 7.1.1　Definition of Instruments

国际贸易货款的
支付基本上都采用各
类金融票据(可以流通
转让的债权凭证,是国
际上通行的结算和信
用工具)来进行支付。

A credit instrument, known as a document of title, is a written or printed paper by means of which rights can be transferred from one person to another. In a broad sense, instruments refer to all kinds of commercial certificates such as invoices, bills of lading, paper money, insurance policies, warehouse warrants, stocks, checks, drafts, promissory notes, etc. In a narrow sense, however, instruments are much unconditionally negotiable securities in writing addressed by one person to another, signed by the drawer, and directed the drawee to pay a specified sum of money to the payee or holder at a define time. Instruments most commonly used in international payments and settlements are negotiable instruments in a narrow sense, i.e., bills of exchange, promissory notes, and checks.

## 7.1.2　Essential Features of Negotiable Instruments

### 1. Negotiability

票据的流通性是指
可将票据视同现金进行
背书转让,其转让无须通
知债务人。

A credit instrument is mere an instrument of the rights representing a unilateral promise to pay a fixed amount of money to the instrument's legal holder. As a negotiable instrument, it may be transferred to another person either by mere delivery or by endorsement and delivery.

When payable to bearer, a negotiable instrument may be transferred by mere delivery; when payable to a named person or order, a negotiable instrument may be transferred by endorsement and delivery; and if the payee is restricted to a named person only, a negotiable instrument will lose its capability of being transferred and the payer will only pay the named payee. An

instrument thus transferred is said to be negotiated without notifying the drawer or drawee.

The person to whom a negotiable instrument is negotiated can sue on it in his own name. He has the full right and legal title to the instrument.

### 2. Non-Causative Nature

A negotiable instrument is independent of the commercial relations, from which it originated itself or its transfer.

It is obvious that there should be a certain reason for a negotiable instrument to be made out. For instance, when a drawer draws a draft on a drawee, there must be a commercial or funds relationship between the drawer and the drawee, say the seller and the buyer. When the payee transfers the draft to a transferee, the transferee will not mind how the instrument was generated and his only concern is that the instrument must be in a qualified form and must contain the essential items required by the relative negotiable instrument law. Just because of the non-causative nature, a negotiable instrument possesses the characteristic of negotiability as its name shows.

票据的无因性是指即使该票据有原因上的缺陷，只要持票人自己是依法取得的，就享有该票据的权利。

### 3. Requisite in Form

A negotiable instrument must contain the prerequisite items required by the law. Different countries have different laws on negotiable instruments and hence different requirements for the form of a negotiable instrument. Despite the differences, the requisites in form are to a great extent very similar. The processing for a negotiable instrument and all acts of a negotiable instrument i.e. issuing, endorsement, presentment, acceptance, must be subjected to the laws on negotiable instruments.

票据的要式性是指票据的形式、内容和处理行为必须符合相关法律要求。

## 7.1.3  Functions of Negotiable Instruments

### 1. As a Payment Instrument

Under non-cash settlements, the major function of a negotiable instrument is to serve as a substitute for money or asset ownership. For example, bills of exchange, promissory notes or checks are commonly used as a payment instrument to settle debts among traders from different countries.

票据的主要功能有支付功能、信用功能和流通功能等。

### 2. As a Credit Instrument

A negotiable instrument itself has no value, but the parties to it provide value for it on credit basis to serve as a payment instrument. For instance, a bill of exchange has no value itself, meanwhile a time draft can even be discounted in money market after acceptance, because it is based on the credit relations among such parties as the drawer, drawee and acceptor, and both the drawer and the acceptor guarantee they pay for the instrument when due. If the acceptor is credit worthy, they will be even more acceptable, thus a bill of exchange is not only a means of payment but also a credit instrument in financing operations.

### 3. As a Means for Offset

Bills act as clearing instruments by way of offsetting settlement of claims and liabilities between the parties.

---

***Example***

A Co. imported from B Co. a shipment of goods valued at US $100,000.00, and B Co. also purchased from C Co. a patch of goods at the same value, i.e., US$100,000.00. When effecting paper-based payment, a piece of draft can offset the claims and liabilities of these two businesses, by which B Co. draws a draft on A Co. to C Co. and meanwhile instructs A Co. to pay the draft amount to C Co., against the draft presented by C Co, who received from B Co.

---

## 7.1.4 The Legal System of Instruments

英美法系是指以英国普通法为基础发展起来的法律的总称。它产生于英国，后扩大到曾经是英国殖民地、附属国的许多国家和地区，包括美国、加拿大、印度、巴基斯坦、孟加拉、马来西亚、新加坡以及非洲的个别国家和地区。英美法系的主要特点是注重法典的延续性，以判例法为主要形式。

There still exists two different bodies of laws on negotiable instruments: British and the U.S.A. legal system and Continental legal system.

### 1. British and the U.S.A. Legal System

Bill of Exchange Act 1882 is the respective laws on negotiable instruments established by the United Kingdom in 1882. The British law covered the British Commonwealth of Nations such as Canada, India, Australia and New Zealand. Although it has been influenced a lot by the United Kingdom, the United States has its own law relating to negotiable instruments, i.e., the Commercial Paper of the U.S.A. Uniform Commercial Code of 1952.

### 2. Continental Legal System

In the late nineteenth century, France and Germany had also established their own respective laws on negotiable instruments, and many countries such as Austria, Hungary, Switzerland, Sweden, Denmark Belgium, the Netherlands, Portugal, Japan, Norway, Poland, Turkey, Yugoslav and Latin American countries were under their influence.

Since the existence of different laws on negotiable instruments caused inconvenience for those dealing with cross border trade, a conference on forming a uniform law on negotiable instruments was held in Geneva in 1930. Delegates from about 30 countries including France and Germany participated in it and signed the Uniform Law for Bills of Exchange and Promissory Notes. As the participants were mainly from the continent of Europe, the result of that conference was known as the civil law. The civil law on negotiable instruments also includes Uniform Law for Checks signed at Geneva in 1931. The Uniform Law for Bills of Exchange and Promissory Notes of 1930 and Uniform Law for Checks of 1931 are also called the Geneva's Uniform Law. The United Kingdom and the United States did not send any delegates to the conference, and have not yet joined the Geneva Convention.

The main controversy on Instrument Law between the Geneva's Uniform Law system and UK & US Law system is how to protect the instrument holder. The former stresses that the right of holder in good faith is to be protected and stipulates that the right of instrument will not be affected if the holder has taken it in good faith even if it was forged endorsement once it is endorsed in a successive form. The latter emphasizes that the right of the real owner is to be fully protected by law and stipulates that the right of holder in due course can be protected by law only on condition that the holder has taken a bill in good faith and for value, regular and complete on the face of it, before overdue and without notice of any defect in the title of the drawer. Meanwhile, any forged endorsement is treated as void and null.

Having recognized the inconvenience caused by the existence of different negotiable instrument laws, the United Nations has been trying to bring the two bodies of laws on negotiable instruments together, and has issued the Draft, Checks in July 1987. The United Nations has formally filed these two documents to different countries for comments.

### 3. People's Republic of China Law on Negotiable Instruments

The thirteenth meeting of the Eighth National People's Congress adopted

大陆法系又称欧陆法系，主要由欧洲大陆的国家(如法国、意大利、德国、荷兰等)及其他受上列国家影响的国家和地区(如日本，拉丁美洲等)采用。大陆法系主要历史渊源是古时罗马帝国的法律，以成文法为主要形式。

1995 年 5 月 10 日，第八届全国人民代表大会常务委员会第十三次会议通过了《中华人民共和国票据法》，并定于1997 年 1 月 1 日起施行。第五章共 8 条对涉外票据的法律适用作了专门的规定：涉外票据的票据行为均采取适用行为地法律和国际惯例的原则。

汇票是由一人签发给另一人的无条件书面命令，要求受票人见票时或于未来某一规定的或可以确定的时间，将一定金额的款项支付给某一特定的人或其指定的人，或持票人的票据。

People's Republic of China Law on Negotiable Instruments on 10th May 1995. The law was implemented on 1st January 1997, which was revised again on 28th August 2004. It is the first People's Republic of China Law on Negotiable Instruments. The "instrument" consists of seven chapters with 111 clauses, which contains the relative definitions and instrumental actions etc. of the bill of exchange, promissory notes and checks.

## 7.2　Bill of Exchange (Draft, Bill)

Bill is a frequently used instrument of payment in international trade. It is a kind of security which is often used as a substitute for cash in circulation. The three mainly adopted bills and notes are bill of exchange (draft), promissory note and check.

### 7.2.1　Definition of Bill of Exchange

#### 1. The Definition from Bills of Exchange Act 1882 in the UK

A Bill of Exchange is defined as an unconditional order in writing, addressed by one person (drawer) to another (drawee), signed by the person giving it, requiring the person to whom it is addressed to pay on demand, or at a fixed or determinable future time, a sum certain in money, to or to the order of a specified person (payee), or to the bearer.

汇票是出票人签发的，委托付款人在见票时或者在指定日期无条件支付确定的金额给收款人或者持票人的票据。

#### 2. The Definition from Negotiable Instruments Law of the People's Republic of China

A draft is a bill signed by the drawer, requiring the entrusted payer to make unconditional payment in a fixed amount at the sight of the bill or on a fixed date to the payee or the holder.

## 7.2.2 Contents of a Bill of Exchange

(1) The terms of "Bill of Exchange" or "Draft" are required to be on the draft to distinguish from other paying instruments (Promissory Note, Check), but it is not required in Bills of Exchange Act.

(2) It is an unconditional pay order, with the unlimited payment, without proviso. For example,

➢ Pay …

➢ Would you please pay …

➢ I should be appreciated if you would pay…

(3) A certain sum, which is indicated in Arabic numbers and words in a definite currency including the interest, not allowed to be described with ambiguous words and approximate sum. For example,

➢ USD10, 000

➢ USD10, 000 or USD11,000

➢ about USD10, 000

(4) Drawer, the one who issues the draft (namely debtee). The property of

金额的文字大写和数字小写同时记载，并且两者要完全一致，否则汇票无效。"Exchange for"后写小写金额，"The sum of"后写大写金额。

the draft is different according to different drawers. The drawer of a commercial draft is an exporter while the drawer of the banker's draft is a bank.

(5) Drawee, the one who is ordered to make payment by the drawer. The drawee of a commercial draft can be the buyer, importer or bank, and the drawee of the banker's draft is definitely a bank.

(6) Payee, who is entitled to the sum of the draft, in the import and export business, can be an exporter, seller, an appointed bank or a normal holder of the draft.

付款人姓名及付款地点写在汇票左下角，如：To …

The payee can be classified into the following three kinds:

(a) Restrictive Order

Writing the words on the draft, like "pay ×× Co. only", or "pay ×× Co., not negotiable". This type of draft is not transferable, and only the payee is qualified to accept the payment. For example,

汇票的抬头主要有以下三种方式：限制性抬头、指示性抬头和来人抬头。

> ➤ Pay somebody not transferable
> ➤ Pay to somebody not negotiable

(b) Demonstrative Order

Writing the words on the draft like "To ×× Co. or to order", and transferable to others with endorsement. For example,

> ➤ Pay to somebody or order
> ➤ Pay to the order of somebody

(c) Payable to Bearer

A draft may be payable to the bearer without a specific person as the payee. This kind of order indicates that the bill can be transferred more freely, as no endorsement is needed. For example,

> ➤ Pay to bearer or holder …
> ➤ Pay to _____
> ➤ Pay to somebody or bearer

(7) Payment Due Date

a. Payment Time Regulation

(a) Payable on demand

Payment at sight refers to that the payment is made by the payer at sight of the draft, and the due date is the day that the payee presents the draft to the payer. The words "at sight" or "on demand" or "on presentation" are indicated on the bill. For example,

➢ At sight pay US$100 to the order of ...

➢ On demand pay Mary only...

➢ On presentment pay US$1000 to bearer...

(b) Payable ×× days after sight

The draft holder makes presentation of the draft to the payer, demanding the payer to accept the draft and make payment on the due date. The due date is confirmed according to the presentation date. For example,

➢ At 45 days after sight pay to ABC bank or order ...

➢ At one and half month after pay to the order of Mary ...

(c) Payable ×× days after date

Payable within ×× days after the draft issuance date. For example,

➢ At 30 days after date pay to ABC Co. or order ...

➢ At two month after date pay to the order of ...

(d) Payable ×× days after B/L date

➢ At 30 days after issuance of B/L pay to the order of ...

(e) Fixed Date

➢ Payable on a fixed date, for example,

➢ On Dec. 27, 2011 pay to Li Ming or order...

➢ At one month after the date of negotiation pay to the order of ...

b. Payment time stipulated in the Negotiable Instruments Law of the People's Republic of China:

(a) Payable at sight,

(b) Payable on a fixed date,

(c) Payable on a fixed date after the draft is issued,

(d) Payable on a fixed date after the sight of the draft.

The time calculation: not including the sight date, the issuance date or B/L date.

*NOTE*: The draft is not recognized if the payment time is not definite or the conditions are attached to it. According to Negotiable Instruments Law of the People's Republic of China, without the specific payment time requirement, the draft will be regarded as being payable at sight.

见票后定期付款(after sight)又称"注期汇票"，在汇票上记载自付款人承兑之日起经过一定期限付款，属远期汇票。

出票后定期付款(After Date)又称"记期汇票"，在汇票上记载自出票日起经过一定期限付款，属远期汇票。

定日付款汇票又称"板期汇票"，在汇票上订明在某年某月某日付款，属远期汇票。

汇票付款日的计算方法：算尾不算头；月为日历月；半月以15 天计算；月初为 1 日，月中为 15 日；先算整月，再算半月；碰到假日顺延。

**Class activities:**

*When shall the exporter deal with the payment if he exports some goods?*
*Date of B/L / Date of draw / Date of presentation / Date of payment*

| 9/30 | 10/7 | 10/18 | |
|------|------|-------|---|
| *at sight* | | | ? |
| *at 30 days after sight* | | | ? |
| *at 70 days after date* | | | ? |
| *at 45 days after date of B/L* | | | ? |
| *at one month after sight* | | | ? |

(8) The Date and Place of Draft Issuance

The issuance date must be written on the draft so as to confirm the qualification of the drawer and calculate the payment date.

The place of draft issuance: written next to the date. It is necessary to write the issuance place in order to confirm the applicable law and complete the draft. According to Negotiable Instruments Law of the People's Republic of China, the issuance place must be written on the draft, which can be the business operation place, the habitation, or the regular dwelling place of the drawer.

(9) Payment Place

It is written next to the name of the payer, namely the place of making payment against the draft. According to Negotiable Instruments Law of the People's Republic of China, the payment place can be the business operation place, the habitation, or the regular dwelling place of the drawer in case that the specific payment place is not written on the draft.

(10) Signature of the Drawer

After signing the draft, the drawer is regarded as the main debtor and to be committed to the draft fulfillment. If the signature is fake or not authorized, the draft is invalid.

(11) Other Items Maybe Written on the Draft

a. The draft is issued in duplicate. The drawee makes payment against one draft, and then the other one is cancelled accordingly.

b. Consideration clause, for value received.

c. The draft is not transferable.

(12) In Negotiable Instruments Law of the People's Republic of China, the draft is regarded as being invalid in case that the following items are not

stated on the draft: ① the word "draft"; ② unconditional appointment; ③ definite sum; ④ name of payer; ⑤ name of payee; ⑥ draft issuance date; ⑦ payment date.

## 7.2.3 The Acts of Bills of Exchange

In a broad sense, acts of bills of exchange refer to the behavior, changes and loss of rights and obligations to a bill of exchange. Generally, there are five stages for a bill of exchange: to issue, to endorse, to accept, to present and to pay under normal circumstance. In exceptional circumstances it may also include acceptance for honor, payment for honor, dishonor, protest, the exercise of right recourse or some other possible stages.

### 1. Issuance

(1) It is made out in written form. The drawer fills in the contents including the payer's name, payment sum, payment time, payment place, payee's name etc., and signs his/her name.

(2) The issuance is regarded to be fulfilled only after the bill is sent to the drawee.

出票是创设票据的行为,是指出票人填写汇票,经签字后交付与持票人的行为。

### 2. Presentation

The holder of the draft presents the draft to the drawee, asking for the acceptance or payment.

(1) Presentation for Payment.

The draft holder presents the draft to the payer asking for the sight payment.

(2) Presentation for Acceptance.

The draft holder presents the draft to the payer asking for the acceptance at sight of the draft and making payment on the maturity time.

提示是持票人向付款人出示汇票,要求其付款或承兑的行为。它包括付款提示和承兑提示两种。

### 3. Acceptance

It is a promise made by the payer that it will make payment against a time draft. The payer writes the word "acceptance" on the bill remarking the acceptance date and affixes its signature, and then returns the bill to the draft holder. The payer is regarded as the acceptor after making acceptance for the draft. The first debtor of the draft is the drawer before making acceptance, and

承兑是远期汇票的付款人承诺负担票据债务的行为。

汇票一经承兑，付款人即成为承兑人，也即汇票的主债务人，必须承担汇票到期无条件付款的责任，而出票人和其他背书人则退居于次债务人的地位。

it changes into the payer after making acceptance while the drawer becomes the second debtor. Before the payer's acceptance, all the bearers are allowed to recourse to the drawer as the draft is transferable.

The acceptance is classified into the following two kinds:

(1) General Acceptance.

The acceptor confirms the payment unconditionally. The normal acceptance is the general acceptance. For example,

ACCEPTED

Date: 1 Sept. 2013

Due: 18 Oct. 2013

For ABC Trading Co.

*Signature*

(2) Qualified Acceptance.

The acceptance result is dependent on the clear expression of the acceptance conditions. The acceptor will not make payment until a certain condition is met.

Legally, there are two key elements for the acceptance: ①the word of "Acceptance" must be written on the bill; ②the acceptance is not fulfilled until the draft with acceptance is sent back to the draft holder. For example,

ACCEPTED

3rd Sept. 2013

Payable on delivery of all documents

For ABC Trading Co.

*Signature*

### 4. Payment

付款(Payment)是付款人或承兑人对到期票据正当付款以结束票据上一切债权债务关系的行为。

For the sight payment, the payer shall make payment against the presentation of the draft; for the time bill, the payer makes payment on the maturity time after the acceptance and all the debts on the draft come to an end after the payment.

### 5. Endorsement

The endorsement of the draft includes two points:

(1) To make endorsement on the overleaf of the draft.

(2) To transfer the bill to the endorsee.

These two points are both necessary for the fulfillment of the endorsement.

In the international market, the draft is a kind of transfer instrument, which is negotiable and transferable in the bill market. The endorsement is one legal procedure of transferring the bill. That is to say, the holder of draft signs its name on the back of the bill or adding the name of the bearer (endorsee), and then transfers the draft to the bearer. After the endorsement, the claim for the payment is transferred to the bearer, too.

The draft can be transferred again and again after endorsements. For the endorsee, all the endorsers and the drawer are its remote holders; for the endorser, all the bearers after its endorsement and transferring are its subsequent parties. The remote holders are committed to the guaranty responsibility of the payment for the subsequent party.

背书是以转让票据权利为目的的票据行为。它是指背书人在汇票背面签名并将已背书的汇票交付给受让人的行为，可分为限制性背书、记名背书和空白背书。

### 6. Discounting

Discounting means that the usance bill after the acceptance but undue is sold to a bank or a discounting house for the immediate with the discounting interest deducted from the payment sum based on a certain discounting rate.

In the international market, in order to receive the payment immediately, a time bill holder may transfer the draft to others by making endorsement before the bill is mature. The procedures are as follows:

贴现是指远期汇票承兑后，尚未到期，由银行从票面金额中扣减一定贴现率计算的贴现息后，将余款付给持票人的行为。

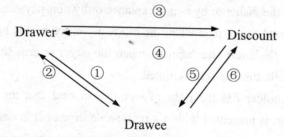

(1) To issue a bill, present it for acceptance;

(2) To accept it;

(3) To sell it to the discounting house;

(4) To pay the amount (i.e., less than the face value);

(5) To present it for payment at maturity;

(6) To pay the face value.

**Class activities:**

*Suppose an exporter draws a bill for USD7,000 payable to himself at two and half months after sight on an importer abroad. At the time that the accepted bill is returned, he finds that the due of the bill is on September 30th and there are still 45 days to go before it becomes due. As he needs the money right now, he may discount the bill. If the discount rate is 10%, the discount interest is calculated as follows:*

$D = V \times t \times d / 360$

*Where: D = discount interest*

*V = face value of the bill*

*t = tenor (days)*

*d = discount rate (% p.a.)*

*Hence:* $D = V \times t \times d \div 360$

$= 7\,000 \times 45 \times 10\% \div 360$

$= USD87.5$

*The amount the exporter can get is:*

$7\,000 - 87.5 = USD6912.5$

在国外，银行计算年利息一年按照 370 天计算，而在中国一般按照 360 天计算。

### 7. Dishonor

It is called the dishonor by non-acceptance or by non-payment in case that bill is not accepted or not paid when the bill is presented by the bill holder for the acceptance. Dishonor also happens when the payer returns the bill, keeps away from the bill, dies, or is bankrupted.

The draft holder has the right of recourse in case that the draft is not accepted when it is presented within a reasonable time or it is not paid on the maturity date. The bill holder has the right to claim for the shipment documents or payment against the endorser and the drawer.

拒付(Dishonor)又称退票，是指当汇票在付款提示或承兑提示时，付款人拒绝付款或承兑的行为。

### 8. Right of Recourse

Upon the dishonor, the bill holder has the right to claim for the settlement of the payment and the relevant charges against the prior endorser (or the

追索(Recourse)是指持票人在付款人拒付时，

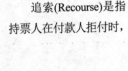

local notary public, bank, chamber of commerce or court testifying that the draft has been dishonored. It is the legal proof with which the bill holder can take the right of the recourse against the prior endorser. If the dishonored bill has been accepted, the bill holder can go to court claiming for the payment against the acceptor.

## 7.2.4　The Classification of the Drawer

### 1. According to the Different Drawer

(1) Banker's Draft

The draft is drawn by a bank, and the drawer is a bank. A banker's draft is sent to payee by remitter, with which the payee can exchange the money from the payer (the bank).

银行汇票一般是指出票人和付款人均为银行。在我国，银行汇票一般为即期。

The characteristics of banker's draft: both the drawer and the drawee are banks.

(2) Commercial Draft

The draft is made out by the seller of one country (exporter) and presented to the importer or the payment bank. Usually, the draft is presented to the importer or the payment bank (L/C opening bank) through the bank in the exporter's place or the correspondent bank of it in the importer's place.

The characteristics of commercial draft: the drawer is a firm or an individual, and the payer (the drawee) is a firm, an individual, or a bank.

### 2. According to the Documents Accompanied

(1) Clean Bill

Without shipment documents to accompany, the banker's draft is usually a clean bill.

(2) Documentary Bill

The draft is accompanied with shipment documents, which is guaranteed by exporter's credit as well as the goods. The commercial draft is usually a documentary bill.

### 3. According to Payment Time

(1) Time Bill or Usance Bill

This is an acceptance order drawn by the exporter on the importer (customer), payable a certain number of days after "sight" (presentation) to the

远期汇票是指出口商开具，要求进口方在"见票"若干天后承兑的汇票。

托收时与汇票一起出具的单据还包括可转让提单、保险凭证和商业发票等。

即期汇票与远期汇票类似,唯一的不同在于,在进口方放款之前,即期汇票将由进口方银行持有。

holder. Think of it as nothing more than IOU(I owe you), or promise to pay in the future.

Documents such as negotiable bills of lading, insurance certificates, and commercial invoices accompany the bill and are submitted through the exporter's bank for collection. When presented to the importer at the bank, the importer acknowledges that the documents are acceptable and commits to pay by writing "accepted" on the draft and signing it. The importer normally has 30 to 180 days depending on the draft's term to make payments to the bank for transmittal.

(2) Sight Bill

A sight bill, or demand bill, is payable at sight, on demand, on presentation. Sight bill is the most common method employed by exporters throughout the world. Sight bill is nothing more than a written order on a standardized bank format requesting money from the overseas buyer. While this method costs less than the letter of credit (defined below), it has greater risk because the importer can refuse to honor the draft.

## 7.2.5 The Order of Making Recourse

(1) According to the law of Britain: the bill holder can exercise the recourse against anyone of his prior endorsers or drawers.

(2) According to the law of Germany: the bill holder can only exercise the recourse against the direct endorser, and then the endorser further takes recourse against his prior endorser in turn.

(3) According to Negotiable Instruments Law of the People's Republic of China, the bill holder shall present the relevant proof about the refusal of the acceptance or payment when it exercises the recourse right, and the acceptor or payer shall be committed to the civil obligation due to the dishonor unless it presents the reason letter for the dishonor of the bill. The bill holder is allowed to get other relevant proofs legally.

The draft without recourse: To avoid the obligation of settling the recourse claim, the drawer or endorser of the bill remarks the word like "without recourse", which kind of bill is hardly discounted or transferred in the market. According to the laws, the payer of the draft cannot exercise the recourse after the payment even though the payment is wrong.

## 7.3　Promissory Note

### 7.3.1　The Definition from Bills of Exchange Act 1882 of the United Kingdom

The promissory note is an unconditional promise in writing made by one person (the maker) to another (the payee) and signed by the maker engaging to pay on demand or at a fixed or determinable future time a sum certain in money to or to the order of a specified person or bearer.

In accordance with "Convention on the Unification of the Law Relating to Bills of Ex-change and Promissory Notes", the promissory note shall include the following contents:

(1) the words of "promissory note";

(2) unconditional payment promise;

(3) the payee or the specified person by the payee;

(4) the drawer;

(5) the date and place of the issuance;

(6) a period for payment;

(7) a sum certain in money;

(8) the payment place.

### 7.3.2　The Definition from the *Negotiable Instruments Law of the People's Republic of China*

The promissory note is the note issued by the drawer, promising to make unconditionally a definite sum of money to the payee or the note holder at sight of the note. It is stipulated in *Negotiable Instruments Law of the People's Republic of China* that the promissory note is named as the bank promissory note, issued and signed by the central bank of China or other financial institutions. There are only bank promissory notes in China but no commercial promissory note.

本票是出票人签发的、承诺自己在见票时无条件支付确定的金额给收款人或持票人的票据。

本票是一个人向另一个人签发的，保证于见票时或定期或在可以确定的将来的时间，对某人或其指定人或持票人支付一定金额的无条件的书面承诺。

> Due 11th July 2017
>
> Promissory Note for <u>GBP 800.00</u> London, 8th April 2017
>
> <u>At 90 days after sight</u> we promise to pay Beijing Art and Craft Corp. or order the sum of Eight hundred pounds Only
>
> To: Bank of Europe
>
> London.
>
> signature

### 7.3.3   The Key Elements in the Promissory Note

a. the words of "promissory note";

b. unconditional payment promise;

c. a sum certain in money;

d. the name of payee;

e. the issuance date;

f. the signature of the drawer.

### 7.3.4   Classification of Promissory Notes

商业本票是指由公司、商号或个人签发的本票。商业本票有即期和远期之分。

(1) Commercial promissory notes are also called general promissory notes, drawn by the commercial firms. The general promissory notes are divided into sight promissory note and time promissory note.

(2) Bank promissory notes are issued and signed by banks. The bank promissory notes are sight, which are mostly adopted in international trade.

银行本票是由银行签发的本票。银行本票都是即期的。

(3) The involved parties to the promissory notes

There are two parties usually: the drawer and the payee. The payer of the promissory note is the drawer himself. The time promissory notes don't need the acceptance.

Some banks issue the promissory note which is at sight, without stating the payee or the words of "to the order". This kind of promissory note is equal to the currency circulated in the market.

(4) The differences of the promissory note and the bill of exchange

a. The promissory note is a promise made by the drawer to make payment to the note holder; the B/E is an order made by one party to the other party requiring it to make payment.

b. There are only two parties in a promissory note, but three parties in a B/E.

c. The drawer of a promissory note is the payer, and a time promissory note doesn't need the acceptance; the drawee of a B/E is the payer.

d. In whatever situation, for a promissory note, the drawer is the first debtor; for a B/E, the drawer is the first debtor before the bill is accepted, the acceptor becomes the first debtor after the acceptance and the drawer turns into the second debtor.

e. The promissory note is made out in only one original; the B/E is made out in duplicate.

## 7.3.5　Differences Between a Promissory Note and a Bill of Exchange

The most fundamental difference between a bill of exchange and a promissory note is that the former is an order to pay by the drawer to the drawee while the latter is a promise by the maker himself to pay. In addition, the difference is mainly manifested in the essential contents of the instrument, bill behavior, and etc. The detailed differences between a bill of exchange and a promissory note are shown in Table 7-1.

Table 7-1　The Differences Between a Bill of Exchange and a Promissory Note

| Bills of Exchange | Promissory Notes |
| --- | --- |
| (1) An order to pay | (1) A promise to pay |
| (2) A three-party (the drawer, the drawee, the payee) | (2) A two-party (the maker, the payee) |

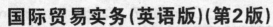

续表

| Bills of Exchange | Promissory Notes |
|---|---|
| (3) the drawer is primarily liable where payable at sight, the acceptor becomes primarily liable where payable at a future time. | (3) The maker is always primarily liable |
| (4) Where payable at a future time, a bill is generally accepted. | (4) Never accepted |
| (5) Foreign bills need protesting on dishonor to retain liability of prior the parties. | (5) Protest is never needed |
| (6) can be drawn in a set | (6) One copy |

# 7.4  Check (Cheque)

## 7.4.1  Definition of Check

英国票据法认为，支票是以银行为付款人的即期汇票。它是银行存款人(出票人)对银行(付款人)签发的授权银行对某人或其指定人或持票人即期支付一定金额的无条件书面命令。

It is stipulated in the Bills of Exchange Act of the UK that a check is a sight B/E with the bank as the payer. That is to say, it is an unconditional order drawn on a banker by the drawer, requiring the banker to pay on demand a sum certain in money to the order of a specified person or to the bearer.

In Negotiable Instruments Law of the People's Republic of China, a check means a bill issued and signed by the drawer, appointing the bank or other financial institutes to make payment of a sum certain in money unconditionally to the payee or the check holder.

我国的票据法认为，支票是出票人签发的，委托办理支票存款业务的银行或其他金融机构在见票时无条件支付确定金额给收款人或持票人的票据。

The key elements in a check according to Negotiable Instruments Law of the People's Republic of China are as follows:

(1) The words of "Check" or "Cheque";

(2) Unconditional payment promise;

(3) A sum certain in money;

(4) The name of payee;

(5) The issuance date;

(6) The signature of the drawer;

(7) The check without any one of stipulated elements is regarded as invalid.

The drawer draws a draft and order the drawee bank or financial institution to pay a certain amount of money to the holder on demand. The drawer shall be committed to the obligation for the check and on the law. The obligation of the check means that the drawer shall take the responsibility of making payment to the payee; the legal obligation refers to the drawer shall keep an account in the paying bank with the deposit not lower than the sum on the check. If the deposit is less, the check will be dishonored when the bearer presents the check to the paying bank for the payment. In this case, the drawer shall be held for the legal responsibility. The check is a special draft and is only at sight.

## 7.4.2   Classification of Check

According to the relevant law of China, checks are classified into cash check and transfer check.

在我国，支票可以划分为转账支票和现金支票。

In other countries, checks are divided into crossed check and uncrossed check. The crossed check is crossed with two parallel lines on the up-left of the check, and the payee cannot cash the check but receive the payment through the bank transfer. There are two kinds of crossed check. They are general crossing and special crossing. The uncrossed check can both cash the money and make transfer.

在其他国家，支票可划分为划线支票和非划线支票。划线支票只能用于转账，而非划线支票既可用于转账也可用于支取现金。

## 7.4.3   Differences Between a Check and a Bill of Exchange

The detailed differences between a bill of exchange and a promissory note are described in Table 7-2.

Table 7-2   The Differences Between a Check and a Bill of Exchange

|  | Check | Bill of Exchange |
| --- | --- | --- |
| payer | bank only | bank or trader |
| tenor | at sight | at sight or time bill |
| acceptance | No | Yes |
| primarily liable | drawer | drawer        (pre-acceptance) |
|  |  | acceptor      (post-acceptance) |

# 【Key Terms and Words】

Drawer　出票人

Drawee　受票人

Payer　付款人

Payee　受款人

Presentation　提示

Acceptance　承兑

Payment　付款

Endorsement　背书

Dishonor　拒付

Protest　拒付证明书

Instrument　支付工具

Check　支票

Bill of exchange/draft　汇票

Banker's bill　银行汇票

Commercial's bill　商业汇票

Clean bill　光票

Time bill / Usance bill　远期汇票

Promissory note　本票

Documentary bill　跟单汇票

Sight bill　即期汇票

# 【Exercises】

I. Please answer the following questions.

1. What are the differences between the commercial bill and the banker's bill?

2. Who are the involved parties in a bill of exchange? Why is the drawer the main debtor (before the acceptance of the draft)?

3. Which one is the payer in the involved parties in B/E, promissory note and check?

4. What is the title of the B/E? How many ways are there for the title of the B/E?

5. What is the endorsement of the B/E? How many types are there for the endorsement?

II. Please answer, fill in the blanks or make choice of the following questions.

1. There are two main kinds of methods of settlements, namely (1) _____ and (2) _____. The remittances is that the funds flow in a _____ direction to the payment instructions transmitted there-from.

2. There are four parties in a remittance, i. e., (1) _____ (2) _____ (3) _____ (4) _____.

3. The remittances which are handled by the home remitting bank are called (1)_____, while those are handled by foreign paying bank are called (2)_____.

4. Remittance through a bank from one country to another may usually be made by one of the following methods: (1) _____ (2) _____ (3) _____.

5. A customer would apply to a remitting bank at Beijing for the outward remittance of GBP1,250.00 to a payee at London, he has provided for USD account with that bank remaining a balance of USD25,000.00. Please calculate how much the bank will draw in USD out of the customer's account.

Exchange rate: GBP/CNY: 13.6762/13.6797

USD/CNY: 8.2753/8.2789

Suppose Bank of China, Tianjin would be the remitting bank of the above remittance, they have:

(1) a branch office—Bank of China, London

(2) an account bank—National Westminster Bank Ltd., London

(3) a correspondent—Barclays Bank Ltd., London

Please select one of the above three banks which will be more applicable to a paying bank.

III. Answer the questions according to the information from the draft.

**DRAFT**

DRAWN UNDER ___BANK OF CHINA, SINGAPORE___ L/C NO. ___774351___

DATED ___5TH MAY 2013___ PAYABLE WITH INTEREST @ .....%...........

NO ..MO789. EXCHANGE FOR _USD729,000.00_ SHANGHAI ___17TH JULY 2013___

AT ___*******___ SIGHT OF THIS FIRST OF EXCHANGE (SECOND OF EXCHANGE BEING UNPAID ) PAY TO THE ORDER OF ..BANK OF CHINA__

THE SUM OF    UNITED STATES DOLLARS SEVEN HUNDRED AND TWENTY NINE THOUSAND ONLY    VALUE RECEIVED

SHANGHAI MACHINERY

IMPORT & EXPORT CORP.

张小明

TO    BANK OF CHINA, SINGAPORE ...

DEPT. MANAGER

(1) 开证行名称：

(2) 信用证号码：

(3) 开证日期：

(4) 汇票金额(小写)和币制：

(5) 汇票金额(大写)：

(6) 付款期限：

(7) 受款人(收款人)：

(8) 付款人(受票人)：

(9) 出票人：

(10) 汇票抬头人：

IV. Answer the questions according to the information from the draft.

Specimen 7-1    The Application of Remittance

汇出汇款申请书(代支款凭证)

APPLICATION FOR  OUTWARD  REMITTANCE

致：中国农业银行        广州 分行

TO:THE AGRICULTURAL BANK OF CHINA

日期　DATE: 2013 年 3 月 8 日

兹委托贵行办理下列汇款。I/We hereby request you to effect the following remittance.

| X 电汇  □ 信汇  □ 票汇    付款地点 | | 银行编号(查询时请引述) |
|---|---|---|
| T/T    M/T    D/D    Drawn on: | | Ref No. TT96785 |
| 收款人 Beneficiary's name 及地址 & address | United Trading Company Hong Kong 70 Wing Tai Road, Chai Wan Hong Kong | 币别及金额 Curr.& Amt. HK Dollars 20,000.00 |
| 账号 A/C No. | 0709166060322-8 | 银行填写栏 BANK USE ONLY |
| 收款银行 Beneficiary's Bank 及地址 & address | PO SANG BANK LTD. HONG KONG | 汇率(Rate) 等值人民币 Equivalent in ¥ |
| 汇款人 By order of | CHINA NAT. METALS & MINERALS I/E CORP. | 手续费(Commission) |
| 附言 Details of Payment | COMM.  UNDER  S/C NO. CT0011-01 | 邮电费(Postage & Cable) 其他费用(Other Charges) 合计 |

国外银行的一切费用由我方/收款人负担(如无说明由收款人负担)。汇款全过程均以电传形式通知。

All foreign bank's charges are to be borne by us/payee(if not specified, all charges are to be borne by payee). All parties in the channel are advised by telex.

□请付敞账(debit my/our account)，账号(a/c No.)

□兹附支票(enclose my/our cheque)，号码为(No.)

付款行(Drawn on)

X 现金支付(I/We pay cash herewith)。　联系电话(TEL) 83738789

申请人签章

张　三

Applicant's

Stamp & Signature

经办：　　　　会计：　　　　复核：　　　　记账：

| | |
|---|---|
| (1) Method of remittance | |
| (2) Remitter | |
| (3) Beneficiary | |
| (4) Amount | |
| (5) Message | |
| (6) Charges for | |
| (7) HHK/CNY=105.53/91(buying rate), HHK/CNY=109.46/87(selling rate), then how much did remitter surrender to remitting bank? | |
| (8) Bank's remission? | |
| (9) What does remitter pay attention to under the current foreign exchange control system? | |

# Chapter 8   International Payment and Settlement

**Lead-in: News Report**

**J.P. Morgan Supports Payment-Versus-Payment Settlement for Foreign Exchange Transactions in Indonesia**

J.P. Morgan Treasury Services today announced that it has developed a solution to facilitate a new currency clearing service for its Indonesian bank clients using Hong Kong's cross-border payment-versus-payment (PvP) settlement system. By having access to this system, J.P. Morgan's clients are able to better mitigate foreign exchange settlement risk and increase operational efficiency.

The PvP infrastructure established by Bank Indonesia and the Hong Kong Monetary Authority links the real time gross settlement (RTGS) systems in both economies to provide simultaneous delivery of Indonesian Rupiah and U.S. Dollar currencies within the Asia business day. This innovative infrastructure represents a new clearing standard between these two currencies. J.P. Morgan also provides clearing services using PvP settlement in Malaysia.

By leveraging J.P. Morgan's Global payment network and leading position in U.S. Dollar clearing, financial institutions also can benefit from optimized liquidity, faster payments and high standards of service delivery.

J.P. Morgan was a key participant in the working group of commercial banks brought together by Bank Indonesia to identify a solution to mitigate settlement risk for foreign exchange transactions between Indonesian Rupiahs and U.S. Dollars and to increase efficiency in the inter-bank market for both currencies. J.P. Morgan was in a unique position to deliver thought leadership and share its experience as a major provider of clearing services to the banking industry in Malaysia since the inception of the PvP settlement services in 2007.

"Beyond the role banks normally play in payment clearing and foreign exchange settlement, we are committed to fostering innovation in the industry and are proud to be part of this initiative led by Bank Indonesia and supported by the Hong Kong Monetary Authority. Our client banks in Indonesia value our successful experience with PvP settlement in Malaysia, where we continue to see a high demand for these services and future developments in this area," said Raof Latiff, managing director and Asia head of Treasury Services clearing and foreign exchange at J.P. Morgan.

"J.P. Morgan Treasury Services is actively engaged in promoting best practices and supporting initiatives aiming to reduce risk and enhance efficiency at an industry level. We are pleased to be able to offer a wider range of cash management services to our clients in Malaysia and Indonesia to meet their most advanced clearing needs," added Simon Jones, managing director and regional Treasury Services executive—Asia Pacific at J.P. Morgan.

J.P. Morgan is the world's largest U.S. Dollar clearing and commercial bank. J.P. Morgan Treasury Services leverages the services and products of the bank's Worldwide Securities Services division, as well as its Investment Bank, Asset Management and Private Bank lines of business to provide its clients with integrated banking solutions.

**About J.P. Morgan Treasury Services**

The Treasury Services business of J.P. Morgan is a top-ranked, full-service provider of innovative payment, collection, liquidity management, trade finance, and commercial card and information solutions to corporations, financial services institutions, middle market companies, small businesses, governments and municipalities worldwide. With more than 100,000 clients and services provided in more than 70 countries and 40 U.S. states, J.P. Morgan Treasury Services is one of the world's largest providers of treasury management services and a division of JPMorgan Chase Bank, N.A., member FDIC.

*(Source: HONG KONG, April 19 2010/PRNewswire-Asia/)*

*Class Activities:*

1. International payment and settlement systems are a core element of a bank. How is the money transferred from one bank to another?

2. What do different banks benefit from international payment and settlement?

3. What kinds of treasury services does J.P. Morgan involve?

# 8.1 Remittance

【Learning Objectives】

By studying this chapter, you should be able to master:

- Definition of remittance
- The classification of remittance
- Reimbursement of remittance cover
- Cancel the remittance or refund the imbursement
- The function of remittance in international trade

## 8.1.1 The Definition of Remittance

汇付又称汇款，是指汇款人向汇出行申请汇款，汇出行接受汇款人的委托，将款项委托书寄交汇入行或以密押电报通知汇入行，授权汇入行按一定金额付款给收款人。

Remittance refers to that the payer makes payment to the payee through a bank or other institutions. For the remittance in the international trade, the buyer makes payment to the seller by bank according to the conditions and the payment time stipulated in the contract.

## 8.1.2 Parties to a Remittance

Parties involved in international bank remittance include the following: the remitter, the payee, the remitting bank and the paying bank.

The remitter is the party who makes payment by remittance. Usually, the importer or the buyer is the remitter; the payee or beneficiary is the party who receives payment; the seller is the payee or beneficiary. The remitting bank is the bank which issues a remittance instruction at the request of the buyer. Usually, the remitting bank is the bank in the importer's country; the paying bank is the bank that transfers the money to the account of the seller following the instruction of the remitting bank; the paying bank is the bank in the exporter's country.

The application form of remittance is a contract concluded between the buyer and the remitting bank, and the paying bank is the agency bank of the remitting bank, committed to the obligation of making payment.

## 8.1.3　The Classification of Remittance

According to different ways to give payment instruction, remittance can be classified as remittance by mail transfer (M/T), remittance by telegraphic transfer(T/T), and remittance by demand draft (D/D).

根据汇款方式不同,汇款可分为电汇、信汇和票汇三种。

### 1. Remittance by Mail Transfer

Mail transfer refers that the remitting bank sends a remittance instruction letter by mail to the paying bank at the request of the payer, authorizing the paying bank to make payment of a sum of money to the payee.

信汇是指汇出行应汇款人的要求,用航邮信函通知汇入行向收款人付款的汇付方式。

● Advantages

(1) The cost is lower.

(2) Control Documents: Specimen of authorized signature book is mostly used.

(3) Funds can be taken up for short time by the bank.

● Disadvantages

It takes a long time to receive the payment.

● The procedure of M/T

The whole process of mail transfer includes many separate steps. Procedure of mail transfer is as shown in Figure 8-1.

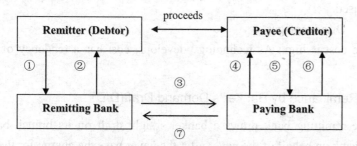

Figure 8-1　The Procedure of M/T

(1) The remitter fills out the application form, submits the proceeds to the bank, and pays the commission for remittance.

(2) Upon receipt of the application form, the proceeds, and the commission, the remitting bank offers the remitter a receipt.

(3) The remitting bank sends a payment order or advice by mail to the paying bank, instructing the paying bank to make payment to the payee.

(4) Upon receipt of the payment order and after authenticating the signature, the paying bank notifies the payee of the payment order or advice.

(5) The payee provides the paying bank with a receipt.

(6) The paying bank makes the payment to the payee.

(7) The paying bank sends the debit advice and the payment receipt from the payee to the remitting bank.

### 2. Remittance by Telegraphic Transfer

电汇是指汇出行接受汇款(申请)人委托后，以电报、电传等方式将付款委托通知收款人当地的汇入行，委托其将一定金额的款项解付给指定的收款人的汇付方式。

Telegraphic transfer refers that the remitting bank sends the remittance instruction to the paying bank by telex, tele-transmission or SWIFT at the request of the payer. It is exactly the same as a mail transfer, except that instruction from the remitting bank to the paying bank is transmitted by telex, tele-transmission or SWIFT instead of by mail. Therefore, it is faster, but more expensive than the main transfer. It is often used when the remittance amount is large and the transfer of funds is subject to a time limit. Thus 90% remittances are done through by SWIFT in practice nowadays.

● Advantages

(1) It is the fastest way to collect funds. It is beneficial to the seller's capital running as it can receive the payment in a short time.

(2) It is safe. The telex and SWIFT are mostly used.

(3) It is easy to control documents: Test Key & SWIFT certificate are mostly used.

● Disadvantages

The cost is high. As technology develops, cost has a tendency of going lower.

### 3. Remittance by Banker's Demand Draft(D/D)

票汇是指以银行即期汇票作为支付工具的一种汇付方式，汇出行应汇款人的申请，开立以其代理行或其他往来银行为付款人的银行即期汇票，列明收款人名称、金额等，交给汇款人自行寄交收款人，凭票向付款行取款的一种汇付方式。

The remitting bank draws a banker's sight draft on its branch bank or agency bank on behalf of the payer after the payer pays the charge for the draft, and sends the draft to the payee; the payee gets the payment from the paying bank with the draft.

The detailed procedure of remitting funds by the demand draft is as shown in Figure 8-2.

(1) The remitter fills out the application form, submits the proceeds to the bank, and pays the commission for remittance.

(2) Upon receipt of them, the remitting bank draws a demand draft and

gives it back to the remitter.

(3) The remitter sends the demand draft directly to the payee.

(4) The remitting bank sends the advice of drawing to the paying bank.

(5) The payee presents the draft for payment to the paying bank.

(6) Upon presentation of the demand draft by the beneficiary, the paying bank should check the authenticity of the draft, and then makes the payment.

(7) The paying bank sends the debit advice to the remitting bank.

在票汇流程中，根据我国票据法的规定，支票有十天的兑付期，在未兑付前，只要有正当理由，出票人可以通知开户银行止付。

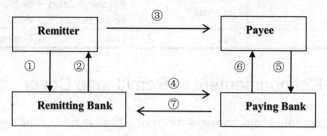

Figure 8-2　The Procedure of D/D

● Advantages

(1) It's convenient for the payee to collect funds since he can go to any correspondent of the remitting bank.

(2) The draft can be negotiated.

(3) The delivery of the draft is outside the banking system. The bank draft should be handed over to the remitter, who may dispatch or even bring it to the beneficiary abroad.

(4) Control documents: the counterfoil is mostly used.

During the remittance by draft (D/D), the exporter should provide banking information to the importer to draw the draft. Supposing the exporter is from Wenzhou City, the banking informing is as follows:

*To: Bank of China, Wenzhou Branch*

*Address: 113 Chan Str., Wenzhou, China*

*Telex: 11357 BOCWZ, CN*

*A/C No.: 112891140*

*Beneficiary: Wenzhou Imp/Exp. Corp*

Comparison of M/T, T/T and D/D is as shown in Table 8-1.

电汇、信汇和票汇的比较。

(1) 从支付工具来看，电汇方式使用电报、电传或 SWIFT，用密押证实；信汇方式使用信汇委托书或支付委托书，用签字证实；票汇方式使用银行及其汇票，用签字证实。

(2) 从汇款人的成本费用来看，电汇收费较高。

(3) 从安全方面来看，电汇比较安全。

(4) 从汇款速度来看，电汇最为快捷。

(5) 从使用范围来看，电汇是目前使用最广泛的方式；信汇方式很少使用；票汇介于两者之间。

汇款的偿付又称汇款头寸偿付，俗称"拨头寸"。

按照国际惯例，汇出行在发出汇款委托书的同时，必须将头寸拨付给付款行，使付款行不致因执行付款指示而垫付头寸。

Table 8-1  Comparison of M/T, T/T and D/D

| Items | T/T | M/T | D/D |
|---|---|---|---|
| Methods of transfer | Cable/telex/SWIFT | Airmail | Mail or carried by remitter |
| Time of transfer | Fastest | Slow | |
| Method of authentication | Test key of SWIFT, authentication key | Authorized signature | Authorized signature |
| Security | Quite safe | Reliable, but may be lost in post | Stop-payment is time consuming |
| Charge | High | Low | Lowest |

## 8.1.4  Reimbursement of Remittance Cover

If the remitting bank consigns the paying bank to release the payment, the former should transfer the funds to the paying bank, which is called as the reimbursement of remittance cover. According to the international regulations, when the remitting bank sends the payment order, it should transfer the funds to the paying bank as well.

There are two types of ways to reimburse the remittance cover:

(1) Make the payment first and then require the reimbursement. When two banks are contracted as correspondent banks, the correspondent arrangement may regulate the ways of reimbursement. However, the paying bank takes a risk of non-payment from the remitting bank under such kind of payment methods. Unless they have given contracts, it is not recommended to use this kind of reimbursement.

(2) Require the reimbursement first and then make the payment. Most of the reimbursement methods adopt this way.

According to the situations of a remitting bank's account and a paying bank's account, there are two kinds of ways for the remitting bank to reimburse the payment.

a) If the paying bank maintains a current account with the remitting bank, or the remitting bank has an a/c with the paying bank, the reimbursement can be effected through crediting the paying bank's vostro account by a remitting bank or debiting the remitting bank's nostro account by a paying bank. In the payment order, it can be written as "in cover, we have credited your a/c with us" or "in cover, please debit our a/c with you".

b) If there is no vostro or nostro account with each other, the remitting bank can find a third bank, with which both the paying bank and the remitting bank maintain current account. When the remitting bank sends the payment order, it should notify the common accountant bank to debit its account and credit the paying bank's account at the same time and then send a credit advice to the paying bank, for example, "In cover, we have authorized Bank A to debit our a/c and credit your a/c with them". If there is no vostro or nostro account with each other, the remitting bank and the paying bank do not maintain current account with a third bank, but the correspondent bank of remitting bank and the correspondent bank of paying bank have account relationships. The cover instructions can be "In cover, we have instructed Bank A to pay the proceeds to your account with the Bank B".

## 8.1.5 Cancel the Remittance or Refund the Imbursement

"Refund" means to cancel the remittance before the payment, which can be effected by the payee or remitter or the paying bank. It is very simple for the payee to refund the imbursement. He or she could simply refuse to receive the payment in respect of M/T or T/T and notify the remitting bank. Then the paying bank will refund the payment order to the remitting bank and the remitting bank will instruct the remitter to get the refund. In terms of D/D, the payee has to mail the draft to the remitter in order to claim the refund of the imbursement.

If the refund of the imbursement is claimed by the remitter, it should be separated into two situations. In respect of M/T or T/T, if the paying bank has not released the payment to the payee, the remitter could notify the remitting bank and the paying bank to stop the payment. When the remitting bank receives the refund request from the remitter, the remitting bank should notify the paying bank by airmail or cable to stop releasing the payment to the payee. If the paying bank has not made the payment, it will agree to do so. If the paying bank has already released the payment to the payee, the paying bank cannot recourse it from the payee and the remitter cannot claim the refund from the remitting bank and the remitter has to negotiate it with the payee directly.

汇款的偿付有两种方式。

(1) 先拨后付：付出行在受理一笔汇款业务后，先将头寸拨给汇入行，汇入行收到头寸以后才向收款人进行解付。这是最主要的头寸调拨方式。

(2) 先付后偿：汇出行受理一笔汇款业务后，先将汇款通知寄给汇入行，汇入行根据通知先垫付资金给收款人，然后向汇出行索偿。除非汇出、汇入两行有先解付、后拨头寸的代理合约，否则不能采用。

退汇是指汇款人或收款人某一方，在汇款解付前要求撤销该笔汇款。在实际业务中，主要有以下原因。

(1) 因收款人名称、账户、地址不清等原因而无法解付汇入款超过3个月，银行将主动退汇。

(2) 汇出行提出退汇的，若查明头寸确已收妥，且汇款未解付的，可办理退汇；若已解付，由汇款人直接与收款人联系退汇事宜。

(3) 因收款人拒收要求办理退汇的，应由收款人说明原因，经银行查实同意后，退还原汇出行。

In terms of D/D, it is very difficult for the remitter to refund the payment. Once the remitting bank issues the draft, the remitting bank has to be responsible for all the holders in due course. If the remitting bank refuses to honor the payment, it may lose the credit of the bank. Suppose the draft has not been sent to the payee, the remitter could claim the refund by returning the draft to the remitting bank. If the draft has been lost in the way by accident, the remitting bank may refund the imbursement after confirming the event. Otherwise, once the draft is delivered to the payee, it is hard to claim the refund of imbursement even if the payee did not clear the draft.

The paying bank may request to refund the imbursement when the payee did not release the payment after a certain period. The valid period of remittance is different across countries, which depends on each country's regulations, generally between half a year to one year. After the valid period, the paying bank will refund the payment to the remitting bank.

## 8.1.6　The Application of Remittance in International trade

Remittance is a method of "clean payments" (as compared with documentary payments, to be described later), which predominate both in size and in number in the developed countries. The main reason is not only that it is a simple method of payment, cheap and flexible for both the buyer and the seller, but that it is also an indication of the underlying general trade pattern. Remittance can be separated into two terms: payment in advance and payment after the arrival of goods.

### 1. Payment in Advance

预付货款是进口商(付款人)在出口商(收款人)将货物或货运单据交付以前将货款的全部或者一部分通过银行付给出口商，出口商收到货款后，再根据约定发运货物。

Payment in advance means that the buyer simply pays at the time of order (cash with order) or prior to shipment of the goods. This term of payment is commonly used in specialized and capital intensive goods with good credit. Payment in advance or cash in advance provides the seller with the most security but leaves the buyer at great risk that the seller will not comply with all the terms of the contract. The cash payment is received before, and independently of, shipment of the goods. If the goods are delayed or in inferior quality, the buyer's last resort is to take legal action based on the sales contract.

In this case, the importer will generally depress the prices of goods and provisions for payment on the payment conditions. For example, the payee or the paying bank to provide a written guarantee by the exporter to fulfill the obligation to deliver within a certain period of time, or refund received payment, and pay the interest.

Advance payment can be divided into: (a) Full payment in advance. The importer pre-pays the full amount of funds to the exporter prior to shipment. (b) Pre-paid part of the amount. The importer deposits a certain percentage of the total amount of contract value as a deposit or pre-paid a batch of commodities to prevent the importer later from changing their mind. It is generally used for sample payment.

Payment in advance places the burden for financing the transaction entirely on the buyer. Actually, this term of payment is the worst choice for the buyer. However, the buyer may change his situation by combining payment in advance with bank guarantee or standby credit so as to minimize his risks.

### 2. Payment after arrival of Goods

Payment after arrival of the goods, also called credit transaction, cash on delivery or open account, means that the seller delivers goods or services to the buyer without receiving cash, a bill of exchange or any other legal binding and enforceable undertaking at the time of delivery, and the buyer is expected to pay according to the terms of the sales contract and the seller's later invoice.

货到付款与预付货款相反，它是进口商在收到货物后，立即或在一定时期以后再付款给出口商的一种结算方式，也被称为延期付款或赊销。

Under payment after arrival of the goods, the payment is not made at the time when the goods are delivered or when the documents are presented, but at the time specified in the contract, such as 30, 70, 90 days or a longer period after shipment. Therefore, open account payment provides the buyer with the greatest security and flexibility but leaves the seller at the greatest risk that the buyer will not comply with the terms of the contract and pay as promised. If the buyer does not pay, the seller's last resort is to take legal action on the basis of the sales contract. Due to the high degree of risk, the seller should always consider whether any other alternatives are available before agreeing to open account terms.

# 8.2　Collection

【**Learning Objectives**】

By studying this chapter, you should be able to master:

- Definition of collection
- Main parties of a collection
- Procedure of documentary collection
- The involved parties in collection
- Types of collection
- The Rules of *URC522*
- Points for Attention for collection
- Risk and protection for exporters and importers
- Financing under the collection

## Lead-in: Case Study

### D/P Changed into D/A

On April 9th, 2015, a remitting bank accepted an outward collection business of D/P at sight with the amount of US $100,000.00. Following the exporter's instructions, the remitting bank mailed the full set of documents together with a collection instruction to a collecting bank in the U.S.A. week later, and the principal claimed that the importer required the remitting bank to change "D/P at sight" into "D/A at 70 days sight". The principal ignored the remitting bank's warning about the high risk of D/A, and insisted on the change, so the remitting bank sent a modification instruction. However, the collecting bank never sent the notice of acceptance. On August 2nd, the principal asked the remitting bank to instruct the collecting bank to send back the documents. On August 19th, the remitting bank received the returned documents and found that one of the three original bills of lading was missing. Through an organization in the U.S.A., the principal learned that the goods had been picked up by the importer. The remitting bank required that the collecting bank either send back the documents in full or make payment by acceptance, but the collecting bank paid no attention to it. Furthermore, the principal was unwilling to solve the problem by legal means. The whereabouts of the payment is still unknown.

***Class Activities：***

1. What are the difference between D/P and D/A?

2. Does the remitting bank have responsibilities in this case?

3. What are lessons from this case?

## 8.2.1　Definition of Collection

Collection is an arrangement whereby the seller draws a draft on the buyer and authorizes its bank to collect the payment.

The definition of the International Chamber of Commerce (ICC) *URC 522*: the collection is the handling by banks, on instructions received, of documents (financial documents and/or commercial documents), in order to: (a) obtain acceptance and/or, as the case may be, payment, or (b) deliver commercial documents against acceptance and as the case may be, against payment, or (c) deliver documents on other terms and conditions.

托收是出口人(债权人)先行发货，开立以买方为付款人的汇票，或随附主要有关单据(如提单、保险单、发票等)，委托出口地银行通过其在进口地的分行或代理行向进口人(债务人)收取货款的一种结算方式。

## 8.2.2　Nature of Collection

Collection is a kind of commercial credit, offered to each other by firms and merchants. The collection bank acts only as the collector of funds on behalf of the seller and is not committed to the obligation whether the buyer makes payment or not. It is dependent on the commercial credit of the buyer if the seller will be paid after the delivery of goods. Therefore, a collection transaction puts the seller under a great risk.

托收是基于商业信用，托收行和代收行的责任仅限于及时向付款人提示汇票，并在遭拒付时及时把详细情况通知委托人，它们对汇票的付款人(受票人)拒绝付款或拒绝承兑不承担任何责任。

## 8.2.3　Procedure of Documentary Collection

The payment method agreed in the sales contract is by collection, in which the seller signs a commission contract with the local bank of the seller's country in form of collection authorization letter, authorizing the local bank of the seller's country (collection bank) to collect the payment through the correspondent bank of it in the buyer's country, then deliver the shipping documents to the buyer, as shown in Figure 8-3.

(1) The buyer and the seller conclude the sales contract, and stipulate the payment made by documentary collection with D/P at sight.

(2) The exporter authorizes the local bank to effect the collection, and submit the full set of shipping documents with draft to the remitting bank.

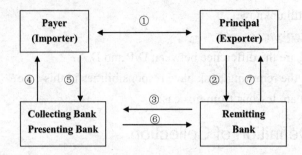

Figure 8-3   The Procedure of Collection

托收当事人法律关系：委托人与托收行之间、托收行与代收行之间都是代理关系，它们的权利和义务应受代理法一般原则的支配，特别是本人(委托人)应补偿代理人的开支，向其支付报酬；代理人应尽职尽责地完成代理事务，并不得越权。

(3) The remitting bank sends the draft and the shipping documents to the collecting bank of the importer's country together with the instructions received from the exporter.

(4) The presenting bank makes presentation of the payment advice to the importer.

(5) The importer makes the payment and gets the documents.

(6) The collecting bank informs the remitting bank and makes transfer of the payment to the remitting bank.

(7) The remitting bank credits the payment to the account of the exporter.

## 8.2.4   The Involved Parties in Collection

During collection, the following parties will be involved:

(1) Principal. Usually, the principal is the seller.

(2) Remitting Bank. The bank in the exporter's country is authorized by the principal to effect the collection on behalf of principal.

(3) Collecting Bank. The collecting bank is the bank in the importer's country who receives the authorization from the remitting bank to collect the funds from the payer.

(4) Payer. Namely the payer is the buyer or the drawee.

(5) Presenting Bank. Presenting bank is the bank who presents the shipment documents with draft to the payer.

## 8.2.5   Types of Collection

The collection is classified into two kinds, which are clean collection and documentary collection. The documentary collection is divided into

Documents against Payment (D/P) and Documents against Acceptance (D/A).

## 1. Documents Against Payment (D/P)

(1) Definition of D/P.

The document against payment refers to that the seller delivers the documents upon receipt of the payment from the buyer (importer). The buyer cannot get the documents until it makes the payment to the seller.

付款交单是出口人的交单必须以进口人的付款为前提条件，即出口人将汇票连同有关货运单据交给银行托收时，指示银行只有在进口人付清款项时才能交出货运单据。

The documents are vital for a documentary collection, for the delivery of documents means the transfer of the ownership of cargoes. The collecting bank in the importer's country will make presentation to the importer with the bill and the documents received from the remitting bank, but will not release the documents to the importer until the importer makes payment to the collecting bank.

(2) Classification of D/P.

● D/P at sight

After the shipment, the seller draws a sight draft and makes presentation of it with the full set of shipment documents to the buyer through the banks, and the buyer makes the payment at sight of the bill; the bank releases the documents to the buyer on receipt of the full payment from the buyer.

付款交单按照支付时间的不同，可分为即期付款交单和远期付款交单两种。

● D/P after sight

After the shipment, the seller draws a usance draft and makes presentation of it with the full set of shipment documents to the buyer through the banks, and the buyer accepts the bill after confirming it and makes the payment on the mature date; then the bank releases the documents to the buyer.

The above shows that only after the payment has been made can the buyer obtain the shipping documents, and take delivery of or resell the goods, whether it is D/P sight or D/P after sight. Therefore, using D/P sight or D/P after sight represents less risk for the seller compared with using remittance.

## 2. About Trust Receipt

(1) The Definition of D/P·T/R and T/R. Under D/P after sight, in order to avoid possible delay and get the goods as soon as possible, the buyer can present a Trust Receipt and borrow the shipping documents from the collecting bank and effect the payment of the goods upon the maturity of the draft, which is called D/P·T/R.

信托收据(T/R)是进口人借单时提供的一种书面信用担保文件，用于表示出票人愿意以代收银行的受托人身份代为提货、报关、存仓、保险、出售，同时承认货物所有权仍属银行。

信托收据是代收行自己向进口人提供的信用便利，与出口人无关。因此，如果代收行借出单据后，汇票到期不能收回货款，则代收行应对委托人负全部责任。如果委托人指示代收行借单，则日后收汇风险由委托人自己承担。

承兑交单是指出口人的交单以进口人的承兑为条件。进口人承兑汇票后，即可向银行取得货运单据，待汇票到期日才付款。承兑交单只适用于远期汇票的托收。

(2) T/R is a written document presented by the buyer to the collecting bank by which he expresses his wish to take delivery of the goods, make customs clearance, effect storing and make sales of the goods on behalf of the collecting bank. He also acknowledges that the title of the goods and the sales proceeds belong to the collecting bank and also he is obliged to make the payment of the goods at the maturity of the draft.

(3) The responsibility of risk. With Trust Receipt (T/R), the buyer can borrow the documents from the bank before the payment. The trust receipt is a kind of credit guarantee document in written form. Acting as an assignee, the remitting bank offers the documents to the buyer according to the regulations in the collection instructions, committed to the obligation of compensation to the seller in case that the buyer fails to pay. However, if the principal agrees that the drawee gets the shipping documents with a Trust Receipt，the risks will be borne by the principal himself which is called D/P·T/R that means D/P at ... days after sight to issue trust receipt in exchange for documents.

### 3. Documents against Acceptance (D/A)

After the shipment, the seller draws a usance bill and makes presentation to the buyer through banks with the full set of documents, and the collecting bank releases the documents to the buyer upon receipt of the acceptance of the buyer. The seller will fulfill the payment when the bill is due. Documents against acceptance means that the buyer obtains the ownership of cargo before making payment, and thus the seller will be put into a great risk. The seller will get into the loss of goods and money in case of the buyer's failure in payment. Therefore, the international trade companies in our country are very cautious about the payment by D/A. Comparison between D/P and D/A is as shown in Table 8-2.

Table 8-2　Comparison between D/P and D/A

|  | Date of Presentation | Date of Acceptance | Date of Payment | Date of Doc. Releasing |
|---|---|---|---|---|
| D/P at sight | 2012.9.17 | — | 2012.9.17 | 2012.9.17 |
| D/P at 30 days | 2012.9.17 | 2012.9.17 | 2012.10.17 | 2012.10.17 |
| D/A at 30 days | 2012.9.17 | 2012.9.17 | 2012.10.17 | 2012.9.17 |

## 8.2.6　The Property, Advantages and Disadvantages

Collection is a kind of commercial credit in favor of the buyer. The payment by collection needn't go through as complicated procedures as the L/C, without the requirement of bank deposit, with lower bank service charges, and not occupying capital. The remitting banks and collecting banks are not committed to the obligation of payment, and thus it is completely dependent on the buyer's credit whether the seller can receive payment or not. The seller is in the risk of failure or delay of being paid in case that the buyer goes bankruptcy, loses the ability of discharging debt or refuses to pay on purpose. Although D/P is to deliver the documents on receipt of payment, the buyer may refuse to make payment and give up the documents when the market is shrinking. In this case, the seller will bear the loss of money and goods as well. The banks are not committed to the obligation of keeping and delivery of the shipment, but the seller has to pay for the settlement charges of delivery, customs clearance, warehouse storage, insurance, resale, auction or shipping back, etc. For the payment by D/A, the risk for the seller is larger.

## 8.2.7　The Rules of *Uniform Rules for Collections 522 (URC522)*

- The instructions of Collection shall write the words like "keep to *URC522*, and D/P after sight is not advisable".
- The usance bill is not allowed and the commercial documents shall be delivered after the payment. For the D/P after sight, it shall be remarked with documents against payment or documents against acceptance.
- The consignee shall not be the banks or to order of bank; banks are only in charge of documents, not responsible for the goods.
- Banks are not responsible for the verification of documents, but in charge of confirming if the quantity of documents is the same as indicated in the collection instruction.
- The presenting bank shall send the advice of dishonor to the remitting bank in case that the collection is dishonored.

国际商会为统一托收业务的做法、减少托收业务各有关当事人可能产生的矛盾和纠纷，修订了 *URC522*。该规则本身不是法律，因而对一般当事人没有约束力。有关当事人只有在事先约定的条件下，才受其约束。

### 8.2.8 Points for Attention for Collection

(1) The seller shall make a detailed investigation about the credit of the buyer before accepting the payment by collection. For the countries that are strict on foreign exchange, it is not advisable to adopt collection as the payment method.

(2) The seller shall have a full understanding of the commercial regulations of the import country. For example, in some Latin American countries, the shipping documents will be released to the buyer on receipt of the acceptance for D/P after sight, which makes no difference with D/A. For these countries, it is not advisable to accept D/P after sight as the payment term.

一些拉美国家在实际业务操作中会把 D/P 远期当作 D/A 来处理。

(3) The exporter shall try to conclude the contract with CIF term if the payment term is by collection. The risk is larger with FOB or CFR in case that the buyer refuses to pay as the seller does not hold the insurance policy. For the exports with FOB or CFR, the seller shall insure for the export credit.

(4) For the collection, the seller shall have a wholesome accounting system with regular examination, urge and settle the unpaid business in prevention of the possible loss.

### 8.2.9 Risk and Protection for Exporters and Importers

#### 1. Risks for the Exporter

(1) The exporter may face the risks of non-acceptance or payment by the importer, if there is a significant drop in market price. Therefore, the exporter should investigate the market trend of exported goods in the importing country.

(2) The exporter may be confronted with the operational risks of an importer, such as bankruptcy, liquidation, sued by the court, etc. It is essential for an exporter to investigate the reputation, creditworthiness and financial standing of the importer before consenting to a documentary collection.

(3) The exporter should take into account the political and economic condition of the importer's country. The D/P or D/A term can be signed only in a politically and economically stable country. If there are foreign exchange restrictions, the exporter must make sure the importers have obtained all

licenses for foreign exchanges.

(4) The exporter should find out from the importer what documents are required for customs clearance in the importer's country. The exporter should then assemble the documents carefully and make sure they are in the required form and endorsed or authenticated as necessary.

(5) Under D/A terms, if the buyer signs the acceptance, takes possession of the goods, and then refuses to pay the bill of exchange at maturity, the seller has given up title to the shipment, and the only recourse is to the buyer, not the banks.

### 2. Risks for the Importer

Comparing with the exporter, the risks of importer is comparatively small, but there are still some risks that may be against to the importer. The main concern of the importer is the quality of the goods and whether the exporter will ship the goods as specified in accordance with the agreement between the buyer and the seller. In order to guarantee the quality of the goods, the importer should also investigate the creditworthiness and reputation of the exporter, carefully specify all documentations required from the seller in the contract, e.g., a certificate of inspection from a reliable third party and inspect the documents to make certain they meet all specifications for customs clearance and for the eventual sale of the goods in his own country.

## 8.2.10 Financing under the Collection

### 1. Financing Provided by the Remitting Bank to the Exporter

Financing provided by the remitting bank to the exporter is also called export bill purchasing under documentary collection or negotiate the bill, which means the remitting bank purchases its customer's draft drawn on the overseas importer before the importer makes the payment and exporter obtains proceeds of the goods in advance.

The original bill is drawn by the exporter to himself on the importer. In the procedure of export bill purchasing, the exporter should endorse the draft and transfer the payee to the remitting bank. After endorsing the bill to the remitting bank, the later becomes the holder in due course and has the right to recourse from the endorser (exporter).

The net proceeds that the exporter can finance from the remitting bank are the face value of the draft minus the interest during the period of collection and some other commission charges.

## 2. Financing Provided by the Collecting Bank to the Importer

There are two kinds of financing provided by the collecting bank to the importer, trust receipt and bank guarantee.

### 1) Trust Receipt

Under the term of D/P at a fixed time after sight, when the goods and documents have both arrived at the importer's place before the draft is mature, the importer may borrow the documents from the collecting bank by writing up an undertaking in order to precede the goods immediately. The undertaking is called trust receipt. Under a T/R, the bank still owns the title of the goods and the importer helps the bank to process the goods.

Upon receipt of the goods, the importer may sell the goods and effects the payment when the draft matures. However, T/R places the collecting bank into a risky position. Once the importer has no abilities to reimburse the payment, the collecting bank has to make a payment to the exporter under a D/P term. Generally, the collecting bank will investigate the creditworthiness of the importer or let the importer deposit up to 100% of the goods value according to the importer's credit before agreeing on releasing documents to the importer against a T/R.

### 2) Bank Guarantee

Bank guarantee is generally used when the goods arrived earlier than the documents. In order to obtain the goods on time, the importer will ask the collecting bank to issue a bank guarantee which guarantees the collecting bank will deliver the documents, especially B/L to the carrier upon the arrival of the documents. With the bank guarantee, the carrier may release the goods to the importer.

It is very risky for the banks to issue a bank guarantee, if the importer refuses (or is unable) to make payment after the documents have arrived or the draft is matured. After issuing a bank guarantee, the collecting bank transfers the ownership of the goods to the importer. When the importer is bankrupted, the collecting bank has to reimburse the payment to the exporter. Therefore, similar to T/R, the collecting bank will investigate the importer's financial

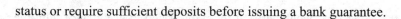

status or require sufficient deposits before issuing a bank guarantee.

***Summary***

Collection is an arrangement whereby the seller draws a draft on the buyer, and/or shipping documents are forwarded to his bank, authorizing it to collect the money from the buyer through its correspondent bank. The basis for this form of payment is that the buyer should either pay or accept the draft, before they gain control over the documents that represent the title of goods. In other words, compared with open account or cash on delivery, this method will protect the exporter from losing the ownership of the goods before obtaining the funds. However, the exporter may still face the non-payment risks by the importer.

According to the payment method, the collection is divided into clean collection and documentary collection. Generally, most of the collection is based on documentary collection. There are two kinds of ways to deliver the documents under documentary collection, say documents against payment (D/P) and documents against acceptance (D/A).

# 8.3   Letter of Credit

【Learning Objectives】

By studying this chapter, you should be able to master:
- Definition of a letter of credit
- The participants in a letter of credit
- Main procedure of the letter of credit
- The characteristics of a letter of credit
- The use of a letter of credit
- Contents of a letter of credit
- The varieties of documentary credit
- Other special credits
- Combined use of different methods of payment

## 8.3.1   Definition of L/C

A letter of credit is a written undertaking issued by a bank (the issuing

信用证是国际贸易中常用的支付方式之一。出口方若能确保所交的单据与信用证的条款完全一致,进口方银行将对其付款。

bank) to the seller (the beneficiary) at the request and in accordance with the instruction of the buyer (the applicant) to effect payment (that is by making a payment, or by accepting or negotiating bills of exchange) up to a stated sum of money, within a prescribed time limit and against stipulated documents. According to *UCP600*, all letters of credit are irrevocable letters of credit, which are the most commonly used methods of payment for imports. Exporters can be sure that they will be paid when they dispatch the goods and importers have proof that the goods have been dispatched according to their instructions. There are various types of letters of credit, including irrevocable L/C, confirmed L/C, unconfirmed L/C, transferable L/C, Back-to-Back L/C, documentary L/C, standby L/C and so on.

## 8.3.2 Parties to a Letter of Credit

All letters of credit have three parties involved: the originator, the beneficiary, and the banks. More details are discussed as follows.

### 1. Applicant or Opener

通常情况下,进口方若没有开证行的银行账户,银行将要求其提供100%的抵押物;如有账户,银行将依此为其建立相应的信用额度。

The applicant or the opener is always an importer or a buyer, who fills out and signs an application form, requesting the bank to issue a letter of credit in favor of an exporter or a seller abroad. He is in duty bound to ensure that the credit is issued in compliance with the terms and conditions laid down in the sales contract within a proper or reasonable time. After the payment is effected by the issuing bank, the opener must pay the bank against correct shipping documents or refuse to pay if the documents are not in order.

### 2. Beneficiary

受益人一般为出口人,是信用证的收件人和信用证的使用者。可以按信用证要求,签发汇票向付款行索取货款。

The beneficiary is the exporter or the seller in whose favor the credit is issued. If there is a discrepancy between the credit opened and the sales contract, the beneficiary may have the option to accept it as it stands or persuade the opener to have it amended so as to be in line with the contract. Once the beneficiary accepts the credit, he must deliver the goods in compliance with the contract. Then he tends to his bank or any other bank all the relevant documents as stipulated in the credit. He is responsible not only for the correctness and genuineness of the documents but also for the goods which must conform to the contract. If the issuing bank does not pay or is in liquidation, the beneficiary can claim from the opener for the payment.

## 3. Issuing Bank or Opening Bank

The issuing bank is the one which issues a letter of credit at the request of an applicant. It undertakes to pay to the beneficiary. If the applicant fails to pay after the issuing bank makes payment, the latter has the right to sell the goods and claim from the applicant if the proceeds are not sufficient. It is primarily liable to the beneficiary, no matter whether the applicant is in default or not.

开证行一般是进口地的银行，开立信用证后，承担第一付款责任。

## 4. Advising Bank

The advising bank is the one which advises the credit to the beneficiary in accordance with stipulations on the credit. It is located in the place of the beneficiary, which is usually the branch or correspondent of the issuing bank, acting as an agent of the opening bank in accordance with the instructions given.

通知行要负责审核信用证的真伪。

## 5. Negotiating Bank

Negotiating means the giving of value for draft(s) and/or documents by the bank authorized to negotiate. The negotiating bank is the one which negotiates or purchases the draft drawn by the beneficiary on the issuing bank or on any drawee bank as specified in the credit. The negotiating bank naturally becomes the holder in due course of the draft after negotiation. And so it normally has a right of recourse against the drawer, namely the beneficiary in the credit, in the event of dishonor by the issuing bank.

议付行又称押汇银行、购票银行或贴现银行，作为善意持票人对出票人(受益人)具有追索权。

## 6. Paying Bank

The paying bank is always the drawee of a draft stipulated in the credit. Or we may say it is a bank nominated by the issuing bank to make payment under the credit. In most cases, the paying bank is the issuing bank itself.

付款行又称受票银行，开证行一般兼为付款行。

## 7. Reimbursing Bank

A reimbursing bank is the agent of the issuing bank. It honors the reimbursement claims of a paying bank or an accepting bank or a negotiating bank under a particular credit in accordance with the instructions or authorization given by the issuing bank.

In a word, all letters of credit have three main parties: the originator, the beneficiary, and the banks. A letter of credit is written by an originator to perform two functions. One of them is to connect the buyer with the seller so that the transaction is performed efficiently and based on the expectations of both sides. The other is to connect the buyers with the banks. This connection is performed so that the issuing bank knows what terms and conditions it needs to look for in the merchandise and establishes it in the letter of credit.

偿付行信用证清算银行，是开证行的偿付代理人，有其存款账户。对代付行或议付行的索偿予以支付，不承担审核单证的义务，发现单证不符，可以追回付款。

In the documentary credit, there is always at least one bank that agrees with the payer to open credit, and in turn, is being placed as principal in the chain of credit. Besides the bank, there may be a multiplicity of additional banks in the chain, which makes a greater or lesser degree of the functions of the issuing bank in respect of documentary credit.

The other obvious participant of any letter of credit is the beneficiary. It is the person that will receive the payment in concept of the purchase of the merchandise, i.e., the exporter.

The beneficiary is the person that has to deliver the goods to the port of entry and who would receive payment for it if the transaction goes according to what the letter of credit establishes. Below are three types of banks that are generally involved in the creation and follow-up of letter of credit.

The issuing bank is the one that writes the actual letter of credit in cooperation with the importer in order to give it to the exporter, which also has the responsibility of informing the corresponding bank whether or not the exporter can receive payment.

保兑行是应开证行请求在信用证上加具保兑的银行，通常由通知行兼任，承担必须付款或议付的责任。

Confirming banks are located in the country of the exporter and are the ones that provide the payment given by the letter of credit, which respond to issuers and confirmers on confirmed letters of credit.

If the bank of the originator does not have a branch in the country of the beneficiary, then the beneficiary uses a notifying bank, which informs the beneficiary if a letter of credit has been open to his or her favor. Notifying banks do not have obligations against the beneficiaries.

### 8.3.3　Procedure of Credit L/C

L/C is an inter-bank communication. The two banks take full

responsibility that both shipment and payments are in order. The main stages an L/C goes through are as shown in Figure 8-4.

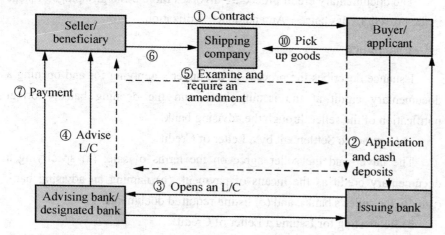

Figue 8-4   The Procedure of L/C

Step 1: A buyer and a seller enter into a sales contract providing payment by a documentary credit.

Step 2: The buyer instructs the issuing bank to issue a documentary credit in favor of the seller.

Step 3: The issuing bank opens a documentary credit according to the instructions of the applicant.

Step 4: The issuing bank asks another bank, usually in the country of the seller, to advise and perhaps also to add its confirmation to the documentary credit.

Step 5: The seller examines the documentary credit, and requires an amendment of the credit if necessary.

Step 6: The seller examines the documentary credit and prepares the required documents.

Step 7: The seller presents his documents to the advising bank for settlement.

Step 8: The designated bank examines the documents and forwards them to the issuing bank, claiming reimbursement as agreed between the two banks.

Step 9: The issuing bank examines the documents and reimburses the designated bank.

Step 10: The buyer redeems the documents and picks up the goods against the documents.

The documentary credit procedure involves three basic groupings of steps in the procedure: Issuance—Amendment—Utilization.

### 1. Issuance

Issuance describes the process of the buyer's applying for and opening a documentary credit at the issuing bank and the opening bank's formal notification of the seller through the advising bank.

1) Contract to Settlement by a Letter of Credit

The buyer and the seller agree on the terms of sale: (a) specifying a documentary credit as the means of payment, (b) naming an advising bank (usually the seller's bank), and (c) listing required documents.

2) Requesting for Issuing a Letter of Credit

The buyer applies to his bank (issuing bank) to open a documentary credit naming the seller as the beneficiary based on specific terms and conditions that are listed in the credit. Before that, the applicant should complete the L/C application form.

3) Opening of a Letter of Credit

After accepting the application, the opening bank shall stipulate L/C clauses strictly conforming to the instructions of the application form and mail or telex or send by SWIFT to the advising bank named in the credit.

4) Advising the Beneficiary

After verifying the authenticity of the credit, the advising bank shall advise the beneficiary of L/C or just transfer the L/C to him, and a copy is usually kept for file.

There are two ways of advising: one is to deliver the L/C directly to the beneficiary, attached with a signed advice note; another one is when the addressee of the L/C is the advising bank, the advising bank shall copy word by word in its own advice note, sign, and deliver it to the beneficiary.

### 2. Amendment

Amendment describes the process whereby the terms and conditions of a documentary credit may be modified after the credit has been issued.

After receiving the documentary credit, the seller must examine it closely to determine if the terms and conditions (a) reflect the agreement of the buyer and seller, and (b) can be met within the time stipulated. Upon examination, the seller may find problems. If the seller still wants to proceed with the transaction, but with modification to the terms of the credit, he or she should contact the buyer immediately and request an amendment.

Amendments must be authorized by the buyer and issued by the issuing bank to the seller through the same channel as the original documentary credit. This can be an involved undertaking so any amendments should be initiated only when necessary and as soon as a problem is identified.

### 3. Utilization

Utilization describes the procedure for the seller's shipping of the goods, the transfer of documents from the seller to the buyer through the banks, and the transfer of payment from the buyer to the seller through the banks as well.

(1) The seller (beneficiary) ships the goods to the buyer and obtains a negotiable transport document (negotiable bill of lading) from the shipping firm/agent.

(2) The seller prepares and presents a document package to the advising bank consisting of documents such as the negotiable transport document, the commercial invoice, the insurance document, the inspection certificate, etc.

(3) The advising bank reviews the document package making certain the documents are in conformity with the terms of the credit and pays the seller. In the case of a credit available by negotiation, the negotiating bank (usually be the advising bank) negotiates the documents with recourse to the beneficiary. After negotiation, the negotiating bank will claim reimbursement from the issuing bank or the reimbursing bank in accordance with the reimbursement terms indicated in the credit and documents will be sent to the issuing bank.

(4) The advising bank sends the document package by mail or by courier to the issuing bank.

(5) The issuing bank reviews the document package making certain the documents are in conformity with the terms of the credit, pays the advising bank and advises the buyer that the documents have arrived.

(6) The buyer reviews the document package making certain the documents are in conformity with the terms of credit, and makes a cash payment (with a sight draft) to the issuing bank, or signs an acceptance (promising to pay at a future date).

受益人收到信用证后，要及时审证，且要将不符点一次性列出，原因是信用证具有有效期。如果与合同不一致的内容没有及时列出并加以修改，将以信用证内容为主，因为信用证具有独立性。信用证的修改内容必须经过相关当事人一致同意后才有效。

(7) The issuing bank sends the document package by mail or courier to the buyer who then takes possession of the shipment.

**More Details to Follow:**

- **How to urge the establishment of an L/C**

When a transaction is concluded, the buyer, as a rule, is under obligation to establish a letter of credit with his bank within the time stipulated in the sales contract (confirmation), so that the seller can have ample time to make preparations for shipment. However, sometimes the buyer fails to establish the L/C, or the L/C does not reach the seller in time, then a letter, usually a telex or fax, has to be sent to the buyer to urge him to expedite the L/C.

---

**Example 1: Request to open an L/C**

*August 3, 2016*

*Dear Sirs,*

*We refer to your order for 2,000 sets of Sewing Machine and our sales confirmation No.112.*

*We like to remind you that the delivery date is approaching and we have not yet received the covering L/C.*

*We would be grateful if you would expedite establishment of the L/C so that we can ship the order on time.*

*In order to avoid any further delay, please make sure that the L/C instructions are in precise accordance with the terms of the contract.*

*We look forward to receiving your response at an early date.*

*Yours faithfully,*

---

- **How to complete an L/C application form**

During the international trade, the importer should open the said letter of credit in accordance with the contract. Before that, the applicant should complete the L/C application form.

When filling in the Irrevocable L/C Application Form, the applicant should make sure that:

(1) All the contents of the sales contract should be included in the irrevocable L/C application form.

(2) All instructions should be complete and precise.

(3) All instructions must state precisely the documents against which payment, acceptance or negotiation is to be made.

- **How to extend an L/C**

Sometimes the seller may fail to get the goods ready for shipment in time or the buyer may request that the shipment be postponed for one reason or another. Then the seller will have to ask for extension of the expiry date as well as the date of shipment of the L/C.

---

**Example 2: Request to extend an L/C**

*August 30, 2016*

*Dear Sirs,*

*Thank you for your letter of credit No.112 issued through the Commercial Bank covering 5,000 sets of computers.*

*We are sorry that, because of a delay in supplies, we will not be able to get the shipment ready before the end of this month. We faxed you earlier today to that effect.*

*We expect that the consignment will be ready in the early part of September. We are arranging to ship it on M/S "Dongfeng" from Dalian on 7 September. Therefore, we have to request you to extend the date of shipment and validity of the L/C to September and validity of the L/C to September 30, respectively.*

*We are looking forward to receiving your faxed extension to the letter of credit so that we can effect shipment of the goods accordingly.*

*We send our sincere apologies for the delay and trust that it will not cause too much inconvenience to you.*

*Yours sincerely,*

---

- **How to request the amendment of an L/C**

The seller, on receiving the L/C, should first of all make a thorough examination to see whether the clauses set forth in the L/C are in full conformity with the terms stated in the sales contract (confirmation). This step is essential. A minor difference between the two, if not discovered of duly amended, may cause the seller much inconvenience because the negotiation bank will refuse the negotiation of the documents according to the instructions given by the opening bank. Therefore, if any discrepancies or some unforeseen special clauses to which the seller does not agree are found in the L/C, the seller should send an advice to the buyer, asking for him to make amendment.

---

**Example 3: Request to amend an L/C**

*October 23, 2016*

*Dear Sirs,*

*We acknowledge your L/C No. 202 covering your order for 200 sets of sewing machine. On examination, we have found some discrepancies from our S/C. Please make the following amendments without the least possible delay:*

*1. Allow partial shipment and transshipment and delete the clause "by direct steamer".*

*2. Increase the amount of your L/C by $480.*

*3. Amendment the quality to read: 200M/T (5% more or less at Seller's option).*

*We hope that in the future you will establish your letters of credit exactly according to the terms and conditions of the relevant sales confirmation. By doing so, you will not only save much trouble, but also help us facilitate shipment of your products.*

*Please see to it that your amendments reach us by 30 October, otherwise shipment will be further delayed.*

*Sincerely yours,*

---

● Some points to amendment of an L/C

(1) Generally speaking, a credit can neither be amended nor cancelled without the agreement of the issuing bank, the confirming bank, if any, and the beneficiary.

注意：(1) 掌握好"改"与"不改"的界限。

(2) 修改信用证的内容要征得开证人的同意,由开证行发改证通知才有效。

(2) The terms and conditions of the original credit (or a credit incorporating previously accepted amendments) will remain in force for the beneficiary until the beneficiary communicates its acceptance of the amendment to the bank that advised such amendment.

(3) Partial acceptance of an amendment is not allowed and will be deemed to be notification of rejection of the amendment.

(4) A provision in an amendment to the effect that the amendment shall enter into force unless rejected by the beneficiary within a certain time shall be disregarded.

(5) All discrepancies should be listed at one time.

● Some issues relating to documents under the credit

(1) Ambiguity as to Issuers of Documents.

According to the UCP Rules, if terms such as "first class" "well-known" "qualified" "independent" "official" "competent" "local" are used in a documentary credit to refer to the issuer of a required document, banks are authorized to accept whatever documents that are presented, provided that they appear on the face to be in compliance with the credit and were not issued by the seller (beneficiary).

(2) Originals.

The originals of specified documents should be provided unless copies are called for or allowed. If more than one original are required, the buyer should specify in the credit how many are necessary.

Unless otherwise noted in the credit, banks are authorized to accept documents as originals, even if they were produced or appear to have been produced on a copy machine, by a computer system, or are carbon copies, provided they have the notation "original" and are, when necessary, signed.

(3) Authentication.

Banks are not responsible for the verification of the certification or authorized signature. Certificates usually bear the signature of the issuer. Unless otherwise stipulated in the credit, banks are authorized to accept documents that appear to satisfy the requirement.

(4) Signature.

Banks are authorized to accept documents that have been signed by facsimile, perforated signature, stamp, symbol, or any other mechanical or electronic method.

(5) Unspecified Issuers or Contents of Documents.

If the credit does not name a specific content of a document (other than transport documents, insurance documents, and commercial invoice), banks are authorized to accept documents as presented so long as the data contained in

(3) 对于需修改的内容应一次性向对方全部提出，以节约改证费用和时间。

(4) 对修改通知书内容只能全部接受或全部拒绝，并立即向通知行表示，不可在未接到修改通知书之前贸然出运货物。

the documents are consistent with the credit and other stipulated documents.

(6) Issuance Date.

Unless otherwise noted in the documentary credit, banks are authorized to accept documents dated prior to the issuance date of the credit, so long as all other terms of the credit are complied with.

### 8.3.4 Characteristics of a Letter of Credit

A letter of credit places a bank's credit instead of a commercial credit. It is guaranteed by the issuing bank's credit worthiness. Its main characteristics are as follows:

开证行负有第一性付款责任，即银行信用代替商业信用。

(1) Primary liability of the issuing bank to make payment. A letter of credit is in their own bank credit to guarantee payment; therefore, in the form of letters of credit, the banks bear the primary responsibility for payment. The letter of credit is to replace the commercial bank credit. This feature greatly reduced as a result of transactions between businessmen of the uncertainty caused by the uncertainty of payment for the import and export's protection.

信用证是一份独立自主的文件。

(2) Separated from the underlying contracts. The credit is separated from the sales or other contracts. The credit and the sales contract are two relationships separated from each other.

信用证是一种纯单据交易，只要单证一致，单单一致，开证行便要付款。

(3) Dealing with documents only. A letter of credit is purely business document trading. Under Article 4 of *UCP600*: In the letter of credit business, all parties concerned are dealing with a document rather than the document involving goods, services or other acts. It shows that the documents and the goods are separated from each other. In credit operation all parties concerned deal with documents instead of goods, services and / or other performances to which the documents may relate. As long as the documents presented by the beneficiary are in compliance with the terms and conditions of the credit, the issuing bank or the bank nominated by the credit shall fulfill the undertaking to pay, accept or negotiate.

Therefore, the credit is a contract independent of other contracts, and if the documents comply with the credit, the issuing bank or the confirming bank (if any) should fulfill its undertaking to pay independently regardless of other parties. Rights and obligations of an issuer to a beneficiary under a letter of credit are independent of the nonperformance of a contract or arrangement.

## 8.3.5  The Use of a Letter of Credit

Letters of credit are found where the buyer and supplier are separated by geography, culture or national borders. It's a way of smoothing over any rough spots in a business transaction before they appear. According to the Surety Information Office, banks usually charge one percent of the price for arranging the letter of credit. The buyer and supplier might share in the cost, and this arrangement would be part of the letter of credit. If there is no mention of cost in the letter of credit, it would be paid in its entirety by the buyer.

### 1. Protection for the Buyer

The letter of credit may outline conditions for successful delivery. The item has to arrive at a certain date in a certain condition before payment can be made. In the event the supplier defaults on the obligation, the money isn't transferred. There can be special conditions in the letter of credit covering unusual circumstances; but, generally, the buyer-protection feature of the letter of credit prevents the money from changing hands. There is no default by the buyer since the buyer has already given the money to the bank, which is in a special account. The letter of credit prevents buyer defaults.

开证行具有双重角色。如果买方能提供与所有信用证条款相符的文件，那么开证行会向出口商支付到期货款。这等于向出口商提供了销售的安全保障。

### 2. Protection for the Supplier

The supplier creates and finishes the item and ships it. The buyer takes delivery and checks to make sure delivery was made according to the conditions outlined in the letter of credit for successful completion of delivery. The buyer notifies his bank that the transaction was successful, then the bank releases the money to the supplier's bank that gives it to the supplier.

开证行代为检查所有文件，只有在与信用证上设定条款相符的情况下才会支付货款。这等于保护了进口商的利益。

## 8.3.6  Contents of a Letter of Credit

At present, most L/Cs are opened by telecommunication. Although the forms are different, their contents are, in the main, the same. The following details are to be found on all credits.

(1) Name and address of the issuing bank.

(2) Type of the credit. Every credit must indicate whether it is revocable or irrevocable. Whether it is a transferable credit or a confirmed credit must also be indicated in the credit.

(3) Name and address of the beneficiary.

(4) Amount of the credit and its currency.

(5) Expiry date of the credit and its place to be expired.

(6) Name and address of the applicant.

(7) L/C number and date of issue.

(8) Drawer and drawee as well as tenor of the draft. The drawer is always the beneficiary; the drawee may be the issuing bank or any other banks.

(9) Full details of the goods.

(10) Full details of the documents to be presented.

(11) Partial shipment permitted/not permitted.

(12) Transhipment allowed/not allowed.

(13) Port of shipment and port of discharge.

(14) Latest date for shipment, and the latest date for presentation of documents.

(15) Instructions to the advising bank, negotiating bank or paying bank.

(16) Other special terms and conditions.

(17) The undertaking clause of the issuing bank.

(18) The indication "This credit is subject to the *Uniform Customs and Practice for Documentary Credit (1993 revision), International chamber of Commerce Publication No. 600.* "

### 8.3.7   The Varieties of Documentary Credit

#### 1. According to the revocability of credit

A credit may be either revocable or irrevocable. Every credit should clearly indicate whether it is revocable or irrevocable. In the absence of such indication, the credit shall be deemed to be irrevocable.

1) Revocable Documentary Credit

信用证可分为可撤销信用证与不可撤销信用证。*UCP600* 规定，凡是信用证均为不可撤销。

Under this form of documentary credit, the issuing bank is authorized to amend the terms or even revoke the letter of credit without the prior consent from the beneficiary. The only commitment of the issuing bank is to notify the documentary credit to the exporter. This type of credit is of course extremely risky for the exporter which explains why it is very rarely used.

2) The Irrevocable Documentary Credit

With the irrevocable credit, the issuing bank is committed to pay the exporter if the documents provided before the expiry date of the credit are matching the terms and conditions stated in the letter of credit.

An irrevocable documentary credit gives the beneficiary greater assurance of payment, though he remains dependent on an undertaking of a foreign issuing bank. The irrevocable documentary credit cannot be cancelled or modified without the express consent from the issuing bank, the confirming bank (if any) and the beneficiary. According to the *UCP600*, all credits should be irrevocable credits.

### 2. According to the Attaching of Documents

#### 1) Clean Credit

A clean credit is a credit against which the beneficiary of the credit may draw a bill of exchange without presentation of documents. Payment will be effected only against a draft without any shipping documents attached thereto or sometimes, against a draft with an invoice alone attached thereto.

根据付款凭证的不同，信用证可分为光票信用证和跟单信用证两种。光票信用证是指开证行仅凭受益人开具的汇票或简单的收据而无须附带货运单据付款的信用证。

#### 2) Documentary Credit

A documentary credit is universally used as a method of payment in international trade. It is a credit under which payment will be made against documents representing title to the goods and thus making the transfer of title possible.

跟单信用证是指凭跟单汇票或仅凭单据付款、承兑或议付的信用证。

### 3. According to the Time of Payment

#### 1) Sight L/C

A letter of credit calling for the presentation of sight drafts is a sight credit, under which the beneficiary (the drawer) is entitled to receive payment at once on presentation of his draft to the drawee bank or to the issuing bank if drawn on the issuing bank, once the relevant documents have been checked and found to be in order.

根据付款时间的不同，信用证可分为即期信用证和远期信用证。

#### 2) Usance or Time Credit

If a letter of credit specifies that drafts are to be drawn at any length of time, such as 30 days, 60 days, 90 days or 120 days after sight, it is called a usance or time credit. Under such credit, the drafts may be drawn on and accepted by the opening bank, or the paying bank as indicated therein. In this case, the exporter issues his draft, and presents it for acceptance, together with all the shipping documents, to the issuing bank or to the confirming bank or to the paying bank, as stipulated in the credit. The draft is accepted means that the accepting bank promises to pay the full amount of the draft at a specified future date. The accepted usance draft can be discounted in the discount market.

### 4. According to the Adding of Confirmation

#### 1) Confirmed Credit

A confirmed credit is a credit which is advised to the beneficiary with another bank's confirmation added thereto. In cases where the financial conditions in the importing country and/or the solvency of the issuing bank are in doubt, the exporter may demand that another bank, preferable in the exporting country, should undertake to honor by adding its confirmation. In this way, the exporter is assured that payment will be made by the confirming bank no matter the issuing bank is insolvent or not. Only the issuing bank can request another bank to add its confirmation.

保兑信用证是指另一家银行, 即保兑行应开证行的请求, 对其所开的信用证加以保证兑付的信用证。

The confirming bank usually adds on the credit such words as "This credit is confirmed by us" or "We hereby add our confirmation to this credit" and then signs thereon. It has the obligation to pay, to accept, or to negotiate a bill without recourse to the drawer and bona fide holder just the same as the issuing bank.

在国际贸易中, 信用证加保兑主要有经济上的原因和政治上的原因, 卖方以此减少开证行拒付的风险。

If the letter of credit originally opened by the applicant is indicating that it is irrevocable and confirmed, the advising bank automatically becomes the confirming bank. When the confirmation is not part of the terms of the letter of credit, it is up to the beneficiary to choose a bank to play this confirming role.

This kind of L/C is more secure; hence it is more often used. It claims our attention that, according to *UCP 600*, if an L/C is not marked as being irrevocable or not, it should be taken as irrevocable.

This step is related to the fulfillment by the bank of its obligation to pay the exporter. In order to address the various requirements of both parties, several forms are associated with the availability of the credit.

#### 2) Unconfirmed Credit

非保兑信用证是指未经除开证行以外的其他银行保兑的信用证。

A letter of credit advised to the beneficiary without adding any other bank's confirmation is called an unconfirmed credit. Usually the word "unconfirmed" is not indicated in the credit.

### 5. According to the method of payment

All credits must clearly indicate whether they are available by sight payment, by deferred payment, by acceptance or by negotiation.

1) Sight Payment Credit

A sight payment credit is a credit available by payment, under which a bank specifically nominated therein is authorized to pay against the shipping documents with or without a draft presented in conformity with the terms of the credit. "Available by payment at sight" is stipulated in sight payment credit.

2) Deferred Payment Credit

Deferred payment credit is a credit available by deferred payment under which payment must be effected on a specified future date. No draft is required for this credit. Provisions like "Available by deferred payment" are stipulated in the credit.

With this mode of fulfillment introduced with the "uniform rules and regulations" of 1994 related to the documentary credit, the exporter receives a promise of payment from the bank designated a pre-agreed date. Such documentary credits are often used for goods which can be sold by the importer prior to its own payment.

3) Acceptance Credit

An acceptance credit is a credit available by acceptance, under which a bank specifically nominated therein is authorized to accept. It must be a usance credit and the draft thereunder must be a time bill drawn on the issuing bank, the advising bank, or any other drawee bank. The clause used in the credit is as follows: "This credit is available by acceptance of draft drawn on the ××× bank". By accepting the draft under the credit, the accepting bank signifies its commitment to pay the face value thereof at maturity. The beneficiary will discount the accepted draft with his own bank or in local money market if he wishes to get paid immediately.

Acceptance credit is usually issued if the contract is on time basis. The beneficiary will receive payment on a specified future date. If he discounts the accepted draft in the money market, discount charges are for account of the beneficiary. This is called seller's usance credit. If the contract is concluded on sight basis, the importer may issue an acceptance or time credit for purposes of financing through discounting the accepted time draft in the

即期付款信用证是指规定受益人开立即期汇票随附单据，或不需要汇票仅凭单据向指定银行提示，请求付款的信用证。

延期付款信用证是指被信用证指定的付款行在收到符合信用证规定的远期汇票和单据时，先在汇票上履行承兑手续，俟汇票到期日再行付款的信用证。

承兑信用证是指信用证指定的付款行在收到符合信用证规定的远期汇票和单据时，先在汇票上履行承兑手续，俟汇票到期日再行付款的信用证。

discount market.

4) Negotiation credit

议付信用证是指开证行中,邀请其他银行买入汇票及/或单据的信用证。议付信用证可分为自由议付信用证和限制议付信用证。

A negotiation credit is a credit under which a bank specifically nominated therein is authorized to negotiate or a credit which is freely negotiable by any bank.

A credit treated as negotiable is either a sight credit or a time credit, calling drafts to be drawn on the issuing bank or on any other drawee bank. A negotiation credit assures any bank negotiating the drafts thereunder that they will be duly honored by the opening bank provided all the terms stipulated therein are complied with.

## 8.3.8  Other Special Credits

There are numerous special letters of credit designed to meet specific needs of buyers, suppliers and intermediaries. Special credits usually involve increased participation by banks, so financing and service charges are higher than those for basic credits. The following is a brief description of some special credits.

### 1. Revolving Credit

循环信用证是指信用证在金额部分或全部使用后,其金额又恢复到原金额并再度使用,周而复始,直至达到该证规定的次数或总金额为止的信用证。

This is a type of credit that renews itself after its amount is drawn. To define it more clearly, it is a credit where, under the terms and conditions thereof, its amount is renewed or reinstated without any specific amendment made thereto.

To facilitate continuous repeated purchases from the same supplier a revolving credit is often used. So far as this type of credit is concerned the opening bank issues, only one letter with a fixed amount is available for each defined calendar period. The delivery of the goods is made in installments and at stipulated intervals. When the drawing is made by the beneficiary, the original credit amount becomes again available for the next period.

### 2. Transferable Credit

The buyer opens the L/C, which states clearly that it is transferable, on behalf of the middlemen as the original beneficiary who in turn transfers all or part of the L/C to the supplier(s). The transfer must be made under the same terms and conditions as those in the original L/C with the following exceptions:

amount, unit price, expiration date, and shipping date. In this instance the buyer and supplier are usually disclosed to each other. This is a common financing tactic for middlemen.

### 3. Assignment of proceeds

The assignment of proceeds method shows a typical letter of assignment. Note that the proceeds of all letters of credit may assign. In this instance the buyer opens the L/C as the beneficiary and relies on the middleman to comply so that the beneficiary can be paid. Any discrepancy in middleman documents will prevent payment under the L/C. The middleman instructs the advising bank to effect payment to the supplier when the documents are negotiated. In this way, buyers and sellers are not disclosed to each other.

### 4. Back-to-back Credit

This is a new credit opened on the basis of an already existing non-transferable credit. It is used by traders to make payment to the ultimate supplier. A trader receives a letter of credit from the buyer and then opens another letter of credit in favor of the supplier. The first letter of credit is used as collateral for the second credit. The second credit makes price adjustments from which come the trader's profits.

### 5. Red Clause Credit

Often an exporter does not have the funds to produce products to fill current orders. A letter of credit may have already been issued by the importer in anticipation of goods being exported. If allowed by the terms of the letter of credit, the exporter may draw upon the letter to obtain funds to produce goods. Once the goods are delivered the exporter may then submit the proper documents to obtain the balance of the letter of credit. This type of interim financing is referred to as coming from a "Red Clause Letter of Credit".

### 6. Letter of Guarantee (L/G)

A letter of guarantee is a subordinate document issued by a bank by which the issuing bank promises to the beneficiary that it will hold itself responsible for the debt, losses caused by the fault or infringement of contract of a third person. It can be used under various occasions. Here we focus on the following two groups.

可转让信用证是开证银行向中间商(受益人)提供对信用证条款权利履行转让便利的一种结算方式。它是指受益人(第一受益人)可以请求授权付款,承担延期付款责任,承兑或议付的银行(转让行);或如果是自由议付信用证时,可以要求信用证特别授权的转让行,将信用证的全部或部分一次性转让给一个或多个受益人(第二受益人)使用的信用证。

背对背信用证中的中间商必须有银行信贷额度,因为不管第一信用证是否得到支付,中间商都有责任支付第二信用证。

"红条款信用证"是指开证行授权付款行在受益人交单以前向受益人预先垫付信用证金额的全部或部分,待受益人交单议付时,再从议付金额中扣还预先垫款的本息,将余款付给受益人的信用证。

银行保证书又称银行保函,是银行向受益人开立的保证文件。由银行作为担保人,以第三者的身份保证委托人未对受益人履行某项义务时,由担保银行承担保证书中所规定的付款责任。

(1) Tender guarantee is issued by a bank upon the application of the bidder, by which the bank promises to the beneficiary (the tender inviter) it will answer for the losses caused by the bidder if he withdraws the bid or makes amendments to his bidding documents before the bidding begins, or refuses to sign or pay the margin after he has been awarded the bidding.

(2) By a performance guarantee, the issuing bank promises to the beneficiary it will pay him a certain sum of money or adopt certain remedial measures if the principal has not duly fulfilled his liabilities in time. In international trade practice, the performance guarantee can be either supplied by the importer or the exporter. Under the former case, the issuing bank will promise the seller that if the importer cannot duly effect payment of the goods, the bank will answer for it. As for the latter case, the issuing bank will promise the buyer that if the exporter cannot make the delivery of the goods in time, the bank will answer for the losses sustained by the buyer.

A letter of guarantee (L/G) is different from an L/C. Under the L/C, the opening bank holds itself for the payment of the goods. But under a letter of guarantee, the issuing bank holds itself responsible only after the principal has not fulfilled its obligations. Under an L/C, the seller can get the payment through negotiation, but he cannot do so under an L/G. Also, under an L/C, the issuing bank handles only the relevant documents, it has nothing to do with the sales contract, but under an L/G, when the beneficiary has presented a written documents declaring that the principal has not fulfilled his obligations and asks the issuing bank for recompense, the bank will have to make clear how and why his principal has not fulfilled his obligations. In this way, he may get involved into the disputes. In some countries, like U.S.A. and Japan, do not allow their banks to get involved in commercial disputes, so the banks of these countries do not issue L/G, instead they use standby L/C.

### 7. Standby L/C

备用信用证是指当支付未在特定期间(通常是30～60 天)完成时,需启用的信用证。

Standby L/C, also called commercial paper L/C, or guarantee L/C, or performance L/C, is a kind of clean L/C. It is a document by which the opening bank promises the beneficiary that it will bear some liabilities on behalf of the applicant if the latter has not duly fulfilled his obligations as required by the contract. Should the applicant have duly fulfilled his obligations, the standby L/C will not be used while if he has not, the beneficiary is to render a written document stating that the applicant has not duly performed the contract and asks the opening bank to make recompense.

Standby L/C is similar to L/G in that they both use bank credit and are both a kind of promise from a bank to the beneficiary that it holds itself responsible if the principal has not duly performed a contract or effected payment. They are different in that under L/G. The opening bank holds itself responsible only if the applicant has not duly performed his liabilities, and in doing so, it might possibly get involved in the disputes between the applicant and the beneficiary, while under a standby L/C, the opening bank will affect the payment if the beneficiary has presented to opening bank the required statement, and the opening bank stands aloof from the contract between its applicant and the beneficiary.

With L/G or standby L/C, progress payment or deferred payment can be used. Progress payment is used when the sale is made by installments. Under such cases, the buyer will first pay a certain sum of front money. The balance of the payment will be made by installments along with the installments deliveries of the goods. Under deferred payment, the buyer first pays a certain sum of earnest money, and then the balance of the payment will be made by installments during a rather long time afterwards. This is in fact a kind of credit sale, by which the buyer can make the purchase by using foreign funds. Deferred payment involves interest, and an interest clause should be given in the contract. Also, the two methods can be used in a combined way; that is, each installment payment under progress payment will not be effected immediately after each delivery. Instead, it will be made some time after each delivery.

### 8. Governing Rules of Letter of Credit

Like bills for collections, letter of credit is governed by a set of rules from the ICC. Used by L/C practitioners worldwide, the *Uniform Customs and Practice for documentary Credits (UCP)* are the most successful private rules for trade ever developed. Bankers, traders, lawyers, transporters, academics and all the like who deal with L/C transactions around the whole world, refer to UCP series on a daily basis. The prevalent version is uniform customs and Practice of Documentary credit, Icc Publication No. 500, 1993

几乎所有的跟单信用证都依循《商业跟单信用证统一惯例》运作，该惯例目前得到了 156 个国家的银行业的认可。

revision, in short, it is known as *UCP500* and, again, over 90% of the world's banks adhere to this document.

However, the latest version which came into being on 25 October, 2006 is *UCP600*, approved by the ICC Banking Commission. *UCP600*, which came into effect on 1 July 2007, contains significant changes that international traders will need to know, including:

- A reduction in the number of articles from 49 to 39.
- New articles on "Definitions" and "Interpretations" to provide more clarity and precision in the rules.
- The replacement of the phrase "reasonable time" for acceptance or refusal of documents by a firm period of five banking days.
- New provisions which allow for the discounting of deferred payment credits.
- A definitive description of negotiation as "purchase" of drafts of documents.

*UCP600* also contains within the text the 12 Articles of the UCP, ICC's supplement to the UCP governing presentation of documents in electronic or part-electronic form.

## 8.3.9 Combined Use of Different Methods of Payment

In international trade, usually only one method is used for a deal, but sometimes more than one method will be used in order to fulfill the payment of the goods. Also, various methods of payment can be combined together for the settlement of payment for various reasons and under various occasions, among them are the combination of L/C with collection, combination of L/C with remittance, the combination of documentary collection with down payment, and the combination of documentary collection with standby L/C.

### 1. Combination of L/C and collection

Payment effected in this way will be made partly by L/C and partly by collection, which will require the buyer to open an L/C for a certain percentage of the whole payment of the goods. The balance is to be collected. Also in the

实际业务中应该是
光票信用证，跟单托收
较合理。

sales contract, it should be declared clearly that the amount of payment under L/C will be available against a clean draft, while the balance of the payment will be available against documentary draft on collection basis. The shipping documents will not be released to the buyer unless he has effected all the payment.

## 2. Combination of L/C and Remittance

Payment made in this way is done partly by L/C and partly by remittance. If the remittance is made before the shipment of the goods, the money is taken as front money or advanced payment. If it is done after the shipment of the goods, it is often used for the balance of the payment for the consignment which can be varied in amount.

## 3. Combination of Documentary Collection and Down Payment

To make sure that the exporter will not sustain much loss because of collection, the seller can ask the buyer to make some down payment. When the shipment has been made, the down payment is to be deducted from the payment to be collected. In this way, if the draft has been dishonored, the exporter can ship the goods back, the loss thus sustained can be compensated by the down payment, but the exporter should make sure that the goods can be shipped back from the importing country.

## 4. Combination of Documentary Collection and Standby L/C

To avoid risks in documentary collection, the exporter can ask the buyer to open a standby L/C. Thus when the payment has been dishonored by the buyer, the seller can ask the opening bank of the standby L/C for payment.

To use this method, the time of validity of the standby L/C must be sufficiently long, so that after the payment has been dishonored, the seller has enough time to ask for the issuing bank for the payment. In filling the form of application for export collection, the exporter should ask the remitting bank to tell the collecting bank to give immediate notice by electronic means once the draft has been dishonored.

实际业务中，此付款方式在中东客户中使用较为常见。因为该地区进口关税率比较高，所以40%为L/C、60%为T/T是普遍的做法。

作用：如买方已支付20%～30%的订金，一般不会拒付托收项下的货款，否则，订金将无法收回，因此，卖方的收汇风险将大大降低。即使买方拒付，仍可以将货物返运回国，订金将用于支付往返费用。

# 【Key Terms and Words】

| | |
|---|---|
| Beneficiary 受益人 | Terms of validity 信用证效期 |
| Guarantor 保证人 | Expiry Date 效期 |
| Collection 托收 | Date of issue 开证日期 |
| Principle 委托人 | L/C amount 信用证金额 |
| Bearer 来人 | L/C number 信用证号码 |
| Payer 付款人 | To open by airmail 信开 |
| Consignee 受托人 | To open by cable 电开 |
| Consignor 委托人 | To open by brief cable 简电开证 |
| Drawer 出票人 | To amend L/C 修改信用证 |
| Principal 委托人 | Sight L/C 即期信用证 |
| Drawee 付款人 | Usance L/C 远期信用证 |
| Consingnee 受托人 | Buyer's Usance L/C 买方远期信用证 |
| Truster 信托人 | Traveler's L/C 旅行信用证 |
| Acceptor 承兑人 | Revocable L/C 可撤销的信用证 |
| Trustee 被信托人 | Irrevocable L/C 不可撤销的信用 |
| Endorser 背书人 | Confirmed L/C 保兑的信用证 |
| Discount 贴现 | Unconfirmed L/C 不保兑的信用证 |
| Endorsee 被背书人 | Transferable L/C 可转让信用证 |
| Endorse 背书 | Untransferable L/C 不可转让信用证 |
| Holder 持票人 | Revolving L/C 循环信用证 |
| Endorsement 背书 | Reciprocal L/C 对开信用证 |
| Bailee 受托人，代保管人 | Back to Back L/C 背对背信用证 |
| M/T 信汇 | Anticipatory L/C 预支信用证 |
| T/T 电汇 | Credit payable by a trader 商业付款信用证 |
| D/D 票汇 | Credit payable by a bank 银行付款信用证 |
| Cash on Delivery (COD) 货到付款 | without recourse 不受追索 |
| Payment in advance 预付货款 | Exporter's Bank 出口方银行 |
| Remitting bank 托收行 | Importer's Bank 进口方银行 |
| Collecting bank 代收行 | Seller's Bank 卖方银行 |
| Letter of Credit (L/C) 信用证 | Buyer's Bank 买方银行 |
| Form of credit 信用证形式 | Paying Bank 付款行，汇入行 |

Remitting Bank　汇出行
Opening Bank　开证行
Issuing Bank　开证行
Advising Bank　通知行
Notifying Bank　通知行
Negotiating Bank　议付行
Drawee Bank　付款行
Confirming Bank　保兑行
Presenting Bank　提示行
Transmitting Bank　转递行
Accepting Bank　承兑行
Pay bearer　付给某人
D/P. TR　付款交单凭信托收据借单
Opening bank's name & signature　开证行名称及签字
Confirmed irrevocable L/C　保兑的不可撤销信用证
Irrevocable unconfirmed L/C　不可撤销不保兑的信用证
Usance credit payment at sight　假远期信用证

Payment against documents　凭单付款
Payment by acceptance　承兑付款
Payment by bill　凭汇票付款
Letter of Guarantee (L/G)　保证书
Bank Guarantee　银行保函
D/P at sight　即期付款交单
Customer's representative　代理
Documents against payment　付款交单
Documents against acceptance　承兑交单
Presenting bank　提示行
D/P after sight　远期付款交单
Trust receipt　信托收据

# 【Exercises】

## I. Answer the following questions.

1. What are the differences between the commercial bill and the banker's bill?

2. Who are the involved parties in a bill of exchange? Why is the drawer the main debtor (before the acceptance of the draft)?

3. Which one is the payer in the involved parties in B/E, promissory note and check?

4. What is the title of the B/E? How many ways are there for the title of the B/E?

5. What is the endorsement of the B/E? How many types are there for the endorsement?

6. What are basic parties and their roles of a collection?

7. Please compare the different terms of releasing documents and explains their advantages and disadvantages.

8. What are the risks of documentary collection?

9. Please list the methods of financing under collection.

10. What is the property of the collection? How is it used in the international trade?

11. What are the differences between D/P after 30 days sight and D/A after 30 days sight?

## II. True or false

1. Remittance refers to the transfer of funds from one party to another among different countries through banks.

2. Mail transfer can be replaced in the time of telecommunication developed rapidly.

3. Under the serial payment method, the instruction to credit a beneficiary account is sent together with the instruction to debit sender's account.

4. The serial payment method cannot, however, delay the payment between different time zones.

5. A collection on the basis of commercial credit is usually processed through banks acting as the intermediary.

6. Banks have responsibility to examine the documents thoroughly.

7. The collecting bank handles the collection business according to the collection instruction.

8. In receipt of dishonor advice, the remitting bank must give appropriate instructions as to the further handling by the collecting bank.

## III. Put the following into English

1. 不可撤销信用证
2. 跟单信用证
3. 商业发票
4. 议付
5. 开立信用证
6. 延期信用证
7. 修改信用证
8. 允许分批装运
9. 销售确认书
10. 贸易条款

## IV. Finish the Following Exercises According to the Irrevocable Letter of Credit

Look at the irrevocable L/C below. Read the explanations of the various sections, and tell which explanation goes with which number in the document. The documentary Letter of Credit is a form payment widely used in foreign trade. Most credits are similar in appearance and contain the following details:

1. (    ) The terms of contract and shipment.
2. (    ) The name and address of the import.
3. (    ) Whether the credit is available for one or several partshipments.
4. (    ) The amount of the credit, in sterling or a foreign currency.
5. (    ) The expiry date.

6. (　) A brief description as to the documents against which payment is to be made.

7. (　) The name and address of the exporter.

8. (　) Precise instructions as to the documents against which payment is to be made.

9. (　) The type of credit (revocable or irrevocable).

10. (　) Shipping details, including whether partshipments and/or transshipments are allowed. Also recorded should be the latest date for shipment and the names of the ports of shipment and discharge.

11. (　) The name of the party on whom the bills of exchange are to be drawn, and whether they are to be at sight or of a particular tenor.

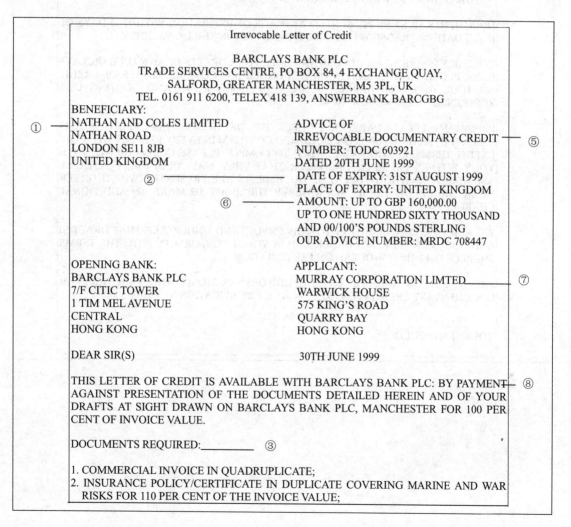

Irrevocable Letter of Credit

**BARCLAYS BANK PLC**
TRADE SERVICES CENTRE, PO BOX 84, 4 EXCHANGE QUAY,
SALFORD, GREATER MANCHESTER, M5 3PL, UK
TEL. 0161 911 6200, TELEX 418 139, ANSWERBANK BARCGBG

① — BENEFICIARY:
NATHAN AND COLES LIMITED
NATHAN ROAD
LONDON SE11 8JB
UNITED KINGDOM

② —————————————

⑥ —————

ADVICE OF
IRREVOCABLE DOCUMENTARY CREDIT — ⑤
NUMBER: TODC 603921
DATED 20TH JUNE 1999
DATE OF EXPIRY: 31ST AUGUST 1999
PLACE OF EXPIRY: UNITED KINGDOM
AMOUNT: UP TO GBP 160,000.00
UP TO ONE HUNDRED SIXTY THOUSAND
AND 00/100'S POUNDS STERLING
OUR ADVICE NUMBER: MRDC 708447

OPENING BANK:
BARCLAYS BANK PLC
7/F CITIC TOWER
1 TIM MEL AVENUE
CENTRAL
HONG KONG

APPLICANT:
MURRAY CORPORATION LIMTED — ⑦
WARWICK HOUSE
575 KING'S ROAD
QUARRY BAY
HONG KONG

DEAR SIR(S)　　　　　　　　　30TH JUNE 1999

THIS LETTER OF CREDIT IS AVAILABLE WITH BARCLAYS BANK PLC: BY PAYMENT — ⑧
AGAINST PRESENTATION OF THE DOCUMENTS DETAILED HEREIN AND OF YOUR
DRAFTS AT SIGHT DRAWN ON BARCLAYS BANK PLC, MANCHESTER FOR 100 PER
CENT OF INVOICE VALUE.

DOCUMENTS REQUIRED:_____　③

1. COMMERCIAL INVOICE IN QUADRUPLICATE;
2. INSURANCE POLICY/CERTIFICATE IN DUPLICATE COVERING MARINE AND WAR
　 RISKS FOR 110 PER CENT OF THE INVOICE VALUE;

3. FULL SET OR CLEAN ON BOARD BLANK ENDORSED PORT TO PORT BILLS OF
LADING MARKED NOTIFY MURRAY CORPORATION LIMITED, WARWICK HOUSE, 575
KING'S ROAD, QUARRY BAY, HONG KONG.

COVERING THE FOLLOWING GOODS:

16. PRINTING MACHINES NATHAN AND COLES MODEL CAXTON EXCELSIOR 1470 ____ ⑨
④—— COST, INSURANCE & FREIGHT HONG KONG
PARTIAL SHIPMENTS: NOT ALLOWED _____ ⑩
TRANSHIPMENTS: ALLOWED
SHIPMENT FROM: UK PORT
NO LATER THAN: 15TH AUGUST 1999 _____ ⑪
FOR TRANSPORTATION TO: HONG KONG

DOCUMENTS MUST BE PRESENTED AT PLACE OF EXPIRATION WITHIN 15 DAYS OF
ISSUE DATE OF TRANSPORT DOCUMENT AND WITHIN THE L/C VALIDITY.

DOCUMENTS ARE TO BE ACCOMPANIED BY YOUR DRAFTS DRAWN ON BARCLAYS
BANK PLC AT SIGHT MARKED 'DRAWN UNDER IRRECOVABLE LETTER OF CREDIT
NO TODC 603921 OF BARCLAYS BANK OF HONG KONG AND QUOTING OUR
REFERENCE NUMBER MRDC 708447.

IMPORTANT: PLEASE CAREFULLY CHECK THE DETAILS OF THIS CREDIT AS IT IS
ESSENTIAL THAT COCUMENTS TENDERED CONFORM IN EVERY RESPECT WITH THE
CREDIT TERMS. IF YOU ARE UNABLE TO COMPLY, PLEASE COMMUNICATE WITH
YOUY BUYERS PROMPTLY IN ORDER THAT THEY MAY ARRANGE A SUITABLE
AMENDMENT WITHOUT DELAY. IF DOCUMENTS ARE PRESENTED WHICH DIFFER
FROM THE CREDIT TERMS, WE RESERVE THE RIGHT TO MAKE AN ADDITIONAL
CHARGE.

WE ADD OUR CONFIRMATION TO THIS CREDIT AND UNDERTAKE THAT DRAFT(S)
AND DOCUMENTS DRAWN UNDER AND IN STRICT CONFORMITY WITH THE TERMS
THEREOF WILL BE HONOURED ON PRESENTATION.

THIS CREDIT IS SUBJECT TO THE UNIFORM CUSTOMS AND PRACTICE FOR
DOCUMENTARY CREDITS (1993 REVISION), ICC PUBLICATION NUMBER 500.


YOURS FAITHFULLY

## V. Complete the Credit Application According to the Following S/C

**SALES CONFIRMATION**

Sellers: <u>GUANGDONG LONGHUA TRADING</u>
<u>CO., LTD.</u>

Address: <u>152, COMPANY ROAD, GUANGZHOU,</u>
<u>CHINA</u>

Buyers: <u>ABC CO., LTD., FINLAND</u>

Address: <u>AKEDSANTERINK AUTO P.O. BOX9,</u>
<u>FINLAND</u>

Contract № <u>C215</u>

Date: <u>Nov. 15, 2003</u>

Signed at: <u>GUANGZHOU, CHINA</u>

TELEX: <u>0835 GDLEA CN</u>

FAX: <u>(020)83869360</u>

TELEX: _____

FAX: 833—675

This Sales Contract is made by and between the seller and the Buyer, whereby the Seller agree to sell and the Buyers agree to buy the under-mentioned goods according to the terms and conditions stipulated below.

| (1) Name of commodity and specification | (2)Quantity | (3)Unit | (4)Unit price | (5)Amount |
|---|---|---|---|---|
| TRIANGLE BRAND 3U-SHAPW ELECTRONIC ENEGY SAVING | | | | |
| TR-3U-A 110V 5W E27/B22 | 5 000PCS | PC | USD 2.50/PC | USD 12 500.00 |
| TR-3U-A 110V 7W E27/B22 | 5 000PCS | PC | USD 3.00/PC | USD 15 000.00 |
| TR-3U-A 110V 22W E27/B22 | 5 000PCS | PC | USD 3.80/PC | USD 19 000.00 |
| TR-3U-A 110V 26W E27/B22 | 5 000PCS | PC | USD 4.20/PC | USD 21 000.00 |
| With 5% more or less both in amount and quantity allowed | Total Amount | | | USD 67 500.00 |

(6) Packing: CARTON    (7) Delivery From GUANGZHOU TO HELSINKI

(8) Shipping Marks: N/M

(9) Time of shipment: Within 30 days after receipt of L/C, allowing transshipment and partial shipment.

(10) Terms of payment: By 100% Confirmed Irrevocable Letter of Credit in favor of the Seller to be available by sight draft to be opened and reach China before Dec. 1, 2003 and to remain valid for negotiation in China until the 15th days after the foresaid Time of Shipment. L/C must mention this contract number. L/C advised by BANK OF CHINA, GUANGZHOU BRANCH. TLX: 44U4K GZBC. CN. All banking Charges outside China (the mainland of China) are for account of the Drawee.

(11) Insurance: To be affected by Sellers for 110% of full invoice value covering F.P.A up to HELSINKI to be effected by the buyers.

(12) Quality / Quantity Discrepancy and Claim:

In case the quality and / or quantity / weight are found by the Buyer to be not in conformity with the contract after arrival of the goods at the port of destination, the Buyer may lodge claim with the Sellers supported by survey report issued by an inspection organization agreed upon by both parties, with the exception, however, of those claims for which the insurance company and or the shipping company are to be held responsible, claim for quality discrepancy should be field by the Buyers within 30 days after the arrival of the goods at the port of destination, while for quality/ weight discrepancy claim should be filed by the Buyers within 15 days after arrival of the goods at the port of destination. The Sellers shall, within 30 days after receipt of the notification of the claim, send reply to the Buyers.

(13) Force Majeure: In case of Force Majeure, the Seller shall not be held responsible for late delivery or non-delivery of the goods but shall notify the Buyers by cable. The Seller shall deliver to the Buyers by registered mail, if so requested by the Buyer, a certificate issued by the China Council for the Promotion of International Trade or/and competent authorities.

(14) Arbitration: All disputes arising from the execution of or in connection with this contract shall be settled amicably by negotiation. In case of settlement can be reached through negotiation, the case shall then be submitted to China International Economic & arbitral award is final and binding upon both parties for setting the dispute. The fee, for arbitration shall be borne by the losing party unless otherwise awarded.

(15) Shipping advice must be sent to buyer within 2 days after shipment advising number of packages, gross & net weight, vessel name, Bill of Lading No. And date, contract No. value.

THE SELLER                                          THE BUYER

   Li  Ming

Please sign and one copy of this sales confirmation to us at your earliest convenience

| IRREVOCABLE DOCUMENTARY CREDIT APPLICATION | |
|---|---|
| To: | Date: |
| Beneficiary ( full name and address) | L/C NO.<br>Ex-Card No.<br>Contract No.<br>Date and place of expiry of the credit |
| Partial shipments<br>☐allowed<br>☐not allowed | Transshipment<br>☐allowed<br>☐not allowed | ☐Issue by airmail  ☐With brief advice by teletransmission<br>☐Issue by express delivery<br>☐Issue by teletransmission (which shall be the operative instrument) |
| Loading on board/ dispatch/ taking in charge at/ from<br><br>not later than<br>for transportation to | Amount ( both in figures and words) |
| Description of goods: | Credit available with<br>☐by sight payment ☐by acceptance ☐by negotiation<br>☐ by deferred payment at Against the documents detailed herein☐and beneficiary's draft for      % of the invoice value<br>at<br>On |
| Packing: | ☐FOB          ☐CFR          ☐CIF<br>☐or other terms |

Documents required: (marked with ×)
1. (   )Signed Commercial Invoice in           copies indicating L/C No. and Contract No.
2. (   )Full set of clean on board ocean Bills of Lading made out to order and blank endorsed, marked
      "freight [   ] to collect/ [   ] to collect/ [   ] prepaid [   ] showing freight amount" notifying
3. (   )Air Waybills showing "freight [   ] to collect/ [   ] prepaid [   ] indicating freight amount" and consigned to
4. (   )Memorandum issued by
5. (   )Insurance Police/Certificate in       copies for    % of the invoice value showing claims payable in China
      In currency of the draft, blank endorsed, covering ( [   ] Ocean Marine Transportation / [   ] Air Transportation / [   ] Over Land Transportation) All Risks, War Risks.
6. (   )Packing List/ Weight Memo in      copies issued by quantity/ gross and net weights of each package and

Packing conditions as called for by the L/C .
7. (   )Certificate of Quantity / Weight in        copies issued by an independent surveyor at the loading port,
      Indicating the actual surveyed quantity / Weight of shipped goods as well as the packing condition.
8. (   )Certificate of Quantity in     copies issued by [   ] manufacturer / [   ] public recognized surveyor / [   ]
9. (   )Beneficiary's certified copy of cable / telex dispatched to the accountees within___hours after shipment
      Advising [   ] name of vessel / [   ] flight No. / [   ] wagon No. , date, quantity, weight and value of shipment.
10. (   )Beneficiary's Certificate certifying that extra copies of the documents have been dispatched according to the
      Contract tems.
11. (   )Shipping Co's Certificate attesting that the carrying vessel is chartered or booked by accountee or their
      shipping agents:
12. (   )Other documents, if any:

      Additional instructions:
1. (   ) All banking charges outside the opening bank are for beneficiary's account.
2. (   ) Documents must be presented within        days after the date of issuance of the transport documents
      but within the validity of this credit.
3. (   ) Third party as shipper is not acceptable. Short Form/ Blank Back B/L is not acceptable.
4. (   ) Booth quantity and amount     % more or less are allowed.
5. (   ) Prepaid freight drawn in excess of L/C amount is acceptable against presentation of original
      charges voucher
      Issued by shipping Co./ Air Line/ or it's agent.
6. (   ) All documents to be forwarded in one cover, unless otherwise stated above.
7. (   ) Other terms, if any:

| | | |
|---|---|---|
| Account No: | with _____ (name of bank) | |
| Transacted by: | (Applicant: name, signature of authorized person) | |
| Telephone No.: | (with seal) | |

## VI. Case Study

A foreign trade company in China reaches an export contract with Country Z's X Company and the term of payment is D/P 45 days of after sight. When the bill of exchange and all the commercial documents are delivered to the collecting bank through the remitting bank, X Company accepts the bills immediately. When the goods arrives in Country Z, X Company signs a trust receipt and borrows the documents from the collecting bank in order to obtain the goods ASAP. After obtaining the documents, X Company releases the goods from the carrier. When the draft is matured, X Company is bankrupted due to inappropriate management and loses the abilities to reimburse the payment to the collecting bank. The collecting bank advises the remitting bank that the bill is dishonored and suggests the trade company to recourse the payment from X Company directly.

***Question:***

Who should undertake the non-payment responsibilities?

**国际贸易实务(英语版)(第2版)**

Specimen 8-1    SWIFT L/C

| APPLICATION HEADER: | | BANK OF CHINA TOKYO (TOKYO BRANCH) |
|---|---|---|
| SEQUENCE OF TOTAL | 27 | 1/1 |
| FORM OF DOC.CREDIT | 40A | IRREVOCABLE |
| DOC.CREDIT NUMBER | 20 | 199900033 |
| DATE OF ISSUE | 31C | 030301 |
| EXPIRY | 31D | DATE 030415 PLACE CHINA |
| APPLICANT | 50 | A.B.C.CO. , LTD. 03029 MATUKAGECHO, NAKAKU, YOKOHAMA, JAPAN |
| BENEFICIARY | 59 | BEIJING VENUS IMP/EXP CO., LTD, NO. 16 HUIXIN STREET BEIJING CHINA |
| AMOUNT | 32B | CURRENCY USD15,000.00 |
| AVAILABLE WITH/BY | 41A | ANY BANK BY NEGOTIATION |
| DRAFTS AT | 42C | DRAFTS AT SIGHT FOR 100PCT OF THE INVOICE VALUE |
| DRAWEE | 42A | BANK OF CHINA TOKYO (TOKYO BRANCH) |
| PARTIAL SHIPMENTS | 43P | ALLOWED |
| LOADING IN CHARGE | 44A | CHINESE PORT |
| FOR TRANSPORT TO | 44B | YOKOHAMA |
| LATEST DATE OF SHIP. | 44C | 030331 |
| DESCRIPT. OF GOODS | 45A | SCHOOL BAG AS PER S/C NO. 03AB0066 PRICE TERM: CIF YOKOHAMA |
| DOCUMENTS REQUIRED | 46A | 1) SIGNED COMMERCIAL INVOICE IN 3 COPIES<br>2) FULL SET OF CLEAN ON BOARD OCEAN BILLS OF LADING MADE OUT TO THE ORDER OF SHIPPER AND BLANK ENDORSED MARKED FREIGHT PREPAID AND NOTIFY APPLICANT<br>3) PACKING LIST IN 3 COPIES<br>4) CERTIFICATE OF ORIGIN GSP-FORM-A<br>5) INSURANCE POLICY FOR ICC(A)FOR 110 PCT OF INVOICE VALUE |
| ADDITIONAL COND. | 47A | ALL DOCUMENTS MUST BE SENT TO US IN LOT BY DHL OR REGISTERED AIRMAIL. |
| DETAILS OF CHARGES | 71B | ALL BANKING CHARGES OUTSIDE JAPAN FOR THE ACCOUNT OF THE BENEFICIARY |
| PRESENTATION PERIOD | 48 | DOCUMENTS TO BE PRESENTED WITHIN 15 DAYS AFTER THE DATE OF ISSUANCE OF THE SHIPPING DOCUMENTS BUT WITHIN THE VALIDITY OF THE CREDIT. |

| CONFIRMATION | 49 | WITHOUT |
|---|---|---|
| INSTRUCTIONS | 78 | ALL DRAFTS DRAWN HERE UNDER MUST INDICATE THE NUMBER, DATE OF ISSUE AND NAME OF ISSUING BANK OF THIS CREDIT. THE AMOUNT OF EACH DRAWING UNDER THIS CREDIT MUST BE ENDORSED BY THE NEGOTIATING BANK ON THE REVERSE HEREOF, WE HEREBY ENGAGE WITH DRAWERS AND BONA FIDE HOLDERS OF DRAFTS DRAWN UNDER AND IN WILL BE DULY HONORED UPON PRESENTATION TO THE DRAWEE. |
| TRAILER: | | ORDER IS (MAC:)… |

Specimen 8-2　Mail L/C

# THE ROYAL BANK OF CANADA

BRITISH COLUMBIA INTERNATIONAL CENTRE

1055 WEST GEORGIA STREET, VANCOUVER, B.C. V6E 3P3

CANADA

CONFIRMATION OF TELEX/CABLE PRE-ADVISED

TELEX NO. 4720688 CA

DATE: APR. 8, 2015

PLACE: VANCOUVER

| IRREVOCABLE DOCUMENTARY CREDIT | CREDIT NUMBER: 98/0501-FTC | ADVISING BANK'S REF. NO. |
|---|---|---|
| **ADVISING BANK:** SHANGHAI A J FINACE CORPORATION 59 HANGKONG ROAD SHANGHAI 200002,CHINA | **APPLICAN:** JAMES BROWN & SONS #304-310 JALAN STREET, TORONTO, CANADA | |
| **BENEFICIARY:** HUAXIN TRADING CO.,　LTD. 14TH FLOOR KINGSTAR MANSION, 676 JINLIN RD., SHANGHAI CHINA | **AMOUNT:** USD 46,980.00 (US DOLLARS FORTY SIX THOUSAND NINE HUNDRED AND EIGHTY ONLY) | |
| **EXPIRY DATE:** MAY 15, 2015 | FOR NEGOTIATION IN APPLICANTS COUNTRY | |

GENTLEMEN:

WE HEREBY OPEN OUR IRREVOCABLE LETTER OF CREDIT IN YOUR FAVOR WHICH IS AVAILABLE BY YOUR DRAFTS AT SIGHT FOR FULL INVOICE VALUE ON US ACCOMPANIED BY THE FOLLOWING DOCUMENTS:

+ SIGNED COMMERCIAL INVOICE AND 3 COPIES

+ PACKING LIST AND 3 COPIES, SHOWING THE INDIVIDUAL WEIGHT AND MEASUREMENT OF EACH ITEM

+ ORIGINAL CERTIFICATE OF ORIGIN AND 3 COPIES ISSUED BY THE CHAMBER OF COMMERCE

+ FULL SET CLEAN ON BOARD OCEAN BILLS OF LADIG SHOWING FREIGHT PREPAID CONSIGNED TO RODER OF THE ROYAL BANK OF CANADA INDICATING THE ACTUAL DATE OF THE GOODS ON BOARD AND NOTIFY THE APPLICANT WITH FULL ADDRESS AND PHONE NO. 77009910

+ INSURANCE POLICY OR CERTIFICATE FOR 130 PERCENT OF INVOICE VALUE COVERING: INSTITUTE CARGO CLAUSES (A) AS PER I.C.C. DATED 1/1/1982

+ BENEFICIARY'S CERTIFICATE CERTIFYING THAT EACH COPY OF SHIPPING DOCUMENTS HAS BEEN FAXED TO THE APPLICANT WITHIN 48 HOURS AFTER SHIPMENT

COVERING SHIPMENT:

4 ITEMS TRMS OF CHINESE CERAMIC DINNERWARE INCLUDING: HX1115 544SETS, HA2012 800SETS, HX4405 443SETS AND HX4510 245SETS

DETAILS IN ACCORDANCE WITH SALES CONFIRMATION SHHX98027 DATED APR.3, 2015.

〖 〗FOB/ 〖 〗CFR/ 〖X〗CIF/ 〖 〗FAS TORONTO CANADA

| SHIPMENT | TO | LATEST | PARTIAL SHIPMENTS | TRANSSHIPMENT |
|---|---|---|---|---|
| FROM  SHANGHAI | VANCOUVER | APRIL 30, 2015 | PROHIBITED | PROHIBITED |

DRAFTS TO BE PRESENTED FOR NEGOTIATION WITHIN 15 DAYS AFTER SHIPMENT, BUT WITHIN THE VALIDITY OF CREDIT.

ALL DOCUMENTS TO BE FORWARDED IN ONE COVER, BY AIRMAIL, UNLESS OTHERWISE STATED UNDER SPECIAL INSTRUCTIONS.

SPECIAL INSTRUCTIONS: ALL BANKING CHARGES OUTSIDE CANADA ARE FOR ACCOUNT OF BENEFICIARY

+ ALL GOODS MUST BE SHIPPED IN ONE 20' CY TO CY CONTAINER AND B/L SHOWING THE SAME

+ THE VALUE OF FREIGHT PREPAID HAS TO BE SHOWN ON BILLS OF LADING

+ DOCUMENTS WHICH FAIL TO COMPLY WITH THE TERMS AND CONDITIONS IN THE LETTER OF CREDIT SUBJECT TO A SPECIAL DISCREPANCY HANDLING FEE OF USD35.00 TO BE DEDUCTED FROM ANY PROCEEDS.

DRAFT MUST BE MARKED AS BEING DRAWN UNDER THIS CREDIT AND BEAR ITS NUMBER; THE AMOUNTS ARE TO BE ENDORSED ON THE REVERSE HEREOF BY NEG. BANK. WE HEREBY AGREE WITH THE DRAWERS, ENDORSERS AND BONA FIDE HOLDER THAT ALL DRAFTS DRAWN UNDER AND IN COMPLIANCE WITH THE TERMS OF THIS CREDIT SHALL BE DULY HONORED UPON PRESENTATION.

THIS CREDIT IS SUBJECT TO THE UNIFORM CUSTOMS AND PRACTICE FOR DOCUMENTARY CREDITS (1993 REVISION) BY THE INTERNATIONAL CHAMBER OF COMMERCE PUBLICATION NO. 600.

DAVID JONE             YOURS VERY TRULY,

                              JOANNE SUSAN

AUTHORIZED SIGNATURE         AUTHORIZED SIGNATURE

# Chapter 9    Inspection, Claims, Force Majeure and Arbitration

---

【Learning Objectives】

By studying this chapter, you should be able to master:

- Definition of Inspection, Claims, Force Majeure and Arbitration
- To explain ways to stipulate the place and time of inspection within the contract
- To master the inspection procedure
- To understand the conditions for breach of contract and settlement of claims
- To describe ways of stipulating claim clauses in the contract
- To be aware of the consequences of force majeure events
- To explain ways to stipulate force majeure clauses in the contract
- To realize the importance of arbitration in the settlement of disputes and claims
- To be aware of the issues to be considered in the negotiation of arbitration
- To describe the ways of stipulating an arbitration clause in the contract

---

## Lead-in: News Report

### HK Role Vital in B&R Arbitration Solution

Hong Kong's status as a regional legal service hub and its international image make the city's role essential in the nation's ambition to establish a Belt and Road-themed arbitration mechanism, legal experts said on Wednesday.

The call came after the nation's top reform decision-making body—the Leading Group for Deepening Overall Reform—approved a guideline for setting up such a procedure and organization in a meeting that concluded in Beijing on Tuesday.

According to the guideline, the dispute-solving procedure and organization should be built with the principle of extensive consultation, joint contribution and shared benefits, and should be based on China's existing judicial, arbitration and mediation institutions.

Wang Guiguo, president of the Hong Kong-based International Academy of the Belt and Road, said Hong Kong is an ideal venue for the organization to operate its business.

Wang, who is also chair professor of Chinese and Comparative Law in the City University of Hong Kong, explained that the principles for the establishment of such an organization emphasized the participation of all countries and regions involved in the Belt and Road Initiative.

Hong Kong, an international city that enjoys the world's freest economy, leading arbitration service and favorable geographic position, would easily win recognition and trust from foreign regions and nations, attracting them to settle disputes in the city, Wang concluded.

Meanwhile, Wang said it would offer an opportunity for Hong Kong to further consolidate its leading role in international arbitration services.

Echoing Wang on Hong Kong's edge, Secretary-General of Hong Kong International Arbitration Center Sarah Grimmer described Hong Kong as a "leading option" for handling Belt and Road disputes. She said the country's move is "very important" to Hong Kong as the city could contribute and benefit from what it has excelled in.

According to Grimmer, the number of cases handled by the HKIAC in 2017 increased by 47 percent from 2016. Among them, approximately a third of the cases involved Chinese enterprises and Belt and Road jurisdictions.

According to a survey by Queen Mary University of London in 2015, the HKIAC ranked the third best arbitral institution worldwide. The number of dispute resolution cases handled by the HKIAC reached 460 in 2016 with the total disputed amount for the administered cases reaching HK$19.4 billion ($2.5 billion).

Raymond Leung Hai-ming, a Hong Kong arbitrator, believes that Hong Kong should team up with arbitration organizations on the Chinese mainland to offer a comprehensive solution for both common law and civil law clients.

*(Source: http://www.chinadaily.com.cn/a/201801/25/WS5a6929bea3106e7dcc1366ce.html)*

***Class Activities:***

1. According to the guideline, what is about the dispute-solving procedure?

2. Why can Hong Kang become a leading role in international arbitration services?

In international trade practice, inspection is considered to be absolutely necessary in the process of commodity transportation. The buyer's right of inspection is clearly stipulated in laws or regulations of various countries. Actually, to clarify the responsibilities between the seller and the buyer, inspection clauses are usually stipulated in the contract.

If there is a dispute arising from breach of contract by either of the seller or the buyer, claim clauses are involved in contract. However, if the breach of contract results from Force Majeure, the party concerned is supposed to be excluded from the responsibility. In this case, whether an event is Force Majeure should be ascertained in the contract beforehand.

When both parties have different views on some cases or clauses and any party shirks liabilities intentionally, arbitration by a third party is required.

# 9.1   Inspection

进出口商品检验是指按照合同的规定，对进出口商品的品质、数量(重量)、包装、卫生、安全等实行检验、鉴定并出具检验证书，作为买卖双方交接货物、银行结算和处理索赔的有效凭证。

Inspection is an indispensable clause of a contract, and its aim is to protect the interests of both the buyer and the seller. Therefore, it is of great significance in international trade. Laws and regulations in various countries as well as international conventions have imposed inspection liabilities on both the sellers and the buyers. The failure in inspection and unfavorable inspection results may result in disputes between the buyers and the sellers and claims lodged by one party against the other.

In export trade, disputes between the buyers and the sellers may arise at anytime despite the fact that both parties of the sales contract work very carefully in the performance of the contract. In such cases, with a view to maintaining good relationship, the two parties of a dispute are normally recommended to rely on friendly negotiation and mediation. However, in case these means are not workable, the disputes may be submitted for arbitration or even litigation.

## 9.1.1   The Implication of Commodity Inspection

Commodity inspection is an indispensable link in the chain of smooth handling of foreign trade transaction. It is quite often the case that export and import goods are subject to damage or shortage in transit because of rough handling in loading and unloading, and the long distance they are traveling. Besides, the quality of the goods received by the buyer may not be in conformity with the contract of sale. All these will surely lead to disputes, and it is necessary to find out who is the right party responsible for that. If the commodity has been inspected and a commodity inspection certificate issued, the certificate will serve to ascertain where the trouble lies and who is to blame.

Internationally, export and import commodity inspections are executed by a third party generally known as surveyor. Some of the surveyors are governmental organs, others are run by individuals or trade associations upon application by the seller or the buyer. The surveyor exercises inspection or analysis over the export or import commodities as to their quality, weight, quantity, packaging, marking, place of origin or damage. As a result of the inspection and notarized appraisal, commodity inspection certificates are issued. They, in foreign trade practice, function as a foundation or basis on which the delivery and acceptance of the goods, the payment of the goods, or the claim and reimbursement for a loss is made between the seller and buyer.

商检机构可以接受对外贸易关系人以及国内外有关单位或外国商检机构的委托，办理规定范围内的进出口商品的鉴定业务，签发各种鉴定证书，作为办理进出口商品的交接、结算、计费、通关、索赔和仲裁等的有效凭证。

## 9.1.2   The Importance of Commodity Inspection

In international trade, the quality and quantity of the goods delivered by the seller should be in conformity with the terms of the contract and the goods should be packaged in the manner required by the contract. In this case, inspection of commodity and the insurance of certificate of inspection are necessary steps in the transfer of the goods.

Inspection may be made by the seller and the buyer themselves. But on most occasions, the seller does not transfer the goods to the buyer face to face. In addition, during the long-distance transit, loading and unloading operation, the loss of or damage to the goods may occur owing to the various kinds of risks or the carriers' fault. For the purpose of identifying liabilities and ascertaining facts, inspection by authoritative, impartial inspection bodies is required, by whom the certificates of inspection are issued. These certificates

检验是商检机构应对外贸易关系人的申请，而对进出口商品的品质、数量、重量、包装和运输工具等查验、鉴定，以确定其是否符合一定的标准。

have been the major basis for transferring the goods, making payments, lodging and settling claims in international trade.

Besides, CISG (United Nations Conventions on Contracts for the International Sale of Goods) and the laws of various countries have made similar stipulations on the buyer's right of inspection.

### 9.1.3 Import and Export Commodity Inspection

报验是指对外贸易关系人要求商检机构对进出口商品的品质、数量、重量、包装和运输工具等进行检验、鉴定的一种申请手续。根据提出申请的时间不同，报验可分为出口商品预检报验和出口商品检验报验。

Import and export commodity inspection covers the inspection of a commodity's quality, quantity, weight, safety and sanitation. All commodities listed in the Catalogue of Import and Export Commodities subject to statutory inspection, or commodities subject to statutory inspection otherwise specified by laws and regulations, must be subject to inspection by the Chinese entry/exit inspection and quarantine authorities or other designated institutions. The consignee of the imports subject to statutory inspection must register with the inspection and quarantine authorities at the port of discharge; and the consignor of the imports and exports subject to statutory inspection shall declare commodity inspection within the period and at the place specified by the inspection and quarantine authorities. Commodities subject to statutory inspection may be marketed or used being inspected, and export commodities may not be exported if found inferior in quality through inspection.

### 9.1.4 Time and Place of Inspection

The inspection of the goods can be conducted at various stages of the trade process. Before delivery, the manufacturers should make a precise and comprehensive inspection of the goods with regard to its quality, specifications, quantity or weight, and issue an inspection certificate certifying the technical data or the result of the inspection. Before shipment, the authorized department in the exporting country will conduct mandatory inspection as to the quality and quantity or weight of the goods and issue the relevant inspection certificates which serve as the basis for the negotiation of payments by the seller. After the arrival of the goods at the destination, the goods may be further inspected by relevant departments in the importing country, the unfavorable result of which serves as the basis for the claim made by the buyer.

Therefore, it is important to make clear when and where inspection should be conducted. CISG provides that unless the parties have agreed, otherwise the buyer has the right to inspect the goods and the time and place of inspection should be stipulated in detail in the contract.

There are generally three ways to stipulate the place and time of inspection in the sales contract: inspection at the factory or at the port of shipment, inspection at the port of destination, and inspection at the port of shipment and re-inspection at the port of destination.

### 1. Inspection at the Factory or at the Port of Shipment

Inspection at the factory or at the port of shipment refers to the inspection conducted by an authorized party agreed upon by both parties of the sales contract to testify the quality, quantity, weight, package, etc. of the goods at the factory or at the port of shipment before the delivery of the goods. Another name for this is known as shipping quality and weight. The inspection certificate(s) thus issued will be considered final for the delivery of the goods by the seller. In other words, the seller will not be obliged to go any change to the goods in transit after the goods have been inspected before delivery. Although the buyer can re-inspect the goods at the port of destination, normally he cannot claim for compensation based on the result of the re-inspection. Therefore, this method is more favorable to the seller.

### 2. Inspection at the Port of Destination

Inspection at the port of destination is also referred to as landed quality and weight. It indicates the inspection conducted by an authorized party within the time period stipulated in the sales contract to testify the quality, quantity, weight, package, etc. of the goods at the port of destination. The inspection certificate(s) issued in the destination country is considered final for the delivery of the goods by the seller. Under this arrangement, if any discrepancies are found between the actual goods and terms described in the sales contract, the buyer can retain the right of claim for compensation. Therefore, the buyer often prefers this method of inspection.

### 3. Inspection at the Port of Shipment and Re-inspection at the Port of Destination

As discussed above, neither way in stipulating time and place for inspection is satisfactory to both parties. To avoid further disputes, a third method has been created, stating that the inspection certificate(s) issued by the authorized party at the port of shipment can be used as one of the documents

检验时间和地点一般分为在工厂或装运港(地)检验、在目的港(地)检验以及在装运港检验,在目的港复验。

在工厂或装运港检验是指货物在工厂或装运港(地)交货前,由合同规定的商检机构验货后出具检验证明作为买方接受货物的最后依据。这种做法又称为离岸品质。离岸重量(数量)货物抵达目的港(地)后,买方无复验权。

目的港检验指货物运达目的港(地)时,由合同规定的检验机构验货后出具检验证明作为最后的依据。这种做法又称为到岸品质,到岸重量(数量)。如经检验证明货物与合同的规定不符,卖方应负责任,即买方有检验权。

装运港检验、目的港复验是以装运港(地)的检验证书作为卖方收取货款的依据，货到目的港(地)后买方行使复验权。即货物在装运前由合同规定的检验机构进行检验，其检验证书作为卖方要求买方支付货款或向银行议付的单据之一；货物运抵目的港(地)后的一定时间内，由合同规定的检验机构复验。若验货后发现货物与合同规定不符，并证明这种不符不属于承运人或保险公司的责任范围，买方可以在规定的时间内凭复验证书向卖方提出异议和索赔。

商品检验标准是检验进出口商品是否合格的依据。对商品检验要明确检验标准。因为可供检验和衡量的标准有很多种，如企业标准、行业标准、国家标准、国际标准等，采用不同的标准就可能得出不同的结论。因此，买卖双方应在合同中明确检验标准。但是，买卖双方约定的标准不能和国家法律法规使用的标准相冲突，否则该项合同就是无效的。

for the seller to settle payment after the delivery of the goods. However, the buyer retains the right to re-inspect the goods at the port of destination. If he obtains from an authorized party designated in the contract at the port of destination the inspection certificate(s) showing that the goods received are not as described in the contract, the buyer has the right to claim for compensation from the seller as long as there are evidences to show that the seller should be responsible for the discrepancies. Obviously, this method benefits both sides to a certain degree and therefore is widely adopted in international trade practice.

## 9.1.5　Inspection Standard

Inspection certificates are issued only when they are proved to be up to certain standards. Then what standards should be followed as far as commodity inspection is concerned?

Inspection on import and export commodities performed by the commodity inspection authorities shall cover quality, specifications, quantity, weight, packing and the requirements for safety and hygiene. If the mandatory standards or other inspection standards which must be complies with are specified in the Law and the Regulations, the inspection, of course, shall be performed according to the standards as specified in the Law and the Regulations.

However, in the absence of the mandatory standards or other inspection standards, the inspection shall be performed according to the standards agreed upon in the international trade contracts. One thing that calls for attention is that if the trade is conducted against the sample, the inspection shall be performed simultaneously according to the sample provided.

In the process of inspection, it is likely that the standards specified in the Law and the Regulations are not consistent with those agreed upon by the seller and buyer in the sales contract. In such cases, if the compulsory standards or other inspection standards specified in the Law and the Regulations are higher than the standards agreed upon in the contract, the inspection shall be conducted subject to the higher standard. If the standards specified in the Law and the Regulations are lower than the standards agreed upon in the contract, the inspection shall be conducted according to the standards agreed upon in the contract. Similarly, if the trade is conducted against the sample, the inspection shall be performed according to the sample provided.

Finally, if the inspection standards are not specified in the Law and the Regulations or the inspection standards are either not agreed upon or unclear in the contract, the inspection shall be conducted according to the standards of the manufacturing country, or relevant international standards or the standards designated by the state inspection agency.

# 9.1.6   Inspection Certificate

After the commodities are inspected and proved up to the standard(s) recognized by the inspection authorities, the inspection authorities then will issue inspection statements. Inspection statements issued by the commodity inspection authorities after the commodities have undergone inspection are called inspection certificates. The inspection certificates usually issued by the Chinese inspection authorities are as follows:

检验证书是进出口商品经由商检机构检验、鉴定后所出具的证明文件。它是卖方交货情况的证明；卖方向买方或其指定银行收取货款的单据；海关通关放行的依据；处理索赔与理赔的依据；进口国实行关税差别待遇的依据等。

(1) Inspection Certificate of Quality

This certifies that the quality and specifications of import and export commodities are in conformity with the contract stipulation.

(2) Inspection Certificate of Weight or Quantity

This certifies that the weight or quantity of import and export commodities is in conformity with the contract stipulation.

(3) Inspection Certificate of Value

This certifies that the price of import and export commodities in the invoice is a true reflection of the value of goods transacted.

(4) Inspection Certificate of Origin

This certifies that the name of the place is where the export commodity has been produced or manufactured.

(5) Sanitary Inspection Certificate

This certifies that foods and animal products for eating are up to standards for export.

(6) Veterinary Inspection Certificate

This certifies that the animals to be exported are in a condition good enough for export.

(7) Disinfection Inspection Certificate

This certifies that animal products to be exported have been disinfected.

(8) Inspection Certificate on Damaged Cargo

This certifies the degree to which the goods imported have been damaged and the causes of the damage.

### 9.1.7　Inspection Clause

In order to clarify the inspection time, place, institution and certificates required, it is necessary to set down the inspection clause in sales contract.

The following is a sample of inspection clause for export cargoes:

---

**Example 1**: *Specimen of Inspection Clause*

It is mutually agreed that the Certificate of Quality and Weight (Quantity) issued by the State General Administration of the People's Republic of China for Quality Supervision and Inspection and Quarantine at the port of shipment shall be part of the documents to be presented for negotiation under the relevant L/C. The buyer shall have the right to re-inspect the quality and weight (quantity) of the cargo.

The re-inspection fee shall be borne by the buyer. Should the quality and weight (quantity) be found not in conformity with that of the contract, the buyer are entitled to lodge with the seller a claim which should be supported by survey reports issued by a recognized surveyor approved by the seller. The claim, if any, shall be lodged within certain days after the arrival of the cargo at the port of destination.

---

### 9.1.8　Inspection Procedures

Inspection and quarantine procedures normally include six steps. They are application for inspection, acceptance of application, calculation and collection of fees, inspection and quarantine, decontamination treatment, and issuance of certificate and release of goods.

E.g., *If an importer asks the beneficiary for an SGS inspection certificate. the main procedure is as follows.*

① Making a deal

② Applying for SGS No. by the importer

③ Authorized inspection by the importer's SGS office

④ Arranging inspection by SGS–CSTC company

⑤ Cooperation with the inspection by the exporter

The Procedure of SGS Inspection Certificate is shown in Figure 9-1.

SGS-CSTC 通标公司，系瑞士通用公证行(SGS)与中国标准技术开发公司(CSTC)共同组建的合资公司。

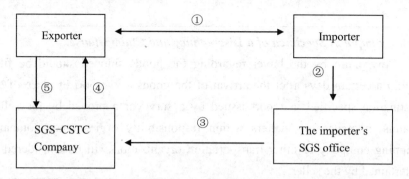

Figure 9-1   The Procedure of SGS Inspection Certificate

## 9.2   Claim

Complaints and claims from the customers, and disputes between the buyers and the sellers occur frequently in international trade. For example, the seller or the buyer may breach the contract, and then claim may arise. Usually a claim will be made, after the disputes, by the injured party. Sometimes the transaction parties may even submit their disputes to arbitration if they cannot resolve them.

索赔是指买卖合同的一方当事人因另一方当事人违约致使其遭受损失而向另一方当事人提出要求损害赔偿的行为。

Generally speaking, there are three types of claims in international trade practice. First, a claim between the seller and the buyer; second, a claim against carrier; third, a claim against the insurer. Previously in Chapter 5, we have roughly talked about the claim within insurance. In this section, we are going to focus on the claim between the seller and the buyer.

Claim can be defined as a demand made upon a person for payment on account of a loss sustained through negligence. In international trade, if the importer (buyer) or the exporter (seller) does not fulfill or wholly fulfill the contract, his act amounts to breach of the contract and the injured party can file a claim. Sometimes the claim made by buyers or customers may be a genuine complaint, however sometimes a claim may not be genuine in order to terminate contract. In import and export business, claims are common, even if the relevant parties tried to execute the contract cautiously. Therefore, it is necessary to include a discrepancy and claim clause in a contract. Normally, a discrepancy and claim clause in a contract goes as follows:

买卖双方应在合同中规定的索赔期内提出索赔。索赔期的长短，由买卖双方根据货物的性质、运输、检验的繁简等情况通过磋商确定。

**Example 2: Specimen of a Discrepancy and Claim Clause**

Any claim by the buyer regarding the goods shipped should be filed within a certain days after the arrival of the goods at the port or place of the destination specified in report issued by a surveyor approved by the seller. Claims in respect of matters within responsibility of insurance company, shipping company or other transportation organization will be considered or entertained by the seller.

In case the goods delivered are inconsistent with the contract stipulations, the buyer should make a claim against the seller within the time limit of re-inspection under the support of an inspection certificate or survey report issued by a nominated surveyor.

If a claim is justified, prompt and well-supported, it can be settled in the following ways: making refund and compensating for other direct losses or expenses; selling the goods at lower prices; or replacing the faulty goods with perfect ones.

Sometimes a penalty clause should be included in the contract in case one party fails to implement the contract such as non-delivery, delayed delivery, delayed opening of L/C. Under this clause, the party who has failed to carry out the contract must pay a fine which may be a certain percentage of total contract value.

罚金条款是指合同中规定的,如由于一方未履行合同或未完全履行合同,而应向对方支付一定数量的约定金额作为赔偿。主要用于卖方延期交货或买方延期接货等索赔。

**Example 3: Specimen of Penalty Clause**

The rate of penalty is charged at 0.8% of the total value of the goods whose delivery has been delayed for every seven days, odd days less than seven days should be counted as seven days. But the total amount of penalty, however, shall not exceed 8% of the total value of the goods involved in the late delivery.

To file or to settle a claim, the following points should be first considered:

a. Whether the claim is justified by the contract.

b. Whether the claim is made in time.

c. Whether the claim is well supported by good documentation.

Failure to have positive answers to all the above would mean difficulties in settling the claim. If it is justified, timely and well-supported, a claim can be settled in one of the following ways:

a. Making refund with compensation for other direct losses and expenses such as banking charges, storage and inspection charges, etc.

b. Devaluating the goods according to the degree of inferiority, extent of damage and amount of losses.

c. Replacing the defective goods with new ones that conform to the specifications, quality and performance as stipulated in the contract.

Therefore, whatever complaints or claims may be, we must handle them quickly, amicably to the satisfaction of all parties concerned without referring them to arbitration. Letters concerning the claims should always be courteous. Even if the complaint is unfounded, the sellers should not say so until they have sufficient and reliable grounds on why to repudiate the claim.

## 9.2.1 Breach of Contract

(1) Breach of contract commonly committed by the seller

a. The seller fails to deliver the goods on time or even no delivery.

b. The documents relating to the goods are incomplete.

c. The goods delivered are not in conformity with contract, etc.

(2) Breach of contract commonly committed by the buyer

a. The buyer fails to pay the price.

b. The buyer fails to take delivery of the goods, etc.

## 9.2.2 Liabilities of Breach of Contract

A claim appears only in the case of breach of contract. Different legal systems differ in their definition of breach of contract:

1. According to the United Nations Convention on Contracts for the International Sale of Goods (CISG), there are two types of breach of contract: fundamental breach, and non-fundamental breach

《公约》违约的法律后果可分为根本违约和非根本违约。

CISG Article 25 provides that "A breach of contract committed by one of the parties is fundamental if it results in such detriment to the other party as substantially to deprive him of what he is entitled to expect under the contract, unless the party in breach did not foresee and a reasonable person in the same circumstances would not have foreseen such a result. In the case of a fundamental breach of contract, the party suffering the losses is entitled to declare the contract void and ask for compensation."

If however, the breach of contract is non-fundamental, the suffering party can only claim damages but not declare the contract void.

英国法从违反合同的条款或规定情况把违约分为违反要件和违反担保。

### 2. The British Law divides the breach of contract into Breach of Condition and Breach of Warranty

Breach of condition refers to the breach of the major terms of the contract, for example, quality, quantity (weight), name of goods, package manners, price amount and so on; the suffering party may declare the contract void and claim damages.

Breach of warranty means breach of the minor terms of the contract, the breach of which gives rise to a claim for damages, but not to a right to reject the goods and treat the contract as repudiate.

美国从违反合同所造成的后果出发把违约分为重大违约和轻微违约。

### 3. The American Law divides it into Material Breach of Contract and Minor Breach of Contract

The main types of breach of contract of American law will be material breach of contract and minor breach of contract. A material breach can be a breach that has serious consequences on the outcome of the contract, while a minor breach can be, for example, a builder who substitutes his own type of materials for specified materials.

## 9.2.3 Valid Term for Claim

索赔的有效期一般为买卖双方规定的复验期。如未规定,《公约》规定索赔的有效期为两年。

The valid term for claim means the period within which the suffering party is entitled to ask for compensation. It is usually decided by the seller and buyer in the contract or may be stipulated by relevant laws. According to CISG, the valid term for a claim is two years from the date that the buyer receives the goods.

> ***Example 4**: Specimen of a Letter of Claim*
> Dear Sirs,
> Concerning LC—2015/7 we have to claim that the cable charges amounting to US $98 mentioned in your fax of this morning should be collected from the LC's applicant and be refunded to us.
> Meanwhile, as the payment was delayed, the delayed payment interest commencing from October 1 to the date of payment November 30 at the interest rate 10 percent p.a. amounting to US $348,000 should also be for the applicant's account.

Will you please advise the applicant and remit the proceeds to Mantrust New York for our credit?

Yours faithfully,
John Brown

# 9.3   Force Majeure

## 9.3.1   Definition of Force Majeure

Force majeure which means superior force in French refers to an event or effect that cannot be reasonably anticipated nor controlled, such as a strike, riot and war. As no fault to both parties, neither the seller nor buyer is obligated to any damage, provided that the contract contains a force majeure clause. To prove the event or effect is force majeure, the breaching party has to show:

(1) That his failure was "due to an impediment beyond his control".

(2) That the impediment was something he could have reasonably taken into account at the time of contracting.

(3) That he remains unable to overcome the impediment or its consequences.

Force majeure clause usually excuses a party who breaches the contract due to the party's performance being prevented by the occurrence of an event that is beyond the party's reasonable control. Typically, "Force Majeure" clauses are usually applicable to performance failures caused by:

(1) Natural disasters or other "Acts of God"(earthquakes, hurricanes, floods)(Acts of God or Act of Nature is a legal term for events outside of human control for which no one can be held responsible. This does not protect those who put others in danger of acts of God through negligence.).

(2) Wars, riots or other major upheaval.

(3) Government restrictions.

(4) Performance failures of parties outside the control of the contracting parties (subcontractors, suppliers and/or carriers).

## 9.3.2   Features of Force Majeure

A force majeure event should have the following features:

不可抗力又称为人力不可抗拒、人力不可抗拒事故。它是指在合同签订后，发生了不是由于任何一方当事人的过失或疏忽、当事人既不能预见和预防，又无法避免和克服的意外事件。在此情况下，合同不能履行或不能按期履行，遭受意外事件的当事人可免除其不履行或不按期履行合同的责任。

导致不可抗力主要有自然原因(如水灾、火灾、冰灾、雪灾、暴风雨、地震等)及社会原因(如战争、罢工、政府禁令等)。

(1) It happens after the contract is signed;

(2) It is not due to the negligence of the buyer or the seller;

(3) Neither the buyer nor the seller can control the situation.

### 9.3.3　Consequences of Force Majeure

不可抗力的后果是：导致合同的终止或合同的变更。

There are usually two consequences of force majeure: termination of the contract and postponement of the contract. Whether terminating the contract or postponing the performance of the contract depends on what degree the force majeure event has affected the performance of the contract, or on the detailed stipulations in the contract.

#### 1. Terminating the Contract

If the occurrence of force majeure event has damaged or destroyed the basis of the contract and makes it impossible to perform, for example, a flood has damaged or destroyed goods ready for shipment, then the contract can only be terminated.

#### 2. Postponing the Contract

In cases of events (such as transportation stoppage caused by an earthquake) that will only delay the fulfillment of a contract, the contract can be postponed but not terminated since it is still possible for the seller to carry out his contract obligations.

### 9.3.4　Force Majeure Clause

#### 1. Content of Force Majeure Clause

概括式不可抗力条款即在合同中不具体规定不可抗力事故的种类，只做笼统的规定。例如，"由于公认的不可抗力的原因……"或"由于不可抗力事故……"。

The force majeure clause usually contains:

(1) The scope of force majeure events. As there is no definite explanation on which events should be regarded as force majeure, the seller and the buyer usually stipulate in their contract about the scope of force majeure events.

(2) Time limit of notifying the other party. In case of a force majeure event, the party seeking to use the clause of force majeure has a duty to inform the other party promptly.

(3) The issuer of the certificate. A force majeure event should be verified by a certificate that attests such an event.

## 2. Three Ways of Stipulating What Constitutes Force Majeure

### (1) Generalization

In this way, the contract does not stipulate what events are included in force majeure in detail.

> **Example 5: *Specimen of Generalization Clause***
>
> If the shipment of the contracted cargo is prevented or delayed in whole or in part due to force majeure, the seller shall not be liable for non-shipment or late shipment of the goods of this contract. However, the seller shall notify the buyer by cable or telex and furnish the latter within 15 days by registered airmail with a certificate issued by China Council for the Promotion of International Trade attesting such event or events.

### (2) Specification

The stipulation of scope of force majeure would be stated in detail in the contract.

> **Example 6: *Specimen of Specification Clause***
>
> If the shipment of the contracted cargo is prevented or delayed in whole or in part by the reason of war, earthquake, flood, fire, storm, and heavy snow, the seller shall not be liable for non-shipment or late shipment of the goods or non-performance of this contract. However, the seller shall inform the buyer by cable or telex and furnish the latter within 15 days by registered airmail with a certificate issued by China Council for the Promotion of International Trade attesting such event or events.

列举式不可抗力条款即逐一列明不可抗力事故的种类。此方法是把双方公认的可以作为不可抗力的事故逐一列出，凡未列出者均不能作为不可抗力事故的援引。

### (3) Combination

This is a way that combines generalization and specification.

> **Example 7: *Specimen of Combination Clause***
>
> If the shipment of the contracted cargo is prevented or delayed in whole or in part by the reason of war, earthquake, flood, fire, storm, heavy snow or other causes of force majeure, the seller shall not be liable for non-shipment or late shipment of the goods or non-performance of this contract. However, the seller shall inform the buyer by cable or telex and furnish the latter within 15 days by registered airmail with a certificate issued by China Council for the Promotion of International Trade attesting such event or events.

综合式不可抗力条款即采用概括式与列举式综合并用的方式。

国际贸易实务(英语版)(第2版)

**Case Study**

*In October, export company A of China signed a contract with a foreign client for the export of agricultural products with the time of delivery in December. However, in July and August of the same year, the producing area suffered great draught and the exporter was unable to make delivery within the time stipulated in the contract. As a result, the exporter asked for the termination of the contract on the basis of force majeure event.*

**Questions:**

*Is the exporter appropriate in asking for the termination? Why or why not?*

# 9.4　Arbitration

解决争议的方式主要有：当事人之间协商解决；通过第三方的调解；提交仲裁或司法诉讼。其中，仲裁是解决国际贸易争议的一种重要方式。

It is quite normal that disputes arise in the course of the execution of a business contract or relating to the interpretation of the provisions of a contract. When disputes between exporter and importer arise in international trade, the two parties often resolve the disputes through amicable negotiations to maintain the goodwill and friendly business relations between them. But in case no settlement can be reached by negotiation, the relevant two parties can resort to mediation, arbitration or even litigation.

When either party is reluctant to make concessions or is in disagreement during negotiation, arbitration becomes an alternative solution to make a settlement.

## 9.4.1　The Definition of Arbitration

仲裁是指买卖双方达成协议，自愿将有关争议交给双方所同意的仲裁机构进行裁决的一种方式。仲裁的裁决是终局的，对双方都有约束力，双方必须执行仲裁的裁决。

Arbitration is a method of settling a dispute between two parties through the medium of a third party agreed by themselves in accordance with certain arbitration rules and make a final decision binding each of the parties based on the arbitration clause concluded previously by them or based on the arbitration agreement the parties have reached after the disputes arose.

SHAC

上海仲裁委员会

280

## 9.4.2 Characteristics of Arbitration

(1) Voluntarily. The litigants submit themselves voluntarily to an arbitrator. The arbitrator is a private, disinterested person or non-official government organization chosen by the parties to a disputed question.

(2) An arbitration agreement in written form is required for arbitration. Arbitration agreement is a contract between two or more parties whereby they agree to refer the subject in dispute to others and to be bound by their award.

(3) Arbitration is simpler in procedures, which is less costly and time consuming than litigation.

(4) The award is final and binding on both parties. Neither party may bring a suit before a law court or make a request to any other organization for revising the arbitral award. But if one party refuses to obey the award, the other can ask a court to enforce the implementation of the award. Another situation is that, when the procedures of arbitration are discovered to be illegal, a lawsuit can be filed in respect of award of arbitration.

## 9.4.3 Arbitration Clauses

Arbitration clauses in the contract will usually include the following terms:

### 1. The Arbitration Body

There are two forms of arbitration: institutional arbitration and ad hoc arbitration.

The arbitration body can be a temporary organized body for specific arbitration and which is dismissed when the arbitration is over, or it may be a permanent arbitration body, such as the Arbitration Court of International Chamber of Commerce (ICC), the London Court of Arbitration, and American Arbitration Association.

In our country, the China International Economic and Trade Arbitration Commission (CIETAC) in Beijing and its chapters in Shenzhen and Shanghai, and liaison offices in Dalian, Fuzhou, Changsha, Chengdu and Chongqing accept arbitration cases according to arbitration rules and regulations, and use the unified Arbitration Rules and panel of arbitrators.

仲裁的重要原则为当事人意思自治，即各方当事人通过签订合同中的仲裁条款或事后达成的仲裁协议，可以自行约定或选择仲裁事项、仲裁地点、仲裁机构、仲裁程序、适用法律、裁决效力，以及仲裁使用的语言等。

仲裁裁决一般是终局的，即裁决做出后，当事人不能上诉。如有一方拒绝执行，可要求法院强制其执行。

### 2. Place of Arbitration

仲裁地点是指进行仲裁的所在地。在商定仲裁协议时，双方当事人一般都力争在本国进行仲裁。

The place of arbitration will decide which arbitration rules or laws are applicable. The arbitration place can be anywhere in the seller's country, the buyer's country or a third country. The concerned parties always try to choose a place of arbitration they know well.

### 3. Arbitration Award

仲裁庭的裁决是终局性的，对双方均有约束力。一经裁决，双方当事人均不可向法院或其他机关提出变更裁决的要求。

An award is the decision made by the arbitration tribunal. It must be in written form with or without explanations or reasons. An arbitration clause must provide that the arbitral award is final, which is the incarnation of excluding the jurisdiction of litigation of courts by the arbitration clause. If an arbitration clause doesn't conclude that the arbitral award is final, CIETAC will not accept the case.

### 4. Arbitration Procedures

The arbitration clause will stipulate how arbitration is to apply, to work, how arbitrators are to be appointed, and how the case will be heard. We can divide the procedures into several steps:

仲裁的程序主要包括提交仲裁申请，组织仲裁院审理案件和做出裁决。

#### 1) Submit Dispute to Arbitration

If a dispute is to be submitted to a permanent organization, the application is sent directly to the tribunal and to the defendant (also called respondent). If the dispute is to be submitted to a temporary organization, the application is sent directly to the defendant.

#### 2) Appoint Arbitrators

Two points must be considered in appointing arbitrators: number of arbitrators and qualifications of arbitrators.

Usually, one or three arbitrators are appointed. The arbitration organization can appoint one arbitrator. Or both the plaintiff (also called claimant) and the defendant appoint one arbitrator and a third arbitrator is appointed by the arbitration organization. Another possibility is that a chief arbitrator is appointed by the arbitration organization and the chief arbitrator appoints two other arbitrators.

It is also important to consider the qualifications of the arbitrators, particularly the nationality and the professional background, to ensure an impartial and quality award.

In case that one party refuses to appoint an arbitrator, the other can either ask the organization to appoint one for the former when there is an arbitration organization or ask a law court to appoint one for the former if no organization has been agreed upon.

3) Hear a Case

Case hearing can be carried out by face-to-face reply or correspondence. In some countries, the tribunal can give the order of interim measures of protection while the arbitration is going on. For example, the subject object can be placed under a third party's control or perishable goods can be sold and the proceeds are placed under the tribunal's control.

4) Issue an Award

An award is the decision made by the arbitration tribunal. It must be in written form with or without explanations or reasons.

## 5. Arbitration fees

Generally, the arbitration clause should provide that the arbitration fees shall be borne by the losing party.

关于仲裁费用，一般规定由败诉方负担；也有规定由双方负担，或按仲裁裁决办理。

> **Example 8: *Specimen of Arbitration Clause in a Contract***
>
> All disputes in connection with the contract or the execution thereof shall be settled through friendly negotiations. If no settlement can be reached through negotiations, the case should then be submitted for arbitration to the Foreign Trade Arbitration Commission of the China Council for the Promotion of International Trade. The decision rendered by the said Commission shall be final and binding upon both parties. The arbitration fee shall be borne by the losing party.

# 【Key Terms and Words】

Discrepancy　差异、差别

Quarantine　检疫

Conciliation　抚慰，调解

Surveyor　鉴定人

Investigation　调查

Litigation　诉讼，起诉

Force majeure　不可抗力

Arbitration　仲裁

Penalty　罚款

Negotiation　商讨，议付

Inspection　检验

Claims　索赔

Arbitration clause　仲裁条款

Arbitrator　仲裁员

Issue an award　做出裁决

Hear a case　听证

Presiding arbitrator　首席仲裁员

Submit dispute to arbitration　提出仲裁申请

International Chamber of Commerce　国际商会

Arbitration Association　仲裁协会

China International Economic & Trade Arbitration Commission
中国国际经济贸易仲裁委员会

# 【Exercise】

**I. Please answer the following questions.**

1. Why is inspection an indispensable part of international trade?

2. Please explain the three major ways of stipulating the place and time of inspection.

3. What are the three types of inspection agency?

4. Please list at least 5 types of inspection certificates.

5. Please list the possible places where reinspection can be conducted.

6. What is the difference between receipt of cargo and acceptance of cargo?

7. What are some of the major characteristics of a force majeure event?

8. What factors need to be considered when drafting the force majeure clause?

II. Decide whether the following statements are true or false by writing "T" for true and "F" for false in the bracket besides each statement.

1. (      )Should cargo be damaged or lost during transit, the carrier bear no responsibility whether or not the damage or loss is due to the carrier's negligence.

2. (      )For one contract, only one method and one standard should be used to ensure consistency in inspection.

3. (      )In international trade, the party that has failed to implement the contract may choose not to carry out his contract obligations if he has paid the required penalty.

4. (      )Arbitration can be used to settle criminal cases as well as civil cases.

5. (      )Usually an arbitration tribunal can consist of one, two or three arbitrators.

6. (      )An arbitration award must be in written form with or without explanations or reasons.

7. (      )When the departure term (EXW) is used, the commodity should be inspected at the factory or warehouse where the delivery is made.

8. (      )If shipping quality is used in inspection, the inspection must be conducted at the seller's factory only.

9. (      )In practice, for small differences (e.g., 0.5% of weight), inspection result at the port of shipment is considered final or the difference is divided between the buyer and the seller.

III. Please briefly define or explain the following terms.

1. claim
2. force majeure
3. arbitration
4. arbitration award
5. arbitration tribunal
6. penalty clause
7. veterinary inspection
8. landed quality
9. shipping quality

IV. Write two letters with the following particulars.

1. A complaint letter for deferred delivery.

(1) Referring to the previous letters, cables or documents about the date shipment;

(2) Stating that the goods have not been received, and didn't catch the selling season;

(3) Stating that the delay makes you suffer some loss and lodging a claim for the loss.

2. A reply to the above letter.

(1) Informing the customer of receiving the letter or cable and express regret for delaying the goods;

(2) Stating the reasons of late delivery;

(3) Promising to make compensation for the customer's loss.

## V. Case study.

1. Company A signed a CIF contract with an American company, importing a piece of equipment. The total amount of the contract was USD8 million. It was stipulated in the contract that "if one of the party of the contract breach the contract, the other party will have the right to lodge a claim for compensation", and that "the party breaching the contract shall pay USD12 million as penalty for compensating the other party for the damages." After the signing of the contract, company A didn't receive the equipment from the American seller, which in turn influenced the production and sale of our own products. As a result, company A lodged a claim against the American seller within the period for claim stipulated in the contract. However, the American seller filed litigation unilaterally to the local court.

**Question:**

Please comment on the case.

2. Company A signed a contract with a foreign importer, exporting agricultural products. The date for signature was September 1 and the time for shipment stipulated in the contract was October, November and December. However, after the mid-September, the domestic price of the contracted product rose to a significant extent. Company A found it would suffer great loss if it exported the goods according to the contract. Upon investigation, the reason for the rising of the price was the serious flood taking place in the producing area in mid-July.

**Questions:**

(1) Can Company A resort to force majeure clause for the avoidance of its contractual obligations?

(2) What lessons can Company A learn from this case?

3. On February 2nd, an exporter signed a CFR contract with a Chinese importer which stipulated that L/C was the term for payment. The Chinese buyer issued L/C and the seller fulfilled shipment and presented a full set of documents required. Later on, the seller issued a Letter of Indemnity, asking the shipping company to release the goods to a company in Shantou of China. On March 24th, the Chinese buyer obtained the full set of document and went to the shipping company to take delivery of the contracted goods. However, he was told the goods had been taken by the Shantou Company on the 18th of the same month. On the 9th of June of the same year, the seller settled payment under the contract with the bank. Despite the efforts, the buyer was still unable to get the contracted goods. As a result, on the 14th of March of the next year, the Chinese buyer asked for arbitration in China.

**Question:**

What award could the arbitrators possibly issue for this case?

# Chapter 10   Business Negotiation and Establishment of Contract

【Learning Objectives】

By studying this chapter, you should be able to master:

- The general process of negotiation
- The meaning and types of a enquiry
- Guidelines for writing enquiries and replies
- The meaning and types of an offer
- Four necessary conditions of a firm offer.
- Time of validity or duration of an offer
- Withdrawal or revocation of an offer
- Termination of an offer
- The meaning of counter-offer
- The requirements of acceptance
- Necessary conditions of an effective contract
- Forms of a written contract
- Structure of a written contract

## Lead-in: Case Study

In October, 2015, country D called for bids on iron oxide yellow. With the intention to submit a tender, Company A in that country inquired Company B in China about this product.

On October 23, Company B sent the following offer: OFFER VALID November 25, IRON OXIDE YELLOW 1,500 M/T AT US$455 PER M/T CIF NET DLVRY FROM AUG-OCT IN 3 SHPMTS OF 450 M/T EACH.

Company A submitted a bid at the price based on the quotation. After bid opening on October 30, Company A was required by the tendering company to compete with another bidder. Eager to win the bid, Company A made a 30% reduction and got the bid. Afterwards, Company A sent a telex asking Company B to cut the price to US$439 per metric ton. Company B replied on November 3 that there was no room for reduction for the price quoted was the lowest. At the same time, Company

B managed to resell the goods to country E at the price around US$516 per metric ton.

In order to fulfill the obligation arising from winning the bid, Company A had to accept the Company B's offer on October 23, and asked the latter to send the contract.

After a careful study, Company B thought that the counteroffer of October 30 made by Company A had rendered the offer of October 23 and the earlier offer was invalid, discharging Company B from the obligation, so the acceptance of November 10 was still invalid. Hence Company B replied on November 14 as follows: due to your counteroffer of October 30, our offer dated October 23 is invalid. Besides, as our stock has been cleared out, please look for supplies elsewhere.

After receiving the message, a group led by the general manager of Company A came to Company B for a negotiation. They made the following arguments: your offer of October 30 remains open till November 25. In spite of our counteroffer of October 30, we have made acceptance within the term of validity. According to our laws, the acceptance is valid and should be enforced. Company B invoked Article 17 of CISG: An offer, even if it is irrevocable, is terminated when a rejection reaches the offeror, which finds its equivalence in both continental law and Anglo-American law system.

In the end, the general manager of Company A accepted the reason given by Company B and gave up his opinion. In consideration of Company A's difficult situation, company B helped to gather 500 metric tons of supplies and offered again at the price quoted on October 23. Company A purchased the rest of goods elsewhere and fulfilled its tender obligation at a loss.

### Class Activities:

1. What is the main process of the negotiation?

2. What do the buyer and the seller focus on in the case?

3. What can we learn from the case?

The word "negotiation" stems from the Roman word *negotiari* meaning "to carry on business or to trade". Negotiation is a kind of basic human activity that people undertake every day to manage the relationship between children and parents, husband and wife, buyer and sellers, business associates and so on. It is a process in which two or more entities come together to discuss common and conflicting interests in order to reach an agreement, solve a problem or make arrangements.

Generally speaking, business negotiation refers to the negotiation that takes place in the business world and deals with business relationships. It can be understood as back-and-forth communication between different companies or economic organizations with the goal of reaching agreements to gain their economic benefits.

## 10.1  The General Process of Business Negotiation

The process of business negotiation is made up of three stages: pre-negotiation, face-to-face negotiation and post-negotiation. Every stage is defined as a specific part of the process and covers all actions and communications by either side. A specific stage comes to an end where both sides decide to proceed on to the next stage or decide to abandon the communication if there is no point in further negotiations.

### 1. Pre-negotiation

The pre-negotiation stage is even more important than the formal negotiations in the business relationship, and it usually starts from the first contact between the two sides whose interest in doing business with each other is shown. From this stage on, both sides begin to form their strategies for face-to-face negotiation. To get fully prepared before the negotiation, both sides should take two aspects into consideration, i.e., environmental factors and information gathering. The environment factors refer to those factors that will affect the negotiation in a direct or indirect way — politics, religious belief, legal system, business practices, social customs, financial state, infrastructure and climate. The information gathering may in some way determine the success or failure of the negotiation, and includes that of markets, science and technology, policy and regulations,

国际贸易实务(英语版)(第2版)

finance and opponents.

### 2. Post-negotiation

At this stage, all the terms and conditions have been agreed upon with the contract being drawn up to be signed. However, we cannot toss the contract into our files and forget about it, because writing the contract and the wording in it is a negotiation process in itself. Any aspect of any contract may need to be re-negotiated, or the details altered to counter a broad variety of changing circumstances. Therefore, it is essential for both sides to make sure that they understand everything they have agreed on before they leave the negotiation table.

### 3. Face-to-face negotiation

At this stage, both sides know that they can work together with the other side for a solution to a joint problem in spite of the fact that each side may view the situation in its own way. It is time for both sides to explore the differences in preferences and expectations so that they can come closer to each other. Some business person prefer to start negotiations by discussing and agreeing on broad principles, and another good way to ensure success at this stage is an initial discussion on items of common interest.

The business negotiation may be carried out through correspondence, such as letters, e-mail, fax, etc. And it may also be conducted orally or both. No matter what way the negotiations are hold, in practice, the business negotiation usually go through four steps, i.e., enquiry, offer, counter-offer, and acceptance. Of course, it is not necessary for every transaction to cover these four stages, sometimes, only offer and acceptance are the two necessary stages which are required for making a contract.

Process of Business Negotiation is shown in Figure 10-1.

交易磋商可以通过信函、电子邮件或传真等形式来进行，也可以采用口头磋商的形式，抑或是口头与书面两种形式结合起来使用。在实际业务中，不管采用哪种形式，贸易磋商通常包括4个环节：询盘、发盘、还盘和接受。当然，不是每一次磋商都必须包括这4个环节，但发盘和接受是两个必不可少的环节。

交易磋商是进出口业务中一个非常重要的步骤。它也是为了让买卖双方达成一致而围绕合同条款进行的。这些条款包括商品的描述、品质、数量、包装、价格、装运、保险、支付、商检、索赔与争议、仲裁与不可抗力等。只有双方对所磋商的条款都无异议，销售合同才能签订。

Figure 10-1   Process of Business Negotiation

290

Business negotiation is one of the most important steps in conducting an export or import transaction. It is also the dealings between seller and buyer in order to reach an agreement on the terms about the description of the goods, quality, quantity, packing, price, shipment, insurance, payment, inspection, claims and disputes, arbitration, force majeure, etc. Only when both parties agree on those terms consulted can the business be done and the contract of sales concluded.

# 10.2  Enquiry

Enquiry refers to intension from a party interested in the purchase or sale of goods specified therein, indicating particular, desirable conditions regarding price and delivery terms, etc., addressed to a prospective supplier or buyer with a view to obtaining an offer or bid.

询盘是指一方为了购买或销售货物而向卖方或买方提出的一些有关价格和运输等交易条件的询问。

In international trade, an enquiry usually serves as the starting point of business negotiation. Both the seller and the buyer can make an enquiry. The enquiry made by the seller is usually called "invitation to offer", and the enquiry made by the buyer is usually called "invitation to bid". The invitation has no legal effect on either the inquirer or the recipient, therefore, the recipient can choose to answer or not. On the other hand, an enquiry can be made to several parties at the same time, in this way the enquirer can choose to trade with the one who has offered the best terms. However, according to practice, the receiver of an enquiry will respond timely in the usual form of a quotation, an offer or a bid.

询盘通常由买方发出，称之为"邀请发盘"，也可由卖方发出，称之为"邀请递盘"。这种邀请对于询盘人和被询盘人都无法律约束力。

## 10.2.1  Types of Enquiry

According to the content, an enquiry may be very simple or is in great details, it can be of two types: general enquiry and specific enquiry. In a general enquiry, the buyer just wants to have a general information of the commodities, such as a catalogue, a price list, a brochure, a sample, etc., which the exporter is in a position to supply. In a specific enquiry, the buyer needs detailed information about a certain commodity he intends to purchase, such as the name of commodity, quality, quantity, specifications, terms of price, terms of payment, time of shipment, packing, discount, etc. An enquiry can be made by letter, e-mail, fax, or even telephone or through face-to-face talk.

## 10.2.2　Guidelines for Writing Enquiries and Replies

Enquiries mean potential business, so both the buyer and the seller should take great care in writing or replying to them.

Enquiries should be concise, courteous, specific and reasonable.

An inquirer should be specific about what he needs, and ask for more information besides the price of the goods.

Replies to enquiries should be prompt, courteous, objective, and entire, and contain all the information customers required.

Do not use over-polite, humble wording in replies.

It's better for the seller to assure that he has full confidence in his products or service.

---

***Example 1: An Enquiry from a Buyer***

Dear Sirs:

Messrs. Armstrong & Smith of Sheffield inform us that you are exporters of cotton bed-sheets and pillowcases. We would like you to send us details of your various ranges, including sizes, colors and prices, and also samples of the different qualities of the materials used.

We are large dealers in textiles and believe there is a promising market in our area for moderately priced goods of the kind mentioned.

When replying, please state your terms of payment and discount you would allow on purchase of not less than 100 dozen of individual items. Price quoted should include insurance and freight to Liverpool.

Yours sincerely,

---

***Example 2: A Reply to the Enquiry***

Dear Sirs,

We are very pleased to receive your enquiry of 15th January and are enclosing our illustrated catalogue and price list giving the details you asked for.

Also by separate post we are sending you some samples and feel confident that when you have examined them you will agree that the goods are both excellent in quality and reasonable in price.

On regular purchase in quantities of not less than 100 dozen of individual items, we would allow you a discount of 2%. Payment is to be made by irrevocable L/C at sight.

Because of their softness and durability, our cotton bed-sheets and pillowcases are rapidly becoming popular and after studying our prices, you will not be surprised to learn that we are finding it difficult to meet the demand. But if you place your order not later than the end of February, we would ensure prompt shipment.

We invite your attention to our other products such as table clothes and table napkins, details of which you will find in the catalogue, and look forward to receiving your first order.

Yours faithfully,

# 10.3　Offer

## 10.3.1　The Meaning of an Offer

An offer is a proposal made by the buyer or the seller to the other party in order to sign a contract. In other words, it means the buyer or the seller explicitly expresses his willingness to do the business according to the terms offered. According to Article 14(1) in *United Nations Convention on Contracts for the International Sale of Goods* (CISG), a proposal to conclude a contract addressed to one or more specific person constitutes an offer if it is sufficiently definite and indicates the intention of the party making the offer to be bound in case of acceptance. "Offeree" is the party addressed, and "offeror" is the party making an offer. In the case of the seller, the offer is called a selling offer, while in the case of the buyer, it is called a buying offer or bid.

《公约》第 14 条第一款对发盘的定义是：向一个或一个以上特定的人提出的订立合同的建议，如果十分确定并且表明发价人在得到接受时承受约束的意旨，即构成发价。

## 10.3.2　Types of an Offer

There are two kinds of offers: firm offer and non-firm offer.

(1) Firm offer

A firm offer is an offer which is made to one or more specific persons to express or imply a definite intention of the offer or to make a contract under a clear, complete and final trade terms. To a firm offer, its contents in terms of description, quantity and price should be indicated definitely, besides, the firm

实盘是发盘人向一个或一个以上特定的对象提出的愿意按明确、完整、无保留的交易条件达成交易的肯定表示。

offer should be made without reservation, and the intention and terms in the offer should clearly be described without ambiguity. Words such as "about", "roughly", "approximately" should not be used.

A firm offer will contain the following points:

a. Description of commodities, including name, quality, quantity and specifications;

b. Price and type of currency;

c. Date of delivery and packaging;

d. Terms of payment and discounts;

e. The time of validity of the offer.

The pattern of an offer is not fixed, it may be complete or brief depending on the specific situations. Normally, the offer shall be in a detailed form when we face a new client, while the offer would be simple when we offer to an acquainted client.

Once a firm offer is accepted by the offeree within its stipulated validity, it can not be withdrawn and is binding on both offeror and offeree, and then the contract is concluded right away. Therefore, firm offer can encourage offerees to make decisions and close business.

---

***Example 3: An Example of Firm Offer Letter***

Dear Sirs,

We thank you for your letter dated June 22 covering our Jianlong Brand automatic washing machine inquiry.

Jianlong Brand is one of the best known trade marks in China. It can run 15,000 times continuously without any breakdown. It first passed through the recognition of America's UL and the qualities have kept the first for more than ten years in succession.

Complying with your request, we take the pleasure in making you a firm offer Jianlong Brand automatic washing machine USD 118 per machine FOB Ningbo, inclusive of your 5% commission. Your reply must reach us before 12 a.m. July 20 our time.

For detailed specification, please refer to the catalogue enclosed. We hope that you will be glad to place a trial order with us.

We are looking forward to your early reply.

Yours faithfully,

---

## (2) Non-firm offer

A non-firm offer is an offer without engagement. It is not binding upon the sellers and the details of the offers may change in certain situation. In most cases, the content of a non-firm offer are not clear and definite, the main terms and conditions are not complete, and there is no time of validity in the non-firm offer. Moreover, the offeror makes the offer with reservation. Such wordings as "subject to our final confirmation" and "subject to goods being unsold" are often used.

A non-firm offer looks more flexible to the offeror than a firm offer, as he can make decision of closing business according to the market situation. However, offerees often pay little attention to it and just regard it as an ordinary business dealing, which does no good to the conclusion of business.

虚盘是指发盘人有保留地向受盘人发出交易条件，愿意签订合同的建议。

---

> **Example 4: An Example of Non-firm Offer Letter**
>
> Dear Sirs,
>
> Thank you for your letter of March 9 enquiring for our tape recorders and your desire to establish direct business relations with us.
>
> As requested, we are sending you our quotation sheet covering the types in which you are interested. Unless otherwise sated, all the products can be supplied within four weeks after receipt of your order and the prices listed are subject to our final confirmation. On an order exceeding 10,000 sets, we usually allow 13% quantity discount.
>
> Some latest catalogues and brochures have also been sent to you under separate cover for your reference. Should any of the items be suitable for your market, please let us know. As soon as your specific enquiry is received, we will make you an offer immediately.
>
> Your early reply will be much appreciated.
>
> Yours faithfully,

---

## 10.3.3   Four Necessary Conditions of a Firm Offer

(1) The offer shall address to one or more specific persons.

According to Article 14(2) in CISG, a proposal other than one addressed to one or more specific persons is to be considered merely as an invitation to make

发盘必须向一个或一个以上特定的人提出。《公约》的第十四条第二款中规定，非向一个或一个以上特定的人提出的建议，仅应视为邀请做出发价，除非提出建议的人明确地表示相反的意向。

offers, unless the contrary is clearly indicated by the person making the proposal.

(2) The offer shall indicate the intention of the offeror to be bound in case of acceptance.

a. The contractual intent may be indicated by stating "offer", "firm offer", or by stipulating the time of validity of the offer, etc.

b. Once the offer is unconditionally accepted by the offeree within its validity, the terms in the offer generally forms a binding contract which is binding on both offeror and offeree.

(3) Contents of the offer shall be sufficiently definite.

a. Contents of the offer shall be clear. An offer should contain the intention and the essential terms of the contract.

b. Trade terms of the offer shall be complete. The CISG stipulates that a sufficiently definite offer should include three basic elements: name, quantity and price. In our foreign trade practice, a complete offer shall include the quality, quantity, packing, price, terms of delivery of the goods and terms of payment.

c. A firm offer shall be final, which means it should be made without any restrictive conditions.

d. As to the completeness of the main terms in a firm offer, it is understood that not all the terms are required in every offer in the following conditions:

- Some general business terms have been agreed upon between the traders;
- A usual practice has been formed between the traders through long business relationships established in the past;
- Invoke the content of the business letters between the traders or the previous contract number.

E.g., REPEAT OFFER 41000 10000YDS MAY SHIPMENT OTHER TERMS SAME AS (AS PER) S/C NO200034 DATED OCT. 18TH.

(4) The offer shall be communicated to the offeree.

According to Article 15 in CISG, an offer becomes effective when it reaches the offeree.

发盘中的贸易条款必须完整。《公约》规定，一项确定的发盘要包括三个基本要素，即名称、数量和价格。在我国的对外贸易实践中，一项完整的发盘要包括质量、数量、包装、价格、货物交货条款和支付条款等内容。

在以下三种情况下，一项发盘的交易条件表面上不完整，而实际上是完整的。

- 交易双方事先已订立"一般交易条件"；
- 交易双方在以前的业务中已形成的习惯做法；
- 援引来往的函电或以前成交的合同号码。

### 10.3.4   Time of Validity or Duration of an Offer

In a firm offer, the date is very important, and in the international trade, any offer has a time of validity. An offer will be effective when it reaches the offeree, and the offer can not revoke or amend it during the time of validity. If the offer is accepted by the offeree during the time, a contract is then concluded.

发盘于送达被受盘人时生效。在有效期内，发盘不能撤回或修改。如果被受盘人在有效期内接受发盘，合同即告成立。

A firm offer usually contains a validity date. However, the time of validity is not an indispensable condition of an offer.

(1) Ways of stipulating the time of validity clearly.

a. Stipulate the latest date for acceptance, for example: "the offer is subject to your reply reaching here on or before 14th, July", "the offer valid until Thursday our time".

b. Stipulate a period of time for acceptance, for example: "the offer is valid for four days", "the offer is subject to your reply in five fifteen days".

(2) If an offer doesn't clearly stipulate a validity date, it would be valid within a reasonable time. What constitutes a reasonable time depends on the circumstances of each case. For example: "reply as soon as possible", "reply promptly". As to this method, there is a question of computing validity time.

Article 20 in CISG stipulates "*A period of time for acceptance fixed by the offeror in a telegram or a letter begins to run from the moment the telegram is handed in for dispatch or from the date shown on the letter or, if no such date is shown, from the date shown on the envelope. A period of time for acceptance fixed by the offeror by telephone, telex or other means of instantaneous communication begins to run from the moment the offer reaches the offeree.*" "*Official holidays or non-business days occurring during the period for acceptance are included in calculating the period. However, if a notice of acceptance cannot be delivered at the address of the offeror on the last day of the period because that day falls on an official holiday or a non-business day at the place of business of the offeror, the period is extended until the first business day which follows*".

(3) According to Article 18(2) in CISG, if the offer is made orally, "An oral offer must be accepted immediately unless the circumstances indicate

otherwise."

(4) Time that an offer becomes effective. There are two main different views of the time that a written form offer becomes effective, one is dispatch theory, and the other one is arrival theory. Both "convention" and our "contract law" adopt arrival theory.

### 10.3.5　Withdrawal or Revocation of an Offer

(1) Withdrawal of an offer

发盘的撤回，指的是撤回通知于发盘到达被发盘人之前或同时送达被发盘人。

Withdrawal of an offer refers to the notice of withdrawal reaching the offeree before or at the same time as offer. The British laws and the American laws have different explanations to withdrawal. Article 15 (2) of CISG stipulates: "*An offer, even if it is irrevocable, may be withdrawn if the withdrawal reaches the offeree before or at the same time as the offer.*" In international practice, the suitable occasion for withdrawal is just when the offer is sent by mail or telegram.

(2) Revocation of an offer

Revocation of an offer usually refers to the notice of cancellation reaching the offeree later than the offer. The general rule is that the revocation is effective only when it is made known to the offeree. If the offeror seeks to revoke the offer, but the offeree accepts the offer before notice of the revocation, a valid contract is created.

As to whether an offer can be revoked or not, different laws have different explanations.

a. The law of the Continental countries rules that the offer cannot be revoked within the time of validity.

b. Stipulation in the British laws and the American laws show that an offer can be revoked at any time before acceptance, except the offer that is made with a consideration or signed and sealed by the offeror.

c. CISG adopts a compromise regulation. Article 16 of CISG stipulates: "*Until a contract is concluded, an offer may be revoked if the revocation reaches the offeree before he has dispatched an acceptance. However, an offer cannot be revoked ① if it indicates, whether by setting a fixed time for acceptance or otherwise, that it is irrevocable; or ② if it was reasonable for the offeree to rely on the offer as being irrevocable and the offeree has acted in reliance on the offer.*"

## 10.3.6   Termination of an Offer

Termination of an offer means the offer is no longer valid. An offer may be terminated in any one of the following ways:

Revocation of the offer by the offeror;

Rejection of offer by offeree;

The offer is not accepted within the validity;

Death or disability of either party;

Performance of the contract becomes illegal after the offer is made.

# 10.4   Counter-offer

If an offeree does not agree with any or some of the terms of the original offer, he would put forward a new offer, i.e., the counter-offer. For example, if an offeree accepts the price, but adds a term by stating that new tires must be put on the car, this is a conditional acceptance and therefore a counteroffer. It can be made verbally or in writing.

还盘是受盘人对原发盘的拒绝，也是受盘人以发盘人的身份提出的一项新的发盘。

According to Article 19 in the CISG:

(1) A reply which purports to be an acceptance but contains additional limitations or other modifications is a rejection of the offer and constitutes a counter-offer.

(2) However, a reply to an offer which purports to be an acceptance but contains additional or different terms which do not materially alter the terms of the offer constitutes an acceptance, unless the offeror, without undue delay, objects orally to the discrepancy or dispatches a notice to that effect. If he doesn't so object, the terms of the contract are the terms of the offer with the modifications contained in the acceptance.

(3) Additional or different terms relating among other things, to the price, payment, quality and quantity of the goods, place and time of delivery, extent of one party's liability to the other or the settlement of disputes are considered

to alter the terms of the offer materially.

Once a counter is made, the original offer made by the offeror would lose its effectiveness. If an offeree wants to accept the original offer after he made a counter-offer, the firm offer is invalid unless the offeror agrees to reinstate it.

The buyer may not agree on the price or packing or shipment put forward by the seller or offeror, and states his own terms instead in the counter-offer, therefore, it is virtually a new offer. The original offeree turns to be the new offeror while the original offeror becomes the new offeree. The new offeree may accept or reject it and even make a counter-offer again.

---

***Example 5: An example of counter-offer letter***

Dear Sirs,

We are in possession of your letter July 1 offering us Jianlong Brand automatic washing machine USD118 per machine FOB Ningbo inclusive of our 5% commission.

While appreciating the quality of your lines, we made a careful study of your offer. We find your prices are too high to be acceptable. In fact, the cost of raw materials has not soared in the past three month. In order to make your products more competitive in our market, we suggest that you reduce prices by 8%. If you will agree to our counter-suggestion, regular orders for large numbers will be placed. Otherwise, we will conduct our business elsewhere.

Please let us have your E-mail confirmation at your earliest convenience.

Yours faithfully,

---

接受的实质是对发盘表示同意。接受一旦生效，合同即告成立，双方都将受合同约束。

# 10.5   Acceptance

In business law, an acceptance is an assent to terms of an offer or counter-offer, required before a contract can be valid. An acceptance of an offer becomes effective at the moment the indication of assent reaches the offeror. Once the offer is accepted, a contract is thereupon concluded.

## 10.5.1　The Meaning of Acceptance

Article 18 of CISG says: "*An acceptance of an offer becomes effective at the moment the indication of assent reaches the offeror.*" However, the laws of some countries stipulate that an acceptance begins to function the moment the letter or cable of acceptance is posted or dispatched. A contract is thus formed at this very moment in spite of the fact that the letter or cable is likely to be lost in the mail or transmission. To avoid subsequent disputes or confusion in this respect, it is the practice to clarify to the offeree that an acceptance would be valid unless the letter or cable is received before the time limit.

An effective acceptance should meet the following requirements:

An acceptance should be made by the specific offeree to whom the offer is delivered.

An acceptance should be clearly expressed by the offeree's verbal or written statement. Silence or inactivity on the part of the offeree is not an acceptance.

An acceptance must accept all the terms that are put forward in the offer. In other word, the acceptance must be unconditional. In principle, if any conditions, modifications or limitations to the offer are made, they are a counter-offer, but not an acceptance.

An acceptance must reach the offeror within the validity of a firm offer.

《公约》第十八条第一款：受盘人声明或以其他行为表示同意一项发盘的，即为接受。

## 10.5.2　Effective Time of Acceptance

According to Article 23 in CISG, a contract is concluded at the moment when an acceptance of an offer becomes effective in accordance with the provisions of this Convention.

## 10.5.3　Late Acceptance

An acceptance which arrives at an offeror after the expiry of the time of validity or exceeds the reasonable time of an offer which doesn't stipulate a validity date is named as a late acceptance. It is generally not valid, but according to the stipulation of CISG, it is effective in the following conditions:

(1) A late acceptance is nevertheless effective as an acceptance if, without

一般的逾期接受无效，但发盘人同意接受，并立即通知对方，仍有效；传递不正常引起的逾期接受有效，但发盘人不同意，并立即通知对方，仍无效。

delay, the offeror orally so informs the offeree or dispatches a notice to that effect.

(2) If a letter or other writing containing a late acceptance shows that it has been sent in such circumstances that if its transmission had been normal it would have reached the offeror in due time, the late acceptance is effective as an acceptance unless, without delay, the offeror orally informs the offeree that he considers his offer as having elapsed or dispatches a notice to that effect.

### 10.5.4   Withdrawal of Acceptance

英美法实行的是投邮主义，接受不可以撤回，除非发盘规定接受到达生效。大陆法采用的是到达主义，接受可以撤回。

(1) The *Common Law* adopts Mail-box Rule, which means the acceptance can not be withdrawn unless the offer stipulates that it would be effective when it reaches the offeree. However, Received the Letter of Acceptance is adopted in the *Civil Law*, acceptance can be withdrawal. In another word, an offer becomes effective when it reaches the offeree.

根据《公约》及《中华人民共和国合同法》的规定，如果撤回通知先于接受通知或于接受通知同时送达发盘人，接受可以撤回。

(2) According to CISG and *Contract Law of the People's Republic of China.* An acceptance can be withdrawn if the withdrawal reaches the offeror before or at the same time as the acceptance would have become effective.

---

***Example 6: An example of Acceptance***

Dear Sirs,

We have received your letter of July 16. It is regretful for us to see that you cut down the price of our Jianlong Brand automatic washing machine too sharp, but in order to develop our market in your place, we have decided to accept your counter-offer as an exceptional case.

We hope you will send us your formal order by return, which we will execute with our best attention.

Yours faithfully,

---

An acceptance dispatched by the offeree after expiration of the period for acceptance constitutes a new offer, unless the offeror timely advises the offeree that the acceptance is valid. If the offeree dispatched its acceptance within the period for acceptance, and the acceptance, which would otherwise have reached the offeror in due time under normal conditions, reaches the offeror after expiration of the period for acceptance due to any other reason, the acceptance is valid, unless the offeror timely advises the offeree that the acceptance has been rejected on grounds of the delay.

## 10.6  Conclusion of Contract

As a rule, a contract is concluded once the offeree accepts the offer. In practice, when the effective acceptance reaches offeror or when the offeree make the behavior of accepting, both parties will enter into a contract conclusion. A contract is an agreement that creates an obligation. It is a binding, legally enforceable agreement between two or more competent parties.

合同是一份具有法律效力的协议，它对双方或多方具有法律约束力。

### 10.6.1  Necessary Conditions of an Effective Contract

(1) Contracting parties should have signing abilities;

(2) The content of the contract should be legal;

(3) The contract should comply with legal formality;

(4) Contracting parties' meaning expresses should be true.

A contract can take in written form, oral form as well as other forms. The parties may choose the proper one according to their need and requirements. In international trade practice, the written form is preferred by parties.

### 10.6.2  Forms of a Written Contract

In international trade, there is no legal requirement for the title or the form of a written contract. Therefore, export and import contracts vary in both names and forms. The most common written text of a business contract has four forms, namely, contracts, confirmation, agreements and memorandums. The first two are used for business whose terms are always detailed and formal, and the memorandum is used for groups and government departments. In our foreign trade business, contracts and confirmation are mainly adopted, for example, the sales contract or confirmation drawn up by the seller, and the purchase contract or confirmation drawn up by the buyer. Although the structures of all types of contracts are basically similar, each type of contract has a specific effect.

### 10.6.3  Structure of a Written Contract

合同一般有正本和副本,内容通常由标题、前言、条文和结语4个部分组成。

A contract generally has the Original and the Copy, and it is usually made up of four parts: Title, Preamble, Body and Remarks.

(1) Title

The title of a contract varies in accordance with the contents, such as Sales Contract, Agency Contract, Compensation Contract, etc. The title can reflect the nature, contents and types of the contract.

(2) Preamble

The preamble of a contract mainly includes number, the date and place of signature of the contract, the names and addresses of signing parties. Besides, it needs to give a brief description of the contract under the name of parties in this part.

**For example:**

*The contract, made out, in Chinese and English, both versions being equally authentic, by and between the seller and the buyer whereby the seller agrees to sell and the buyer agrees to buy the undermentioned goods according to the terms and conditions stipulated below.*

(3) Body

The body of a contract will provide specific terms. It usually consists of commodities and specifications, quality and quantity, price, packing, time of shipment, port of shipment and port of destination, shipping mark and payment. And it also includes those clauses concerning insurance, inspection, claims, force majeure and arbitration, etc. Each term must be concrete, clear and complete in order to avoid disputes.

(4) Remarks

The remarks of a contract generally state the concluding sentences, which includes copies, words and validity of the contract. Signature and seal of related parties are required in this part. Furthermore, if there is an appendix or any supplement, it should be given here.

Specimen 10-1    Examples of written contract

**Sales Contract**

S/C No.：HY98CS004

Date：March 27, 2009

Signed at：Shanghai, China

| The Seller: | The Buyer: |
|---|---|
| Datung Trading Co., Ltd | Universal Trading Co., Ltd. |
| No. 165, Cense Road, Yangon Myanmar | RM.1201-1216, Mayling Plaza, 131 Dongfang Road, Shanghai CHINA |
| Tel：+ (95) 1-651866 | Tel：86-21-58818844 |
| Fax：+ (95) 1-651877 | Fax：86-21-58818840 |

This contract is made by and among the Buyers, the end-user and the Sellers; whereby the Buyers acting as the import agent agree to buy on behalf of the end-users and the Sellers agree to sell the under-mentioned commodity according to the terms and conditions stipulated below:

1.

| No. | Name of Commodity & Specifications | Quantity | Unit Price | Total Amount |
|---|---|---|---|---|
| 1 | ACE CENTER MODEL: MB-67VB | 1 SET | | US$239,105.00 CIF SHANGHAI |
| Total Value : | CIF SHANGHAI    US$239,105.00 | | | |

2. Country of Origin OR Manufacturers: Myanmar, Yangon, Datung Trading Co.,Ltd.

3. Packing: To be packed in strong wooden case(s), which should be quarantine or fumigated, marked "IPPC" stamp, or in carton(s), suitable for long distance ocean transportation and to change of climate, well protected against moisture and shocks. The Sellers shall be liable for any damage of the commodity and expenses incurred on account of improper packing and for any rust attributable to inadequate or improper protective measures taken by the Sellers in regard to the packing. One full set of service and operation

instructions concerned shall be enclosed in the case(s).

4. Shipping Marks: The Sellers shall mark on each package with fadeless paint the package number, gross weight, net weight, measurement and the wordings: "KEEP AWAY FROM MOISTURE", "HANDLE WITH CARE", "THIS SIDE UP", etc., and the shipping mark:

KMC100515B

SHANGHAI，CHINA

5. Time of Shipment: By May 31, 2009

6. Port of Shipment: SHANGHAI, CHINA

7. Port of Destination：YANGON MYANMAR

8. Insurance: TO BE COVERED BY THE SELLER FOR 110% INVOICE VALUE

9. Payment: 40% by T/T, 60% by L/C

(1) Within two weeks after the contract is made, Advance 10% of the total contract price i.e. US$23,910.50 and Bank guarantee for the 10% of the total contract should be issued at the same time.

30 percent (%) of the total contract price i.e. US$71731.50 by the end of August and Bank guarantee for the 30% of the total contract should be issued at the same time.

(2) The Buyers shall, upon receipt from the Sellers of the delivery advice, 30 days prior to the date of delivery, open an Irrevocable 60% of the contract value Letter of Credit In favor of the Sellers. There including:

a) 50 percent (%) of the total contract price i.e. US$119552.50 , shall be paid at sight by the Buyers to the Sellers after receipt of the negotiation documents specified in Clause 10 hereof.

b) 10 percent (%) of the total contract price i.e. US$23,910.50 shall be paid by the Buyers to the Sellers after the Acceptance Certificate for the goods is issued and not later than 7 days from the date receipt by the Buyers from the Sellers of the documents stipulated as follows:

a. Five copies of commercial invoice

b. One copy of the Final Acceptance Certificate issued and stamped by representatives of the Buyers, the Seller.

10. Documents:

(a) 2/3 set of on board ocean bills of lading marked "Freight Prepaid"

made out to order blank endorsed notifying the Buyer. Another 1/3 one will be directly airmailed to the buyers by express immediately after the shipment is made.

(b) Commercial Invoice in 5 copies indicating contract number, made out in details as per relative contract.

(c) Insurance Policy/Certificate in one original and one copy for 110% of the invoice value showing claims payable in China in currency of the draft, blank endorsed, covering All Risks and War Risks.

(d) One original and one copy of draft.

(e) Certificate of origin in one original and one copy issued by correlative government department.

(f) Packing list in 2 copies issued by the Manufacturers.

(g) Certificate of Quality and Quantity issued by the Manufacturers.

(h) Copy of fax to the Buyers advising particulars of shipment immediately after shipment is made.

(i) One copy of Certificate treatment(fumigation)if packing in wooden case.

In addition, the Sellers shall, within 2 days after shipment, send by airmail one copy set of the aforesaid documents to the buyer (Including one original Certificate of quarantine or heat treatment(fumigation)if packing in wooden case) .

11. Shipment: The Sellers shall ship the goods within the shipment time from the port of shipment to the port of destination. Partial shipment is not allowed. Transshipment is not allowed.

12. The Sellers shall, immediately upon the completion of the loading of the goods, advice by fax the Buyers of the Contract No., commodity, quantity, invoice value, gross weight, name of vessel and date of sailing etc..

13. The Sellers guarantee that the commodity hereof is made of the best materials with first class workmanship, brand new and unused, and complies in all respects with the quality and specification stipulated in this Contract. The warrantee period should be 12 months after the date of the Final Acceptance Certificate issued or 18 months after the shipment date, whichever is occurred first.

14. Claims: Within 90 days after the arrival of the goods at destination, should the quality, specification, or quantity be found not in conformity with

the stipulations of the Contract except those claims for which the insurance company or the owners of the vessel are liable, the Buyers shall, on the strength of the Inspection Certificate issued by the Jiangsu Commodity Inspection Bureau, have the right to claim for replacement with new goods, or for compensation, and all the expenses ( such as inspection charges, freight for returning the goods and for sending the replacement, insurance premium, storage and loading and unloading charges, etc. ) shall be borne by the Sellers. As regards quality, the Sellers shall guarantee that if within 12 months from the date of arrival of the goods at destination, damages occur in the course of operation by reason of inferior quality, bad workmanship or the use of inferior materials, the Buyers shall immediately notify the Sellers in writing and put forward a claim supported by inspection Certificate issued by the Jiangsu Commodity Inspection Bureau.

The Certificate issued shall be accepted as the base of a claim. The Sellers, in accordance with the Buyers' claim shall be responsible for the immediate elimination of the defect(s), complete or partial replacement of the commodity or shall devaluate the commodity according to the state of defect(s). If necessary, the Buyers shall be at liberty to eliminate the defect(s) themselves at the Sellers' expenses. If the Sellers fail to answer the Buyers within one month after receipt of the aforesaid claim, the claim shall be reckoned as having been accepted by the Sellers.

15. Force Majeure: The Sellers shall not be hold responsible for the delay in shipment or non-delivery of the goods due to Force Majeure, which might occur during the process of manufacturing or the course of loading or transit. The Sellers shall advice Buyers immediately of the occurrence mentioned above and within fourteen days thereafter, the Sellers shall send by air mail to the Buyers for their acceptance a certificate of the accident issued by the Competent Government Authorities where the accident occurs as evidence thereof. Seller's inability in obtaining export license shall be considered as Force Majeure.

Under such circumstances the Sellers, however, are still under the obligation to take all necessary measures to hasten the delivery of the goods. In case the accident lasts for more than 10 weeks, the Buyers shall have right to cancel the Contract.

16. Late Delivery and penalty: Should the Sellers fail to make delivery on time as stipulated in the Contract, with exception of Force Majeure causes specified in the above clause, the Buyers shall agree to postpone the delivery on condition that the Sellers agree to pay a penalty which shall be deducted by the paying bank from the payment under negotiation. The penalty, however, shall not exceed 5% of the total value of the goods involved in the late delivery. The rate of Penalty is charged at 0.5% for every seven days, odd days less than seven days should be counted as seven days. In case the Sellers fail to make delivery ten weeks later than the time of shipment stipulated in the Contract, the Buyers shall have the right to cancel the contract and the Sellers, in spite of the cancellation, shall still pay the aforesaid penalty to the Buyers without delay.

17. Arbitration: All disputes in connection with this Contract or the execution thereof shall be settled friendly through negotiations. In case no settlement can be reached, the case may then be submitted to China International Economic and Trade Arbitration Commission for arbitration which shall be conducted by the Commission in Beijing or by its ZHEJIANG Sub-Commission in ZHEJIANG or by its Shanghai Sub-Commission in Shanghai at the Claimant's option in accordance with the Commission's arbitration rules in effect at the time of applying for arbitration. The arbitral award is final and binding upon both parties; Both parties shall not seek recourse to a law court or other authorities to appeal for revision of the decision. The arbitration fees shall be borne by the losing party unless otherwise awarded by the Commission.

18. Two original ones of this contract will be held by the Buyer, and the Seller respectively. The Chinese version shall govern if there are any discrepancies between two versions.

The Seller:
Datung Trading Co., Ltd.
No. 165, Cense Road, Yangon
Myanmar

Tel：+ (95) 1-651866
Fax：+ (95) 1-651877

The Buyer:
Universal Trading Co., Ltd.
RM.1201-1216, Mayling
Plaza, 131 Dongfang Road,
Shanghai CHINA
Tel：86-21-58818844
Fax: 86-21-58818840

# 【Words and Phrases】

Amendment 修正　　　　　　　Specific enquiry 具体询盘
Supplement 附件　　　　　　　Invitation to offer 发盘邀请
Enquiry 询盘　　　　　　　　Invitation to bid 邀请递盘
Offer 发盘　　　　　　　　　Trade terms 交易条件
Reservation 保留　　　　　　Firm offer 实盘
Offeror 报盘人　　　　　　　Non-firm offer 虚盘
Offeree 受盘人　　　　　　　Time of validity 有效期
Quotation 报价　　　　　　　Duration of an offer 发盘的有效期
acceptance 接受　　　　　　　Withdrawal of an offer 发盘的撤回
Confirmation 确认书　　　　　Revocation of an offer 发盘的撤销
Agreement 协议　　　　　　　Termination of an offer 发盘的终止
Order 订单　　　　　　　　　Counter-offer 还盘
Memorandum 备忘书　　　　　Conclusion of contract 合同签订
Preamble 序文、前言　　　　　Sales contract 销售合同
Body 正文　　　　　　　　　Sales confirmation 销售确认书
Packing 包装　　　　　　　　Purchase contract 购货合同
Insurance 保险　　　　　　　Purchase confirmation 购货确认书
Claim 索赔　　　　　　　　　Time of shipment 装运期
Arbitration 仲裁　　　　　　Terms of payment 支付条款
Lapse 失效　　　　　　　　　Commodity inspection 商品检验
Business negotiation 交易磋商　Force majeure 不可抗力
General enquiry 一般询盘

# 【Exercises】

Ⅰ. Put the following into English.

1. 询盘　　　　　　　　　　　6. 受盘人
2. 还盘　　　　　　　　　　　7. 发盘的撤销
3. 虚盘　　　　　　　　　　　8. 发盘的撤回
4. 实盘　　　　　　　　　　　9. 有效期
5. 发盘人　　　　　　　　　　10. 发盘的终止

II. Answer the following questions with T or F.

1. ( ) According to the CISG, once the offeror stipulates the validity on the offer, the offeror can still cancel the offer.

2. ( ) Offer and acceptance are two indispensable links for reaching an agreement and concluding a contract.

3. ( ) During the negotiation, the offer is made by the seller and acceptance is made by the buyer.

4. ( ) Enquiry, offer, counter-offer and acceptance are indispensable part of a negotiation.

5. ( ) Same to the offer, acceptance also can be cancel.

6. ( ) According to CISG, there is firm offer and non-firm offer.

7. ( ) Once an offer being accepted, the seller can not change it no matter what kind of reason it would be.

8. ( ) A firm offer should include at least three specific conditions: name of commodity, quantity of commodity and price of commodity.

9. ( ) A firm offer must indicate that once it has been unconditionally accepted by the offeree within its validity, the offer is binding on both parties.

10. ( ) According to CISG, an offer, if it is irrevocable, may not be withdrawn if the withdrawal reaches the offeree before or at the same time as the offer.

11. ( ) Claim and arbitration clause must be included in the written contract.

12. ( ) Once signed, any amendments and supplements to the present contract could not be accepted.

13. ( ) Written form of contract has a lot of advantages in disputes resolving, so every contract should be conducted in written form.

14. ( ) In most cases, in order to get a contract, both the buyer and the seller will experience many rounds of offer and counter-offer.

15. ( ) Usually terms of trade are stipulated in the trade contract and clearly indicate both parties' responsibilities.

III. Please fill in the Sales Confirmation form in English based on the conditions stated below.

After several rounds of negotiations on the terms of the transaction, a Chinese corporation—Huaxin Trading Co., Ltd (address: 14th Floor Kingstar Mansion, 676 Jinlin Rd., Shanghai) and a Canada company—James Brown & Sons (address: #304-310 Jalan Street, Toronto, Canada) have reached a consensus. The details are as follows:

## 国际贸易实务(英语版)

| 货 号 | 品 名 | 成交数量 | 成交单价(USD) |
|---|---|---|---|
| HX115 | 35-Piece Dinnerware and Tea Set | 542 sets | US$23.50/set |
| HX201 | 20-Piece Dinnerware Set | 800 sets | US$20.40/set |
| HX445 | 47-Piece Dinnerware Set | 443 sets | US$23.20/set |
| HX451 | 95-Piece Dinnerware Set | 254 sets | US$30.10/set |
| 成交价格条件: | CIFC5% TORONTO | | |
| 包装条件: | 纸箱包装, HX201 一箱装两套, 其他的三个货号一箱装一套。 | | |
| 唛头: | TORONTO NO.1-UP | | |
| 交货/装运条件: | 货物用集装箱自中国经海运至加拿大多伦多港, 装运期为 2017 年 4 月, 允许转运, 不允许分批装运 | | |
| 保险条件: | 由卖方按 CIF 成交金额的 110% 投保中国人民保险公司海运货物水渍险和战争险 | | |
| 付款条件: | 不可撤销即期信用证付款。信用证议付有效期为货物装船后第 15 天在中国到期 | | |

## Sales Confirmation

S/C No: SHHX98027

Date: 15-July-2017

The Seller: _____

Address: _____

The Buyer: _____

Address: _____

The Sellers agree to sell and the Buyers agree to buy the undermentioned goods according to the terms and conditions as stipulated below.

| Art. No. | Commodity | Unit | Quantity | Unit Price (US$) | Amount (US$) |
|---|---|---|---|---|---|
| | | | | | |
| | | | | | |
| | | | | | |
| | | | | | |

Total Contract Value: _____

Packing: _____

Shipping Marks: _____

Port of Loading & Destination: Delivery from _____ to _____

Time of Shipment:

To be effected _____ with _____ and _____.

312

Terms of Payment:

_____ shall_____ a _____ to reach the Seller before July 25, 2008 Valid for negotiation in _____ until _____.

Insurance: _____ shall cover insurance against _____and _____for _____ as per_____.

Inspection: The Inspection Certificate of Quality/Weight issued by _____shall be taken as basis for the shipping Quality/Weight.

Force Majeure: If shipment of the contracted goods is prevented or delayed in whole or in part due to Force Majeure, the Sellers shall not be liable for nonshipment or late shipment of the goods under this Contract. However, the Sellers shall notify the Buyers by fax or telex and furnish the latter within 15days by registered airmail with a certificate issued by the competent authorities at the place of occurrence attesting such event or events.

Arbitration: All disputes arising out of the performance of, or relating to this Contract, shall be settled amicably through negotiation. In case no settlement can be reached through negotiation, the case shall then be submitted to the China International Economic and Trade Arbitration Commission for arbitration in accordance with its arbitration rules. The arbitral award is final and binding upon both parties.

Confirmed by:

The Seller:

    (Signature)

The Buyer:

    (Signature)

## IV. Case study

An export company in China made an offer on grain to a Canadian importer. Aside from all the essential conditions, it was also indicated in the offer that "packing in sound bags". Within the validity period, the Canadian importer gave a reply: "refer to your telex first accepted, packing in new bags". After receiving this, the export company started to prepare the goods. A few days later, when the price of grain plummeted in the international market, the Canadian importer claimed in its telex: the contract is invalid because you have not confirmed our alteration to the offer. But the export company insisted that the contract was valid. A dispute was thus aroused.

**Questions:**

(1) In this case, how could the export company handle the situation?

(2) Try to support your argument.

# Chapter 11   Exporting and Importing Procedures

【Learning Objectives】

By studying this chapter, you should be able to master

- The basic exporting and importing procedures
- The performance of international trade export contracts
- How to examine L/C in accordance with the contract before the goods are delivered
- How to prepare and present documents required to the bank for negotiation within the validity of L/C

## Lead-in: News Report

### China flays US on false WTO claims

China on Thursday took strong exception to recent reports in the United States that pointed fingers at its membership in the World Trade Organization and said such claims are not only false but also ignore the fact that the country is an open and market-oriented economy.

Last week, the US Trade Representative's office issued two reports on China's WTO compliance saying that the country has made little progress in aligning its economy with the commitments it made prior to joining the WTO. The reports said the US had mistakenly supported China's WTO membership in 2001.

Gao Feng, a spokesman for the Ministry of Commerce, said China strongly opposes the arguments made in the reports, which exhibit tendencies of protectionism and unilateralism.

"Many arguments in the reports not only ignore but also falsify the facts, and are self-contradictory," he said at a news conference in Beijing.

A genuine and reasonable market economy, Gao said, should be an economic system where the "market plays a decisive role in the allocation of resources, and is suitable for that country's national conditions, rather than those based on the standards in other countries."

Gao cited several references to enumerate China's historic achievements in building a market economy.

"Since China's accession to the World Trade Organization, tariffs have declined from 15.3 percent to 9.8 percent. More than 50 access restrictions in the manufacturing industry have been removed. In addition, the country has also opened, to varying degrees, about 120 subsectors out of the 160 in the services industry," he said.

Taking strong exception to the US stance, leading experts have suggested that China should take necessary measures to thwart the US, while continuing to seek redress for its grievances under the WTO dispute mechanism.

"China should continue to obey and safeguard the WTO rules," said Yu Yongding, an economist with the Chinese Academy of Social Sciences.

"When problems arise in the US, they often use domestic laws to override the WTO rules. China should not rule out the use of reciprocal retaliatory measures, but use them prudently. It is in accordance with international law," Yu said at the China Finance Annual Forum.

Wei Jianguo, former vice-minister of commerce, said the US itself does not adhere to the WTO rules. He was referring to the US opposition for market economy status to China and its use of Section 301 of the US Trade Act to override global trade rules.

"We clearly do not want a trade war ... but if the US sticks to protectionism, we can cope with it," he said. "Do not bully China to test the country's endurance."

Wei's comments come at a time when available data indicated that China was the largest victim of global trade remedy investigations in 2017, despite the number and value of cases falling by 37 percent and 23 percent year-on-year, respectively.

Last year, 21 countries and regions launched 75 trade remedy investigations against exports of Chinese enterprises, the data showed.

*(Source:http://www.chinadaily.com.cn/a/201801/26/WS5a6a64e2a3106e7dcc136aca.html)*

### Class Activities:

1. Is protectionism evil? Why did the US issue two reports on China's WTO compliance?

2. What should we do to achieve the balance between protectionism and free trade?

3. What is the key value that nations should pursue in their economic development amid globalization?

The export and import trades are two sides of the same coin. One country's export is another country's import. The contract serves as the guideline throughout the entire procedure of international trade. Generally speaking, from the very beginning to the end of a transaction, the whole procedure of international trade undergoes the following stages: preparation of a transaction, negotiation of the contract and performance of the contract.

# 11.1 Exporting Procedures

履行出口合同的4个基本环节：准备货物(货)、落实信用证(证)、安排装运(运)和制单结汇(款)。

Ocean transportation is by far the chiefly used transportation mode in international trade. In this part, the basic exporting procedure under a CIF contract with the L/C payment is to be shown in the following Table 11-1 for learners' reference.

Table 11-1　The Basic Exporting Procedure (CIF, L/C)

| Procedures | Content | Focus |
|---|---|---|
| I. Preparation stage | ● Selecting target markets<br>● Finding potential buyers<br>● Acquiring Export License | Market |
| II. Negotiation stage | ● Enquiry　● Offer<br>● Counter-offer　● Acceptance | Contract |
| III. Performance stage | (1) Preparation goods for shipment | Goods(货) |
| | (2) Urging, examining and amending L/C | L/C(证) |
| | (3) Inspection and customs clearance | |
| | (4) Insurance | |
| | (5) Arranging for shipment | Shipment(运) |
| | (6) Preparing documents for negotiation<br>① Bill of exchange<br>② Commercial invoice<br>③ Packing list<br>④ Bill of lading<br>⑤ Insurance policy<br>⑥ Inspection certificate<br>⑦ Certificate of origin or GSP form A<br>⑧ Shipping advice<br>⑨ Beneficiary's declaration | Payment(款) |
| | (7) Tax refund | |
| | (8) Settlement of dispute | |

## 11.1.1 Preparation Stage of Export Contract

Before business negotiation, the exporter should make full preparation for the transaction, including selecting target markets, selecting prospective buyers and acquiring export license.

### 1. Selecting target markets

To start a business, the exporter needs to do some research on target markets. Different countries have different political system, economic situation and different customs and preferences. It is necessary to know something about them. Market research is a process of conducting research into a specific market for a particular product. That is to say, the exporter is to investigate the market of his target country, carefully select the products he wants to export and study current export trends. Through research, the exporter can select the right target markets and decide the export products and methods.

### 2. Finding potential buyers

At the same time, by doing the market research, the exporter should find some potential buyers for his products. There are some channels to make contacts with prospective buyers.

(1) Self-introduction by email or Skype;

(2) Enquiries from friends or other business connections in foreign countries;

(3) Participating in international trade fairs and exhibitions, including Canton Fair, Berlin Trade Fair and so on;

(4) Consulting embassies, Commercial Counselor's Office, Chamber of Commerce and taking note of addresses of importers, such as International Chamber of Commerce (ICC), China Council for the Promotion of International Trade (CCPIT) etc;

(5) Mutual visits by trade delegations;

(6) Collecting information from trade directories, periodicals or Journals, such as *Economist*, *Financial Times*, and *Wall Street Journal*;

(7) Searching websites, such as Alibaba (www.alibaba.com), Ebay (http://www.ebay.com), Globalsources (www.globalsources.com), Euro-pages (www.europages.com), Bosslink (http://www.bosslink.com/) etc.

After the exporter has approached potential buyers, it is important to investigate their reputation, business operations and financial status. To acquire the necessary information, he may consult the bank in target country or even his counterparts in this market.

与国外客户建立业务关系时，外贸人员需充分利用互联网——低成本而有效的运作方式。

一方发盘经另一方有效接受后，买卖双方即构成合同关系。

● **Acquiring export license**

When business relations have been established, it is still too early to start a business negotiation. The exporter should know the government policy and whether the products he intends to sell are within some certain export controls. If so, he has to deal with them before negotiation. Many areas and countries around the world have exercised export controls over certain merchandise. Even in economic free zones such as Hong Kong, export control is not viewed as unusual. Therefore, in some business, the export should ensure whether he needs or could obtain export license (see Specimen 11-1) from the government. It is the exporter's duty to obtain export license and the quota before arranging a contract.

出口管制最常见和最有效的手段是实行出口许可证制度。

Specimen 11-1 Export License of the People's Republic of China

中华人民共和国出口许可证

| 1. 出口商(Exporter):<br>宏昌国际股份有限公司<br>Grand Western Foods Corp. | | | 3. 出口许可证号(Export license No.): | | |
|---|---|---|---|---|---|
| 2. 发货人(Consignor):<br>宏昌国际股份有限公司 | | | 4. 出口许可证有效截止日期( Export license expiry date): | | |
| 5. 贸易方式(Terms of trade):<br>一般贸易 | | | 8. 进口国(地区)(Country/Region of purchase):<br>加拿大 | | |
| 6. 合同号(Contract No.):<br>Contract01 | | | 9. 付款方式(Payment):<br>L/C | | |
| 7. 报关口岸(Place of clearance):<br>南京 | | | 10. 运输方式(Mode of transport):<br>海运 | | |
| 11. 商品名称(Description of goods):<br>CANNED SWEET CORN<br>CANADA<br>C/NO.1-800<br>MADE IN CHINA | | | 商品编码(Code of goods):<br>20058000 | | |
| 12. 规格、型号<br>Specifications | 13. 单位<br>Unit | 14. 数量<br>Quantity | 15. 单价( )<br>Unit Price | 16. 总值( )<br>Amount | 17. 总值折美元<br>Amount in USD |
| Canned sweet corn 3060g×6tins/ctn | carton | 800 ctn | USD 14 | USD 11200 | |
| 18. 总计 Total | | 800 ctn | | USD 11200 | |
| 19. 备注：<br>Supplementary details | | | 20. 发证机关签章<br>Issuing authority's stamp & signature<br>21. 发证日期<br>License date | | |

商务部监制　　　　　　　　　　　　　　　本证不得涂改，不得转让

## 11.1.2    Negotiation stage of export contract

Before the contract is concluded, much work has to be done during the business negotiation. Negotiation of the contract generally consists of four procedures, which are enquiry, offer, counter-offer and acceptance. Among them, offer and acceptance are the two indispensable procedures. Since these four steps have been discussed in Chapter 10, efforts are made to review some tips for business negotiation.

交易磋商主要包括询盘、发盘、还盘和接受四个环节。其中发盘和接受两个环节不可缺少。

- **Negotiating with prospective buyers**

The seller should possess necessary skills for negotiating with his potential buyers. While conducting business negotiations, he should avoid conflict, controversy and criticism with the importers or trade agents. His attitude in conversation is of vital importance to achieve effective communication. There should be coherence, creativity, compromise, consensus, commitment and compensation in business negotiation. As overseas buyers generally insist for samples before placing confirmed orders, the seller should carefully prepare informative and attractive samples for the buyer's reference.

一方发盘经另一方有效接受后，买卖双方即构成合同关系。

- **The pricing problem**

During the negotiation stage, the most sensitive issue the exporter may face must be the pricing problem. One of the buyer's contentions is that prices are too high. Thus the seller should tactfully postpone the price issue, until other issues have been discussed and mutually agreed upon. From the very beginning the seller should determine the importer's real interest in the product. Only by doing so, may he be able to solve problems which might arise. Later, in case the buyer requests some modifications in presentation of the product, the seller should show his willingness to meet such request, and most important of all figure out a profitable counter proposal. All in all, being the most important sales tool, price has to be properly developed and presented.

一方发盘经另一方有效接受后，买卖双方即构成合同关系。

- **Conclusion of the contract**

At the end of business negotiation, the contract can be established, which contains matters both parties have agreed upon during their negotiation. Such matters include the major terms and conditions of the contract and even some clauses involving inspection, claim, force majeure and arbitration. As Article 23, CISG stipulates that "a contract is concluded at the moment when an

一方发盘经另一方有效接受后，买卖双方即构成合同关系。

# 国际贸易实务(英语版)(第2版)

acceptance of an offer becomes effective," the contents of offer and acceptance serves as terms and conditions of contract.

There is no legal requirement for the form of contract. According to Article 11 of CISG, "a contract of sale need not be concluded in or evidenced by writing and is not subject to any other requirement as to form. It may be proved by any means, including witnesses." Nevertheless, sales contract (see Specimen 11-2) and sales confirmation are the two widely used written form in international trade practice.

Specimen 11-2　Sales Contract 销售合同

## GRAND WESTERN FOODS CORP.

Room 2501,Jiafa Mansion, Beijing West road, Nanjing 210005, P.R.China

### SALES CONFIRMATION

| Messrs: | Carters Trading Company, LLC<br>P.O.Box8935, New Terminal, Lata. Vista, Ottawa, Canada | | | | **No.** Contract01 | |
| | | | | | **Date:** 2004-08-19 | |

Dear Sirs,

　　We are pleased to confirm our sale of the following goods on the terms and conditions set forth below:

| Choice | Product No. | Description | Quantity | Unit | Unit Price | Amount |
|---|---|---|---|---|---|---|
| | | | | | [CIF] [Toronto　] | |
| ○ | 01005 | CANNED SWEET CORN<br>3060Gx6TINS/CTN | 800 | CARTON | USD14 | USD11200 |
| | | | | | | |
| | | | Total: 800 | CARTON | [添加][修改][删除]<br>[USD] [11200 ] | |

| Say Total: | U.S.DOLLARS ELEVEN THOUSAND TWO HUNDRED ONLY |
|---|---|
| Payment: | L/C ▾ [By 100% irrevocable sight letter of credit in our favor. ] |
| packing: | 3060Gx6TINS/CTN<br>Each of the carton should be indicated with Item No., Name of the Table, G.W., and C/No. |
| Port of Shipment: | Nanjing |
| Port of Destination: | Toronto |
| Shipment: | All of the goods will be shipped on or before Sep. 20, 2004 subject to L/C reaching the SELLER by the end of August, 2004. Partial shipments and transhipment are not allowed. |
| Shipping Mark: | CANNED SWEET CORN<br>CANADA<br>C/NO.1-800<br>MADE IN CHINA |
| Quality: | As per sample submitted by seller. |
| Insurance: | The SELLER shall arrange marine insurance covering ICC(A) plus institute War Risks for 110% of CIF value and provide of claim, if any, payable in Canada, with U.S. currency. |
| Remarks: | The Buyers are requested to sign and return one copy of this Sales Confirmation immediately after receipt of the same. |

| BUYERS | SELLERS |
|---|---|
| Carters Trading Company, LLC | GRAND WESTERN FOODS CORP. |
| *Carter* | *Minghua Liu* |
| (Manager Signature) | (Manager Signature) |

320

## 11.1.3　Performance stage of export contract

According to Article 30, CISG stipulates that "the seller must deliver the goods, hand over any documents relating to them and transfer the property in the goods, as required by the contract". As soon as the contract is concluded, the exporter should fulfill his duty to deliver the goods and transfer the ownership of the goods to the importer. The following steps are what an exporter needs to go through in performance of his contract.

履行合同既是经济行为又是法律行为。买卖双方需遵循"重合同、守信用"原则。

### 1. Preparing goods for shipment

As soon as the contract is signed, the exporter should start to prepare the goods for shipment and check them against the terms stipulated in the contract. He must get the goods ready for shipment before the stipulated delivery time. He must prepare the goods in the exact quality and quantity that the contract has stipulated. At the same time, the packing and marks of the goods should be strict in line with stipulations in the contract. Also, the exporter's legal ownership to the goods should be guaranteed. The shipment should not be claimed by third party according to intellectual property.

出口商备货时需注意：按时、按质、按量、按合同规定包装和拥有货物的所有权问题。

### 2. Urging, examining and amending the L/C

#### ● Urging the L/C

If the contract is under the payment of L/C, the exporter cannot make shipment until he has received the L/C (see Specimen 11-3). The importer, as a rule, undertakes his duty to establish the L/C on time, but sometimes he may delay for various reasons. For the safe collection of payment, it is necessary and important for the exporter to urge the importer to expedite the opening of L/C.

#### ● Examining the L/C

The exporter, upon receipt of the notification of L/C (see Specimen 11-4), need to examine it very carefully to make sure that all terms and conditions are stipulated in accordance with the contract. This step is very essential. If any discrepancy happens, the exporter should contact the importer immediately so as to guarantee the smooth execution of the contract. Examination of the L/C can be carried out in two ways.

### Overall examination of the L/C

(1) When examining the L/C, the seller should make sure that L/C is in conformity with the trade agreements between the two trading countries, and it doesn't carry deprecatory clauses or clauses which contain political bias.

信用证总的方面的审核要点：
①政策上审核；
②对开证银行资信情况的审核；
③信用证有无限制性条款等的审核。

(2) The credit status of the issuing bank should also be checked. Technically speaking, issuing banks with poor credit position and dishonest operating style should be rejected. In China, it is usually the notifying bank's duty to examine the status position of the issuing bank. Thus, if the exporter receives the L/C directly, he should present it to the notifying bank for further examination.

(3) It should be examined that whether the L/C contains any restrictive or self-contradictory clauses. Restrictive clauses are as follows: "this credit is not operative until the buyer has got the import license"; "we shall make payment only after the goods have passed the inspection at the port of destination."; or "we shall make the payment after the goods arrival at the destination." And if insurance policy is required under the FOB contract for negotiation, it is obviously self-contradictory. Under such conditions, these clauses should be deleted, for they add unnecessary difficulties for the exporter to get payment.

### Individual examination of the L/C

信用证专项审核时，需保证其内容与合同的内容一致。

Most important of all, the exporter should examine individual clauses of the L/C one by one, and bear in mind that they should all correspond with the contract. It is difficult to mention all the clauses listed in the L/C, and specials are required on the following items.

(1) Applicant and beneficiary

Name and address of the applicant and beneficiary should be correctly given and spelt in the L/C.

(2) Amount of the credit and its currency

Amount of credit should correspond with that given in the contract and in the same currency.

(3) Latest date of shipment, validity of the credit and documents presentation period

Latest date of shipment should be the same as that given in the contract.

According to *UCP 600* Article 14(c), if no such time is given, the shipping documents should be made within 21 days after the shipment has been made. If the time for shipment is too short, such as 2 days, it is usually unacceptable. It is acceptable when the date of shipment given in L/C is later than that given in the contract. The exporter should ask for extension of the date of shipment, if he cannot make shipment timely.

There should be a period of time between the validity of L/C and date of shipment, so that the exporter can obtain sufficient time to prepare documents and present them for negotiation. Usually, the validity of the credit should be later than the latest date of shipment.

What's more, documents should be presented to the negotiating bank within the validity of the credit. If documents presentation period has not been described in the L/C, the exporter, as a rule, has to present documents to the negotiating bank within 21 days after the date of shipment.

When L/C contains stipulation like "due at the exporting place", "due at the importing place", "due at a third country", the exporter normally chooses the first one because the latter two are difficult for him to control.

(4) Partial shipment and transshipment

If the sales contract states that transshipment or partial shipment is allowed, the L/C should bear the similar clause. According to *UCP 600*, if "transshipment prohibited" or "partial shipment prohibited" is not stated in the L/C, it should be considered that transshipment or partial shipment are allowed.

(5) Description of the goods

Descriptions of the goods should be in line with that of the contract, such as name, quantity, packing, unit price and specification.

(6) Documents required

The seller should check whether documents required in the L/C are reasonable and feasible. Relevant documents including bill of exchange, commercial invoice, bill of lading, insurance policy, certificate of origin should not pose unnecessary barriers to the deal. What matters is that when examining those items, the seller must bear in mind all the documents must not conflict with each other.

(7) Additional conditions

Additional conditions in the L/C should also be noted, such as banking

最迟装运日、信用证有效期和交单期：①信用证中的最迟装运日，应与合同规定一致；②信用证有效期应在最迟装运日之后；③交单期不得迟于信用证有效期。如果信用证没有明确规定交单期，那么按惯例，银行有权拒受迟于运输单据 21 天后提交的单据。

charges and instructions to negotiation bank. Usually, instructions to the negotiation bank may include endorsement clause, method of reimbursement, method of dispatching documents and engagement/undertaking clauses.

● **Amending the L/C**

Once the exporter found the L/C containing discrepancies which did not agree with the contract, he should ask the importer to amend it when necessary. Basically, the totally unacceptable clauses should be amended without delay. The exporter can send an advice to the importer, requiring the opening bank to make amendments, in order to guarantee collection and avoid disputes.

Yet if the discrepancies are of minor significance and the deal can be performed smoothly, perhaps it will not be necessary to make amendments. The exporter can send an advice to importer, requiring the issuing bank to accept such minor discrepancies, so as to save time and expenses.

Sometimes the amendment is made by the importer himself. If the exporter cannot accept the amendment, he should reject it within 3 days, or it will be taken that the exporter has agreed with the amendment. Once the amendment is made, it becomes part of the L/C and the deal is to be executed accordingly.

注意：

1. 掌握好"改"与"不改"的界限。

2. 修改信用证的内容要征得开证人的同意，由开证行发改证通知才有效。

3. 对于需修改的内容应一次向对方全部提出，以节约改证费用。

4. 对修改通知书内容只能全部接受或全部拒绝，并立即向通知行表示。不可在未接到修改通知书之前贸然出运。

## Specimen 11-3 Irrevocable Documentary L/C 不可撤销跟单信用证

```
                        LETTER OF CREDIT
----------------------- MESSAGE TEXT -----------------------
:27:SEQUENCE OF TOTAL
1/1
:40A:FORM OF DOCUMENTARY CREDIT
IRREVOCABLE
:20:DOCUMENTARY CREDIT NUMBER
STLCN000001
:31C:DATE OF ISSUE
040820
:31D:DATE AND PLACE OF EXPIRY
041015 IN THE BENEFICIARY'S COUNTRY
:51A:APPLICANT BANK
THE CHARTERED BANK

:50:APPLICANT
CARTERS TRADING COMPANY, LLC
P.O.BOX8935,NEW TERMINALI, LATA. VISTA, OTTAWA, CANADA
:59:BENEFICIARY
GRAND WESTERN FOODS CORP.
ROOM2501,JIAFA MANSION, BEIJING WEST ROAD, NANJING 210005, P.R.CHINA
:32B:CURRENCY CODE, AMOUNT
[USD            ] [11200                              ]
:41D:AVAILABLE WITH BY
NANJING COMMERCIAL BANK BY NEGOTIATION

:42C:DRAFTS AT
SIGHT

:42A:DRAWEE
ISSUE BANK

:43P:PARTIAL SHIPMENTS
NOT ALLOWED
:43T:TRANSHIPMENT
NOT ALLOWED
:44A:ON BOARD/DISP/TAKING CHARGE
NANJING
:44B:FOR TRANSPORTATION TO
TORONTO
:44C:LATEST DATE OF SHIPMENT
040920
:45A:DESCRIPTION OF GOODS AND/OR SERVICES
01005 CANNED SWEET CORN, 3060Gx6TINS/CTN, QUANTITY: 800 CARTON
CIF TORONTO, PRICE: USD14/CTN
:46A:DOCUMENTS REQUIRED
+SIGNED COMMERCIAL INVOICE IN 6 COPIES INDICATING CONTRACT NO. CONTRACT01
+FULL SET OF CLEAN ON BOARD BILLS OF LADING MADE OUT TO ORDER AND BLANK ENDORSED, MARKED "FREIGHT TO PREPAID"
NOTIFYING THE APPLICANT
+INSURANCE POLICY/CERTIFICATE IN 3 COPIES FOR 110 % OF THE INVOIECE VALUE SHOWING CLAIMS PAYABLE IN CANADA IN
CURRENCY OF THE DRAFT, BLANK ENDORSED, COVERING ALL RISKS, WAR RISKS
:47A:ADDITIONAL CONDITIONS




:71B:CHARGES
ALL BANKING CHARGES OUTSIDE THE OPENING BANK ARE FOR BENEFICIARY'S ACCOUNT
:48:PERIOD FOR PRESENTATION
DOCUMENTS MUST BE PRESENTED WITHIN 21 DAYS AFTER DATE OF ISSUANCE OF THE TRANSPORT DOCUMENTS BUT WITHIN
THE VALIDITY OF THIS CREDIT
:49:CONFIRMATION INSTRUCTIONS
WITHOUT
:57D:ADVISE THROUGH BANK
```

Specimen 11-4    Notification of Documentary L/C    信用证通知书

**南京商业银行**

**Nanjing Commercial Bank**

No.19 Lane 32 I Sen Rd, Nanjing 210014, P.R.China
FAX:86-25-27203335

信 用 证 通 知 书

**NOTIFICATION OF DOCUMENTARY CREDIT**

日期: 2004-08-22

| TO 致: | WHEN CORRESPOND NG | AD94001A40576 |
|---|---|---|
| GRAND WESTERN FOODS CORP. ROOM2501,JIAFA MANSION, BEIJING WEST ROAD, NANJING 210005, P.R.CHINA | PLEASE QUOTE OUT REF NO. | |
| ISSUING BANK开证行 THE CHARTERED BANK P.O.Box99552,Riyadh 22766,KSA | TRANSMITTED TO US THROUGH 转递行  REF NO. | |

| L/C NO.信用证号 | DATED 开证日期 | AMOUNT 金额 | EXPIRY PLACE 有效地 |
|---|---|---|---|
| STLCN000001 | 040820 | [USD ] [11200.00          ] | CANADA |
| EXPIRY DATE 有效期 | TENOR 期限 | CHARGE 未付费用 | CHARGE BY 费用承担人 |
| 041015 | SIGHT | RMB0.00 | BENE |
| RECEIVED VIA 来证方式 | AVAILABLE 是否生效 | TEST/SIGN 印押是否相符 | CONFIRM 我行是否保兑 |
| SWIFT | VALID | YES | NO |

DEAR SIRS 敬启者:
WE HAVE PLEASURE IN ADVISING YOU THAT WE HAVE RECEIVED FROM THE A/M BANK A(N) **LETTER OF CREDIT**, CONTENTS OF WHICH ARE AS PER ATTACHED SHEET(S).
THIS ADVICE AND THE ATTACHED SHEET(S) MUST ACCOMPANY THE RELATIVE DOCUMENTS WHEN PRESENTED FOR NEGOTIATION.
兹通知贵公司, 我行收自上述银行信用证一份, 现随附通知。贵司交单时, 请将本通知书及信用证
一并提示。

REMARK备注:
    PLEASE NOTE THAT THIS ADVICE DOES NOT CONSTITUTE OUR CONFIRMATION OF THE ABOVE L/C NOR DOES IT CONVEY ANY ENGAGEMENT OR OBLIGATION ON OUT PART.

THIS L/C CONSISTS OF          SHEET(S), INCLUDING THE COVERING LETTER AND ATTACHMENT(S).
本信用证连同面函及附件共      纸。

IF YOU FIND ANY TERMS AND CONDITIONS IN THE L/C WHICH YOU ARE UNABLE TO COMPLY WITH AND OR ANY ERROR(S), IT IS SUGGESTED THAT YOU CONTACT APPLICANT DIRECTLY FOR NECESSARY AMENDMENT(S) SO AS TO AVOID AND DIFFICULTIES WHICH MAY ARISE WHEN DOCUMENTS ARE PRESENTED.
如本信用证中有无法办到的条款及/或错误, 请迳与开证申请人联系, 进行必要的修改, 以排除交单时可能发生的问题。

THIS L/C IS ADVISED SUBJECT TO ICC UCP PUBLICATION NO.500.
本信用证之通知系遵循国际商会跟单信用证统一惯例第500号出版物办理。

此证如有任何问题及疑虑, 请与结算业务部审证科联络, 电话:   86-25-27293344

YOURS FAITHFULL

FOR _____  *Nanjing Commercial Bank*

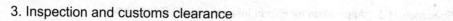
### 3. Inspection and customs clearance

#### ● Inspection

If required by the stipulation of the states or the contract, the exporter should apply for inspection to the inspection organization within the stipulated time limit. Usually, the goods will be released only after the insurance of inspection certificate by the inspection organization. Thus, inspection needs to be carried out before the customs clearance.

通常，只有取得商检部门发给的合格检验证书后，货物才能被海关放行。所以，一般出境货物最迟应于报关前报检。

In china, China Entry-Exit Inspection and Quarantine (CIQ) Bureau is one kind of inspection organization. Regarding to the exit goods subject to statutory inspection, the exporter shall apply for inspection to the local inspection authority within

the stipulated time limit. After completion of the application form (see Specimen 11-5), the exporter should submit necessary documents like copy of contract, packing list, bill of lading and L/C to the inspection bureau. After the goods have passed inspection, the same authority will issue inspection certificate (see Specimen 11-6) and sign it. Inspection certification is one of the documents that the exporter needs for customs clearance at the customs.

Besides China Inspection and Quarantine Bureau, there also exist some other famous inspection associations, such as Technischer Überwachungs-Verein(TÜV), Intertek Testing Services (ITS), Societe Generale de Surveillance S.A.(SGS ) and Nemko.

China

# 国际贸易实务(英语版)(第2版)

Specimen 11-5　Application for Export Inspection 出境货物报检单

中华人民共和国出入境检验检疫

## 出境货物报检单

| 报检单位 (加盖公章): 宏昌国际股份有限公司 | | | | | * 编　号 STEPC000001 | |
|---|---|---|---|---|---|---|

报检单位登记号：　19576254　　联系人：刘铭华　　电话：86-25-2350121 报检日期：2004 年 8 月 20 日

| 发货人 | (中文)　宏昌国际股份有限公司 | | | | | |
|---|---|---|---|---|---|---|
| | (外文)　GRAND WESTERN FOODS CORP. | | | | | |
| 收货人 | (中文) | | | | | |
| | (外文)　Carters Trading Company, LLC | | | | | |

| 选择 | 货物名称（中/外文） | H.S.编码 | 产地 | 数/重量 | 货物总值 | 包装种类及数量 |
|---|---|---|---|---|---|---|
| ○ | 甜玉米罐头 每箱6罐，每罐3060克 CANNED SWEET CORN 3060Gx6TINS/CTN | 20058000 | China | 800CARTON | USD11200 | 800CARTON |
| | | | | | | |

［添加］［修改］［删除］

| 运输工具名称/号码　Zaandam | | 贸易方式　一般贸易 | 货物存放地点　Nanjing CY | |
|---|---|---|---|---|
| 合同号　Contract01 | | 信用证号　STLCN000001 | 用途 | |
| 发货日期　2004-09-20 | 输往国家(地区)　Canada | 许可证 / 审批号 | | |
| 启运地　Nanjing | 到达口岸　Toronto | 生产单位注册号 | | |

集装箱规格、数量及号码

| 合同、信用证订立的检验 检疫条款或特殊要求 | 标记及号码 | 随附单据（划"√"或补填） | |
|---|---|---|---|
| | CANNED SWEET CORN CANADA C/NO.1-800 MADE IN CHINA | ☑合同 ☑信用证 ☑发票 □换证凭单 ☑装箱单 □厂检单 | □包装性能结果单 □许可/审批文件 □＿＿ □＿＿ □＿＿ □＿＿ |

| 需要证单名称（划"√"或补填） | | *检验检疫费 | |
|---|---|---|---|
| □品质证书　　＿正＿副 | □植物检疫证书　　＿正＿副 | 总金额 （人民币元） | |
| □重量证书　　＿正＿副 | □熏蒸/消毒证书　＿正＿副 | | |
| □数量证书　　＿正＿副 | □出境货物换证凭单 | | |
| □兽医卫生证书　＿正＿副 | ☑通关单 | 计费人 | |
| □健康证书　　＿正＿副 | □＿＿＿＿＿ | | |
| ☑卫生证书　　2正 2副 | □＿＿＿＿＿ | 收费人 | |
| □动物卫生证书　＿正＿副 | □＿＿＿＿＿ | | |

| 报检人郑重声明： 1.本人被授权报检。 2.上列填写内容正确属实，货物无伪造或冒用他人的厂名、标志、认证标志，并承担货物质量责任。 签名：刘铭华 | 领　取　证　单 | |
|---|---|---|
| | 日　期 | |
| | 签　名 | |

注：有"＊"号栏由出入境检验检疫机关填写　　　　　　　◆国家出入境检验检疫局制

[1-2 (2000.1.1)]

328

Specimen 11-6   Inspection Certificate 检验证书

中华人民共和国上海进出口商品检验局

SHANGHAI IMPORT & EXPORT COMMODITY INSPECTION BUREAU
OF THE PEOPLE'S REPUBLIC OF CHINA

地址：上海市中山东一路13号

Address: 13 Zhongshan Road      检 验 证 书      No.

(E.1.), Shanghai      INSPECTION   CERTIFICATE      日期 Date:

电报：上海 2914

Cable: 2914 SHANGHAI      QUALITY

电话 Tel. 63211285

发货人：

Consignor  Grand Western Foods Corp.

收货人：

Consignee  Carters Trading Company, LLC

CANNED SWEET CORN
CANADA

品 名：            标志及号码：      C/N0.1-800

Commodity  Canned sweet corn      Mark & No      MADE IN CHINA

报验数量/重量：

Quantity/Weight

Declared            800 ctns

检验结果：

RESULTS OF INSPECTION:

We hereby certify that the goods are of the above-mentioned

quantity and of sound quality.

主任检验员 李焕

Chief   Inspector:

## ● Customs clearance

The export goods can not be loaded for shipment until they are cleared for export. Certain procedures in customs formalities have to be completed. Nowadays, the exporter or his agent can clear the custom through the EDI system and submit all the documents needed for custom clearance.

In order to declare the export goods to the customs, the exporter or his agent should fill in Declaration Form for Export Goods ( see Specimen 11-7) and submit appropriate documents such as commercial invoice, packing list, copy of contract and L/C. Only  when the customs confirms the export goods, should the goods be loaded on board. Once the goods are cleared, the shipment can be made anytime.

无纸化报关实施以来，企业只需登录报关系统，提交报关所需材料的电子材料，由海关审核，审核通过发放通关凭条(参见样表 11-8)，此时报关完成。

Specimen 11-7    Declaration Form for Export Goods  出口货物报关单
***Old version:***

JG02

## 中华人民共和国海关出口货物报关单

预录入编号：                                          海关编号：

| 出口口岸 | | 备案号 | | 出口日期 | | 申报日期 |
|---|---|---|---|---|---|---|
| 经营单位 | | 运输方式 | 运输工具名称 | | 提运单号 | |
| 发货单位 | | 贸易方式 | | 征免性质 | | 结汇方式 |
| 许可证号 | | 运抵国(地区) | | 指运港 | | 境内货源地 |
| 批准文号 | | 成交方式 | 运费 | | 保费 | 杂费 |
| 合同协议号 | | 件数 | 包装种类 | | 毛重(千克) | 净重(千克) |
| 集装箱号 | | 随附单证 | | | | 生产厂家 |

标记唛码及备注

| 项号 | 商品编号 | 商品名称、规格型号 | 数量及单位 | 最终目的国(地区) | 单价 | 总价 | 币制 | 征免 |
|---|---|---|---|---|---|---|---|---|
| | | | | | | | | |
| | | | | | | | | |
| | | | | | | | | |

税费征收情况

| 录入员 | 录入单位 | 兹声明以上申报无讹并承担法律责任 | | 海关审单批注及放行日期(签章) | |
|---|---|---|---|---|---|
| 报关员 | | | | 审单 | 审价 |
| 单位地址 | | 申报单位(签章) | | 征税 | 统计 |
| 邮编 | 电话 | 填制日期 | | 查验 | 放行 |

*New version:*

JG02

<h1 style="text-align:center">中华人民共和国海关出口货物报关单</h1>

预录入编号：　　　　　　　　　　　　　　　海关编号：

| 收发货人 | | 出口口岸 | | 出口日期 | | 申报日期 |
|---|---|---|---|---|---|---|
| 生产销售单位 | | 运输方式 | 运输工具名称 | | 提运单号 | |
| 申报单位 | | 监管方式 | | 征免性质 | 备案号 | |
| 贸易国(地区) | 运抵国(地区) | | 指运港 | | 境内货源地 | |
| 许可证号 | 成交方式 | 运费 | | 保费 | 杂费 | |
| 合同协议号 | 件数 | 包装种类 | | 毛重(千克) | 净重(千克) | |
| 集装箱号 | 随附单证 | | | | | |
| 标记唛码及备注 | | | | | | |

| 项号 | 商品编号 | 商品名称、规格型号 | 数量及单位 | 最终目的国(地区) | 单价 | 总价 | 币制 | 征免 |
|---|---|---|---|---|---|---|---|---|
| | | | | | | | | |
| | | | | | | | | |
| | | | | | | | | |
| | | | | | | | | |

| 录入员　　　　录入单位 | 兹申明对以上内容承担如实申报、依法纳税之法律责任 | 海关批注及签章 |
|---|---|---|
| 报关人员 | 申报单位(签章) | |

Specimen 11-8　Notice for EDI Customs Clearance Notice 通关无纸化出口放行通知书

## 通关无纸化出口放行通知书

宁波市 报关代理有限公司:

你单位申报的货物(报关单 000000001164877395)于 2016年08月20日 业经通关无纸化放行,请及时办理后续海关手续。

特此通知。

宁波海关

2016-08-20

预录入编号:　517848680　　海关编号:　310120160517848680　　　　310120160517848680

| 出口口岸　　(3104)<br>北仑海关 | | 备案号 | 出口日期 | 申报日期<br>2016-08-20 |
|---|---|---|---|---|
| 经营单位　(3311 216)<br>台州市 工贸有限公司 | 运输方式<br>水路运输 | 运输工具名称<br>MARGRETHE MAERSK/633W | | 提运单号<br>580587401 |
| 发货单位　(3311 216)<br>台州市 工贸有限公司 | 贸易方式　　(0110)<br>一般贸易 | 征免性质　(101)<br>一般征税 | | 结汇方式 |
| 许可证号 | 运抵国(地区)　(302)<br>丹麦 | 指运港　　(1797)<br>奥尔胡斯 | | 境内货源地　　(33119)<br>台州 |
| 批准文号 | 成交方式<br>FOB | 运费 | 保费 | 杂费 |
| 合同协议号<br>FB-3310 | 件数<br>1075 | 包装种类<br>纸箱 | 毛重(千克)<br>2524 | 净重(千克)<br>2273 |
| 集装箱号<br>MWCU6881517 * 1(2) | 随附单证 | | | 生产厂家 |

| 项号 | 商品名称、规格型号 | 数量及单位 | 最终目的国(地区) | 单价 | 币制 |
|---|---|---|---|---|---|
| 1 | 圣诞灯/5800PCS, PVC, 铜丝, 电线, LED泡 | 5800套 | 丹麦 | 5.0841 | 美元 |
| | | | | | |
| | | | | | |
| | | | | | |
| | | | | | |
| | | | | | |
| | | | | | |
| | | | | | |
| | | | | | |
| | | | | | |
| | | | | | |
| | | | | | |
| | | | | | |
| | | | | | |

## 4. Insurance

Under CIF term, the exporter covers insurance at his own expense as agreed in the contract. Therefore, before the shipment, he can contact insurance company or his agents to arrange for insurance. To effect insurance, the exporter needs to fill in an application for cargo transportation insurance (see Specimen 11-9) and prepare commercial invoice. The insurer, upon receiving the required insurance documents, will produce insurance policy (see Specimen 11-10) for the insured.

Specimen 11-9 Application for Cargo Transportation Insurance 投保单

## 货 物 运 输 保 险 投 保 单

投保人: 宏昌国际股份有限公司                    投保日期:    2017-08-25

| 发票号码 | STINV000001 | 投保条款和险别 | |
|---|---|---|---|
| 被保险人 | 客户抬头<br>宏昌国际股份有限公司<br><br>过户<br>Carters Trading Company, LLC | ( ) PICC CLAUSE<br>(√) ICC CLAUSE<br>( ) ALL RISKS<br>( ) W.P.A./W.A.<br>( ) F.P.A<br>(√) WAR RISKS<br>( ) S.R.C.C | |
| 保险金额 | [USD        ][12320                    ] | ( ) STRIKE<br>(√) ICC CLAUSE A | |
| 启 运 港 | Nanjing | ( ) ICC CLAUSE B | |
| 目 的 港 | Toronto | ( ) ICC CLAUSE C | |
| 转 内 陆 |  | ( ) AIR TPT ALL RISKS<br>( ) AIR TPT RISKS<br>( ) O/L TPT ALL RISKS | |
| 开航日期 | 2017-09-10 | ( ) O/L TPT RISKS<br>( ) TRANSHIPMENT RISKS | |
| 船名航次 | Zaandam, DY105-09 | ( ) W TO W<br>( ) T.P.N.D. | |
| 赔款地点 | Canada | ( ) F.R.E.C.<br>( ) R.F.W.D. | |
| 赔付币别 | USD | ( ) RISKS OF BREAKAGE | |
| 保单份数 |  | ( ) I.O.P. | |
| 其 他 特<br>别 条 款 |  |  | |
| 以 下 由 保 险 公 司 填 写 | | | |
| 保单号码 |  | 签单日期 | |

Specimen 11-10　Insurance Policy　保险单

**PICC　中国人民保险公司**

The People's Insurance Company of China Shanghai Branch

总公司设于北京　　　　一九四九年创立

Head Office Beijin　　　Established in 1949

货物运输保险单

**CARGO TRANSPORTATION INSURANCE POLICY**

发票号（INVOICE NO.）STINV000001　　　　　　　　　　保单号次

合同号（CONTRACT NO.）Contract01　　　　　　　　　　POLICY NO.

信用证号（L/C NO.）　STLCN000001

被保险人：

Insured:　　　　　　　　　　　　　宏昌国际股份有限公司

中国人民保险公司（以下简称本公司）根据被保险人的要求，由被保险人向本公司缴付约定的保险费，按照本保险但承保险别和背面所列条款与下列条款承保下述货物运输保险，特立本保险单。

THIS POLICY OF INSURANCE WITNESSES THAT THE PEOPLE'S INSURANCE COMPANY OF CHINA(HEREIN AFTER CALLED "THE COMPANY")AT THE REQUEST OF THE INSURED AND INCONSIDERATION OF THE AGREED PREMIUM PAID TO THE COMPANY BY THE INSURED,UNDERTAKES TO INSURED THE UNDERMENTIONED GOODS IN TRANSPORTATION SUBJECT TO THE CONDITIONS OF THIS POLICY AS PER THE CLAUSES PRINTED OVERLEAF AND OTHER SPECIAL CLAUSES ATTACHED HEREON.

| 标　记 MARKS & NOS. | 包装及数量 QUANTITY | 保险货物项目 DESCRIPTION OF GOODS | 保险金额 AMOUNT INSURED |
|---|---|---|---|
| CANNED　SWEET CORN CANADA C/NO.1-800 MADE IN CHINA | 800 CARTON | CANNED SWEET CORN | USD12320 |

总保险金额：

TOTAL AMOUNT INSURED: SAY US DOLLARS TWELVE THOUSAND THREE HUNDRED AND TWENTY ONLY

保费：　　　　起运日期　　　　　　　　　　　　　　　　装载运输工具：

PREMIUM:_____　DATE OF COMMENCEMENT　2004-09-10　PER CONVEYANCE:　Zaandam, DY105-09

自　　　　　　　　经　　　　　　　　　　　至

FROM　Nanjing　　　　　VIA　　　　　　　　　　TO　　　　Toronto

承保险别：

CONDITIONS:　　ICC Clause A and War Risk

所保货物，如发生保险单项下可能引起索赔的损失或损坏，应立即通知本公司下述代理人查勘。

IN THE EVENT OF LOSS OR DAMAGE WHICH MAY RESULT IN A CLAIM UNDER THIS POLICY IMMEDIATE NOTICE MUST BE GIVEN TO THE COMPANY'S AGENT AS MENTIONED HEREUNDER.

中国人民保险公司上海分公司

The People's Insurance Company of China

Shanghai Branch

赔款偿付地点　　　　　　　　　　　　　　　　　何黔芝

CLAIM PAYABLE AT___Canada in USD_____

出单日期

ISSUING DATE___2004-08-25_____　　　　　　　General Manager

地址：中国上海中山东一路23号　TEL:3234305 3217466-44 Telex:33128 PICCS CN.

Address: 23 Zhongshan Dong Yi Lu Shanghai, China Cable: 42001 Shanghai

**Endorsement Grand Western Foods Corp.**

## 5. Arranging for shipment

Based on CIF contract, the exporter undertakes the obligation of chartering and booking space. Chartering is used for goods of large quantity which needs full shipload, and for bulk goods in small quantities space booking would be enough. In China, the exporter usually asks the freight forwarder to book the shipping space.

The procedure of booking space is as follows. First, the exporter needs to complete the booking note (see Specimen 11-11) and present commercial invoice and packing list to the freight forwarder. After obtaining the receipt of the exporter's booking note, the freight forwarder will deliver shipping note to the shipping company. Accepting the space booking, the shipping company will then mark name of vessel, vessel No. and Dock Receipt (D/R) No. on the shipping order ( see Specimen 11-12) and finally return it back to the forwarder.

Shipping Order (S/O) is quite essential for the exporter to ensure the loading of the goods, and get Bill of Lading (B/L) from the carrier. Only when the customs confirms the export goods and stamps on the shipping order, should the goods be loaded on board. After the goods are loaded on board, the shipping company or ship's agent will issue bill of lading ( see Specimen 11-13), which is a receipt evidencing the loading of the goods on board.

Upon completion of the shipment, the exporter should send the importer the shipping advice (see Specimen 11-14) to enable the latter to arrange insurance (if necessary), payment and receipt of the goods.

The following are some famous shipping companies.

订舱流程：①在货证齐备后，出口商缮制"订舱委托书"(Booking Note)，随附发票和装箱单委托货代代为订舱。②货代接受订舱委托后，缮制"托运单"(十联单)，随同发票、装箱单向船公司办理订舱。③船公司如接受订舱则在"十联单"（其中包括装货单）填上船名、航次并签署，返还给货代。④货代留存第八联，将装货单等交给出口商。

装货单(S/O)，又称关单，是船公司或船代向其负责人(船长或大副)和集装箱装卸作业区签发的一种通知其接受装货的指示文件。海关对货、证核查无误后，在装货单上加盖"放行"章，托运人才可凭以装船。

注意：

实施无纸化报关之后，"装货单"通常由"通关无纸化出口放行通知书"(参见样表)替代，意即出口货物报关已通过，可以装船。

## 货物出运委托书
### (出口货物明细单) 日期: 2017-09-10

根据《中华人民共和国合同法》与《中华人民共和国海商法》的规定，就出口货物委托运输事宜订立本合同。

| | | | | |
|---|---|---|---|---|
| 合 同 号 | Contract01 | | 运输编号 | STINV000001 |
| 银行编号 | dst01 | | 信用证号 | STLCN000001 |
| 开证银行 | THE CHARTERED BANK | | | |

| 托运人 | 宏昌国际股份有限公司<br>南京市北京西路嘉发大厦2501室 | 付款方式 | L/C | | |
|---|---|---|---|---|---|
| | | 贸易性质 | 一般贸易 | 贸易国别 | Canada |
| 抬头人 | To order of Carters Trading Company, LLC | 运输方式 | 海运 | 消费国别 | Canada |
| | | 装运期限 | 2016-09-20 | 出口口岸 | Nanjing |
| 通知人 | Carters Trading Company, LLC<br>P.O.Box8935,New Terminal, Lata. Vista, Ottawa, Canada | 有效期限 | 2016-10-15 | 目 的 港 | Toronto |
| | | 可否转运 | NO | 可否分批 | NO |
| | | 运费预付 | YES | 运费到付 | NO |

| 选择 | 标志唛头 | 货名规格 | 件数 | 数量 | 毛重 | 净重 | 单价 | 总价 |
|---|---|---|---|---|---|---|---|---|
| ○ | CANNED SWEET CORN<br>CANADA<br>C/NO.1-800<br>MADE IN CHINA | CANNED SWEET CORN<br>3060Gx6TINS/CTN | 800CARTON | 800CARTON | 16156.8KGS | 14688KGS | USD14 | USD11200 |
| | | | | | | | | |

| | | | | | | | |
|---|---|---|---|---|---|---|---|
| **TOTAL:** | [800 ][CARTON | ] [800 ][CARTON | ] [16156.8 ][KGS | ][14688 ][KGS | ] | [USD ][11200 | |

[ 添 加 ][ 修 改 ][ 删 除 ]

| 注意事项 | | FOB价 | [USD ][ 7509.58 ] |
|---|---|---|---|
| | | 总体积 | [ 20.5888][CBM ] |
| | | 保险单 险别 | ICC(A)<br>WAR RISKS |
| | | 保险单 保额 | [USD ][ 12320 ] |
| | | 赔偿地点 | CANADA |
| | | 海关编号 | 0000000003 |
| | | 制单员 | 刘铭华 |

受托人(即承运人)

名称: _____

电话: _____

传真: _____

委托代理人: _____

委托人(即托运人)

名称: 宏昌国际股份有限公司

电话: 86-25-23501213

传真: 86-25-23500638

委托代理人: 刘铭华

Specimen 11-12  Shipping Order  装货单

| Shipper (发货人)<br>GRAND WESTERN FOODS CORP.<br>Room2501, Jiafa Mansion, Beijing West road, Nanjing 210005,<br>P.R. China | | | | D/R No.（编号） | | |
|---|---|---|---|---|---|---|
| consignee (收货人)<br>To order of Carters Trading Company, LLC | | | | **Shipping order**<br>**装货单** | | |
| Notify Party (通知人)<br>Carters Trading Company, LLC<br>P.O.Box8935, New Terminal, Lata. Vista, Ottawa, Canada | | | | | | |
| pre-carriage by (前程运输) | | Place of Receipt (收货地点) | | | | |
| Vessel (船名) Voy. No.(航次)<br>Zaandam        DYI105-09 | | Port of loading(装货港)<br>Nanjing | | | | |
| Port of discharge(卸货港)<br>Toronto | | Place of Delivery(交货地点) | | Final Destination for the Merchant's<br>Reference (目的地) | | |
| Container No.<br>(集装箱号)<br><br><br>COSU455961 | Seal No. (封志号)<br>Marks & No.<br>(标志与号码)<br>CANNED SWEET<br>CORN<br>CANADA<br>C/NO.1-800<br>MADE IN CHINA | No. of contain<br>-ers or packages<br>(箱号或件数)<br><br>800 CARTON | Kind of Packages:<br>Description of<br>Goods<br>(包装种类与货名)<br>CANNED SWEET<br>CORN | Gross<br>Weight<br>毛重<br>16156.8<br>KGS | Measurement<br>尺码 | |
| TOTAL NUMBER OF CONTAINERS        SAY EIGHT HUNDRED CARTONS ONLY<br>OR PACKAGES（IN WORDS)<br>集装箱数或件数合计（大写） | | | | | | |
| FREIGHT  & CHARGES<br>（运费与附加费) | Revenue Tons<br>（运费吨) | RATE<br>（运费率) | Per<br>（每) | Prepaid<br>（运费预付) | Collect<br>（到付) | |
| Ex. Rate:<br>（兑换率) | Prepaid at （预付地点)<br>Total Prepaid<br>（预付总额) | Payable at (到付地点)<br>No. of Original B（s）/L<br>（正本提单份数) | | Place of Issue （签发地点) | | |
| Service Type on receiving<br>□-CY. □-CFS. □-DOOR | Service Type on Delivery<br>□-CY. □-CFS. □-DOOR | Reefer-Temperature Required<br>（冷藏温度) | | | F | C |
| TYPE<br>OF<br>GOODS | □Ordinary  □Reefer<br>（普通)    （冷藏)<br>□ Liquid □Live Animal<br>（液体)   （活动物) | □Dangerous<br>（危险品)<br>□Bulk □_____<br>（散货) | □Auto<br>（袋装车辆) | 危<br>险<br>品 | Class:<br>Property:<br>IMDG Code Page:<br>UN No. | |
| 可否转船: PROHIBITED  可否分批: PROHIBITED | | | | | | |
| 装期: | 效期: | 中华人民共和国上海海关 | | | | |
| 金额: | | | | | | |
| 制单日期: | | | | | | |

Specimen 11-13   Bill of Lading  提单

| | |
|---|---|
| 1)SHIPPER<br><br>GRAND WESTERN FOODS CORP.<br>Room2501, Jiafa Mansion, Beijing West road, Nanjing 210005, P.R. China | 10)B/L NO.<br>**CARRIER**<br><br>COSCO<br>**中国远洋运输(集团)总公司**<br><br>CHINA OCEAN SHIPPING(GROUP)CO.<br><br>*ORIGINAL*<br><br>COMBINED TRANPORT BILL OF LADING |
| 2)CONSIGNEE<br>  To order of Carters Trading Company, LLC | |
| 3)NOTIFY PARTY<br>Carters Trading Company, LLC<br>P.O.Box8935, New Terminal, Lata Vista, Ottawa, Canada | |

| 4)PLACE OF RECEIPT | 5)OCEAN VESSEL<br>Zaandam |
|---|---|
| 6)VOYAGE NO.<br>DY105-09 | 7)PORT OF LOADING<br>Nanjing |
| 8)PORT OF DISCHARGE<br>Toronto | 9)PLACE OF DELIVERY |

| 11)MARKS | 12)NOS.&KINDS OF PKGS | 13)DESCRIPTION OF GOODS | 14)G.W.(kg) | 15)MEAS(m3) |
|---|---|---|---|---|
| CANNED SWEET CORN<br>CANADA<br>C/NO.1-800<br>MADE IN CHINA | 800 CARTON | CANNED SWEET CORN | 16156.8 KGS | |

16)TOTAL NUMBER OF CONTAINERS OR PACKAGES(IN WORDS)

SAY EIGHT HUNDRED CARTONS ONLY

| FREIGHT & CHARGES | REVENUE TONS | RATE | PER | PREPAID | COLLECT |
|---|---|---|---|---|---|
| PREPAID AT | PAYABLE AT | | 17)PLACE AND DATE OF ISSUE | | |
| TOTAL PREPAID | 18)NUMBER OF ORIGINAL B(S)L | | | | |

| LOADING ON BOARD THE VESSEL<br><br><br>19)DATE | 20)BY<br>中国外轮代理公司上海分公司<br>CHINA OCEAN SHIPPING AGENCY,<br>SHANGHAI BRANCH<br>常途用 |
|---|---|

Specimen 11-14　Shipping Advice　装船通知

## SHIPPING ADVICE

Messrs.

Carters Trading Company, LLC

P.O.Box8935,New Terminal, Lata. Vista, Ottawa, Canada

Invoice No. STINV000001

Date:　　2004-09-10

Particulars

1.L/C No. STLCN000001

2.Purchase order No. Contract01

3.Vessel: Zaandam

4.Port of Loading:　　Nanjing

5.Port of Dischagre: Toronto

6.On Board Date: 2004-09-10

7.Estimated Time of Arrival: 2004-09-22

8.Container:　　20' X 1

9.Freight:　[USD　　]　[3582　　　　　]

10.Description of Goods:

CANNED SWEET CORN
3060Gx6TINS/CTN

11.Quantity:[800　　　　　　　] [CARTON　　]

12.Invoice Total Amount: [USD　　　] [11200　　　　]

Documents enclosed

1.Commercial Invoice: 1

2.Packing List: 1

3.Bill of Lading: 1(Duplicate)

4.Insurance Policy: 1(Duplicate) 2 Copies

Very truly yours, GRAND WESTERN FOODS CORP.

Minghua liu

Manager of Foreign Trade Dept.

## 6. Preparing documents for negotiation

去银行交单议付时，出口商所提交的单据必须严格遵照"单单一致，单证一致"的原则。

After the shipment, the exporter is to assemble all kinds of documents required by the L/C and present them to the bank for negotiation within the validity of the L/C. All the required documents must be completed with absolute accuracy and clarity. They should be made out in full conformity with the L/C terms, such as types of documents, number of original and copies, items of the documents. Generally, the following documents may be required to present to the bank:

(1) Bill of exchange (see Specimen 11-15)

(2) Commercial invoice (see Specimen 11-16)

(3) Packing list (see Specimen 11-17)

(4) Bill of lading (see Specimen 11-13)

(5) Insurance policy (see Specimen 11-10)

(7) Inspection certificate (see Specimen 11-6)

(8) Certificate of origin or GSP Form A (see Specimen 11-18)

(9) Shipping advice (see Specimen 11-14)

(10) Beneficiary's declaration (see Specimen 11-19)

议付行代开证行"垫付"款项给受益人，议付本身就是一种"垫付"行为。

Under a complying presentation, the negotiating bank purchases the draft and documents by advancing or agreeing to advance funds to the beneficiary. After negotiation, the negotiating bank reimburses from the issuing bank. However, if any discrepancy occurs, the exporter must make corrections immediately within the validity of the L/C. Otherwise, the negotiating bank will refuse to make the payment.

Specimen 11-15　Bill of Exchange 汇票

### BILL OF EXCHANGE

No. STDFT000001　　　　　　　　　　　　　　Dated 2004-08-30

Exchange for　USD　　11200

　　　At　----　　　　　　　　　　　Sight　of　this　　FIRST　　of　Exchange

(Second of exchange being unpaid)

Pay to the Order of Nanjing Commercial Bank

the sum of U.S.DOLLARS NINE THOUSAND SIX HUNDRED ONLY

Drawn under L/C No. STLCN000001　　　　　　Dated 2004-08-20

Issued by　THE CHARTERED BANK

To　THE CHARTERED BANK
　　P.O.BOX99552,RIYADH 22766,KSA

　　　　　　　　　　　　　　　　　　GRAND WESTERN FOODS CORP.

　　　　　　　　　　　　　　　　　　　　(Authorized Signature)

Specimen 11-16  Commercial Invoice 商业发票

<table>
<tr>
<td colspan="3">ISSUER<br><br>GRAND WESTERN FOODS CORP.<br>Room2501,Jiafa Mansion, Beijing West road,<br>Nanjing 210005, P.R.China</td>
<td colspan="4" align="center"><br>商 业 发 票<br>COMMERCIAL INVOICE</td>
</tr>
</table>

| ISSUER | 商 业 发 票 |
|---|---|
| GRAND WESTERN FOODS CORP.<br>Room2501,Jiafa Mansion, Beijing West road,<br>Nanjing 210005, P.R.China | COMMERCIAL INVOICE |

| TO | | |
|---|---|---|
| Carters Trading Company, LLC<br>P.O.Box8935,New Terminal, Lata. Vista, Ottawa, Canada | **NO.**<br>STINV000001 | **DATE**<br>2004-08-20 |
| **TRANSPORT DETAILS** | **S/C NO.**<br>Contract01 | **L/C NO.**<br>STLCN000001 |
| From Nanjing to Toronto on Sep. 10, 2004 By Vessel. | **TERMS OF PAYMENT**<br>L/C | |

| Choice | Marks and Numbers | Description of goods | Quantity | Unit Price | Amount |
|---|---|---|---|---|---|
| | | | | CIF TORONTO | |
| ○ | CANNED SWEET CORN<br>CANADA<br>C/NO.1-800<br>MADE IN CHINA | CANNED SWEET CORN<br>3060Gx6TINS/CTN | 800CARTON | USD14 | USD11200 |
| | | | | | |

[ 添 加 ][ 修 改 ][ 删 除 ]

**Total :** [ 800 ][CARTON]  [USD][ 11200 ]

**SAY TOTAL:**  U.S.DOLLARS ELEVEN THOUSAND TWO HUNDRED ONLY

(写备注处)

GRAND WESTERN FOODS CORP. (公司名称)

Minghua Liu (法人签名)

Specimen 11-17   Packing List 装箱单

| ISSUER | | | | | |
|---|---|---|---|---|---|
| GRAND WESTERN FOODS CORP.<br>Room2501,Jiafa Mansion, Beijing West road,<br>Nanjing 210005, P.R.China | | | 装 箱 单<br>PACKING LIST | | |
| TO<br>Carters Trading Company, LLC<br>P.O.Box8935,New Terminal, Lata. Vista, Ottawa, Canada | | | INVOICE NO.<br>STINV000001 | | DATE<br>2004-08-20 |

| Choice | Marks and Numbers | Description of goods | Package | G. W | N. W | Meas. |
|---|---|---|---|---|---|---|
| ○ | CANNED SWEET CORN<br>CANADA<br>C/NO.1-800<br>MADE IN CHINA | CANNED SWEET CORN<br>3060Gx6TINS/CTN | 800CARTON | 16156.8KGS | 14688KGS | 20.5888CBM |
| | | | | | | |
| | | | | [ 添 加 ] | [ 修 改 ] | [ 删 除 ] |

Total : [800        ] [16156.8    ] [14688    ] [20.5888    ]
        [CARTON  ] [KGS        ] [KGS      ] [CBM        ]

SAY TOTAL:   EIGHT HUNDRED CARTONS ONLY

(写备注处)

GRAND WESTERN FOODS CORP.(公司名称)

Minghua Liu(法人签名)

## Specimen 11-18　GSP Form A 普惠制原产地证书

**ORIGINAL**

| | |
|---|---|
| 1.Goods consigned from (Exporter's business name, address, country)<br><br>GRAND WESTERN FOODS CORP.<br>Room2501,Jiafa Mansion, Beijing West road, Nanjing 210005, P.R.China | Reference No.　STGSP000001<br><br>**GENERALIZED SYSTEM OF PREFERENCES<br>CERTIFICATE OF ORIGIN**<br>(Combined declaration and certificate) |
| 2.Goods consigned to (Consignee's name, address, country)<br><br>Carters Trading Company, LLC<br>P.O.Box8935,New Terminal, Lata. Vista, Ottawa, Canada | **FORM A**<br><br>Issued in　**THE PEOPLE'S REPUBLIC OF CHINA**<br>(country) |
| 3.Means of transport and route (as far as known)<br><br>From Nanjing to Toronto On Sep. 10, 2004 By Vessel. | 4.For official use |

| Choice | 5.Item number | 6.Marks and numbers of packages | 7.Number and kind of packages; description of goods | 8.Origin criterion (see Notes overleaf) | 9.Gross weight or other quantity | 10.Number and date of invoices |
|---|---|---|---|---|---|---|
| ○ | 1 | CANNED SWEET CORN<br>CANADA<br>C/NO.1-800<br>MADE IN CHINA | 800 CARTONS (EIGHT HUNDRED CARTONS ONLY) OF CANNED SWEET CORN<br>3060Gx6TINS/CTN | "P" | 16156.8KGS | STINV000001<br>Aug 20, 2004 |

| 添加 | | 修改 | | 删除 |

| | |
|---|---|
| 11.Declaration by the exporter<br>**It is hereby certified, on the basis of control carried out, that the declaration by the exporter is correct.**<br><br><br><br><br><br><br><br>**Place and date, signature and stamp of certifying authority** | 12.Certification<br>**The undersigned hereby declares that the above details and statements are correct, that all the goods were**<br>produced in ──── **CHINA** ────<br>(country)<br>and that they comply with the origin requirements specified for those goods in the Generalized System of Preferences for goods exported to<br>──── CANADA ────<br>(importing country)<br><br>NANJING, JIANGSU AUG. 25, 2004<br><br>**Place and date, signature and stamp of authorized signatory** |

Specimen 11-19    Beneficiary's Declaration  受益人声明

# GRAND WESTERN FOODS CORP.

Room2501, Jiafa Mansion, Beijing West road, Nanjing 210005, P.R. China

## BENEFICIARY'S DECLARATION

TO: Carters Trading Company, LLC
L/C No: STLCN000001
Invoice No.: STINV000001
S/C No: Contract01

This is to certify that one full set of non-negotiable copies of documents has to be sent by airmail directly to Carters Company, LLC, P.O.Box8935, New Terminal, Lata. Vista, Ottawa, Canada.

GRAND WESTERN
FOODS CORP.
SALES MANAGER
ASSISTANT
Catherine

### 7. Tax refund

为推进贸易便利化，国家外汇管理局、国家税务总局和海关总署决定自 2012 年 8 月 1 日起调整出口报关流程，取消出口收汇核销单，简化出口退税凭证。企业无须再办理出口收汇核销手续。

To further promote trade facilitation, State Administration of Foreign Exchange (SAFE), State Administration of Taxation (SAT) and General Administration of Customs jointly launched the reform on August 1st, 2012. The reform includes adjusting export declaration formalities, cancelling the verifying and writing-off instrument and simplifying tax refund certificates. Thus companies do not need to go through verifying and writing-off procedures.

In China, the export trade differs from domestic trade in the aspect that indirect taxes such as value-added tax and consumption tax will be returned or rebated to the exporter after the conclusion of export business. This is to encourage exporting and earn foreign exchange.

To complete tax refund, the exporter should fill in Export Tax Refund Application Form and submit related documents to the local branch of SAT. Documents required include a page of "export goods declaration form (for export refund only)", value -add tax invoice and export invoice. The SAT announced that applicants who fail to meet the application deadline of tax refund and exemption on export would be treated as those of domestic sales, unless otherwise specified.

出口退税(一单两票):
    出口货物报关单中的出口退税专用联、增值税专用发票、出口发票。

### 8. Disputes settlement

Any disputes arising from the execution of the contract should be settled through negotiation. If no settlement can be reached through negotiations, the dispute will be submitted to an arbitration commission specified in the contract. The award rendered by the commission shall be final and binding upon both parties. In one word, once disputes arise, it is advised that arbitration is better than litigation, and negotiation is better than arbitration.

## 11.2   Importing procedures

The basic importing procedure is similar to that of export, including preparation stage, negotiation stage and performance stage. In this part, the basic importing procedure under a CIF contract with the L/C payment is to be shown in the following Table 11-2 for learners' reference.

进口贸易基本程序可概括为:交易前准备阶段,交易磋商和合同签订阶段,合同履行阶段。

Table 11-2   The basic importing procedure (FOB, L/C)

| Procedures | Content | | Focus |
|---|---|---|---|
| I. Preparation stage | ● Acquiring import license<br>● Finding the right supplier overseas | | Market |
| II. Negotiation stage | ● Enquiry<br>● Counter-offer | ● Offer<br>● Acceptance | Contract |
| III. Performance stage | ① Opening L/C | | L/C |
| | ② Preparing for shipment | | Shipment |
| | ③ Insurance | | |
| | ④ Checking documents and making payment | | Payment |
| | ⑤ Inspection and customs clearance | | |
| | ⑥ Taking delivery and reinspection | | |
| | ⑦ Disputes settlement | | |

## 11.2.1   Preparation stage of import contract

Before business negotiation, the importer should make full preparations for the transaction, like finding the right supplier overseas and acquiring import license.

● Acquiring import license

Normally, countries have more import controls than export controls on commodities in international trade. Importers in China should refer to the Ministry of Foreign Trade and Economic Cooperation's (MOFTEC) current list of "restricted goods" that require import licenses.

An import license is most often required where:

(1) Goods is listed by MOFTEC as a "restricted good" that requires an import license;

(2) An importer does not have foreign trade rights;

(3) Or a Federal Trade Commission (FTC) imports goods that are beyond its business scope as authorized by the government.

Before the importer starts the transactions, he must make sure whether the import license is needed and can be obtained. If needed, he should submit the license application letter to the import office of the local government. Acquiring the import license (see Specimen 11-20) , the importer can start to send his order, make payment and submit application for customs clearance based on the import license.

Specimen 11-20  Import License of the People's Republic of China 中华人民共和国进口许可证

| 1.我国货物成交单位<br>Importer | | | | 3.进口许可证编号<br>Licence No. | | |
|---|---|---|---|---|---|---|
| 2.收货单位<br>Consignee | | | | 4.许可证有效期<br>Validity | | |
| 5.贸易方式<br>Terms of trade | | | | 8.进口国家(地区)<br>Country of destination | | |
| 6.外汇来源<br>Terms of foreign exchange | | | | 9.商品原产地<br>Country of origin | | |
| 7.到货口岸<br>Port of destination | | | | 10. 商品用途<br>Use of commodity | | |
| 唛头—包装件数<br>Marks & numbers—number of packages | | | | | | |
| 商品名称<br>Description of commodity | | | | 商品编码<br>Commodity No. | | |
| 13.商品规格、型号<br>Specification | 14.单位<br>Unit | 15.数量<br>Quantity | 16.单价(USD)<br>Unit price | 17.总值(USD)<br>Amount | 18.总值折美元<br>Amount in USD | |
| | | | | | | |
| | | | | | | |
| 19.备注<br>Supplementary details | | 20.发证机关盖章<br>Issuing authority's stamp & signature<br><br>发证日期<br>Date　　年　月　日 | | | 进口许可证专用章<br>上　海 | |
| 商务部监制 | | 本证不得涂改，不得转让 | | | | |

● Finding the right supplier overseas

Importing for the first time directly or even indirectly can be daunting. So it is important that you devote time to find exactly the right overseas supplier for your requirements.

Personal recommendation is always a good route to a reliable supplier. Relationships are no less important. If the importer plans to place a big order with a company, he needs to be sure that he can trust the person responsible for delivering the order. If personal recommendation is not available, the importer could try consulting any trade associations or business-support organizations for pointers. National embassies, trade fairs and exhibitions can also be a useful source of help. In addition, the importer can look through the trade press and directories for names of suppliers.

## 11.2.2 Negotiation stage of import contract

Negotiation of the import contract generally covers four procedures — enquiry, offer, counter-offer and acceptance. Here efforts are made to mention some tips for negotiating the right deal with suppliers.

### ● Setting objectives when negotiating with suppliers

There's a range of key considerations the importer needs to bear in mind when setting objectives for purchase negotiations. These might include price, delivery, terms of payment, quality, after-sales service and maintenance arrangements.

At the start of negotiation, the importer should be cleared about which aspects of specification are essential and which provide room for negotiation. And he should decide what he has and has not prepared to compromise on.

### ● The danger of squeezing prices

If the importer squeezes the price too low, perhaps by threatening to walk away from the negotiations, he may end up getting a poor deal. The supplier may have to cut costs elsewhere, in an area such as customer service, which could prove costly to the importer in the long run.

Even if the importer is a supplier's main customer and enjoy most of the bargaining power, forcing it to meet low prices at which it could go out of business will damage his reputation as a highly valued customer. The supplier will soon look for other customers and is likely to feel resentful.

### ● Drawing up a contract

Once all the points have been negotiated and a deal has been agreed, a written contract will be drawn up and signed by both parties. Although verbal contracts are acceptable and legally binding, they are very hard to rely on in court.

The importer should make sure that he has agreed all the key issues, such as price, delivery and payment terms. Depending on who holds the bargaining power in the negotiations, the terms and conditions used in the contract may be the importer's, the supplier's or a mixture of the two.

## 11.2.3    Performance stage of import contract

### 1. Opening L/C

When the business is concluded with the payment by L/C, it is the importer's duty to open the L/C. By filling in Irrevocable Documentary Credit Application (see Specimen 11-21), the importer applies to his issuing bank for the opening of L/C in favor of the exporter. The issuing bank will then charge him fees for issuing the L/C. Usually, the issuing bank will requests the importer to deposit a sum of money to a maximum equivalent to the price of the goods to be imported.

出口商应在合同规定的期限内向开证行办理开证申请手续，信用证内容须与合同一致，否则应立即向开证行提出修改申请。

When opening L/C, the importer should follow the time stipulated in the contract. It might not be earlier or later than that in the contract. Earlier, the importer will increase his expense. Later, it will cause his failure in contract obligation and may delay the exporter's shipping operation. The importer should also make sure that terms of the L/C are in strict conformity with the contract. If any discrepancies found in the L/C, the exporter will ask for amendments and the importer needs to request the issuing bank to make appropriate amendments according to the contract agreed by both parties.

进口商应在合同规定的期限内办理开证申请手续，而且信用证内容应该与合同一致，否则应向开证行提出修改申请。

### 2. Preparing for shipment

Under FOB terms, it is the importer's obligation to book the shipping space and accept goods at the stipulated place. After receiving notice from the exporter and knowing that the exporter has got the goods ready for shipment, the importer should charter or book shipping space with the carrier.

The space booking procedure is similar to the procedure operated by exporter under CIF terms. After booking the shipping space, the importer should advice the exporter within 45 days to deliver and load the goods in time. He should also give the exporter sufficient notice of information such as the name of vessel, the name of the loading port and the required delivery time so as to enable the exporter to deliver the goods to the carrier smoothly and without delay.

进口业务中，凡以FOB 贸易术语成立的合同，由进口商安排运输，负责租船或订舱工作。

### 3. Insurance

It is important for the importer to assess and plan for different risks that he may invariably face during his business practice. So the importer must take into account the following factors, such as possible loss or damage of goods in transportation, storage of goods in warehouses, currency fluctuations etc.

FOB, CFR, FCA, CPT 条件下的进口合同，由进口商负责向办公室办理货物的运输保险。

The responsibility for effecting insurance can be shared between the importer and exporter, or be taken on by just one of them. Under the FOB, CFR, FCA and CPT terms, the importer is responsible for affecting the insurance for the goods after receiving the shipping advice. And he should timely notify the insurance company of the commodity name, quantity, port of loading, port of discharge, date of shipment etc.

Specimen 11-21　Irrevocable Documentary Credit Application　信用证开证申请书

### IRREVOCABLE DOCUMENTARY CREDIT APPLICATION

TO: THE CHARTERED BANK　　　　　　　　　　　　　　　　DATE:　040819

| | |
|---|---|
| ☐ Issue by airmail　☐ With brief advice by teletransmission<br>☐ Issue by express delivery<br>☑ Issue by teletransmission (which shall be the operative instrument) | Credit NO.　STLCA000001<br><br>Date and place of expiry　041015 in the beneficiary's country |
| Applicant<br>CARTERS TRADING COMPANY, LLC<br>P.O.BOX8935, NEW TERMINALI, LATA. VISTA,<br>OTTAWA, CANADA | Beneficiary (Full name and address)<br>GRAND WESTERN FOODS CORP.<br>ROOM2501, JIAFA MANSION, BEIJING WEST ROAD,<br>NANJING 210005, P.R.CHINA |
| Advising Bank<br>NANJING COMMERCIAL BANK<br>NO.19 LANE 32 I SEN RD, NANJING 210014, P.R.CHINA | Amount<br>[USD　][11200.00　]<br>U.S.DOLLARS ELEVEN THOUSAND TWO HUNDRED ONLY |

| | | | |
|---|---|---|---|
| Parital shipments<br>☐ allowed　☑ not allowed | Transhipment<br>☐ allowed　☑ not allowed | Credit available with<br>NANJING COMMERCIAL BANK<br>By<br>☐ sight payment　☐ acceptance　☑ negotiation<br>☐ deferred payment at | |

Loading on board/dispatch/taking in charge at/from
NANJING

not later than　040920

For transportation to:　TORONTO

☐ FOB　　☐ CFR　　☑ CIF
☐ or other terms

against the documents detailed herein
☑ and beneficiary's draft(s) for　100　% of invoice value
at　****　sight
drawn on　ISSUE BANK

Documents required: (marked with X)

1.( X ) Signed commercial invoice in　6　copies indicating L/C No.　and Contract No.　Contract01
2.( X ) Full set of clean on board Bills of Lading made out to order and blank endorsed, marked "freight [　] to collect / [ X ] prepaid [　] showing freight amount" notifying　THE APPLICANT
　(　) Airway bills/cargo receipt/copy of railway bills issued by　showing "freight [　] to collect/ [　] prepaid [　] indicating freight amount" and consigned to
3.( X ) Insurance Policy/Certificate in 3　copies for 110　% of the invoice value showing claims payable in CANADA　in currency of the draft, blank endorsed, covering All Risks and War Risks
4.( X ) Packing List/Weight Memo in　3　copies indicating quantity, gross and weights of each package.
5.(　) Certificate of Quantity/Weight in　copies issued by
6.(　) Certificate of Quality in　copies issued by [　] manufacturer/[　] public recognized surveyor
7.( X ) Certificate of Origin in 3　copies issued by MANUFACTURER
8.(　) Beneficiary's certified copy of fax / telex dispatched to the applicant within　hours after shipment advising L/C No., name of vessel, date of shipment, name, quantity, weight and value of goods.

Other documents, if any

Description of goods:
01005 CANNED SWEET CORN, 3060Gx6TINS/CTN
QUANTITY: 800 CARTON
PRICE: USD14/CTN

Additional instructions:
1.( X ) All banking charges outside the opening bank are for beneficiary's account.
2.( X ) Documents must be presented within 21　days after date of issuance of the transport documents but within the validity of this credit.
3.(　) Third party as shipper is not acceptable, Short Form/Blank B/L is not acceptable.
4.(　) Both quantity and credit amount　% more or less are allowed.
5.(　) All documents must be forwarded in
　(　) Other terms, if any

## 4. Checking documents and making payment

After the goods are delivered, the exporter receives documents proving that he has made the delivery of the goods. The necessary documents are handed over by the exporter to the negotiating bank. After checking these documents, the negotiating bank pays the sum that the importer owes to the exporter directly even if something happens to the merchandise in practice. Then the negotiating bank sends the documents to the issuing bank for reimbursement. Through the issuing bank, the documents finally reach the importer, who can use these documents to collect the shipped goods. Finally, the importer pays the amount owed to the issuing bank.

Relevant documents required for negotiation have been mentioned in 11.1.3 as follows: ①bill of exchange, ②commercial invoice, ③packing list, ④B/L, ⑤insurance policy, ⑥inspection certificate, ⑦GSP form A, ⑧shipping advice and ⑨ beneficiary's declaration etc. The negotiating bank will pay the money to the exporter only if the documents presented are in strict accordance with the L/C.

为了保证进口商的权益，审单工作必须认真做好。审单是银行与企业的共同责任，因此必须密切联系，加强配合。

---

### L/C Fraud: Fake Documents

*A fraudulent seller sends fake shipping documents to the opening or advising bank to prove that the goods were shipped. In fact, the goods never left the sellers warehouse or, more likely, never existed at all. Other documents like the invoice, packing list, export declaration, even Certificate of Origin can be easily produced by the scammer. In many L/Cs the only documents needed for the L/C to be paid are the invoice and shipping documents. If the seller's bank believes that the papers are authentic and pays the scammer, the buyer will never see the goods and will spend much time in discussions with his bank.*

**Discussion: As an importer, how to protect yourself?**

---

L/C plays a significant role in international trade, but it is likely to be tricked for it adopts the way of pure document. L/C fraud has become an increasing non-violent crime which severely influences international trade. So the importer can always ask the seller to fax the drafts of all the papers which are supposed to be sent to the bank. Check them carefully. Most of the shipping lines have online tracking system, where by entering the container number the importer can see when the cargo actually left the port and to which destination. If everything is in good order, ask the seller to issue the originals and send copies to you by fax or e-mail. It is a good idea for the importer to ask the opening bank to send the copies of the documents received. Then he can check them before the bank pays the seller.

### 5. Inspection and custom clearance

根据《海关法》的
规定，进口货物除因特
殊原因经海关总署批
准的以外，都应当接受
海关的查验。

If necessary, the importer or his agency would apply for the inspection for the import goods. He will submit documents like the copy of contract, invoice, packing list, B/L after completion of the application form (see Specimen 11-22). The inspection institution would carry out the inspection at the stipulated place according to the contracts and relevant laws. If the goods are qualified, the institution will issue the inspection qualification certificate and sign it.

Specimen 11-22　Application for Import Inspection 入境货物报检单

中华人民共和国出入境检验检疫

入境货物报检单

| | | | | * 编　号 STIPC000001 | | |
|---|---|---|---|---|---|---|
| 报检单位 (加盖公章)：Carters Trading Company, LLC | | | | | | |
| 报检单位登记号：36572596 | 联系人：Carter | 电话：001613789350 | 报检日期：2005年 9 月 22 日 | | | |

| | | | 企业性质(划 " √ ") □ 合资 □ 合作 □ 外资 | | | |
|---|---|---|---|---|---|---|
| 收货人 | (中文) | Carters Trading Company, LLC | | | | |
| | (外文) | | | | | |
| 发货人 | (中文) | 宏昌国际股份有限公司 | | | | |
| | (外文) | GRAND WESTERN FOODS CORP, | | | | |

| 选择 | 货物名称 (中/外文) | H.S.编码 | 原产国(地区) | 数/重量 | 货物总值 | 包装种类及数量 |
|---|---|---|---|---|---|---|
| C | CANNED SWEET CORN 3060Gx6TINS/CTN | 20058000 | Nanjing | 800CARTON | USD11200 | 800CARTON |
| | | | | | | |

[ 添加 ][ 修改 ][ 删除 ]

| 运输工具名称号码 | Zaandam | | | 合　同　号 | Contract01 |
|---|---|---|---|---|---|
| 贸易方式 | 一般贸易 | 贸易国别(地区) | China | 提单/运单号 | STBLN000001 |
| 到货日期 | 2005-09-22 | 启运国家(地区) | China | 许可证/审批号 | |
| 卸毕日期 | 2004-09-22 | 启运口岸 | Nanjing | 入境口岸 | Toronto |
| 索赔有效期至 | 2004-09-30 | 经停口岸 | | 目的地 | |
| 集装箱规格、数量及号码 | TBXU3605231*1*20' | | | 货物存放地点 | |
| 合同订立的特殊条款 以及其他要求 | | | | 用途 | |

| 随附单据 (划 " √ " 或补填) | | 标记及号码 | *外商投资财产(划 " √ ") □ 是 □ 否 | | |
|---|---|---|---|---|---|
| ☑合同 | □到货通知 | CANNED SWEET CORN | *检验检疫费 | | |
| ☑发票 | ☑装箱单 | CANADA | | | |
| ☑提/运单 | □质保书 | C/NO.1-800 | 总金额 (人民币元) | | |
| □兽医卫生证书 | □理货清单 | MADE IN CHINA | | | |
| □植物检疫证书 | □磅码单 | | 计费人 | | |
| □动物检疫证书 | □验收报告 | | | | |
| □卫生证书 | □ | | 收费人 | | |
| □原产地证 | □ | | | | |
| □许可/审批文件 | □ | | 领　取　证　单 | | |
| 报检人郑重声明： 1. 本人被授权报检。 2. 上列填写内容正确属实。 | | | 日　期 | | |
| | | 签名：Carter | 签　名 | | |

注：有 " * " 号栏由出入境检验检疫机关填写　　　　　　　◆国家出入境检验检疫局制

[1-2 (2000.1.1)]

After the inspection, the importer can apply for customs clearance and pay for import duties according to the customs requirement. The importer can clear the custom through the EDI system and submit all the documents needed for custom clearance. The importer has to fill in Declaration Form for Import Goods (see Specimen 11-23) and get the documents needed for customs clearance prepared, such as B/L, invoice, packing list, copy of contract, certificate of origin, import license, insurance policy etc. The customs will check the goods and the documents to see whether the goods are complied with documents. Only after the customs stamps on the transport document, can the consignee or its agent take delivery of import goods.

结关，又称放行，是指进口货物在办完向海关申报的手续，接受查验，缴纳关税后，由海关在货物单据上签字或盖章放行，收货人持此货运单据提取进口货物。

### 6. Taking delivery and reinspection

After making the payment and getting the shipping documents, the importer can take delivery of the goods from the carrier after the arrival of the goods at the destination. However, it should be noted that the importer should inspect the goods to ensure that the goods delivered conform to the description of the goods in the sales contract.

Usually the buyer has reasonable chance to reinspect import goods to see whether they are complied with contract. If the specification and quantity of the goods are found not in conformity with the stipulation in the sales contract, the buyer has the right for compensation, or even to reject the goods. If some damages of the goods are found, the importer should bring forward the related inspection certificates issued by independent public inspection authority accepted by both parties. However, if the buyer has accepted the goods, or has reinspected the goods without indicating rejection of goods, the buyers then cannot reject goods.

### 7. Disputes settlement

Sometimes disputes inevitably arise in spite of the careful performance of contract by the exporter and importer. In international trade, most of the claims are made by the importer. Therefore, upon reinspection of the goods at the destination, should any problem arise, the importer would reserve the right to reject the goods totally or lodge a claim against the relevant party. If problems concerning weight shortage, inferior quality or wrong shipment are found and attributed to the exporter, the importer should lodge claims against exporter. However, if the loss of or damage to the goods is found to be caused by the negligence of the carrier, the importer should make claims against the carrier. If the loss of damage is due to the risks in transit and has been covered by the insurance, the claim should be made against the insurance company.

In one word, claims should be filed within the time limit stipulated in the contract and the importer has to present all documents necessary for the claims. Once disputes arise, it is advised that arbitration be better than litigation, and negotiation be better than arbitration.

Specimen 11-23　Declaration Form for Import Goods　进口货物报关单

## 中华人民共和国海关进口货物报关单

| 预录入编号： | | | 海关编号： | | | |
|---|---|---|---|---|---|---|
| 进口口岸　TORONTO CUSTOMS | | 备案号 | | 进口日期 2004-09-22 | 申报日期 2004-09-23 | |
| 经营单位　CATERS TRADING COMPANY, LLC 5102852098 | | 运输方式 江海运输 | 运输工具名称 Zaandam | | 提运单号 STBLN000001 | |
| 收货单位　CATERS TRADING COMPANY, LLC 5102852098 | | 贸易方式 一般贸易 | | 征免性质 一般征税 | 征税比例 | |
| 许可证号 | 起运国（地区） China | | 装货港 Nanjing | | 境内目的地 | |
| 批准文号　091323588 | 成交方式 CIF | 运费 [　　] | | 保费 [　] [　] | 杂费 [　] [　] | |
| 合同协议号　Contract01 | 件数 800 | 包装种类 CARTON | | 毛重(公斤) 16156.8 | 净重(公斤) 14688 | |
| 集装箱号　TBXU3605231*1 | 随附单据 | | | 用途 | | |
| 标记唛码及备注 CANNED SWEET CORN CANADA C/NO.1-800 MADE IN CHINA | | | | | | |

| 选择 | 项号 | 商品编号 | 商品名称、规格型号 | 数量及单位 | 原产国(地区) | 单价 | 总价 | 币制 | 征免 |
|---|---|---|---|---|---|---|---|---|---|
| ○ | 1 | 20058000 | CANNED SWEET CORN3060Gx6TINS/CTN | 800CARTON | China | 14 | 11200 | USD | 一般征税 |

[ 添 加 ] [ 修 改 ] [ 删 除 ]

| 税费征收情况 | | | |
|---|---|---|---|
| | | | |

| 录入员　录入单位 | 兹声明以上申报无讹并承担法律责任 | 海关审单批注及放行日期(签章) | |
|---|---|---|---|
| 报关员　Carter 申报单位（签章） | | 审单 | 审价 |
| 单位地址　P.O.Box8935,New Terminal, Lata. Vista, Ottawa, Canada | | 征税 | 统计 |
| 邮编　　电话 00161378935( 填制日期 2004-09-22 | | 查验 | 放行 |

# 【Key Terms and Words】

Quotas　配额

Discrepancy　不符点

Export control　出口管制

China Entry-Exit Inspection and Quarantine Bureau　中国出入境检验检疫局

Irrevocable documentary L/C　不可撤销跟单信用证

Insurance policy　保险单

Freight forwarder　货代

Shipping company　船公司

Booking note　订舱委托书

Dock receipt　场站收据

Shipping order　装货单

Bill of lading　提单

Voyage No.　航次

Port of loading　装运港

Port of discharge　卸货港

Shipping advice　装船通知

Inspection association　检验机构

GSP Form A　普惠制原产地证书

Certificate of origin　原产地证

Beneficiary's declaration　受益人证明

Tax refund　出口退税

Value-added tax invoice　增值税发票

the State Administration of Taxation　国税局

Import license　进口许可证

Ministry of Foreign Trade and Economic Cooperation(MOFTEC)　对外贸易经济合作部

Bargaining power　议价能力

# 【Exercises】

I. Find in the text the English equivalents to the following terms.

1. 装货单 _____     6. 增值税发票_____

2. 保险单 _____     7. 出口许可证 _____

3. 装箱单 _____     8. 受益人证明 _____

4 出口退税 _____     9. 出口货物报关单 _____

5. 原产地证 _____     10. 普惠制原产地证书 _____

II. Decide whether the following statements are true or false by writing "T" or "F" in the blanket beside each statement.

1. (     )  If the contract is under the payment of L/C, the exporter can make shipment before he has received the L/C.

2. (     )  The issuer of a commercial invoice should be the beneficiary of the relevant credit.

3. (     )  Both the sales contract and L/C are the legal documents which bind upon both the buyer and the seller, and bind upon the opening bank and the beneficiary.

4. (     )  All the discrepancies in an L/C should be amended.

5. (     )  The L/C can be amended directly by the applicant and be transferred to the beneficiary.

6. (     )  The exporter should submit relevant documents to the local branch of the State Administration of Taxation (SAT) for verification and writing-off.

7. (     )  When there are more than two changes in L/C amendment, the beneficiary can only accept all or refuse all.

8. (     )  The accordance between documents and L/C and between documents and documents is necessary in L/C settlement.

9. (     )  The documents shall be sent to the buyer by the exporter directly under L/C settlement.

10. (     ) Once disputes arise, it is advised that arbitration is better than litigation, and conciliation is better than arbitration.

III. Answer the Following Questions.

1. Please list out relevant parties involved in export and import transaction.

2. Suppose you are an exporter, briefly describe the main procedures in exporting.

3. Suppose you are an importer, briefly describe the main procedures in importing.

4. What documents are needed in export transaction under a CIF contract with the L/C payment ?

5. As an exporter, you have received the notification of documentary L/C. What should you do then?

## IV. Case Study

Company A signed a sales contract with Company B in Jan. 2009 on CIF basis. The term of payment was by confirmed irrevocable letter of credit payable by draft at sight. B issued the L/C through his bank in March, 2009. After checking L/C, A found it complying with the contract. In the L/C, the insurance amount was 110% of CIF invoice value. While A was preparing for the goods, B issued a notification of amendment in which the insurance amount was changed to 120% of CIF invoice value. A disregarded it and effected insurance as per the stipulation of original credit. The negotiating bank forwarded full set of documents to the issuing bank. But the issuing bank rejected payment on account that discrepancy between insurance policy and notification of amendment exists.

**Question:**

Is the issuing bank reasonable for non-payment? Why? Please analyze the case and give your problem-solving plan.

# Chapter 12   Modes of International Trade

## Lead-in: News Release

### China e-commerce market to grow 19 pct in 2017

The e-commerce market in China is expected to grow by about 19 percent year on year in 2017, a report said on Thursday.

China has entered "a new retail era" characterized by online and offline (O2O) retail that has created huge potential and demand, especially for customized products, according to a report released by consulting firm McKinsey & Company Thursday.

Many e-commerce traders that are expanding into online social networks, however, often offer lower quality service compared with that provided by major online shopping sites, the report said.

There is huge market potential if they can just improve their services, it said. After years of explosive growth, China has emerged as the world's largest e-commerce

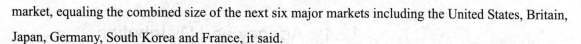

## Chapter 12　Modes of International Trade

market, equaling the combined size of the next six major markets including the United States, Britain, Japan, Germany, South Korea and France, it said.

Last year, China's e-commerce market expanded 19.8 percent year on year to 26.1 trillion yuan (3.82 trillion U.S. dollars), accounting for 39.2 percent of the world's total, according to the Chinese Ministry of Commerce.

*(Source: Xinhua/2017-06-22 22:36:57/Editor: Liangyu)*

***Class Activities:***

1. What is the main problem of China's e-commerce?
2. Do you know what other modes of international trade?

# 12.1 Agency and Distribution

## 12.1.1 Agency

代理是指代理人按照委托人的授权，代表委托人与第三方订立合同，可分为佣金代理、独家代理和总代理。

Agency is a relationship in which one party (the agent) acts on behalf of and under the control of another (the principal) in dealing with third parties. It has its roots in ancient servant-master relations. Agency becomes a legal issue when the agent injures or wrongs a third party.

A vast amount of international trade is handled not only by direct negotiations between the buyers and the sellers but also by means of agencies. An important reason for appointing a foreign agent is that he has all necessary knowledge of local conditions and of the market in which he will operate. He knows what goods are best suitable to his area and what price the market will bear. Therefore, agents and intermediaries often play a very important role in foreign trade.

In foreign trade practice, there are many different types of agents and there are no rigid rules about the use of names. The major forms of agents are as follows:

### 1. Sole Agent

A sole agent is also called an exclusive agent. The agency relationship endows the holder exclusive rights to sell a product or service in a particular territory for a specified period.

### 2. General Agent

A general agent is a person who is legally authorized to represent a company or individual on all kinds of business. General agents can represent single companies or work as representatives of multiple companies and individuals. And they are empowered to act on the basis of agreements made with the people they represent.

Many people and companies need agents to represent them when people normally tasked with decision making are not available, for a variety of reasons ranging from illness to time zone conflicts. The agent is empowered to take action quickly in situations where rapid responses are needed and can also respond to routine business inquiries to reduce the workload for company officers and business people.

### 3. Commission Agent

A commission agent is an agent specializing in buying or selling goods for a principal in another country for a commission. Commission agents possess a fair amount of freedom when it comes to purchasing or selling materials for a principal. Usually, principals outline their material needs and a project's purchase budget, or the desired price of sale, along with a set of preferred conditions for a deal. The commission agent is responsible for meeting the ideal conditions requested by the principal, and must stay within the provided budget or the price of sale. As long as commission agents conform to these stipulations, they possess the freedom to act and make deals as they choose.

Commission agents are protected by the laws of their home country regarding issues with their principals, but they must adhere to the laws of the nation in which they work, as well as international regulations.

## 12.1.2   Distribution

Distribution is a commonly used mode of export promotion in international trade. Exporters can establish a business relationship with overseas clients by signing distribution agreement. It is the process of moving products or services from its manufacturing source to its customers, which consists of distributors, wholesalers and retailers besides manufacturers.

分销是国际贸易中一种常见的出口推销方式。出口商通过与国外客户签订分销协议来建立双方的业务关系。分销实际上就是一个将产品或服务从生产者手中传递给顾客的过程。这个过程主要由生产商、分销商、批发商和零售商等成员构成。

### 1. Distributor

A distributor can be defined as an entity that buys noncompeting products or product lines, warehouses them, and resells them to retailers or direct to the end customers. Most distributors provide strong manpower and cash support to the supplier or manufacturer's promotional efforts. They usually also provide a range of services (such as product information, estimates, technical support, after-sales services and credit) to their customers.

In the practice of international trade, the following two kinds of distributors are generally used:

(a) Sole or exclusive distributor.

It refers to a distributor who is the only one in an area that is allowed by the manufacturer to sell a specific product or service.

(b) Non-exclusive distributor.

There may be several non-exclusive distributors appointed by the principal or supplier in one territory.

### 2. Wholesaler

Wholesalers buy mostly from producers and sell mostly to retailers, industrial consumers, and other wholesalers. As a result, many of the largest and most important wholesalers are largely unknown to final consumers.

### 3. Retailer

Retailer is a business or person that sells goods or services to end consumers, as opposed to a wholesaler or supplier, who normally sell their goods to another business. Retailers come in many different shapes and sizes, and new retail types keep emerging.

# 12.2 Consignment

## 12.2.1 Definition

It means that the consignor delivers the goods to the place of consignment abroad first, then entrusts the consignee with the task to sell the goods according to the conditions and methods stipulated in the agreement of consignment.

## 12.2.2 Features

The features of consignment are as follows.

(1) The consignor shall first deliver the goods to the agent or consignment agent.

(2) Before the commission agent sells out the goods, the title to the goods still belongs to the consignor.

(3) The commission agent is commissioned to sell the goods for the consignor and he will deal with the goods according to the order of the consignor only.

(4) The consignment agent will not under any risks and expenses and he only charges commission for his service.

寄售是一种委托代售的贸易方式。它是指委托人(货主)先将货物运往寄售地,委托国外一个代销人(受托人)按照寄售协议规定的条件由代销人代替货主进行销售,在货物出售后,由代销人向货主结算货款的一种贸易方式。

寄售的特点:

(1) 寄售是先出运、后成交的贸易方式。

(2) 出口商与寄售商之间是委托代销关系。

(3) 寄售不是出售,在寄售商未将商品出售以前,商品的所有权仍属委托人(出口商)。

(4) 寄售商几乎不承担任何风险和费用。

## 12.2.3 The Advantages and Disadvantages of Consignment

### 1. Cost Savings

Consignment saves the consignor money, because it doesn't have to buy inventory before selling. The consignor thus avoids the overhead costs of managing inventory, such as storage, insurance and transportation. Also, because the consignor doesn't have to pay for consigned goods until after the sale, it collects revenue before paying for merchandise. This is desirable sequence of cash flows, because it means the consignor can conserve its funds and reduces the need to borrow money to pay for its inventory, thereby saving interest expense. By the same reasoning, these cash flows are less desirable for the consignee.

### 2. Convenience

Consignment arrangements offer the consignor time-saving conveniences. If you are a consignor, you don't need to spend time reordering stock, because the consignee will promptly replenish sold items. Naturally, this serves the consignee's purposes by ensuring its stock is always available for sale. If you normally order merchandise to complete a sale—for example, in a business that displays but does not stock inventory—you will have fast and easy access to consigned goods because the consignee will do everything possible to facilitate a sale. Often, consignees will physically arrange their wares for display in the consignor's store, saving the storeowner time and labor costs.

### 3. Market Penetration

A consignee benefits from the consignment method by gaining an opportunity to display its wares to the public and build demand. A retailer might be more amenable to showing new products from a consignee than from a conventional wholesaler because of the many benefits of consignment. Consignors might be more willing to temporarily stock seasonal or holiday items that it otherwise might not bother with because of limited demand. By explaining the benefits of consignment to a shop owner, a consignee might be able to compete with items sold through conventional means.

寄售的优点:

(1) 节约成本: 代销人不负担风险与费用, 一般由寄售人垫资, 代销人不占用资金, 可以调动其经营的积极性。

(2) 便利: 寄售方式是凭实物买卖。货物与买主直接见面, 利于促进成交。

(3) 市场渗透: 寄售货物出售前, 寄售人持有货物的所有权, 有利于随行就市。

# 12.3   Tenders and Auction

## 12.3.1   Tenders

招标是指一方发出招标通告，提出准备购买的商品的名称、规格、数量和有关的交易条件。

A tender is an offer or proposal to purchase a specified quantity of a commodity for a specified price. The procedures of tender involve four basic steps: issue the tender notice, bid, declare the party who wins the bid and sign the contract.

It includes two parts, one is invitation to tender, and the other is submission of tender.

### 1. Invitation to tender

Invitation to tender refers that one party issues out a tender notice to show the name of commodity they would like to purchase, as well as the specification, quantity and trade conditions.

Invitations to tender should be written in plain language and avoid the overuse of unnecessary technical terms. The invitation to tender should, as a minimum, include:

(1) Instructions to tenders which set out when and how tenders must be submitted, in what format and where queries should be addressed to at the Council.

(2) The specification/technical details of the subject matter of the contract.

(3) The contract terms and conditions which will apply.

(4) The tender evaluation criteria.

(5) The process for awarding the contract.

There are many types available for invitation to bid. The most popularly adopted types are as follows:

(1) As per territories: It can be classified into international tender offering and domestic tender offering.

(2) As per degrees of competitiveness: It includes competitive tender offering, noncompetitive tender offering or negotiating tender offering, unlimitedly competitive tender offering, limitedly-competitive tender offering or selective tender offering or inviting for tender, exclusive tender offering, two-stage tender offering or tender offering consisting of open and selective stages.

(3) As per ranges of plant-engineering. It may be classified into tender offering for turn-key plant-engineering, tender offering for product-in-hand plant-engineering, tender offering for construction of plant-engineering and installation of equipment, tender offering for purchase of equipment and materials, parallel tender offering, sequential tender offering.

(4) As per modes of valuation of plant-engineering. It is usually classified into tender offering for fixed-total-price plant-engineering, tender offering for unchanged-unit-price plant-engineering, tender offering for cost-and commission plant-engineering.

### 2. Submission of tender

Submission of tender refers that the other party who bids the tender according to the requirement of the tender.

投标是指投标人应招标人的邀请，按照招标的要求和条件，在规定的时间内向招标人递价，争取中标的行为。

Once submission of tenders has come to an end, the employer should hold a ceremony for bid opening within the stipulated time limit at the named place. The employer usually entrusts the institution on invitation of bidding or an advisory company with the responsibility for bid opening within 90 days after the closing date of tender.

In accordance with the specific conditions, there are three modes that can be adopted: bid opening in public, bid opening in private and bid opening secretly.

## 12.3.2   Auction

An auction is a process of buying and selling goods or services by offering them up for bid, taking bids, and then selling the item to the highest bidder. In economic theory, an auction may refer to any mechanism or set of trading rules for exchange.

拍卖是一个通过将货物进行叫价竞购，然后把货物卖给出价最高的买主的商品交易过程。

Auctions are used to sell many things in addition to antiques and art. Although this method of sales originated several hundred years ago, it is, to some extent, still in use today. All around the world there are auctions of commodities such as tobacco, fish, cattle, racehorses, and just about anything else where there's a market of multiple people interested in buying the same thing. That's the key to an auction—a bunch of people who are interested in buying the same object, and taking turns offering bids on the object. The right to buy that object will go to the highest bidder.

Different auction formats exist, varying according to how prices are quoted and bids tendered, among which the most commonly known one is the English Auction, which is commonly used for artworks and wine. This auction is also called the ascending price or open-outcry auction. The best known auction houses, Sotheby's and Christie's, were founded in the eighteenth century, but written records of auctions go back to ancient times. Economists specializing in game theory have investigated the theory of bidding strategies for an auction, and how these strategies depend upon the rules and procedures of the auction. In the business arena, these experts are sometimes hired as consultants for important auctions, for example, at the time that the Unites States government sold wireless spectrum licenses by auction. Depending on the auction, bidders may participate in person or remotely through a variety of means, including telephone and the internet.

## 12.4　Counter Trade

对等贸易也称对销贸易、反向贸易或互抵贸易，一般认为这是一种以货物或劳务(包括工业产权和专有技术等无形财产)作为偿付贷款手段的贸易方式。

对等贸易有多种形式，但其基本形式主要有易货贸易、互购、补偿贸易、转手贸易等。

Counter trade is a reciprocal trading arrangement in which the seller is required to accept goods or other instruments or trade in partial or whole payment for its products. Besides tangible product, the objects of counter trade can include service, technology and so on. Current counter trade can be categorized as follows: barter, counter purchase, buyback, switch trade and offset. It is an alternative means of structuring an international sale when conventional means of payment are difficult, costly or nonexistent.

The terminology counter trade employed today can be traced to the pre-World War II years when normal trade relations were breaking down. Counter trade is a peculiar form of transaction which is popular in less developed countries and in centrally planned economies. It has become the generic term to describe a set of cross-border contracts that link a seller's exports to imports from the buyer, and it is often associated with policy objectives of relevant economies like dealing with foreign exchange shortages and promotion of exports.

## 12.4.1　Main Reasons Why Counter Trade Is Employed

Historically, countertrade was mainly conducted in the form of barter, which is a direct exchange of goods of approximately equal value, with no money involved.

Counter trade is significant because of credit shortages and a lack of hard currency in many countries. Nowadays, it plays a part in 20~25 percent of world trade in practice.

The main reasons why counter trade is employed are as follows:

(1) Increasingly, countries and companies are deciding that sometimes counter trade transactions are more beneficial than transactions based on financial exchange, especially in the markets which are unable to pay for imports.

(2) Counter trade is viewed as an excellent mechanism to gain entry into new markets, and it is a good way to protect or stimulate the output of domestic industries.

(3) As a reflection of political and economic policies, it seeks to plan and balance overseas trade.

(4) Many countries are responding favorably to the notion of bilateralism.

## 12.4.2　Specific Forms of Counter Trade

The counter trade can be divided into different forms, the main forms are barter trade, counter purchase, compensation trade/buyback, switch trade and offset trade.

### 1. Barter Trade

Barter is the oldest form of trade, which is a direct exchange of goods and/or services between two parties without a cash transaction. It is viewed as the most restrictive counter trade arrangement, and it is used primarily for one-time-only deals in transactions with trading partners who are not creditworthy or trustworthy. For those countries which do not have enough

传统的易货贸易，一般是买卖双方各以等值的货物进行交换，不涉及货币的支付，也没有第三者介入，易货双方签订一份包括相互交换抵偿货物的合同，把有关事项加以确定。

在国际贸易中，使用较多的是通过对开信用证的方式进行易货，即由交易双方先订易货合同，规定各自的出口商品均按约定价格以信用证方式付款。

互购又称为对购贸易或平行贸易。互购是指一方向另一方出口商品或劳务的同时，承担以所得货款的部分或全部向对方购买一定数量或金额商品或劳务的义务。

补偿贸易是指在信贷基础上进口设备，然后以回销产品或劳务所得价款，分期偿还进口设备的公款及利息。

转手贸易又称三角贸易。这是一种特殊的贸易方式。在记账贸易的条件下，人们采用转手贸易作为取得硬通货的一种手段。

foreign exchange, they can solve the problem by choosing barter trade. In practice, however, the supply of the principal export is often released only when the sale of the bartered goods has generated sufficient cash. This means if country A sells medical equipment to country B in return for cigars, they will probably hold some of the medical equipment back until they have made some good profit from the cigars.

### 2. Counter Purchase

Counter purchase, also called reciprocal trade or parallel trade, is a reciprocal buying agreement. It occurs when a firm agrees to purchase a certain amount of materials back from a country to which a sale is made.

The contract of counter purchase is usually stipulated to be fulfilled within a given period of time, e.g., 5 years, and the goods or services received in return are usually pre-specified in a list and are subject to availability and changes made by the original importing country. In essence, then, counter purchase is an intertemporal direct exchange of goods and services. For example, in 1977 Volkswagen sold 12,000 cars to the former East Germany and agreed to purchase goods from a list set up by the importer over the following 2 years, up to the value of the cars sold to the former East Germany.

### 3. Compensation Trade/Buyback

Compensation trade or buyback means that one party provides the other party with equipment and technology, the payment of which is made by the goods manufactured with the equipment and technology, or by other goods.

The important difference between counter purchase and buyback is that in buyback the goods and services taken back are tied to the original goods exported whereas that is not the case in counter purchase. Another important difference is that a buyback deal usually stretches over a longer period of time (as long as 15 to 20 years) than a counter purchase deal.

### 4. Switch Trade

Switch trade is exporting and importing through a third nation, where the currency paying for the goods can be easily exchanged into one acceptable to the seller. Switch trade is a relatively more complicated form of barter, and it involves a chain of buyers and sellers in different markets.

Switch trading occurs when a third-party trading house buys the firm's counter purchase credits and sells them to another firm that can better use them. A switch arrangement permits the sale of unpaid balances in a clearing account to be sold to a third party, usually at a discount, which may be used for producing goods in the country holding the balance. Therefore, it is closely linked with the bilateral clearing agreements between governments.

### 5. Offset

Offset means that the exporter agrees to use goods and services from the buyer's country in return for the products being sold. Offset has traditionally been used by governments around the world when they have made major purchases of military goods but nowadays is becoming increasingly common in other sectors, and it is becoming more and more important.

Offset is a practice in which the seller has to undertake some sort of activity favorable to the importer in addition to the supply of the capital goods. It is similar to counter-purchase as one party agrees to purchase goods and services with a specified percentage of the proceeds from the original sale. The difference is that this party can fulfill the obligation with any firm in the country to which the sale is being made.

Whether companies become involved in the complexities offset trade depends mainly on the strength of demand for their products, whether they have alternative sources of supply, and the extent of foreign-exchange problems in the buying country.

There are two distinct types of offset trade. One is direct offset which involves compensation in related goods and usually involves some form of co-production, license or technology transfer. The other is indirect offset which involves goods and services unrelated to the aerospace/defence material being sold.

The impression one gets is that bundled trade takes place where the market institution is imperfect. It can be said to generally take place between mature market economies and economies with a less sophisticated market system. Under such circumstance there are several presumed advantages in counter trade, for example, it is implemented to deal with foreign exchange

抵销贸易是指一方在进口设备时，以先期向另一方或出口方提供的某种商品和/或劳务、资金等抵销一定比例进口价款的做法。

从本质上看，这种方式已突破商品交换的范围，成为直接投资，是通过贸易推动生产国际化进程的一种特殊方式。

shortages, reduce the risks, provide mutual benefits, promote exports, gain entry into new markets and create stability for long-term sales.

However, counter trade can be very risky business. By concealing the real prices and costs of transactions it may conceal and help perpetuate economic inefficiencies in the market place. Companies may suffer losses because they could not get rid of products of poor quality. Finally, counter trade may be considered as a form of protectionism.

# 12.5　Futures Trading

## 12.5.1　Introduction to Futures Trading

期货贸易实际上是期货合同贸易。根据合同的规定，在将来的某个时候进行交易时，可以按照事先约定的价格买卖特定的股票、商品或者此类资产。

Futures trading is the trading of futures contracts which allows specific stocks, commodities or such assets to be traded at a pre-determined price in future. Futures trading is a form of investing that is best suited for more advanced investors who have the time and funds available to devote to tracking futures movement. Because futures trading relies on predicting market swings and movement, investors who utilize futures trading need to be active and involved investors.

Futures trading can trace its history back to farming and agriculture and in particular to the grain and cattle markets of the mid-west around Chicago, where even today many of the largest futures exchanges are still based. Futures trading was used by producers and buyers of agricultural commodities to

protect themselves against seasonal price fluctuations. They traded with each other at the current price on the terms of forward delivery before the harvest. For instance, a farmer may short a futures contract on his 5,000 bushels of corn grains at the price of $0.30 per bushel to a buyer of corn grains. By doing so, the farmer has guaranteed himself the price of $0.30 per bushel for his corns when harvest time comes. The buyer would also have guaranteed himself the purchase price of $0.30 per bushel. In this case, the farmer is clearly hedging against a drop in price of corns, and the buyer doesn't need to worry about the rise of price. Of course, this is merely a simple mode of how futures work.

The most popular and recognized commodities that are traded on the futures market are grains, metals and foods. Additional items traded in the futures market include gold, soybeans, cattle and other goods that fluctuate in value.

## 12.5.2　Main Types of Futures Traders

There are four main types of futures traders in the futures market, creating the liquid futures trading environment that we see today. No matter what you choose to do in futures trading, you will inevitably fall in one or more of these types. Based on the purpose of the trades, futures traders in the futures trading market can be classified into four types, which are: Hedgers, Speculators, Arbitrageurs and Spreaders.

### 1. Hedgers

Hedgers do with futures contracts what futures contracts were initially designed to do when it was first developed along the rivers of Chicago, which is to hedge against price risk. When a trader goes short on futures contracts while owning the underlying asset or other futures contracts of the same or related underlying in order to protect his existing positions against price fluctuations, he plays a role of a hedger.

### 2. Speculators

Speculators form the backbone of the futures trading market we see today. They provide liquidity and activity in the futures trading market through their day trading or swing trading strategies, buying and selling futures contracts outright in order to speculate on a strong directional move. This is also the most dangerous way of trading futures as the price of the underlying asset could just as easily come around and put speculators position in a loss.

根据交易者交易目的的不同，可将期货交易行为分为三类：套期保值、投机和套利。

套期保值就是买入(卖出)与现货市场数量相当、但交易方向相反的期货合约，以期在未来某一时间通过卖出(买入)期货合约来补偿现货市场价格变动所带来的实际价格风险。

投机是指根据对市场的判断，把握机会，利用市场出现的价差进行买卖，从中获得利润的交易行为。投机者可以"买空"，也可以"卖空"。投机的目的很直接，就是获得价差利润。投机是有风险的。

套利是指同时买进和卖出两张不同种类的期货合约。交易者买进自认为是"便宜的"合约，同时卖出那些"高价的"合约，从两合约价格间的变动关系中获利。在进行套利时，交易者注意的是合约之间的相互价格关系，而不是绝对价格水平。

### 3. Arbitrageurs

Arbitrageurs are futures traders that are in the market in order to spot price anomalies between futures contracts and their underlying assets in order to reap a risk free return. Arbitrage is another huge source of volume and liquidity in the market as it typically takes an extremely big fund and big trading volume in order to return a worthwhile profit in arbitrage. Arbitrage is such a competitive area right now that super computers with powerful programs to spot such opportunities are set to perform such arbitrage automatically.

### 4. Spreaders

Spreaders are futures traders that specialize in trading futures contracts in combination with other futures contracts or underlying in order to reduce risk and to extend profitability. This is a very professional and specialized field that has only recently been made known to the general public and makes use of the difference in price and rate of change in price of different offsetting futures contracts in order to create futures positions that move within certain limits and have a much higher chance of profit with a lot lower commissions.

## 12.5.3 Danger of Futures Trading

You may have heard successful stories about people getting rich by way of futures trading, but as with all types of investments, there is a risk involved. Futures traders who buy futures contracts purely for leveraged speculation frequently lose more money than what they put in when prices move against them. Many a multi-million corporations have gone bankrupt due to abuse of futures trading. Too many futures traders have abused the leverage of futures trading by buying futures contracts with almost all their money, expecting prices to go straight up without keeping a reasonable reserve to serve margin calls for those short term price fluctuations. These futures traders frequently lose all their money and more, casting a shadow on futures trading, making futures more dangerous than it really is. A smart futures trader usually takes the right way to have some patience before starting to trade.

## 12.6   E-commerce

With developments in the Internet and Web-based technologies, distinctions between traditional markets and the global electronic marketplace are gradually being narrowed down. In the emerging global economy, e-commerce and e-business have increasingly become a necessary component of business strategy and a strong catalyst for economic development. The integration of information and communications technology in business has revolutionized relationships within organizations and those between and among organizations and individuals. And it also has enhanced productivity, encouraged greater customer participation, and enabled mass customization, besides reducing costs.

## 12.6.1   Definition of E-commerce

E-commerce is short for "electronic commerce". It refers to a wide range of online business activities for products and services. It also pertains to "any form of business transaction in which the parties interact electronically rather than by physical exchanges or direct physical contact."

电子商务是指在组织与组织之间以及组织与个人之间的交易活动中，使用电子沟通的方式和数字信息处理技术来建立相互的关系，并进行关系的转换及重新定位以创造价值。

E-commerce is usually associated with buying and selling over the Internet, or conducting any transaction involving the transfer of ownership or rights to use goods or services through a computer-mediated network. However, this definition is not comprehensive enough to capture recent developments in this new and revolutionary business phenomenon. A more complete definition is: E-commerce is the use of electronic communications and digital information processing technology in business transactions to create, transform, and redefine relationships for value creation between or among organizations, and between organizations and individuals.

Although sometimes e-commerce and e-business are used interchangeably, they are distinct concepts. In e-commerce, information and communications technology is used in inter-business or inter-organizational transactions (transactions between and among firms/organizations) and in business-to-consumer transactions (transactions between firms/organizations and individuals). In e-business, on the other hand, information and communications technology is used to enhance one's business. It includes any process that a business organization (either a for-profit, governmental or non-profit entity) conducts over a computer-mediated network. A more comprehensive definition of e-business is: "The transformation of an organization's processes to deliver additional customer value through the application of technologies, philosophies and computing paradigm of the new economy."

## 12.6.2　Types of E-commerce

电子商务商业模式按照交易对象分为三类：商业机构对商业机构的电子商务(B2B)，商业机构对消费者的电子商务(B2C)，以及消费者对消费者的电子商务(C2C)。

An e-commerce model aims to make the best of the unique qualities of the Internet and World Wide Web. Based on the different type of participants in the transaction, e-commerce can be classified into three major types: business-to-business (B2B), business-to-consumer (B2C) and consumer-to-consumer (C2C).

### 1. B2B E-commerce

B2B 是指一个互联网市场领域的一种，是企业对企业之间的营销关系。它通过 B2B 网站将企业内部网与客户紧密结合起来，利用网络的快速反应，为客户提供更好的服务，从而促进企业的业务发展。近年来，B2B 发展势头迅猛，并趋于成熟。

B2B e-commerce transactions are those where both the transacting parties are businesses, e.g., manufacturers, traders, retailers and the like. It is simply defined as e-commerce between companies. This is the type of e-commerce that deals with relationships between and among businesses. About 80% of e-commerce is of this type, and most experts predict that B2B ecommerce will continue to grow faster than the B2C segment.

The B2B market has two primary components: e-frastructure and e-markets. E-markets are simply defined as Web sites where buyers and sellers interact with each other and conduct transactions.

The more common B2B examples and best practice models are IBM, Hewlett Packard (HP), Cisco and Dell. Cisco, for instance, receives over 90% of its product orders over the Internet.

## 2. B2C E-commerce

B2C e-commerce refers to commerce between companies and consumers. It is the process of exchanging public consumer goods and services via computer networks, supported by electronic payment. So B2C e-commerce is in essence a kind of electronic retail.

B2C 即企业通过互联网为消费者提供一个新型的购物环境——网上商店。消费者通过网络在网上购物、在网上支付。这种模式节省了客户和企业的时间和空间，因而大大提高了交易效率。

It is the second largest and the earliest form of e-commerce. Its origins can be traced to online retailing (or e-tailing). Thus, the more common B2C business models are the online retailing companies such as Amazon.com, Drugstore.com, Beyond.com, and Barnes and Noble.

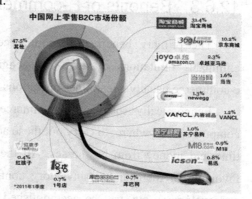

The more common applications of this type of e-commerce are in the areas of purchasing products and information, and personal finance management, which pertain to the management of personal investments and finances with the use of online banking tools.

B2C e-commerce reduces transactions costs by increasing consumer access to information and allowing consumers to find the most competitive price for a product or service. B2C e-commerce also reduces market entry barriers since the cost of putting up and maintaining a Web site is much cheaper than installing a "brick-and-mortar" structure for a firm. In the case of information goods, B2C e-commerce is even more attractive because it saves firms from factoring in the additional cost of a physical distribution network. Moreover, for countries with a growing and robust Internet population, delivering information goods becomes increasingly feasible.

## 3. C2C e-commerce

C2C is simply commerce between private individuals or consumers. Some of the earliest transactions in the global economic system involved barter—a

C2C 是指个人与个人之间的电子商务。

type of C2C transaction. But C2C transactions were virtually non-existent in recent times until the advent of e-commerce. Auction sites are a good example of C2C e-commerce.

Although there is little information on the relative size of global C2C e-commerce, C2C figures of popular C2C sites such as eBay and Napster indicate that this market is quite large. These sites produce millions of dollars in sales every day.

### 12.6.3　Benefits of E-commerce

The primary benefits of ecommerce revolve around the fact that it eliminates limitations of time and geographical distance. In the process, e-commerce usually streamlines operations and lowers costs.

Economically speaking, e-commerce is a cheap way, by connecting computers everywhere, to carry out those activities which used to cost so much time and money from businesses. All these actions like product promotion, invoicing of merchandise, inventory control, communication with suppliers and customers, etc. can be accomplished over the Internet. A part of these lowered costs could be passed on to customers in the form of discounted prices.

If you have a physical store, you are limited by the geographical area that you can service. With an e-commerce website, the whole world is your playground. Besides, with the help of Internet, you can communicate with your boss or employees as conveniently and efficiently as if you were in the same city even they were two thousand kilometers away.

Unlike the traditional mode of business, e-commerce websites can run all the time. From the merchant's point of view, this increases the number of orders they receive. From the customer's point of view, an "always open" store is more convenient. What's more, customers can browse multiple e-commerce merchants and find the best prices by the aid of several online services.

The market used to leave too little room for small businesses. However, things are different for the e-commerce. Small and medium scale enterprises have the opportunity to compete with large and capital-rich businesses. In e-commerce, so long as the business—no matter it is big or small—can move onto the electronic highway, you just go ahead with your business. It is up to the e-commerce consumers to decide which company they like and what products they would like to buy. In a way we may say that e-commerce has brought a "revolution" to businesses in an all-round way.

## 12.6.4   Limitations of E-commerce

What do you concern when you go shopping online? It might be poor commercial credit, lack of mutual trust, or security of your private information, etc. Accordingly, despite all the benefits, there are some limitations of e-commerce.

### 1. Customers can not experience the product before purchase

For those customers who choose online shopping, they cannot touch the fabric of the garment they want to buy, and they cannot check if the pair of shoes feels good on the feet. In many cases, customers want to experience the product before purchase. E-commerce does not allow that.

### 2. Many goods cannot be purchased online

Despite its many conveniences, there are some goods that you cannot buy online. Most of these would be in the categories of "perishable" or "odd-sized". For example, you cannot order a popsicle online. Further more, even though it could be ordered online, the inconvenience should be considered. The popsicle would have to be transported in refrigerated trucks. Unless the seller was willing to make a huge loss, the cost of shipping that popsicle would far exceed the cost of the popsicle.

### 3. Lack of skills and infrastructure

As we know, there still have a certain percentage of customers who do not know how to use the computer and the Internet, and some customers even do not have the infrastructure or equipment. Therefore, e-commerce is not a good channel for every customer.

### 4. Lack of security of online transactions

Security is one of the most important factors in the future growth of e-commerce. When we make an online purchase, we have to provide at least our credit card information and mailing address. In many cases, e-commerce websites are able to harvest the relative information about our online behavior and preferences. This could lead to credit card fraud, or worse, identity theft. That is the reason why many users worried about the security of online transactions.

### 5. Legal protection is insufficient

In China, although there have been more than thirty kinds of rules and regulations regarding Internet development and e-business, there have been no other laws, except the *Electronic Signature Law of the People's Republic of China* passed on August 28, 2004.

On the one hand, it can be said that there is a huge potential market and a very bright future of e-commerce, while on the other hand, we must acknowledge that there are deficiencies of effective supervision on e-commerce. There is a long way to go for the e-commerce.

## 12.6.5 Tips for Running a Successful E-commerce Business

Different e-commerce businesses face different challenges. However, successful e-commerce businesses tend to have some common characteristics. From which we can get some useful tips for running a successful e-commerce business.

(1) Differentiate the business.

Do you ever think about the questions like: Why should a customer visit you? Do you sell exclusive merchandise? Do you offer the lowest price? Does your customer service set you apart? Every business needs to differentiate itself. As an e-commerce business, we cannot hope to sell everything to everybody.

One way to differentiate the business is to solve at least one problem that customers face—especially a problem that no one else is solving.

(2) Get the technology right.

With the kind of robust e-commerce software and hosting available these days, there is no excuse for e-commerce websites that don't work. However, getting technology right is not just about having a bug-free website, it is also about using technology to achieve business ends.

(3) Don't make customers run around in circles.

Common sense dictates that a business should make purchase convenient as possible as it can. However, some e-commerce websites complicate the purchase.

Even the most successful e-commerce businesses find that 20% to 30% of their customers abandon their shopping carts before paying up. The message is loud and clear: many customers refuse to run around in circles.

(4) Be cost effective.

As gross margins reduce to single-digits, e-commerce businesses are selling more but reducing profits. This is not sustainable. All e-commerce businesses are tempted to cut prices. Some businesses choose to price high, while others offer deep discounts. Only e-commerce businesses with effective cost control processes will survive.

## 12.6.6　The Future of E-commerce

We all know that the Internet has become the lifeline of any business. E-commerce have dramatically changed the way brands reach customers, making it faster and easier for consumers to make purchases on the fly while avoiding the hassles of going to the store. In recent years, the concept of e-commerce has been catching on with raging speed just like wildfire in a forest. There are stories all over the place about people becoming millionaires by selling on the net. International trade has become easier and so have the procedures and processes associated with import or export of goods and services.

Among emerging economies, China's e-commerce presence continues to expand. With 538 million internet users, China's e-commerce sales topped one trillion dollars for the first time in history in 2012. One of the reasons behind the huge growth has been the improved trust level for shoppers. The Chinese retailers have been able to help consumers feel more comfortable shopping online.

It should come as no surprise that e-commerce is growing rapidly and changing the way customers shop, and it has become an important tool for businesses worldwide not only to sell to customers but also to engage them.

## 12.7　Cross-border E-commerce

Unrestricted by geographic borders, today's consumers are buying from international merchants more than ever before. Cross-border e-commerce now accounts for over 25 percent of total global e-commerce sales. Millions of

international shoppers, particularly those in emerging markets, search online for discounts or items unavailable domestically. With this in mind, online merchants would benefit from expanding their business into new geographical areas and offering a wider product portfolio to service a global market.

It is expected that China would be one of the world's largest cross-border e-commerce markets in 2020. Many multinationals will spare no efforts in promoting cross-border e-commerce.

♦ **Definition of cross-border e-commerce**

跨境电商通常指的是国际在线贸易。它涉及跨越国界的在线买卖。买卖双方分属不同的国家和关境，使用不同的货币和语言。

The term cross-border e-commerce generally defines international online trade. It entails the sale or purchase of products via online shops across national borders. Buyer and seller are not located in the same country and are often not ruled by the same jurisdiction, use different currencies, and speak different languages.

Cross-border e-commerce can refer to online trade between a business (retailer or brand) and a consumer (B2C), between two businesses, often brands or wholesalers (B2B), or between two private persons (C2C), e.g. via marketplace platforms such as Amazon or eBay.

♦ **Advantages of cross-border e-commerce**

Cross-border e-commerce offers advantages for both buyers and sellers. Sellers can expand their business outside their home market and tap into new markets. Selling abroad also provides the opportunity to seize the potential of different product ranges compared to the domestic market.

For buyers, the advantages of ordering products on foreign websites are often perceived to be a better price and the availability of products that are not available in the home market. In addition, consumers can choose to shop directly from the online shop of their preferred brand.

◆ **Challenges of cross-border e-commerce**

Cross-border e-commerce is springing up in recent years, and technology helps determine the efficiency of cross-border e-commerce. Nevertheless, serving e-commerce customers in other countries often face challenges with market selection, customs procedures, regulatory requirements and taxation issues.

### 1. Selection of adequate markets

Blindly investing in expansion to a new market is dangerous, sellers should make clear what markets can provide reasonable chances to set up a profitable business. In order to select the right markets for an online expansion, the target countries should be profiled to determine their potential.

### 2. Trust of consumers

Online shopping depends a lot on trust. Consumers want to know if the product is the right one they need, how long delivery takes, how the return process works and the means of payment.

### 3. Obstacles of logistics

Research reveals that many of the obstacles to cross-border shopping are delivery-related, thus, designing a well-streamlined logistics procedure is very important.

### 4. Inconsistency of regulation

Some countries treat their domestic companies differently from those incorporated abroad, and every country has its unique set of dos and don'ts about what can be sold online, so sellers should understand the regulation of the target country and meet the requirements when they sell products to a specific country online.

# 【Key Terms and Words】

Agent　代理

Distribution　分销

Distributor　分销商

Wholesaler　批发商

Retailer　零售商

Tender　投标

Bid　出价

Offset　抵销贸易

Hedgers　套期保值者

Speculator　投机商

Arbitrageurs　套汇商

Barter　易货贸易

Broker　经纪人

International trade modes　国际贸易方式

Sole agent　独家代理

Exclusive agent　独家代理人

General agent　总代理人

Commission agent　佣金代理商

Non-exclusive distributor　定销商

Invitation to tender　招标

Submission of tender　投标

Counter purchase　互购

Direct offset　直接抵销

Indirect offset　间接抵销

Futures trading　期货贸易

Futures traders　期货交易员

Future exchange　期货交易所

Future contract　期货交易合同

Margin system　保证金制度

Clearing house　清算所

Counter trade　对销贸易

E-commerce　电子商务

Compensation trade /buyback　补偿贸易

Switch trade　转手贸易

Buy back　回购

Cross-border ecommerce　跨境电商

# 【Exercises】

Please answer the following questions.

1. What is consignment and what are about its advantages and disadvantages?

2. What are the benefits and danger of futures trading?

3. In which case will a company turn to counter trade?

4. What are the main differences between counter purchase and buyback?

5. How to run a successful e-commerce business?

6. What are the challenges of cross-border e-commerce?

# References

[1] BRANCH, A.E. *Export Practice and Management*[M]. 5th Edition. 北京：清华大学出版社，2008.

[2] Dr. Carl A. Nelson. 进出口业务[M]. 丁崇文，等，译. 北京：人民邮电出版社，2011.

[3] Leo Jones, Richad Alexander. *New International Business English*[M]. 北京：华夏出版社，2007.

[4] Paul R. Krugman, Maurice Obstfeld. 国际经济学(理论与政策)[M]. 北京：清华大学出版社，2005.

[5] Joseph P. Daniels, David D. VanHoose. 国际货币与金融经济学[M]. 范小云，改编. 北京：高等教育出版社，2005.

[6] 傅海龙，丛晓明，邵李津. 国际贸易实务双语教程[M]. 2 版. 北京：对外经济贸易大学出版社，2015.

[7] 甘鸿. 外经贸英语函电[M]. 上海：上海科学技术文献出版社，2004.

[8] 耿秉钧. 商用英语与国贸实务[M]. 北京：中国纺织出版社，2008.

[9] 国际商会中国委员会. 2000 年国际贸易术语解释通则[M]. 上海：中信出版社，2000.

[10] 国际商会中国委员会. 2010 国际贸易术语解释通则(英汉对照)[M]. 北京：中国民主法治出版社，2011.

[11] 李月菊. 进出口实务与操作(英文版)[M]. 北京：对外经济贸易大学出版社，2008.

[12] 廖国强. 英汉双语国际贸易实务[M]. 北京：国防工业出版社，2009.

[13] 刘法公. 国际贸易实务英语[M]. 杭州：浙江大学出版社，2002.

[14] 齐俊妍，唐丽. 简明国际贸易实务(英文版)[M]. 北京：清华大学出版社，北京交通大学出版社，2012.

[15] 秦定，高蓉蓉. 国际结算(英文版)[M]. 北京：清华大学出版社，2010.

[16] 帅建林. 国际贸易实务(英文版)[M]. 成都：西南财经大学出版社，2013.

[17] 滕美荣，许楠. 外贸英语函电[M]. 5 版. 北京：首都经济贸易大学出版社，2017.

[18] 黄锡光，吴宝康. 国际贸易实务(英文)[M]. 3 版. 上海：复旦大学出版社，2011.

[19] 吴百福，徐小薇. 进出口贸易实务教程[M]. 7 版. 上海：上海人民出版社，2015.

[20] 谢桂梅. 国际贸易实务(英文版)[M]. 2 版. 北京：清华大学出版社，2015.

[21] 熊伟，陈凯. 国际贸易实务英语[M]. 3 版，武汉：武汉大学出版社，2017.

[22] 徐小贞，程达军，李延玉. 国际贸易实务：国际商务英语[M]. 2 版. 北京：高等教育出版社，2017.

[23] 易露霞，方玲玲，陈原. 国际贸易实务双语教程[M]. 3 版. 北京：清华大学出版社，2011.

[24] 赵宏，杨春梅. 国际贸易实务(英文版)[M]. 北京：中国铁道出版社，经济科学出版社，2009.

[25] 张雪莹，华欣. 新编国际贸易实务(英文版)[M]. 北京：清华大学出版社，2009.

[26] 张素芳. 国际贸易理论与实务(英文版)[M]. 3 版. 北京：对外经济贸易大学出版社，2013.

[27] 周瑞琪，王小鸥，徐月芳. 国际贸易实务(英文版)[M]. 3 版. 上海：对外经济贸易大学出版社，2015.